DATE DUE

DE 18'98			

DEMCO 38-296

The Second Gold Rush

The Second
Gold Rush

Oakland and the East Bay
in World War II

Marilynn S. Johnson

UNIVERSITY OF CALIFORNIA PRESS

Berkeley / Los Angeles / London

University of California Press
Berkeley and Los Angeles, California

University of California Press, Ltd.
London, England

© 1993 by
The Regents of the University of California

Library of Congress Cataloging-in-Publication Data
Johnson, Marilynn S.
　　The second gold rush : Oakland and the East Bay in World
War II / Marilynn S. Johnson.
　　　　p.　　cm.
　　Includes bibliographical references and index.
　　ISBN 0-520-08191-9 (alk. paper)
　　1. Oakland (Calif.)—History.　2. San Francisco Bay Area
(Calif.)—History.　3. Rural-urban migration—California—
Oakland—History—20th century.　4. Rural-urban migration—
California—San Francisco Bay Area—History—20th century.
5. World War, 1939–1945—California—Oakland.　6. World War,
1939–1945—California—San Francisco Bay Area.　I. Title.
F869.02J64　　1993
979.4′66053—dc20　　　　　　　　　　　　　　　　92-41889
　　　　　　　　　　　　　　　　　　　　　　　　　　　CIP

Printed in the United States of America

9 8 7 6 5 4 3 2 1

The paper used in this publication meets the minimum requirements
of American National Standard for Information Sciences—
Permanence of Paper for Printed Library Materials, ANSI
Z39.48-1984. ∞

Contents

Plates following page 142

Acknowledgments

This book is dedicated to the East Bay residents who shared their time, memories, and living rooms with me during the course of this project. Their insights provided not only vital information on the wartime experience but also enriched this story with a human dimension and drama rarely available in the written record. The informants' generosity and enthusiasm were a continuing source of inspiration through five long years of research and writing.

During this time, I accumulated untold debts to my academic colleagues. As dissertation advisers at New York University, Daniel Walkowitz and Susan Ware provided prompt, critical readings of each chapter draft, and their insightful criticisms improved the manuscript at every stage. Thomas Bender, Mary Nolan, and Marilyn Young also read the entire manuscript, offering numerous suggestions for revision. On the sticky subject of crime and public order, Claire Potter helped me rethink the difficult issues raised in chapter 6.

On the West Coast, Stephen Aron, Nancy Bristow, Gerda Ray, Lucy Salyer, and other members of our Berkeley dissertation group read various chapter drafts and provided constructive criticism and emotional support. As specialists in California history, Charles Wollenberg and James Gregory saved me from many errors. I am especially grateful to the latter for convincing me—despite my initial reluctance—to pursue the intricacies of East Bay urban politics in the 1940s. Sheila Levine, Monica McCormick, and Amy Klatzkin at the University of California Press have been patient and persistent editors, while Stephanie Fowler

viii   ACKNOWLEDGMENTS

used great care and sensitivity in copyediting. As my undergraduate adviser at Stanford, Estelle Freedman first kindled my enthusiasm for social and women's history and has offered ongoing support and encouragement over the past fifteen years.

Although this study deals with the East Bay, I owe thanks to librarians and archivists around the country including those at the National Archives in Washington, D.C., the Blues Archives at the University of Mississippi, and the Country Music Foundation in Nashville, Tennessee. In the East Bay, I am grateful to Richard Hill at the Richmond Public Library, Bill Sturm at the Oakland Public Library, Drew Johnson at the Oakland Museum, Katherine MacMahon at the Oakland Police Department, and the many knowledgeable staff at the Bancroft Library. I am also indebted to the Regional Oral History Office at the University of California, Berkeley, and especially to Judith K. Dunning, whose oral histories with Richmond residents proved so valuable to this study.

For financial support, I am grateful to New York University for a Dean's Dissertation Fellowship and History Department Dissertation Grant; to Southern Methodist University for a Dedman College summer research grant; to the American Historical Association for an Albert J. Beveridge grant; and to the Sourisseau Academy for a State and Local History Grant. At Southern Methodist University, funds provided by Dedman College underwrote the photographic research and acquisition for this book, while my colleagues in the history department offered professional advice and encouragement through the latter stages of the project.

My husband, Dan Zedek, has given more to this project than I can recount. His sharp criticism and insights helped improve the manuscript; he lent his technical expertise in creating charts and redrawing maps; and he enthusiastically shared my love of Bay Area blues and country music. Most important, his unfailing love and patience helped see me through the ordeal of turning a vague idea into a finished book.

Introduction

When the local Chamber of Commerce published its laudatory history of Richmond, California, in 1944, it concluded its account with before-and-after photographs. Taken only six months apart, the two pictures captured the dramatic transformation of one city during the tumultuous era of World War II (see plates 1 and 2). The earlier photograph, taken in June 1942 from a hilltop in south Richmond, reveals a pastoral scene of fields and marshes. The later picture, taken in January 1943, provides a startlingly different view of the same terrain. Here, virtually every lot is covered with barrackslike war housing projects that stretch as far as the eye can see.[1]

Offering a unique before-and-after perspective, the two photographs illustrate the sweeping impact of World War II on one West Coast city. They show at a glance the rapid burgeoning of defense industries, war housing, and accompanying urban development that transformed many American cities during the war years. What the pictures do not show, however, are the people involved in this transformation—the thousands of workers who migrated to war production centers between 1941 and 1945 and the longtime residents of such besieged communities.

Most urban historians have portrayed World War II in similar terms. Focusing on structural changes in the economy and the dynamics of urban development, these scholars have shown how the war significantly affected urbanization in America. In *The Martial Metropolis,* a collection of essays on the impact of militarization on American cities, Roger W. Lotchin concludes that recent wars and defense spending brought lasting changes to many cities, accelerating the development of some, precipitating the decline of others.[2] This study adds to the body of literature on war and urbanization but takes a somewhat different tack. In focusing on a single urban area, I hope to move beyond the structural dynamics of wartime cities to explore the human dimension of the war experience as well.

In West Coast cities, defense migration and the human drama of the war boom would be the most enduring legacy of World War II. Between 1940 and 1945, millions of war migrants headed for the Pacific Coast, increasing the racial and cultural diversity of its cities and transforming social relations and cultural life. World War II migration, in fact, was one of the most powerful forces in the spatial rearrangement of the population in the twentieth century. According to the Census Bureau in 1948, "Probably never before in the history of the United States has there been internal population movement of such magnitude as in the past seven eventful years."[3]

Between 1940 and 1947, some twenty-five million people (21 percent of the total population) migrated to another county or state in search of new opportunities in the military and civilian sectors. By comparison, only 13 percent had moved in 1935–1940 and even less during the early thirties. A considerable percentage of war migrants were nonwhite, far more so than during the depression.[4] Although some of the wartime movement was for the duration only, many migrants remained in their new destinations, extending the process of chain migration to friends and relatives into the postwar period.

Surprisingly, though, we know relatively little about this dynamic period of internal migration. Social historians have amply demonstrated the significance of rural-urban migration in shaping early American community life. Herbert Gutman and other historians of the working class have likewise examined the key role of European immigration in northern cities of the nineteenth and early twentieth centuries.[5] Little attention has been given, however, to the renewed importance of internal migration in the post-1920 period, particularly for cities in the South and West.

Recently, a few historians have begun to address this issue, most notably Jacquelyn Dowd Hall et al. in *Like a Family: The Making of a Southern Cotton Mill World* and James N. Gregory in his study of California and the dust bowl migration.[6] These historians demonstrate the significance of rural and regional migration in shaping the social and cultural life of industrial communities in the South and West. Their work describes the effects of migration and settlement on southern families, but also shows how migrants created their own social world through distinctive religious, familial, and cultural practices. By focusing on the World War II years, this book seeks to contribute to an understanding of internal migration in the twentieth century, evaluating its impact on migrants and nonmigrants alike.

In focusing on the war era, this study is also an attempt to address the ongoing historical debate over the impact of the Second World War. Looking at the national level, historians of the home front have reached conflicting conclusions about the significance of the war as an agent of social change. More recent studies of specific localities have yielded greater insights by probing beneath such net national findings to examine the divergent patterns of various regions and communities. Alan Clive's study of Michigan and Gerald D. Nash's work on the West during World War II demonstrate the importance of the war in expanding regional economies, accelerating urbanization, and transforming local racial and gender relations.[7] They do not, however, provide the individual personal perspectives and detailed sociological focus of a community study.

In 1988 historian Marc S. Miller published the first community-based study of World War II, *The Irony of Victory*. Focusing on the economically declining community of Lowell, Massachusetts, Miller argues that the war was a temporary boom phenomenon in the long-term downward course of the city. As such, he finds, it essentially perpetuated prewar social and economic trends, resulting in the eventual abandonment of the city by employers and workers.[8]

In many ways, this book is the flip side of the Lowell story—the more positive, growth-oriented saga of western cities that grew at the expense of those in the Northeast. At the receiving end of this exchange, western cities gained major new industries, housing, and inmigrant populations. Unlike Lowell, the East Bay experienced more change than continuity, more possibility and hopefulness than decline and despair. In time, however, West Coast communities would experience their own difficulties, many of which grew out of the unresolved conflicts of the war boom era. Neither "Sunbelt" nor "Rustbelt," the Bay Area exhibited elements of both types of economies, allowing us to see how western cities and their residents coped with wartime social change and the postwar dislocations that followed.

The Case of the East Bay

As one of the nation's largest shipbuilding centers, the San Francisco Bay Area offers a good window on the wartime experience of West Coast cities. The East Bay region in particular hosted an extensive zone of shipyards and other defense industries that attracted hundreds of thousands of war migrants—both black and white—from around the country.

Defense migration, more than the economic changes that triggered it, permanently transformed life in the East Bay. The massive wartime influx changed the racial and regional composition of the population, enriching the cultural life of East Bay communities. In the workplace, the arrival of unskilled migrants and other new workers prompted a radical restructuring from skilled crafts to mass production. In response, shipyard unions tightened their control of the membership, resulting in undemocratic practices and new forms of labor organization.

Federal government programs, meanwhile, transformed the spatial and social relations of these communities. The construction of war housing projects with corresponding social service systems served to isolate defense migrants within certain sectors of the city, augmenting their physical and psychological separation from the native community. Migrants, though, would construct their own social world within the confines of these new federal ghettos, cultivating regional subcultures that would eventually permeate the larger community.

As Louis Wirth and other sociologists observed in the 1940s, mass defense migration resulted in bitter conflicts between natives and newcomers over material resources, political power, social prestige, and public behavior.[9] Unlike their more immediate predecessors in the East Bay, most war migrants were native-born southerners and midwesterners; the "natives" they most often encountered were former immigrant and white ethnic workers. World War II thus reversed the historic roles of native and immigrant, creating a complex and unstable social hierarchy. Old-timers of the native-born middle class contributed to antimigrant sentiment as well, primarily out of class-based fears of public disorder. For old-timers of all classes, the wartime influx of black migrants provoked fears of social unrest and a disintegration of established racial boundaries in the community.

As in earlier episodes of urban class and ethnic conflict, wartime struggles between newcomers and old-timers were played out on city streets under the banner of crime control. As downtown areas turned into raucous boomtowns, local elites mobilized to reassert control of public space through law-and-order campaigns aimed at migrants and other groups whose social autonomy grew with the war. In the postwar era, wartime campaigns to control public space provided the ideological underpinnings for urban redevelopment and helped fuel white flight to the suburbs. Throughout these struggles, the federal government was an active intermediary, seeking to facilitate the war effort and postwar reconstruction.

Although the newcomer–old-timer dichotomy is a compelling model, it has limitations as a tool for explaining all wartime conflict. First, newcomers and old-timers were themselves internally divided over issues of race, class, age, and gender. Conflicts occurred within families and among migrant neighbors, and newcomers and natives sometimes formed alliances based on race or other common characteristics. In the postwar period especially, newcomer–old-timer boundaries proved to be quite permeable. Many white migrants found social acceptance in nearby suburbs, so that by the 1950s the remaining battle lines were largely racial ones. Racial conflict, which had not been as visible a problem in the prewar era, would become the most troublesome legacy of the war.

World War II also presented opportunities for a class-based challenge to the conservative business interests that had long ruled East Bay cities. The influx of thousands of new working-class voters and the corporatist nature of municipal politics during the war enabled a coalition of labor, black, and other progressive forces to mount a sustained attack against conservative rule. Under the leadership of a united labor movement, the progressive coalition would grow to become a major contender in postwar urban politics, particularly in Oakland. Although these challenges ultimately failed by the 1950s, they nonetheless demonstrated the powerful potential of the war as an agent of social and political change.

Unlike national studies, a sharply focused community study enables us to see these conflicts by exploring social relations within the family, neighborhood, and city. This approach allows us to move beyond the structural preoccupations of most urbanists to understand the social experiences of different individuals and community groups. From this perspective, we can better understand the options and limitations of East Bay residents and their families and the choices made by urban policymakers both during and after the war. In wandering through the shipyards and housing projects of the East Bay, the historian also has an opportunity to examine the ways in which the federal government constructed and reshaped local communities and institutions during those years.

The East Bay region offers a good locale for exploring the wartime transformation of urban life. Like other urban centers around the country, the San Francisco Bay Area grew at the expense of the nation's less developed interior. Nationally, the defense boom augmented the historical shift from rural to urban areas. From 1940 to 1947, U.S. farm areas lost more than three million inhabitants, or one in every eight residents living on farms in 1940.[10] More generally, population in counties outside metropolitan areas declined dramatically—with a nationwide loss of nearly five million civilians between 1940 and 1943 alone. Smaller cities, towns, and rural areas of the nation's interior—the North Central and South Central census regions—contributed the greatest number of urban migrants (see table 1). The wartime population of the Bay Area reflected these shifts, drawing the bulk of its newcomers from precisely those areas. Furthermore, the racial mixture of East Bay migrants mirrored national trends and allows for a comparative analysis of defense migration by race and region.

The Bay Area also represents one of the fastest-growing urban areas of the war era. As noted earlier, World War II helped redistribute urban populations away from northeastern cities and toward newer urban centers in the South and West. From 1940 to 1943, the civilian population of metropolitan counties in the Northeast dropped by 1,023,000 while those in the South and West grew by 2,314,000 (table 1). Despite an overall population decline in the South due to heavy outmigration from rural areas and small towns, southern cities continued to grow, particularly shipbuilding and military centers along the Atlantic and Gulf coasts.[11]

The most spectacular growth, however, occurred in the West. While all other regions experienced a net loss of population, the West grew by 14 percent between 1940 and 1947. The most marked increase occurred in the Pacific Coast states, where population jumped by almost 40 percent. Unlike the East, which converted existing urban industries to defense production, the West expanded its industrial facilities along the perimeter of strategically located coastal cities. Primarily distribution and processing centers for raw materials in the prewar era, West Coast cities developed into major shipbuilding and aircraft manufacturing centers during World War II. In the Northwest, the population

Table 1 *Changes in Civilian Population, April 1, 1940, to March 1, 1943*

Regions (census grouping)	Counties outside metropolitan areas*			Metropolitan areas*		
	Pop. 1940 (000s)	% change since 1940	Net loss/gain	Pop. 1940 (000s)	% change since 1940	Net loss/gain
New England (Me., Mass., N.H., R.I., Vt., Conn.)	1,935	−6.3	−122,000	6,468	−2.4	−157,000
Mid-Atlantic (N.Y., Pa., N.J.)	5,550	−6.9	−382,000	21,944	−3.9	−866,000
S. Atlantic (Del., N.C., Md., S.C., D.C., Va., Ga., Fla., W.Va.)	11,923	−4.7	−560,000	5,800	+13.6	+791,000
E. N. Central (Ohio, Mich., Ind., Wis., Ill.)	11,902	−6.6	−790,000	14,697	+1.9	+272,000
W. N. Central (Minn., N.Dak., Iowa, S.Dak., Mo., Nebr., Kans.)	8,734	−12.9	−1,127,000	4,762	+1.2	+59,000
E. S. Central (Ky., Ala., Tenn., Miss.)	8,486	−8.2	−700,000	2,277	+9.4	+213,000
W. S. Central (Ark., Okla., La., Tex.)	9,550	−8.5	−811,000	3,468	+11.3	+390,000
Mountain (Mont., N.M., Idaho, Ariz., Wyo., Utah, Colo., Nev.)	3,286	−5.2	−172,000	847	+8.4	+73,000
Pacific (Wash., Ore., Calif.)	3,132	−1.6	−51,000	6,544	+12.9	+847,000

SOURCES: All statistics derived from U.S. Bureau of the Census, *Estimates of the Civilian Population of the United States, by Counties: March 1, 1943*, issued October 31, 1943. Table based on Catherine Bauer, "Cities in Flux," *American Scholar* 13 (Winter 1943–44):74. Copyright © 1943 by the Phi Beta Kappa Society.

*"Metropolitan counties," as used by the Census Bureau, include cities of 50,000 or more plus the urbanized counties around them. "Counties outside metropolitan areas," therefore, include smaller cities as well as villages and rural areas.

of the Seattle region grew by 30.5 percent and the Portland area by 33.6 percent. The San Diego area experienced the most dramatic population gain with a 110.5 percent increase. Los Angeles added 17.8 percent and the San Francisco Bay Area 39.9 percent. The Bay Area, then, was the second fastest-growing urban center on the West Coast.[12]

California, more than any other state, reaped the benefits of wartime defense development. Of $360 billion in total federal expenditures in the period 1940–1946, the U.S. government spent some $35 billion in California, accounting for 45 percent of the personal income of state residents. California likewise received more interstate migrants than any other state, absorbing more than 1.5 million newcomers between 1940 and 1944. Nearly one-third of these migrants settled in the San Francisco Bay Area.[13]

The majority of these newcomers settled outside of central cities in suburban and urban satellite communities closest to new war industries. Unlike the congested urban core, the urban periphery offered large expanses of undeveloped land that permitted rapid industrial and residential development. In fact, in all of the nation's ten busiest defense centers, the greatest proportional population growth occurred in outlying areas. World War II, then, hastened the process of metropolitan growth, favoring the suburbs at the expense of the central cities.[14]

The East Bay region offers a prime example of this type of outlying metropolitan growth. During the war years, the majority of migrants settled there adjacent to massive shipyards and military installations that sprang up along the San Francisco Bay. By 1945, the population of East Bay counties surpassed those on the opposite side of the bay, including San Francisco and its peninsula suburbs. The regional focus of this study also reflects the emergent commuter economy of the mid-twentieth century that connected East Bay cities not only economically but also physically and psychologically. This pattern of metropolitan growth was typical of West Coast defense centers, including the industrial corridors of Seattle-Tacoma and Portland-Vancouver and the southern and western suburbs of Los Angeles.[15]

For the purposes of this study, the East Bay encompasses the coastal areas of Contra Costa and Alameda counties bounded by the towns of San Pablo on the north and San Leandro on the south (see map 1). It includes the shipyard boomtowns of Richmond, Oakland, and Alameda, as well as the quieter communities of Berkeley, Albany, El Cerrito, and Emeryville. In the prewar era, this territory was known as the "Oakland metropolitan area," reflecting the city's dominance of the

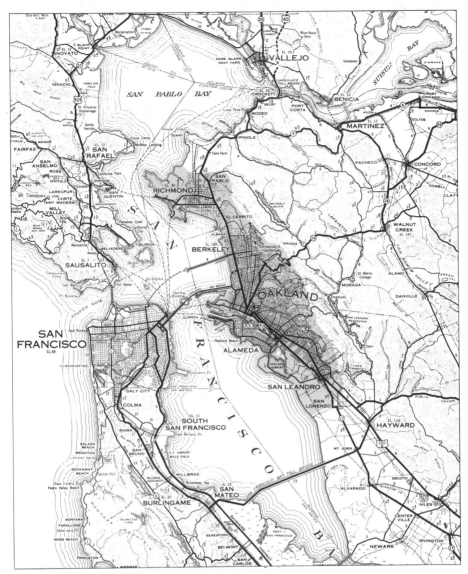

Map 1. East Bay Study Area, 1935

region prior to the completion of the San Francisco–Oakland Bay Bridge in 1936. During the war, the East Bay shared many common characteristics with other shipyard suburbs such as South San Francisco, Marin City, and Vallejo. The East Bay experience, then, parallels that of the Bay Area generally and offers insights into the wartime transformation of Seattle, Portland, Los Angeles, and San Diego.

In terms of sources, cities and counties offer new documentation for the study of wartime society. Reports of housing authorities, city crime commissions, school districts, social welfare organizations, and local newspapers have all enriched this project by providing detailed information on community development, social conflicts, and urban decision-making. In addition, the personal recollections of local residents, when balanced with written sources, provide invaluable insights into wartime family and community strategies.

In some respects, however, reliance on local sources can be problematic. Most western cities do not maintain municipal archives, and many city and county agencies routinely discard their records after a decade. The bureaucratic frenzy of wartime cities only aggravated this problem. Stretched to the breaking point under the strain of ballooning population and service needs, local agencies often could not keep pace with routine record-keeping. Consequently, many of the records that survive are less substantive than those from before or after the war. In some cases, information on local communities appears in the records of federal war agencies. At other times, the historian must splice the story together from a combination of newspapers and other sources.

Fortunately, the notoriety of East Bay boomtowns generated a considerable amount of national and academic interest. Government officials dubbed Richmond the "Purple Heart City" in 1944 because of the war's damaging effects on the community. Postwar observers produced an abundance of documentation about the city's wartime experience, and racial strife in the 1960s encouraged renewed interest in the city's past. The proximity of the University of California at Berkeley also resulted in a number of useful graduate student theses on housing, social welfare, and urban planning in the 1940s and 1950s. Similarly in Oakland, Mills College students canvassed local neighborhoods, reporting on employment, housing, crime, and other community issues. This fortuitous combination of sources offers the historian a bird's-eye view of the East Bay during and after World War II. Whenever possible, I have also tried to place the East Bay in a larger, comparative perspective by offering data and observations on other West Coast cities.

There are other sources that I have chosen not to explore for this study, in particular, those dealing with the environmental impact of wartime growth. As Gerald Nash and other historians have pointed out, urban-industrial development during World War II had critical effects on western cities, including increased air pollution in Los Angeles and water pollution and loss of wetlands in the Bay Area. These issues are timely and important but deserve a separate and thorough treatment. This book, then, will be limited to the social, cultural, and political aspects of the war experience.

Beginning in the prewar era, the study starts with a historical overview of East Bay history, outlining the major political, economic, and social developments in the region from the 1840s to the eve of World War II. This discussion sets the stage for chapter 2, which examines the coming of war and its impact on industrial development, labor recruitment, and migration in East Bay cities. The next two chapters describe the reorganization of work, labor organization, and housing in and around local shipyards, emphasizing the structural segregation of newcomers and old-timers. Focusing on the internal dynamics of new migrant neighborhoods, chapter 5 explores the social experience of migrant families and communities. This section also describes migrants' attempts to sustain their own cultural traditions in the face of a comprehensive corporate welfare program designed to instill modern urban-industrial values.

The focus of the last three chapters shifts away from migrants to examine the social and political conflicts that plagued war boomtowns both during and after the war. Chapter 6 traces the development of newcomer–old-timer conflicts in East Bay cities and the response of local leaders who attempted to tighten control over downtown areas. Focusing on municipal politics, chapter 7 traces the wartime development of a progressive labor coalition and its rise to power in the postwar era. The final chapter examines the unraveling of war boom society, showing how social and political developments of the late forties led to the defeat of urban progressives and their vision for the postwar reconstruction of the city. As with other aspects of war-born change, however, the political transformations of World War II foreshadowed future trends in urban affairs both in the East Bay and throughout the country.

1

Prelude to War

Prior to the Second World War, there were two competing images of the East Bay: a quiet bedroom suburb of San Francisco versus a thriving industrial metropolis.[1] For the most part, the conflicting images accurately reflected the historical reality. Since the mid-nineteenth century, the East Bay had developed in the shadow of San Francisco, the largest and most prominent city in the frontier West. Its location across the bay from San Francisco made the East Bay an ideal site for suburban development. But with the selection of Oakland as the terminus of the transcontinental railroad, a transportation and manufacturing boom began. Over the years, the industrial trend accelerated, aided by the San Francisco earthquake, further railroad and port development, and two world wars.

Dubbed "Contra Costa" (opposite shore) by the Spanish, the East Bay attracted its first white settlers in the 1840s. Like other early California settlements, the East Bay—and the town of Oakland in particular—experienced rapid development in response to the gold rush of 1849. Incorporated in 1852, Oakland served as a popular departure point for stagecoach trips to the Sierra gold fields. Although most forty-niners merely passed through the East Bay, their need for transportation and supplies provided steady income for early Oakland residents.

Compared with San Francisco, an "instant city" dominated by transient gold-seekers, prostitutes, saloons, and hotels, Oakland was staid and tranquil. Although most early settlers were male, the town soon gained a reputation as the "bedchamber" of San Francisco. In contrast to the raucous, boomtown life of "the City," Oakland's more sedate environment attracted families who brought with them churches, schools, clubs, and other community institutions. Among the most significant was the College of California, the state's first institution of higher education, founded by Henry Durant in 1860. When the school relocated to more spacious surroundings north of the city, local civic leaders established the town of Berkeley in 1873. During the same period, residents south of Oakland founded the adjoining towns of Alameda and Brooklyn (now east Oakland).[2]

The selection of Oakland as the terminus for the nation's first transcontinental railroad, however, heralded a new era for the city. With the arrival of the Central Pacific Railroad in 1869, Oakland became the transportation hub of the region. Nearly all freight to and from San Francisco and other Northern California towns was unloaded, sorted, and reloaded onto other rail and ship lines. Over the next thirty years, dozens of manufacturing and processing industries developed in the Oakland area to take advantage of the city's transportation network. As a result, the city's population grew from 1,543 in 1860 to 10,500 in 1870, jumping to 36,500 in 1880, and showing steady growth thereafter (see table 2).[3]

A similar industrial boom occurred in nearby Richmond around the turn of the century. Largely farm and marshland in the nineteenth century, Richmond was incorporated in 1905 following its speculative development as the terminus of the Santa Fe Railroad. In 1905, the Standard Oil Company selected Richmond as the site for a new refinery and storage facility to serve the Northern California area. The Pullman Company, Western Pipe and Steel, and several smaller industries soon followed.[4] The arrival of the Santa Fe line also spurred industrial development along the railroad corridor between Oakland and Richmond, primarily in west Berkeley and Emeryville.

Standard Oil and other companies that moved into the East Bay during the early twentieth century were mainly large, national corporations with headquarters located in the East. The dominance of this type of "national capitalism," as John T. Cumbler has termed it, would have serious implications for the future of East Bay cities. Led by distant home offices reacting to national and international market trends, most East Bay industries operated with little regard for the overall welfare of the community. Unlike the nineteenth-century eastern cities that most social historians have studied, the economic destiny of West Coast

Table 2 *Population History of Four East Bay Cities, 1900–1940*

City & year	Total population	% foreign-born white	% foreign-born parentage	% black	% Chinese & Japanese
Alameda					
1900	16,464	25.4	35.5	0.9	2.2
1910	23,383	23.8	34.5	0.9	3.1
1920	28,806	20.4	20.6	0.8	2.6
1930	35,033	18.1	18.0	0.8	2.6
1940	36,256	13.9	—	0.7	—
Berkeley					
1900	13,214	24.3	35.1	0.5	2.2
1910	40,434	18.9	17.6	0.6	2.9
1920	56,036	17.1	16.7	0.9	2.2
1930	82,109	14.8	14.8	2.7	2.0
1940	85,547	12.6	—	4.0	—
Oakland					
1900	66,960	25.8	35.5	1.5	1.7
1910	150,174	24.5	21.9	2.0	3.4
1920	216,261	21.4	20.4	2.5	3.0
1930	284,063	17.4	18.6	2.6	1.8
1940	302,163	14.1	—	2.8	1.7
Richmond*					
1910	—	—	—	—	—
1920	16,843	21.4	18.0	0.2	—
1930	20,093	17.1	16.4	0.2	—
1940	23,642	14.7	—	1.1	—

SOURCES: U.S. Bureau of the Census, *Twelfth Census of the United States, 1900: Population*, vol. 1, pt. 1, "California"; *Thirteenth Census of the United States, 1910: Population*, vol. 2, *Reports by States*, "California"; *Fourteenth Census of the United States, 1920: Population*, vol. 3, *Composition and Characteristics of the Population by States*, "California"; *Fifteenth Census of the United States, 1930: Population*, vol. 3, *Reports by States*, pt. 1, "California"; *Sixteenth Census of the United States, 1940: Reports on Population*, vol. 2, *Characteristics of the Population*, pt. 1, "California."

*Incorporated in 1905

Table 3 *Country of Origin of Foreign-Born Whites in Oakland, 1900–1940*

	% of foreign-born population				
	1900	*1910*	*1920*	*1930*	*1940*
Canada	10.2	8.5	8.4	10.6	10.7
England	11.7	10.1	10.0	10.6	9.4
Germany	15.9	14.9	10.3	9.7	8.6
Ireland	18.5	11.3	8.1	6.4	5.5
Italy	3.5	10.3	11.3	12.8	13.4
Portugal	5.9	9.1	9.5	7.8	7.6
Scandinavia	11.3	13.9	13.2	14.1	13.4
Scotland	4.1	3.6	3.8	4.9	4.7
All others	18.9	18.3	25.4	23.1	26.7

SOURCES: U.S. Bureau of the Census, *Twelfth Census of the United States, 1900: Population*, vol. 1, pt. 1, "California"; *Thirteenth Census of the United States, 1910: Population*, vol. 2, *Reports by States*, "California"; *Fourteenth Census of the United States, 1920: Population*, vol. 3, *Composition and Characteristics of the Population by States*, "California"; *Fifteenth Census of the United States, 1930: Population*, vol. 3, *Reports by States*, pt. 1, "California"; *Sixteenth Census of the United States, 1940: Reports on Population*, vol. 2, *Characteristics of the Population*, pt. 1, "California."

cities was largely shaped by external forces. This dynamic has led some observers to describe the pre–World War II western economy as "colonial" and its cities as distant outposts of eastern capitalism.[5] Although the argument is somewhat overstated—there were a growing number of indigenous western corporations before World War II—the characterization is essentially accurate.

Eastern and western corporations alike brought a succession of racial and ethnic groups to East Bay cities. From the 1870s until after the turn of the century, the Irish and Germans predominated in railroad and industrial employment. The East Bay also attracted large groups of Scandinavians, Canadians, and British islanders (see table 3). With the completion of the transcontinental railroad, a small community of Chinese laborers settled in the area, primarily along the Oakland estuary and in the downtown area that is still known as Chinatown today.[6] Many of these early workers were men, but over time they brought women and families so that by the late nineteenth century the city's sex ratio was approaching parity. With the development of a large food-processing industry, many women found employment in local canneries and processing plants.

As in many West Coast cities, the black community in Oakland originated as a "Pullman car colony" at the terminus of a transcontinental rail line. In the 1870s, the Pullman Company began its Palace Car Service to the West Coast and hired black porters for the sleeping cars to serve their first-class customers. Over the years, black Oaklanders also found employment as section hands, car cleaners, cooks and waiters on dining cars, and as redcaps who handled baggage. By 1929, the railroad employed approximately one-third of all black wage earners in Oakland. Though pay was low, railroad work offered job security, travel, and the opportunity to save and buy homes. Along with a small number of black professionals, the waiters, redcaps, and porters constituted the core of Oakland's black middle class. Most of them settled in the railroad-dominated community of west Oakland along with other immigrant workers.[7]

By the turn of the century, Italians, Portuguese, and other Southern and Eastern Europeans followed earlier immigrants in seeking work on Oakland's waterfront and rail yards. By 1920, Italians would become the largest ethnic group in the Bay Area, surpassing earlier groups of Germans, Irish, and Scandinavians (see table 3).[8] The population of west Oakland shifted accordingly and included a growing number of black residents. Along with Los Angeles, Oakland became the major center of black settlement in California. Compared with eastern cities, however, Oakland's black population was very small—less than 3 percent until World War II (see table 2). Oakland also hosted small but growing communities of Japanese immigrants who settled in and around the Chinatown neighborhood and Mexicans who resided near the Point in west Oakland.[9] Richmond and Berkeley developed a similar ethnic mix of Europeans, blacks, Asians, and Hispanics, particularly in west-side neighborhoods along the Santa Fe tracks.

The influx of new industries and residents profoundly affected the political organization of East Bay cities. Since their inception, East Bay municipal governments had been dominated by business elites intent on promoting economic growth. With the rise of new industrial concerns, however, a growing group of working-class residents, many of them foreign-born, challenged the prerogatives of the ruling elite. Bringing with them European craft traditions and socialist sympathies, immigrant workers helped spark a radical movement that challenged local business leadership. As in the nation generally, the Socialist party reached its peak influence in the East Bay during the Progressive Era. In Oakland, Socialist candidates in the 1911 city elections nearly took control of the city council, polling 9,837 votes to the business candidates' 11,732. In neighboring Berkeley, voters elected a Socialist candidate, J. Stitt Wilson, for mayor in 1911.

To counteract this threat and to create a favorable climate for business, local elites initiated a series of charter reform measures. Like other American cities in this period, Oakland and other East Bay cities adopted the nonpartisan commission form of government in 1911. By forbidding the use of party labels on the ballot and replacing the ward system with citywide elections, the commission form of government diluted the electoral power of ethnic and working-class voters. Not surprisingly, the new system effectively decimated the Socialist party vote in 1913.[10]

Although business interests would hereafter dominate city government, different business factions continued to fight among themselves. In Oakland, there were two competing factions, one led by John Davie, longtime mayor of the city (served 1895–1897 and 1915–1930), and his allies Mike Kelly and Harry Williams, and the other headed by Joseph P. Knowland, publisher of the *Oakland Tribune*. Knowland's machine was strongest on the county and state levels but less influential in city politics. To put an end to the commission form of government that supported his rivals, Knowland and other banking and business leaders initiated a second round of charter reform in 1928. The establishment of the council-manager form of government in 1931 helped defeat Knowland's opponents and put his business machine in firm control of the city.[11] During the same years, merchants, newspaper editors, and other downtown business leaders lobbied successfully for council-manager systems in Richmond, Berkeley, and Alameda as well.

With the consolidation of business power, East Bay cities pursued an aggressive program of industrial expansion. Ironically, the tragic San Francisco earthquake kicked off this "golden age" of East Bay industry. On April 13, 1906, a massive earthquake estimated at over 8.0 on the Richter scale struck the Bay Area, leaving San Francisco in smoldering ruins. In the months following the disaster, East Bay towns provided emergency relief sites for thousands of homeless families from San Francisco. With relatively light structural damage, these communities resumed normal life more quickly and attracted many permanent settlers from among the refugees. Between 1900 and 1910, Oakland's population grew from 67,000 to over 150,000, and other East Bay cities showed comparable gains (see table 2).[12]

Equally significant was the relocation of many businesses and industries. Among the largest of these was Moore Shipbuilding Company, which moved its yards from San Francisco to Oakland in 1906. The postearthquake commercial boom and the city's long-sought acquisition of private waterfront lands accelerated port development during this period, including the completion of the Tidal Canal on the Oakland Estuary, the construction of the Howard Terminal, and the development of a network of municipal piers, wharves, and railroad connections. These improvements enabled Oakland to compete with San Francisco in cargo capacity and to share in increased trade resulting from the opening of the Panama Canal in 1914.

With the advent of World War I, shipping and shipbuilding grew even more sharply. At Moore shipyards, a work force of over 13,000 completed thirty ships for the federal government between 1917 and 1920.[13] Bethlehem Shipbuilding Corporation and several smaller yards in Oakland and Alameda also participated in large-scale construction projects during this period. Although the mobilization was short-lived and far less dramatic than the World War II effort would be, the war precipitated one of many economic booms that attracted both capital and labor to the area.

World War I, in fact, brought a diverse flow of immigrants and other new workers to the East Bay. The flurry of shipbuilding activity and the dominance of Scottish shipwrights and other skilled workers earned Oakland the nickname "Glasgow of the West."[14] Although some blacks found temporary work in the shipyards, white ethnics occupied the majority of skilled jobs and consolidated their strength in unions like the Boilermakers, the Shipwrights, and the Machinists. Some of them would still be employed during the far more dramatic boom of the Second World War, offering leadership—and sometimes hostility—to the next wave of defense migrants.

The improvements in port facilities during the 1910s and 1920s enabled city leaders to lure new industries to Oakland, many of them branch plants of eastern and midwestern concerns. During the 1920s, city boosters dubbed Oakland "the Detroit of the West" with the arrival of auto assembly plants for companies such as Chevrolet, General Motors, Willys, Faegeol, and Caterpillar Tractor. Numerous other industries, including food processing and chemical, electrical, and paint products, also appeared in these years.[15]

Once again, Richmond followed this pattern a few years later. After years of behind-the-scenes negotiations with a Bay Area real estate developer, Fred Parr, the city contracted for major port improvements and the construction of the Parr Terminal in 1926. Because of the new deep-water port and generous financial incentives from the city, Ford Motor Company located a new assembly plant in Richmond in 1931.[16]

The Depression Years

Coming on the heels of the 1920s boom, the depression curtailed industrial development in the East Bay. Although West Coast boosters insisted on the relative healthiness of their cities, such claims were groundless. According to the State Unemployment Commission, the jobless rate for the San Francisco Bay Area topped 30 percent in the depth of the depression. Despite its recent industrial growth, the East Bay still engaged primarily in transportation and distribution, activities that were hard hit by the depression. Railroad and waterfront operations laid off thousands of workers, and most auto manufacturers reduced production dramatically. Local relief was quickly exhausted, and unemployed transients thronged city streets, parks, and railroad lines.[17]

With the election of Franklin D. Roosevelt in 1932, New Deal relief programs helped ease some of the economic hardships affecting urban residents. Like many other communities, the East Bay benefited from numerous public works projects administered by New Deal agencies. Although conservative business interests often resisted federal intervention, organized labor and the unemployed pressured their governments to undertake federally funded projects such as the Broadway (Caldecott) Tunnel, Berkeley Aquatic Park, new bridges on Park and High Streets in Alameda, and the Treasure Island Fair Grounds. Federal funding from the Reconstruction Finance Corporation also underwrote the construction of the long-awaited Bay Bridge. Under the Wagner-Steagall Housing Act of 1937, the Public Works Administration began building hundreds of public housing projects in cities throughout the United States, including three in Oakland and two in Richmond. These federally financed construction projects established a strong federal presence in East Bay cities, providing organizational precedents for the extensive federal-local cooperation accompanying World War II. In the short term, they provided much-needed employment and income for local workers and their families.

Despite such relief measures, thousands of unemployed left East Bay cities to seek work elsewhere. These urban refugees sought work in mining towns in the Sierra Nevada, in the agricultural areas of the Central and coastal valleys, and on the Boulder, Shasta, and other new federally funded dam projects. In such areas, former city dwellers joined a growing army of migrant workers and their families, including many from out of state.

The most visible newcomers were the so-called Okies—white migrants from the southwestern states of Oklahoma, Texas, Missouri, and Arkansas.[18] Although southwestern migration to California had begun with the collapse of crop prices following World War I, the stream of migrants became a flood in the mid-thirties. In the midst of droughts, dust storms, and other environmental calamities of these years, southwesterners also suffered the effects of New Deal agricultural programs that encouraged farm mechanization and ravaged the tenant system. The collapse of farming triggered a chain reaction of economic decline in southwestern cities, displacing urban manufacturing and service workers as well.

Some three to four hundred thousand southwesterners came to California in the 1930s, the majority of them settling in the San Joaquin Valley and the greater Los Angeles area. In the agricultural valleys, where thousands of Okie families followed the seasonal harvests, local residents gave them a decidedly cool reception. Bitter anti-Okie feelings developed, fed by economic competition and cultural differences. In many areas, assimilation was difficult, with most migrant families living in separate farm labor camps or in "Little Oklahomas" on the edge of town. Unfamiliar with or unsympathetic to the migrants, natives denounced them as ignorant, backward, lazy, and immoral, and groups like the California Citizens Association worked to bar newcomers from the state.[19]

John Steinbeck's *The Grapes of Wrath* and the photographs of Dorothea Lange had brought the Okie problem to state- and nationwide attention. Although only 9.2 percent of California-bound southwesterners settled in the Bay Area, local residents were quite familiar with the highly publicized Okie controversy.[20] A few years later, when defense industries began luring southwesterners into coastal cities, the earlier Okie debate would inform local attitudes toward all migrants, regardless of their origins. During the depression, however, southwestern migrants entered East Bay communities largely unnoticed.

Bay Area leaders were in fact preoccupied with more pressing problems during these years. Beginning in May 1934, local longshoremen, seamen, and other maritime workers engaged in an eighty-three-day strike led by Harry Bridges and other union militants and Communists. In Oakland and Alameda, striking workers threw picket lines around municipal docks while city police escorted scab workers to their jobs. On May 23, Oakland police opened fire on union members who gathered at the Cromwell Stevedore Association to protest the group's strikebreaking activities. Two workers were wounded, and relations between labor and the city's governing elite deteriorated.

The most serious confrontation, however, occurred in July in San Francisco when police killed two strikers in what became known as "Bloody Thursday." In response to these killings, some one hundred thousand Bay Area workers joined in a four-day general strike, including members of more than seventy East Bay locals. In Oakland, the Amalgamated Streetcar Workers not only walked off the job but also threatened to take over the Key System and make it "a mass transportation system for working people." Business leaders reacted with alarm; as one employer representative said, "We felt this was the first step in class conflict that might lead to anything." Despite its militancy, however, the strike ended on an ambiguous note when American Federation of Labor (AFL) leaders agreed to government arbitration over strong opposition by the rank and file. The "Big Strike," however, did galvanize support for unions on the waterfront and reinvigorated the more staid "uptown" unions as well.[21]

One of the most significant legacies of the strike was the opening of the Pacific waterfront to black workers. Traditionally barred from most maritime employment except as strikebreakers, black workers first entered the San Francisco local of the International Longshoremen's Association (ILA) in 1934. When Bridges took the ILA local over to the Committee for Industrial Organization (CIO) in 1937, the new International Longshoremen's and Warehousemen's Union (ILWU) joined other CIO unions in spearheading the fight against racial discrimination. That same year, the Pullman Company recognized the black Brotherhood of Sleeping Car Porters, granting its members higher wages, shorter hours, and increased political clout for A. Philip Randolph, the union president, and C. L. Dellums, a local business agent. Black labor leaders like Dellums thus gained important contacts and experience that would later influence civil rights organizing during the war. Several prominent civil rights leaders also emerged from south Berkeley's middle-class black community during the thirties, including Walter Gordon, Frances Albrier, William Byron Rumford, and Tarea Hall Pittman.[22]

Perhaps the most significant labor activities of the depression years were the organizing efforts of the newly formed CIO unions. In the East Bay, CIO activists sought to organize workers in auto plants, steel mills, canneries, oil refineries, shipyards, and rubber plants; they also founded unions for service workers such as newsboys, bootblacks, newspaper writers, public employees, and domestic workers. Dissidents in the CIO sometimes worked within existing AFL and company unions to address pressing rank-and-file issues. In the late thirties, East Bay dissidents in the unions for hospital workers, teamsters, carpenters, and retail clerks sought to reaffiliate their locals with the rival CIO.

As in the nation generally, the AFL leadership bitterly resented CIO competition in the East Bay, and major feuding ensued. AFL internationals revoked the charters of several dissident locals, and the Alameda County Central Labor Council purged dozens of CIO unions in 1937. In Contra Costa County, where CIO supporters had successfully infiltrated the Central Trades and Labor Council, the organization rejected orders from the national AFL to oust its CIO affiliates. The AFL promptly disbanded the council and established its own rival organization. The Teamsters and other conservative AFL unions also went on the offensive, staging raids on left-wing CIO unions such as the United Auto Workers and the ILWU.[23]

AFL leaders relied on their close ties with local business interests to help suppress CIO organizing drives. With the rise of the Knowland machine in the early thirties, conservative AFL leaders were offered limited participation in Oakland politics in return for their loyalty. The most visible labor politician was James Quinn, a Republican council member, the president of the Alameda County Building Trades Council, and the editor of the AFL's *East Bay Labor Journal*. Quinn's paper regularly endorsed probusiness candidates such as Congressman William F. Knowland (Joseph's son) and District Attorney Earl Warren, both Republicans known for their staunch antilabor views. In return for its loyalty, the CIO claimed, city police looked the other way when AFL thugs attacked CIO organizers. Quinn and other AFL council members likewise remained silent when city police intervened on the side of employers during CIO labor actions.

Organized labor in the East Bay was so divided in this period that even Labor Day parades became controversial. In 1937 AFL representatives used their influence with Oakland officials to have the CIO barred from participating in the traditional Labor Day morning parade. The city issued a special permit to the CIO, allowing its members to hold a separate parade in the afternoon. The following year, the city rejected this arrangement and called for the AFL and CIO to march together. The AFL flatly refused and boycotted the event. In a time of unprecedented labor activism and growth, the Labor Day fiasco revealed the depth of local labor disunity.[24]

Infighting between the AFL and CIO ultimately hindered effective political action during these years. Labor's Non-Partisan League, a political organization founded by CIO members in several U.S. cities, was the most visible labor group in East Bay politics. The Alameda County branch, which also included some members of the AFL, the Communist party, and the Railroad Brotherhoods, worked to "Bring the New Deal to California" by pressuring recalcitrant local officials to accept federal funding for public housing and public works projects. The league also endorsed federal, state, and county political candidates who promised to implement New Deal programs. On the municipal level, however, labor unity disintegrated as powerful AFL leaders formed a rival political league to back local machine candidates. In Oakland, dissident labor and Communist candidates periodically challenged city council incumbents but were easily swept aside. A similar situation prevailed in Berkeley, where New Deal Democrats on the county level made little headway in municipal politics.[25]

In Richmond, a veritable company town, labor had even less influence. Here, Standard Oil and allied business interests held a firm grip on local government. In 1940, most of the city's highest officials had been in office for twenty years or more. Historically, Standard Oil executives had supplied many of the city's mayors and council members, while the corporation's use of company unions and corporate welfare programs had undermined labor's political power. Describing the situation in 1945, even the staid AFL Boilermakers Union felt that the Richmond government left much to be desired: "The city government was essentially conservative and its council, through the then existing conservative 'machine,' had practically perpetuated itself in office for about fifteen years. Labor had been given lip-service, but was not yet recognized as a force in the economic life of the community. Strikes were unknown. In summary, it is safe to say that Richmond was a smug little town."[26]

Richmond and other "smug" cities would have the hardest time adjusting to the massive disruptions that accompanied World War II. Smaller cities were the least prepared to handle the mass influx of wartime industry and workers, and conservative leaders had a notably adverse reaction to the flood of newcomers who threatened to transform the social and political life of the community. Oakland, by contrast, offered a somewhat more open political climate. Here, certain labor and progressive forces would be more sympathetic toward the newcomers and their attempts to adjust to urban life in the West. In both cities, though, the experience would not be an easy one as the powerful forces of war roused the East Bay from its provincial past into national and international prominence.

The East Bay on the Eve of World War II

Nearly a hundred years after the arrival of the first gold rush settlers, the East Bay continued to vacillate between suburban growth and urban-industrial development. Prior to the construction of the Bay Bridge in 1936, the East Bay had developed relatively auton- omously, looking more toward Oakland than toward San Francisco. Up until the postwar era, in fact, Oakland remained the industrial, business, and financial center of the East Bay. Although many residents commuted to San Francisco, the majority found employment closer to home. All train and streetcar lines led to downtown Oakland, and ma- jor department stores, theaters, and cultural events provided amuse- ments not available in the smaller East Bay towns. Although always in competition with "the City" across the Bay, Oakland maintained its position as a vital urban center with more than three hundred thousand residents in 1940.

With its many factories and transportation lines, the East Bay had also become one of California's chief industrial centers. In 1940, both Oakland and Richmond were predominantly blue-collar communities; approximately 14 percent of residents were foreign-born, and immi- grants and their children made up an estimated 30 percent of the total population.[27] Flatland neighborhoods closest to the rails and docks were established working-class communities. Skilled white workers in- habited the more desirable neighborhoods such as Point Richmond and Oakland's East-of-the-Lake district. Italians, Portuguese, Mexi- cans, Eastern Europeans, blacks, and other recent migrant groups oc- cupied the oldest waterfront areas of west Oakland, south Berkeley, and north Richmond.

Old-timers from these areas recall different ethnic and racial groups living alongside one another in predominantly single-family homes, many of them owner-occupied. Marguerite Williams, a prewar black resident of west Oakland, described the area as a cohesive, multiracial neighborhood: "We all lived together in a little community. The kids would go across the street and play basketball together . . . there wasn't any racial fights." This multicultural quality was even more pronounced in north Richmond, where, as Shirley Ann Moore has shown, long-time black residents mingled freely with their white and Hispanic neighbors. North Richmond blacks learned to make tamales, dance the polka, and wager on local bullfights; some even learned to speak Spanish, Italian, or Portuguese. The relatively small number of prewar black residents in East Bay communities made for a more fluid and tolerant social climate.[28]

Farther inland, more affluent middle-class neighborhoods housed native-born and second-generation white ethnic residents. These areas, roughly coterminous with the old streetcar suburbs of the nineteenth century, included much of north and east Oakland and the newer neighborhoods on Richmond's east side. Finally, the exclusive East Bay hills were home to the area's corporate and financial elite. Fashionable hillside neighborhoods and independent enclaves such as Piedmont, Kensington, and El Cerrito served as bedroom communities for the area's most prosperous residents. East Bay cities were thus vertically stratified according to social and economic class.

The public life of downtown commercial districts mirrored the social stratification of East Bay cities. Downtown Oakland, especially, offered a wide variety of amenities and gathering spots for local residents. In the heart of downtown and along Lake Merritt, the city's elite gathered for meetings at the Athens Club, the Oakland Forum, and the City Club. Framed by imposing edifices reflecting the civic pride of the Progressive Era, these institutions formed the heart of Oakland "society." Farther uptown, palatial art deco movie houses, department stores, and restaurants provided public arenas for a broader middle-class clientele. For the less prosperous, more congenial meeting places could be found down near the waterfront and in flatland neighborhoods, where various ethnic groups had established their own businesses and gathering spots.

Looking back on the prewar era, old-time Oakland residents remembered their city somewhat nostalgically as a stable, "well-ordered" community. Steady economic growth during the 1910s and 1920s had, in fact, fostered a gradual expansion of downtown trade and services to keep pace with residential growth. Ethnic and racial minorities had

likewise developed their own commercial districts, venturing downtown periodically for items unavailable in their own neighborhoods.
The *Oakland Observer,* a conservative society weekly, proudly described
prewar Oakland as "pretty well settled down. The various elements of
the city stayed in their localities and were fairly well satisfied."[29] The
city's black and working-class residents echoed this sense of prewar
self-sufficiency, celebrating the accomplishments of their churches,
clubs, and other civic organizations. None of these groups would be
prepared to cope with the colossal changes and confusion that war
would bring to their communities.

Residents of Richmond viewed their community somewhat differently and with even greater nostalgia. Here, old-time residents
described prewar Richmond as a small, self-sufficient town where "everybody knew everybody." According to one visiting journalist, downtown street life was friendly and casual, and "marketing on Macdonald
Avenue left plenty of time for chatting on street corners and admiring
the view of Mount Tamalpais across the Bay." Even during the Christmas rush, Stanley Nystrom recalled, "you would go downtown shopping, and you would bump into everybody that you knew." Another
prewar resident, Marguerite Clausen, remembers Richmond as "a very
self-contained little town" where you could find "anything you needed."
As the Planning Commission described it, "There was a sense of identity with Richmond, and a feeling of belonging that comes naturally to
a small, established city."[30]

Although Richmond natives tended to romanticize their small-town
past—particularly in the wake of the war boom—there was some validity to their claims. Prior to World War II, Richmond was a relatively
small, pastoral community by East Bay standards. Despite its industrial
growth, the city had a population of less than twenty-four thousand in
1940 and abundant open space along its south side. Open fields covered the area south of Cutting Boulevard, where poorer families grazed
goats and other livestock during the depression years.[31] The downtown
itself was fairly small, encompassing the main thoroughfare of Macdonald Avenue and a few cross streets. Many Richmond residents did
know one another, and personal contacts often characterized downtown shopping and other public activities.

The small-town climate also prevailed in the nearby suburban communities of Alameda, Albany, and Berkeley. Alameda, originally a peninsula extending off of east Oakland, became an island when the Tidal

Canal was constructed in 1901. The island subsequently developed as a relatively insulated, middle-class community of white-collar home-owners, many of whom worked in Oakland and San Francisco. On Oakland's northern border, the city of Berkeley also housed a large white-collar population. A significant number of these residents, like those in adjoining Albany, were affiliated with the University of California, the institution around which the town had grown. Although south and west Berkeley had industrial and working-class neighborhoods, the city overall was more sedate and middle-class than its blue-collar neighbors, Oakland and Richmond. Finally, on the extreme ends of the metropolitan area were the urban fringe communities of San Pablo on the north and San Leandro on the south. Future suburban development would be concentrated in these areas.

Although Oakland's urban-industrial economy continued to dominate these smaller communities in 1940, changes were on the horizon. The opening of the Bay Bridge in 1936 and the Golden Gate Bridge in 1937 ensured the emergence of San Francisco as the undisputed commercial capital of the region. For the East Bay, the completion of the Bay Bridge signaled a shift of commercial and financial power from Oakland to San Francisco. This consolidation of the Bay Area economy and easier commuting to San Francisco accelerated the suburbanization of the East Bay. To avoid central city congestion and resurgent labor problems, business leaders also expressed interest in outlying suburban areas for new plant locations. Beginning in 1935, the Oakland Chamber of Commerce de-emphasized central city industrial development, focusing instead on the "Metropolitan Oakland Area," including rural lands in central and southern Alameda County. Although few new industries located in these areas prior to World War II, the direction of future economic growth was evident.[32]

The most significant change, though, would come in response to international events. In the late thirties, a rising tide of fascism in Germany, Italy, and Japan began to erode U.S. isolationism, allowing Roosevelt to begin a rearmament program that would eventually boost the fortunes of the East Bay and other American communities. Although the president had promised to keep American boys out of foreign wars, the German invasion of Poland, Belgium, Holland, and France convinced Roosevelt and Congress to approve the Lend-Lease Act in March 1941. The $7 billion of military appropriations provided by the act brought Henry Kaiser, a local construction magnate, and many other industrialists into the defense business overnight.

When the Japanese attacked Pearl Harbor on December 7, 1941, the United States entered the war, triggering the greatest defense buildup in American history. Supported by massive government subsidies, the East Bay would experience a boom as great as any since the earthquake. As in Detroit, Los Angeles, Seattle, and many other defense centers, the consequences of this event would shape the course of urban development well into the postwar era.

2

The Second Gold Rush

"The Second Gold Rush Hits the West," announced the
San Francisco Chronicle in the spring of 1943. Echoing the words of
shipbuilding magnate Henry Kaiser, the *Chronicle* hailed "the coming
industrial empire in the West" and dubbed migrant workers "the argo-
nauts of today."[1] In many ways, the comparison to the gold rush was
an apt one; not since 1849 had the economy and population of the
Bay Area grown so rapidly or dramatically. Indeed in California,
World War II was to the twentieth century what the gold rush had
been to the nineteenth. Unlike the earlier boom, however, the federal
government now played a key role in directing and facilitating the flow
of migration.

Although Bay Area boosters had been wooing U.S. government
projects since the early twentieth century, it was not until the 1930s
that significant federal involvement occurred in the region. Much of
this involvement grew out of New Deal economic programs for work
relief, housing, and public works. The coming of the war, however,
rapidly expanded this federal influence as the United States invested
billions of dollars in new defense spending. Beginning gradually under
the rearmament program of the late 1930s, mobilization intensified in
1942 following the attack on Pearl Harbor. One of the federal government's most important activities was the coordination of industrial
production and labor recruitment that would shape urban migration
and development throughout the country.

East Bay defense contractors initially turned to traditional sources of labor within Northern California, drawing on the sizable pool of unemployed men in the late 1930s. But as the labor shortage intensified, employers worked with the federal government in recruiting hundreds of thousands of additional workers, including women, youth, the elderly, and the handicapped. Most important, Kaiser and other shipyard managers scoured the country for potential labor, importing workers and their families from all forty-eight states and abroad. The vast majority, including a significant number of black families, came from southern and midwestern states.

The resulting migration was the most dramatic in Bay Area history since the gold rush. Traditionally a land of migrants, California underwent marked demographic shifts during 1940–1944 in age, sex, race, and region of origin. Most noticeably, war migration increased the racial and cultural diversity of the population, making the East Bay and other urban centers more black and more southern than ever before. The surge of new urban dwellers—more so than the industries that brought them—constituted the most significant change for these cities. Although many defense industries would close down with the end of the war, most of the migrants would stay, permanently altering the composition of the urban population.

As historian Roger Lotchin has shown, California cities had been cultivating a "metropolitan-military" relationship with the federal government since the early twentieth century. Beginning in the 1910s, West Coast cities fiercely competed for new naval bases and other military facilities as the U.S. Navy expanded its Pacific fleet. In the San Francisco area, however, rivalries between urban boosters in neighboring cities stalled the military buildup until the mid-1930s. As a result, many federal installations were not completed until the eve of World War II.

The earliest signs of the defense boom appeared in Oakland and Alameda in 1938, when the federal government selected two sites for new military installations as part of the rearmament program. Located midway down the Pacific Coast at the terminus of three transcontinental railroads, Oakland was a logical supply and distribution point for the Pacific war basin. Construction of the Alameda Naval Air Station (an aircraft base and repair facility) and the nearby Naval Supply Base in Oakland began in 1938. These projects were soon followed by plans for new army facilities along Oakland's outer harbor, including the

Camp Knight training center and the Quartermaster's Supply Depot. In Albany, on the grounds of the Golden Gate Fields racetrack, the navy constructed the Naval Landing Forces Equipment Depot to service incoming vessels.

By the end of 1940, the federal government had spent more than $60 million to construct these facilities and had hired thousands of military and civilian personnel to staff them. Not surprisingly, World War II marked the beginning of the Bay Area's reliance on direct federal government employment; for the first time, the federal government offered more jobs than the state and local governments combined.[2]

The major source of wartime industrial growth in the region was, of course, shipbuilding. The Merchant Marine Act of 1936 laid the groundwork for the wartime construction boom by establishing the United States Maritime Commission to coordinate the development of an expanded merchant fleet. With the start of the emergency construction program in 1941, Bay Area shipbuilding moved into high gear. As the nation's number one shipbuilding center, the region received nearly $5 billion in contracts from the navy and the Maritime Commission. By peak employment in 1943, Bay Area shipyards employed nearly 80 percent of those who worked in the region's heavy industry.[3] The East Bay employed well over half of these workers at twelve shipyards located between Alameda and Richmond, making it the largest producer of cargo ships on the West Coast. Among the most significant operations was Oakland's Moore Dry Dock Company, which expanded its ship conversion facilities into two new yards and employed more than thirty-five thousand workers at peak production. General Engineering Company, Pacific Bridge Company, Bethlehem Steel, and Pacific Coast Engineering Company in Alameda also each employed several thousand workers.

The most important development in East Bay shipbuilding, however, was the empire of Henry Kaiser that grew up overnight along the undeveloped Richmond shoreline. Kaiser's construction career had begun in the 1920s with a road-paving business that had progressed into major bridge and dam building by the mid-1930s. In order to gain lucrative federal government contracts for such projects as the San Francisco–Oakland Bay Bridge and the Hoover, Grand Coolee, Shasta, and Bonneville dams, Kaiser had joined with several other major construction contractors to form a conglomerate known as the Six Companies. Through experience with the Six Companies, Kaiser learned to negotiate the bureaucratic waters of Washington, D.C., and had earned the respect of New Deal administrators.[4] Kaiser was thus in a good position when in 1940 the federal government sought bidders for a contract to build thirty cargo ships for the British under what would become the lend-lease program.

Construction of Yard One in Richmond began in December 1940 under the management of Kaiser's Todd-California Shipbuilding Corporation. Shortly after the United States entered the war, the government awarded Kaiser the first of many contracts for Maritime Commission Liberty ships, large merchant vessels used to supply Allied troops. To complete these contracts, the newly organized Kaiser and Permanente corporations constructed three more yards adjacent to the first. During the same period, Kaiser's empire also included major shipyard operations in Portland, Oregon, and Vancouver, Washington; a steel foundry in Southern California; and partial interests in Calship, Todd-Bath, and several other shipyards around the country. In Richmond alone, Kaiser produced 727 cargo ships, including one-fifth of all Liberty ships in the United States. At peak production, the Richmond yards employed 90,634 people—7.3 percent of all manufacturing employees in California at that time. The Kaiser shipyards were clearly the most influential development of World War II in the East Bay economy.[5]

While more than one hundred fifty thousand people worked in East Bay shipyards, a smaller but significant number worked in related defense industries. In the last six months of 1943, Alameda County had 353 prime contracts valued at $5,489,880 and another 192 subcontracts totaling $2,345,574, exclusive of shipbuilding. Auto manufacturing, food processing, railroads, electrical plants, and oil refining all saw major expansion. In adjacent Contra Costa County, Richmond had more than fifty-five defense contractors in 1943 with some thirty thousand workers.[6] Finally, there were the uncounted thousands of nonessential workers in the trade and service sectors who met the needs of a greatly expanded population.

Attracted by shipyards and other defense industries, the civilian population of the Bay Area swelled by over half a million, or 25.9 percent, from 1940 to 1945—the highest growth rate of all the state's metropolitan areas excluding San Diego. Over half of these newcomers settled outside of San Francisco in the East and North Bay. Small industrial cities like Richmond became world-famous boomtowns; from a prewar population of 23,642 in 1940, Richmond grew to over 93,738 in 1943. Oakland developed at a more manageable rate but also had a major population gain, growing from 302,163 in 1940 to 345,345 in 1944 (see table 4). In addition, Oakland's role as a central supply point and port of embarkation for the Pacific theater resulted in an estimated floating population of fifteen to twenty thousand military personnel in a given twenty-four-hour period. In general, the towns with the higher growth rates received the largest numbers of out-of-state migrants.

Labor Recruitment

World War II migration occurred not as a single event but as successive waves that originated at progressively distant points as the war continued. The recruitment program of the Kaiser Richmond yards, some of whose records and statistics have survived, provide insights into this migration.

Shipbuilding, like most major industries during World War II, fell under the jurisdiction of the newly formed War Labor Board (WLB), the federal agency charged with resolving wartime labor-management disputes. In the shipbuilding industry, Kaiser and other employers joined with shipyard unions in forming the Shipbuilding Stabilization Committee and forged an eight-point agreement designed to increase production, control migration, and smooth labor relations. Labor, dominated by the American Federation of Labor (AFL) in West Coast shipyards, agreed to a no-strike pledge in exchange for maintenance of membership provisions that effectively created a closed shop and wage rates that were among the nation's highest within the manufacturing sector: $1.05 per hour for all journeyman trades, increasing to $1.20 by 1943 (the average U.S. hourly wage in manufacturing in December 1943 was $.99).[7]

The agreement also established the AFL's International Brotherhood of Boilermakers, Iron Shipbuilders and Helpers Union as chief labor representative in West Coast shipyards. Under the stabilization agreement, the Boilermakers gained control of hiring and, in effect, seniority, skills, and advancement within most shipyard trades. Kaiser, with the help of the new federal War Manpower Commission (WMC), conveyed new laborers to the hiring halls; the union directed their movement after that point.

Table 4 *Population Growth of Four East Bay Cities, 1940–1950*

City	1940 Total population	1943–1944* Total population	1943–1944* % increase over 1940	1950 Total population	1950 % increase over 1944	1950 % increase over 1940
Alameda	36,256	43,909	21.1	64,430	46.7	77.7
Berkeley	85,547	97,790	14.3	113,805	16.4	33.0
Oakland	302,163	345,345	14.3	384,575	11.4	27.3
Richmond	23,642	93,738	296.5	99,545	6.2	321.1

SOURCES: U.S. Bureau of the Census, *Sixteenth Census of the United States, 1940*, vol. 2, *Characteristics of the Population*, pt. 1, "California"; *Seventeenth Census of the Population, 1950*, vol. 2, *Characteristics of the Population*, pt. 5, "California"; *Population*, ser. CA-3, *Characteristics of the Population, Labor Force, Families, and Housing*, no. 3, "San Francisco Bay Congested Production Area"; *Special Census of Richmond, California: September 14, 1943*, ser. P-SC, no. 6, located in Record Group 212, Committee for Congested Production Areas, central files, San Francisco Area, box 114; *San Francisco Chronicle*, March 10, 1943, p. 13.

*Oakland figures based on federal estimates from April 1944; Alameda and Richmond figures based on federal estimates from March and September 1943, respectively.

Prior to the attack on Pearl Harbor in December 1941, migration had proceeded slowly and was discouraged by both labor and government. With unemployment still exceeding 13 percent in 1940, the Bay Area market offered an ample supply of labor. Since the yards sought mainly skilled workers, they also drew on former Bay Area workers who had left the region to work on dams and other construction projects. One survey of Oakland migrants indicated that 22 percent were former residents of Alameda County who had left the area for four or more years during the depression. These and other workers, nearly 60 percent of whom were from California, came primarily from construction, manufacturing, and trades. At the Richmond yards, management recruited skilled workers from other Kaiser projects such as the Hoover and Grand Coolee dams.

By 1941, however, Richmond authorities were becoming alarmed at the growing influx of unskilled workers. They feared that these workers, like the depression-era Okies, would burden county relief rolls. In February, the *Richmond Independent* applauded the California Federation of Labor for launching a public relations campaign to discourage out-of-state migration, noting that "the man who thinks he will get a job building ships because he built a woodshed somewhere is doomed to disappointment." Within months, however, the Kaiser shipyards would be recruiting just that sort of worker.[8]

With the entry of the United States into the war, orders for new Liberty ships turned a labor abundance into a shortage virtually overnight. Interestingly, some longtime East Bay residents did not rush to apply for higher-paying jobs in the shipyards. According to one longtime resident, Marguerite Clausen, her family preferred to stay in more stable sectors of the work force, despite the lower wages. "When the war is done," she said, "you're out of a job. If you stay where you are, you're getting seniority." In fact, Clausen added, "We didn't know anybody that worked in the shipyards in preference to their own jobs." Other old-time residents like Stanley Nystrom moved into defense work but carefully selected jobs and installations that would continue operation after the war. Nystrom actually took a four-dollar-a-day pay cut from his job at Standard Oil to become an electrician's apprentice at Mare Island Navy Yard in Vallejo. His apprenticeship turned into a permanent job that lasted thirty-seven years.

Later in the war, when the shipyards began recruiting black workers, some longtime black residents expressed similar reservations. Writing in the Oakland-based black newspaper *California Voice*, Louis

Campbell urged black men to "look before they leaped," warning that when the war was over, they would be "cast adrift in the army of the unemployed." Some local residents, it seems, accurately anticipated the dislocations that would occur in the postwar period, carefully selecting or rejecting new work opportunities.[9]

With the rapid expansion of emergency shipyards, employers and the federal government attempted to meet labor demands by importing workers from out of town. The War Manpower Commission took over the state employment office in Richmond and began scouring the state for available workers. The largest number of workers came from agricultural and mining areas in Northern California. Unemployed farm workers in the Central Valley, including many recent Okie migrants, were recruited through U.S. Employment Service (USES) offices in Fresno, Sacramento, and Bakersfield. With the cessation of gold mining in the northern mountains, many small-town mine workers also headed to Bay Area shipyards. By September 1943, Harry T. Krantz, western regional director of the U.S. Civil Service Commission, reported that inland California had "practically no one left who is available for any particular Federal use."[10]

Kaiser also recruited urban workers from the Los Angeles area, a program that became progressively unpopular with local governments. Beginning in June 1942, Kaiser and USES recruited unemployed Southern Californians to work in Richmond, sending several hundred per month. The Los Angeles program was the least successful of any of the recruitment drives, with a 50 percent attrition rate. Management blamed the problem on "the type of workman" coming from the area, where any "desirable type of man" would have already been working in local defense industries.[11] Los Angeles employers, who were struggling with a labor shortage of their own, also resented these efforts to "pirate away" local labor.

Perhaps at the instigation of Southern California employers, Los Angeles County announced a "work for drunks" program in the fall of 1942. Under this program, judges gave suspended sentences to vagrants and other petty offenders who agreed to sign on at the Richmond yards. On October 22, 1942, seventy-four "drunks" arrived by bus in Richmond; three were immediately arrested for public intoxication. Richmond Police Chief L. E. Jones denounced the practice, claiming that the local jail was "too small to handle the output of the Southern California cities." Management and labor blamed one another for the policy, and Kaiser temporarily suspended all Los Angeles recruiting under pressure from the Maritime Commission. The suspension prompted the company to turn its recruiting efforts out of state in November 1942.[12]

With the help of the WMC, Kaiser targeted dozens of southern and midwestern cities where excess labor was available. The company employed more than 170 paid recruiters to procure workers for the Richmond and Portland yards. Twenty-one recruiters worked east of the Mississippi, and many more covered the Midwest and the South Central states.[13] In late 1942 and early 1943, a Kaiser Industrial Relations report indicated that the largest number of recruits came from Minneapolis, followed by Memphis; Little Rock; Saint Louis; Chattanooga, Tennessee; Omaha; Fort Smith, Arkansas; Phoenix; and Sikeston and Cape Girardeau, Missouri. In the peak recruitment days of 1943, more than one hundred men per day left Minneapolis, Kansas City, Chicago, and Memphis, many of whom had been bused in from smaller towns in the region. By the end of the war, Kaiser had brought 37,852 workers to Richmond, fronting their train fare; another 60,000 came on their own with recruiter referrals.[14]

Working out of a central office, recruiters canvassed their regions, visiting small and large towns along the way. As the military absorbed the supply of single men, recruiters signed on increasing numbers of married men. Management wanted these men to leave their families behind for fear of aggravating local housing and transportation problems. But recruiters, who worked on a per-person commission basis, painted a rosy picture of life in the East Bay, downplaying the housing shortage and other potential problems. A Kaiser recruiting pamphlet suggests how recruiters made their pitch:

With or without experience, there's a job of vital importance to your country waiting for you in the Richmond shipyards. And it opens a rare opportunity. You can learn a trade, get paid while you're learning, and earn the highest wages for comparable work anywhere in the world. . . . Richmond is less than an hour from San Francisco—the city you've always wanted to see. You'll be living where the sun shines 275 days a year—never a snowstorm, never too hot for comfort. . . . your job will be for the duration and indefinitely beyond. The United States is committed to building a huge Merchant Marine after the war. . . . There is every indication that shipbuilding has returned to the Pacific Coast to stay.

Potential employers thus played on a recruit's sense of patriotism, the desire for economic security, and a mythic "California dream" long cultivated by state boosters.[15]

Those who signed on were given train tickets and travel advances that were deducted from their first months' pay at a rate of $10 per week. Others, especially those with families, received work clearances and came in their own cars. Recruits were required to bring at least $25 in cash to pay union initiation fees before beginning work. Overall, the recruitment program was not highly efficient; many workers defected along the way, others quit after one or two shifts. A Kaiser auditor reported in June 1943 that the company had spent $600,000 to bring 8,000–9,000 workers to Richmond of whom only 2,500 were still on the job.[16] At an average investment of $60 per person, the company lost hundreds of thousands of dollars. Only the requisites of war and the flexibility of the cost-plus system, which passed along cost overruns to the federal government, kept the recruitment going.

In early 1943, Kaiser's Industrial Relations Department conducted an investigation of the contract recruit program to determine the causes of the high attrition rate. The report provides a rare glimpse of the migration as well as employer attitudes toward the new workers. A minor, if persistent, problem were those who signed on with the company for "a free ride" to California, never intending to work in the shipyards. Others set out for California but either disappeared en route or were put off the train as "troublemakers," "mental patients," and so forth. Some hirees spent their advances on alcohol, the company reported, making "their first stop in Richmond at a bar, and never [finding] the time to stagger in to the Hiring Hall." On the whole, however, the men in these categories accounted for a very small percentage of total manpower losses. The vast majority of recruits, the company noted, were "sincerely anxious to build ships."[17]

The hardships of the trip, unfulfilled expectations, and the difficulties of adjusting to wartime living conditions accounted for the bulk of personnel losses. Averaging three to four days, the train trip from the South or Midwest was crowded and uncomfortable, offering little opportunity to eat or sleep. After a long trip in the "cattle cars," as recruits termed them, the men arrived in Richmond "in a despondent mood . . . feeling that Kaiser [had] given them a bad deal." Some arrived in ill health with colds, sore throats, and pneumonia, and many were too weak to stand in line as required. Others were simply disappointed with the town; Richmond in the rainy season could not measure up to the glorious vision of California propagated by the recruiters and other boosters. A number of recruits also expected more skilled crafts work, not understanding the nature of mass-production shipbuilding. In fact, the company reported that more than 150 fully equipped woodworking toolboxes lay unclaimed in the baggage room of Richmond's Southern Pacific depot. For these and other reasons, thousands of men hopped the first train back home or drifted on to other defense jobs.[18]

The greatest difficulty for new recruits, though, was navigating the bureaucratic complexities of war boomtowns. From the moment of their arrival, new recruits stood in line "first, at the information desk; second, at the housing desk; third, at the union; fourth, to sign in; and fifth, at the various departments any new employee may be required to see." Oftentimes, recruits waited in line for hours "only to have the window closed in their face." This "runaround" was particularly frustrating to the many recruits who came from small towns and rural areas and were unaccustomed to dealing with urban bureaucracies.

Finding affordable housing was another chore, and many found they could not meet the costs of transportation, eating out, and paying rent. The burden was particularly great for those supporting two households at once. Some of these men sent for their families to join them; others returned home after a short time.[19]

One group of discontented recruits confronted Kaiser directly in December 1942. Protesting what they felt was false advertising, these men signed a petition objecting to Kaiser recruitment pamphlets which claimed that "thousands of families of shipyard workers occupy pleasant homes at moderate rentals, with plenty of opportunity to enjoy outdoor life in California's sunshine." At the very least, Kaiser had promised them dorm rooms for $3.75 per week and an accessible cafeteria. Instead, they explained, they were paying more than $5.00 per week for lodging in town and had to walk two and a half miles to the Yard Two cafeteria and then wait in line for more than an hour. The petitioners stated that unless the company took corrective measures by Christmas they would consider their contracts invalid and return home. There is no indication if the dispute was resolved, but the petition symbolized the widespread discontent felt by many out-of-state recruits.[20]

In their investigation, Kaiser officials found significantly higher attrition rates among southern white recruits. Noting a 5 percent loss among recruits from Memphis and Little Rock compared with 3 percent among those from Minneapolis, management observed that southerners were more prone to heart ailments and other health problems due to poor diets and medical treatment. More important, they continued, southern recruits were "of a very different character than those from the Middle West" and were continually grumbling about conditions. Many southerners, they said, complained that they did not like Richmond, that the cost of living was too high, or that they wanted their wives brought out. In short, "they [were] homesick." Furthermore, they said, "the men from the South complain more about the fact that the shipyards employ, and they must mingle with, all races, creeds, and colors."[21] Such comments suggest that southern whites more actively resisted the new wartime regime and resented the more liberal social mores of western cities.

Annoyed by the constant "griping," company officials clearly favored workers from the northern Midwest over those from the South. Once employment opportunities in Bay Area shipyards made headlines, however, migration took on its own dynamic. As recruitment drives served to publicize new work opportunities, hundreds of thousands of families around the country set off for West Coast cities. In 1945, William Martin Camp, a writer for the *San Francisco Chronicle,* described this phenomenon in *Skip to My Lou,* a popular novel about an Arkansas family's odyssey to Richmond. There were, he said, "whole sections of the country being loaded into cars and trucks and trailers, busses, and trains. . . . At night the highways were dotted with their campfires, and the roadhouses and trailer camps were crowded with them."[22] U.S. Routes 40 and 66, the main arteries to California, carried a steady stream of westbound caravans in 1942–1943.

In Oklahoma, Texas, and Arkansas, the departing caravans were a familiar sight; there had been a continuous exodus from these states since the mid-thirties because of the dust storms, farm mechanization, and New Deal agricultural programs. But as Davis McEntire, an economist, explains, "the drought-depression–impelled movement of the 1930s, which aroused so much anxiety in California, only set the stage for the much larger movement to come." This "larger movement" especially affected the coastal cities, whose growth rates had slowed dramatically during the depression. From 1941 to 1945 the number of inmigrant settlers in Oakland increased 67.3 percent over the 1935–1940 period, and the increases in smaller boomtowns like Richmond were far greater.[23]

For the first time in Bay Area history, migrants from southern states made up the largest proportion of new urban dwellers. Census figures from 1944 show that the largest number of out-of-state settlers— 97,790, or 29 percent—came from the West South Central states of

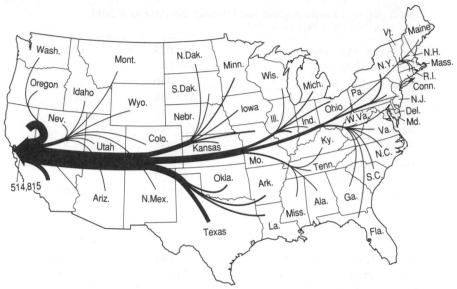

Map 2. Origins of Defense Migrants to the San Francisco Bay Area, 1944
    SOURCE: Sample census taken for the Committee for Congested Production
    Areas by the U.S. Bureau of the Census, spring 1944.

Texas, Arkansas, Oklahoma, and Louisiana (see map 2). In addition,
uncounted thousands of depression-era Okie migrants moved from the
Central Valley and other agricultural areas into coastal cities during the
war years. Agnes Ginn Moore, for instance, first left Arkansas in 1939
for the Salinas Valley, where she worked packing vegetables. After the
war broke out, she and her siblings moved to the Bay Area, where they
found jobs in the Richmond yards. Since the 1944 census counted only
recent arrivals to the state, the impact of this two-stage migration remains unknown.[24]

The second largest group of out-of-state migrants came from the
West North Central region (Minnesota, Iowa, Missouri, Nebraska,
Kansas, and the Dakotas). These states, which sent 74,620, or 22 percent, of interstate migrants, had been the leading region of origin for
Bay Area migrants during 1935–1940. Although no migration statistics are available prior to the 1940 census, demographers believe that
the West North Central states have figured significantly in Bay Area migration since the 1920s.[25] If so, the Bay Area's decades-long association with migrants from the northern Midwest helps to explain their
better reception by employers and other natives during the war. Fur-

Table 5 *Migrant Residents of the San Francisco Bay Area as of 1944,*
by Place of Residence in 1940

From within California	160,825	31.3%
Northern California	103,845	20.2
Southern California	56,980	11.1
From other regions in U.S.*	337,785	65.6
New England	5,810	1.1
Middle Atlantic	22,785	4.4
South Atlantic	11,935	2.3
East North Central	35,525	6.9
West North Central	74,620	14.5
East South Central	9,870	1.9
West South Central	97,790	19.0
Mountain	54,810	10.7
Pacific	24,640	4.8
From foreign countries	16,205	3.1
Total inmigrants	514,815	100.0%

SOURCE: U.S. Bureau of the Census, *Population,* ser. CA-3, *Characteristics of the Population, Labor Force, Families, and Housing,* no. 3, "San Francisco Bay Congested Production Area, April 1944," 14.

*New England: Me., Vt., N.H., Mass., Conn., R.I.; Middle Atlantic: N.Y., N.J., Pa.; South Atlantic: Md., Del., W.Va., Va., N.C., S.C., Ga., Fla.; East North Central: Wis., Mich., Ill., Ind., Ohio; West North Central: Minn., Iowa, Mo., N.Dak., S.Dak., Nebr., Kans.; East South Central: Ky., Tenn., Miss., Ala.; West South Central: Okla., Ark., Tex., La.; Mountain: Mont., Idaho, Wyo., Nev., Utah, Colo., Ariz., N.M.; Pacific: Wash., Ore.

thermore, this group included significant numbers of Scandinavians whose ethnic associations provided a cultural bridge for incoming defense migrants.

During the war, the West Central states (northern and southern) accounted for more than half of all interstate migrants to the Bay Area. For the first time, however, migration from the West South Central region eclipsed that of the northern Midwest. The presence of these southwesterners was even more evident in the shipyards; Moore Dry Dock reported that they made up approximately 20 percent of its work force, and Kaiser reported over 25 percent. Among *all* Bay Area migrants (inter- and intrastate) in 1944, 19 percent were from the West South Central states, 14.5 percent from the West North Central states, 16.7 percent from states east of the Mississippi River, and 31.2 percent from California (see map 2 and table 5).[26] Not surprisingly, southwestern migrants gained a new visibility in East Bay boomtowns.

The preponderance of southwesterners in Bay Area migration helps to explain why observers frequently described newcomers in a stereotyped and distorted fashion. Referred to as "hicks" and "Okies," local residents and media characterized war migrants as poor, rural, and uneducated. In fact, however, less than 16 percent of Bay Area migrants had lived on farms in 1940. The majority had moved from towns and small cities, where they had worked in manufacturing, trade, and construction. Among southwesterners, however, over 30 percent had resided on farms in 1940—the highest percentage of any regional group.[27] In addition to those migrants who had come from farms, an undetermined but undoubtedly large percentage came from smaller southern and midwestern towns and would find urban life in the East Bay a different experience.

War migrants moved to the Bay Area for a variety of reasons of which patriotism was only one aspect. As Katherine Archibald, a sociologist who worked at the Moore shipyards in Oakland, observed, "I met no man who had entered the industry for patriotic reasons alone. Indeed, most of the young men quite openly admitted that they were in the yards to escape the draft."[28] Although essential defense work did provide temporary draft deferment for men aged eighteen to thirty-eight, allegations of draft dodging among migrants were probably exaggerated, reflecting more generalized antimigrant sentiment in the community. According to worker surveys, the most significant reasons for migrating were the higher wages and increased occupational mobility available in the Bay Area. Along with Seattle and Detroit, the San Francisco Bay Area offered the highest wages of the nation's defense centers. As early as 1941, over 10 percent of migrants to Oakland moved from unskilled to skilled or semiskilled positions; the percentage increased steadily as the war continued.[29]

In many cases, defense migrants had been unemployed in their home towns. Recruiters targeted high unemployment areas, but even relatively healthy economies witnessed temporary dislocations as a result of the war. One woman from Oklahoma told how her husband had lost two nonessential jobs back home before agreeing to move to California. Others, still recovering from the financial setbacks of the 1930s, saw defense work as a chance to recoup their losses. A former Oklahoma oil-field worker who moved to Oakland to work in the shipyards described how he spent his earnings: "I paid off an accumulation of debts made during the lean years which I am sure they had written off a long time ago."[30]

Some families even managed to pay off their mortgages back home, a fact that concerned federal officials as migrants began leaving western defense centers in late 1943. In one incident in Oakland, Civil Service officials reported that a group of men "broke up the furniture" at the local Office of Price Administration because they were denied gasoline to return to their farms after earning enough in the shipyards to pay off their mortgages. At the time, new amendments to the Selective Service Act had allowed for agricultural deferments, which prompted additional countermigration. Although relatively few migrants repaid their mortgages or even owned homes, many did leave the East Bay during the war, either to return home or to find better job and housing opportunities in other defense areas.

According to government estimates, more than twice as many people moved through the East Bay during the war years than were ever counted at one time.[31] Unusually high turnover rates required a constant stream of inmigrants to replace those who were leaving. Both Moore and Kaiser shipyards reported a turnover rate of 10 percent to 15 percent per month; smaller industries were even more vulnerable. An exit survey of workers at Kaiser's Yard One in the spring of 1942 revealed that 26 percent were leaving for other jobs, 13 percent were entering the military, and 10 percent were simply "leaving town." Other reasons for quitting included sickness and housing and transportation problems.[32]

The turnover was most acute among skilled workers, whose experience was sought by hundreds of competing contractors in the Bay Area alone. By August 1942 the situation had become so grave that the federal government declared the Bay Area a critical labor shortage area and instituted a series of labor freeze measures. Thereafter, to change jobs, workers had to present to prospective employers clearances from their former employers, who issued them only in cases of absolute necessity. Management was lax in enforcing such measures, however, and most workers continued to move around in search of more desirable jobs.

The Family Work Force

Up until mid-1942, employers had tended to hire white male migrants over local black and women residents. By the fall, however, critical labor demands opened the shipyard gates to these workers as well. Faced with a serious housing shortage, inadequate transportation, and other community problems caused by migration, the federal government ordered defense employers to reorient their hiring efforts toward local residents, including women, youth, African-Americans, and other minority workers. In practice, though, many of these new nontraditional employees came from families who had migrated in response to new work opportunities in East Bay shipyards. As the war progressed, then, increasing numbers of migrant women, youth, and black workers joined single white males in West Coast defense plants.

The first clear indication of this change came in the summer of 1942 when East Bay shipyards began hiring and recruiting women workers. Following the lead of the Boilermakers Union, which barred women from membership, U.S. shipbuilders had refused to hire women yard workers for the first few months of the war. As the labor shortage intensified, however, both employers and women pressured the union to change its policy. In July 1942, a group of women seeking shipyard employment staged a demonstration at the Boilermakers' headquarters in San Francisco. Shortly afterward, the union amended its constitution to admit women, and by the end of the year thousands of women were working in East Bay yards at a variety of trades.

Contrary to government propaganda, middle-class housewives did not flock to defense plants to join the ranks of "Rosie the Riveter"; rather, local working-class women and middle-to-low-income migrant women took up the call. As Archibald explained, shipyard women were the wives and daughters of men who worked "on the farm or in the factory, or at best, as office clerk or small-time salesman."[33]

Local working women quickly moved into war jobs, but migrants constituted the largest new female labor pool in the Bay Area. In fact, in 1944 approximately three-quarters of all new women workers were newcomers to the area. Overall, migrant women made up 46 percent of all Bay Area working women while they represented only 27 percent of the total female population.[34] Migrant women thus were particularly influential in the development of the wartime economy.

As in the nation's defense centers generally, female civilian migration to California and the Bay Area exceeded that of men. For every one hundred women who moved to the Bay Area during World War II, only ninety-four men made the trip. This female-dominated migration pattern was fairly unique in California history; since the 1850s, male migrants had consistently outnumbered women with only a few exceptions.[35] The draft was largely responsible for this shift, as the armed services absorbed many potential male migrants.

Moreover, the Bay Area and other West Coast metropolitan centers were particularly attractive destinations for female migrants. Like other West Coast cities, the Bay Area's dramatic expansion of industry and employment attracted women from around the country, especially those who were supporting families. More than half of Bay Area women workers were married, and the Kaiser and Moore shipyards found that one-third to one-half of their women employees had children. The percentage of married women workers was noticeably greater on the West Coast—55 percent in the Bay Area and 54 percent in Seattle, compared with 45 percent in Detroit and 43 percent in Baltimore. In late 1944, Pacific Coast shipbuilders employed 36 percent of all shipyard labor nationwide but hired 55 percent of the nation's women workers.

The availability of jobs and higher rates of pay on the West Coast account for part of the attraction, but the location was also significant. Many female family heads reported moving to the Bay Area to be near husbands or other male relatives stationed in the area. With the surge in Pacific theater activity, Oakland's role as port of embarkation made the East Bay an especially popular spot. High rates of employment among the wives of migrant war workers also contributed to the West's abundance of married women workers.[36]

The influx of migrant women into the Bay Area was also part of a long-standing trend of urban migration among single mothers. Unlike rural areas, cities offered women a variety of work opportunities—albeit low-paying—in industrial and service occupations. Wartime cities offered even greater opportunities and thus attracted many widowed, divorced, and unmarried mothers. The State Division of Child Welfare reported in 1943 that the number of adoptions in California had doubled in the previous year due to an influx of young, unmarried mothers to coastal defense centers. Such women gravitated to cities like Oakland and San Francisco where they could find work and live unobtrusively among other single mothers.[37]

With the release of the film "Rosie the Riveter" in 1980, the East Bay became known for its role in the history of World War II working women. East Bay shipyards were among the major employers of women on the West Coast, employing more than thirty thousand at peak hiring. In June 1944, Kaiser found that women made up more than 27 percent of its shipyard labor force, and Moore reported more than 20 percent in the same period. Although the shipbuilding, iron, and steel industries employed the largest number of women in the manufacturing sector, thousands also worked in machine shops, auto plants, military supply and ordnance, communications, electrical parts plants, and food processing.[38]

As in the prewar period, though, the largest number of women worked in the service sector. Defense contractors expanded their clerical divisions along with their industrial force, and consumer services grew—somewhat sluggishly—to serve the needs of an expanded population. During the war, more than half of all service, wholesale, and retail trade workers were women. In Bay Area stores and restaurants, women's share of employment grew from 20 percent to 80 percent in four years. Many women chose service jobs, despite their lower wages, because of part-time shifts that allowed them to combine work and family responsibilities.[39]

Among black women, the pattern was somewhat different due to the double barriers of race and sex. Until late in the war, black women were excluded from shipyard employment except as janitors, cafeteria workers, and rest-room attendants. Beginning in 1944, black women were hired as burners, chippers, and shipfitters' helpers in East Bay yards, but never in large numbers. They were more successful in other industries, such as military supply, railroads, and canneries, all of which offered roughly half the wages of shipbuilding. Nevertheless, the war enabled many of these women to move out of domestic service, a field that employed more than 25 percent of Bay Area black women in 1940.[40]

A few months after women's entry into the shipyards, East Bay defense contractors started recruiting teenage youth into the labor force as well. In September 1942, Oakland officials announced the beginning of the nation's first part-time work program for high school students aged sixteen to eighteen. Nicknamed the "Four and Four" program, the plan was conceived as another means of stemming inmigration and its attendant community pressures. The program allowed students to drop four hours per day of nonessential courses, such as music and gym, in favor of four hours of work in local services or industry. In some cases students shared jobs; in others they participated in special apprenticeship programs designed to teach job skills that would be useful after they graduated.

By mid-1943, more than half of all high school boys worked part-time, many as helpers in technical fields and small plants. Girls, who were barred from employment in heavy industry under the California Minor's War Employment Act, worked overwhelmingly in the service sector as store clerks, office workers, and telephone operators in special wartime training programs.[41] The Four and Four program, which drew heavily on children of the nonmigrant population, was limited almost exclusively to low-paying service jobs and work in lighter, smaller defense industries. Similar programs were established in Richmond, Berkeley, and other East Bay cities.

Local students were also recruited for agricultural work and food processing during their summer vacations. Churches, clubs, and service organizations organized a variety of summer harvest brigades to work in Contra Costa County, Napa, and the Sacramento Valley. Ironically, East Bay students were replacing the very workers who had left these areas months before for work in the shipyards and other coastal defense industries. East Bay canneries also hired high school students over the summer months, abetted by a ruling of the State Board of Education to open schools three weeks later than usual because of the critical farm labor shortage.[42] Like the Four and Four program, summer harvest work drew mainly on children of prewar families and offered substantially lower pay than defense work. Although their children obtained more education and long-term job training, old-timer families expressed resentment at the better jobs and higher wages earned by migrant youth, who were rapidly cornering the market on shipyard employment.

From the outset, defense contractors and federal officials sought to lure young migrant males into the shipyards through the establishment of special youth programs. Initially, Kaiser and other California contractors used the apparatus of the National Youth Administration (NYA), a New Deal job training program. With the declaration of war, the NYA converted three of its California facilities (including one in Richmond) into training programs for shipyard welders. Company officials recruited young men, ages sixteen to twenty-four, from throughout the country to participate in a four-week resident training regime that paid $33.50 per month minus room and board. From 1941 to 1943, Kaiser obtained more than fifteen hundred employees through this program. The presence of large groups of single young men in their communities, however, displeased local officials and helped influence Congress to terminate the NYA altogether in mid-1943.[43]

But the ongoing demand for labor ensured the reincarnation of youth work programs, this time under local auspices. With the implementation of full-time work permits for sixteen and seventeen year olds in 1942, local school boards and defense contractors in the East Bay offered continuation school programs that would meet the state requirement of four hours of class time per week. California also required an additional four hours of vocational training, which could be fulfilled through in-plant training programs. Moore Dry Dock and other shipyards thus worked with Oakland and Alameda public schools to offer evening continuation classes for young defense workers.[44]

In Richmond, where the adult continuation school had been closed in April 1942 because of poor attendance, Kaiser established an on-site school in the shipyards to replace the defunct NYA. Several other continuation classes were scattered around the city, located in plants where significant numbers of young people worked. By the 1943–1944 school year, enrollment had mushroomed to 2,790 students and some thirty teachers. Migrants dominated the classes: more than 65 percent of the students were from Oklahoma, Texas, Arkansas, and Missouri and more than 10 percent from other states. Because girls under eighteen were barred from work in heavy industry, the continuation schools were overwhelmingly male. The Richmond school had only 166 female students, less than 6 percent of its total enrollment. Out of some two thousand workers under eighteen in the Richmond yards in 1944, only thirteen were girls, all of whom worked in clerical positions.[45]

The preponderance of single male migrants in continuation school programs posed new social problems for East Bay communities. As in the previous NYA programs, continuation schools attracted hundreds of teenage male migrants, unattached to families or other relatives, and concentrated them in nearby dormitories. Rising concerns about juvenile delinquency (discussed further in chapter 6) focused on this group and its effect on local youth in the community. More generally, the easy availability of work for sixteen to eighteen year olds created a more fluid, permissive environment for all youth. High school became "like college," with increased freedom to come and go. More mature-looking fourteen and fifteen year olds often obtained forged work permits enabling them to work part-time. In Richmond, the forgery problem became so acute in 1943 that school authorities launched a major crackdown on underage employees among service and retail establishments.[46]

New work roles for women and youth tended to strain traditional family relationships as we shall see in chapter 5. At the same time, however, the family helped to accommodate workers to their new roles in the defense industry. In many cases, single male migrants to the East Bay discovered that local employers were hiring women and teenagers and wrote to their families urging them to follow. Consequently, a rapid chain migration pattern developed, extending to siblings, grandparents, and other relatives. Once war housing was available, defense employers encouraged this pattern by offering preferential occupancy to multiworker families.[47] *Fore 'N' Aft,* the Kaiser shipyard newspaper, featured dozens of stories on model migrant families with three generations of shipyard workers. Union officials also commented on how entire families turned out together at the hiring halls their first day.

The prevalence of family work units among migrants became a standard "Okie" joke, according to Katherine Archibald. "Why, they'd put their five year old to work if they could get him through the hiring office as a midget," one old-timer quipped. Among migrants, however, family work units in the shipyards were an extension of working-class and rural work patterns or, in some cases, a temporary collective effort to regain financial ground lost during the depression. World War II migration was thus predominantly one of families, a significant departure from the male-dominated pattern of the gold rush, railroad, and other labor migrations in western history.

The infusion of young migrant families also changed the age composition of the population, both in the Bay Area and in California generally. In 1944, only 19.3 percent of migrants were over forty-five years old, compared with 36.9 percent of natives. The increase in young migrant families together with an overall rise in marriage and birth rates reversed California's long-standing trend toward an aging population. The abundance of young war migrants would later have serious implications for education and other urban services by disproportionately increasing the number of school children. In addition, by swelling the younger, high-risk age groups, problems of crime and disorder seem to have risen accordingly.[48] For the East Bay and other war boomtowns, the infusion of young workers would require a reordering of law enforcement and social service priorities to keep pace with a younger, more volatile population.

Black Migration

Defense migration also altered the racial composition of East Bay cities. Along with other West Coast urban areas, the East Bay constituted part of the "new frontier of race relations" in America.[49]

Between 1940 and 1945, the black population of the Bay Area grew from 19,759 to 64,680, or by more than 227 percent. In Oakland, where the prewar black community numbered 8,462 in 1940, the black population mushroomed to 21,770 by 1944, accounting for about a third of the total black population increase in the Bay Area. In the smaller communities of Alameda and Richmond, the black population grew by 1,539 percent and 2,001 percent, respectively. In nearly all East Bay cities, the black share of the total population increased from less than 3 percent in 1940 to more than 6 percent in 1944, and to more than 11 percent by 1950 (see table 6). More than ever before, the East Bay became a visible and important area of black settlement on the West Coast.

Unlike white migrants from the West South Central states, black migrants did not head for California in large numbers until the war years, when urban defense employment provided the financial means to relocate. Much of this movement was self-initiated. According to the War Manpower Commission in 1943, nearly three-fourths of blacks who settled in the Bay Area came west on their own without any direct contact with recruiters. More than 65 percent came from the southwestern states of Louisiana, Texas, Oklahoma, and Arkansas, with less than 15 percent from outside the South. In the shipyards, black southwesterners made up more than 80 percent of black workers. Records from one Bay Area shipyard indicate that the largest percentage, approximately one-half of these black workers, came from Louisiana; another one-quarter came from Texas; and Arkansas and Oklahoma contributed one-quarter combined.[50]

As in the first Great Migration of the early twentieth century, World War II migration to western cities followed the informal networks of family, neighborhood, and church. As Shirley Ann Moore discovered in her interviews with black Richmond residents, letters sent home by friends and relatives were the most common factor encouraging chain migration. Moore suggests that porters and other railroad workers were also important messengers, dispensing information on California job opportunities in the South through the Southern Pacific and Santa Fe lines. Church connections were commonly cited as influencing migration. According to War Manpower Commission officials, a black Baptist church in Shreveport, Louisiana, became a coordinating center for aspiring Bay Area migrants. In several instances, preachers followed their flocks westward as their home congregations dwindled. In a few cases, whole towns picked up and headed for California. At Moore

Table 6 *Black Population Growth in Four East Bay Cities, 1940–1950*

City	Black pop.			% increase		Blacks as % of total pop.		
	1940	1944	1950	1940–44	1944–50	1940	1944	1950
Alameda	249	4,082	5,312	1,539.4	30.1	0.7	6.0	8.2
Berkeley	3,395	6,129	13,289	80.5	116.8	4.0	6.3	11.7
Oakland	8,462	21,770	47,562	157.3	118.5	2.8	6.3	12.4
Richmond	270	5,673	13,374	2,001.1	135.7	1.1	6.1	13.4

SOURCES: Commonwealth Club of California, *The Population of California* (San Francisco: Parker Printing Co., 1946), 127; U.S. Bureau of the Census, *Census of Population, 1950*, vol. 2, *Characteristics of the Population*, pt. 5, "California," 97, 101–2.

shipyards in Oakland, Katherine Archibald noted a large network of black workers from Bastrop, Louisiana, a town of five thousand near the Arkansas border.[51]

Like white southwesterners, black migrants came from a mixture of rural areas, towns, and cities. Wilson Record, a journalist who conducted a postwar survey of black families in Richmond, found that 30 percent had migrated from rural agricultural areas and 50 percent from towns and small cities. The remaining 20 percent had come from large cities such as Dallas, Memphis, New Orleans, Little Rock, Tulsa, and Saint Louis. As with most self-selected migrant groups, black arrivals to the Bay Area were relatively advantaged compared with their southern counterparts. In a study of 150 black migrant families in the Bay Area in 1944, the sociologist Charles S. Johnson reported an average of 8.64 years of education among the adults—a significantly higher level than he found among southwestern natives generally. He also found a high degree of property ownership, with 23 percent owning homes or land in California or back home.[52]

Although the southern economy was improving during the early war years, the growing prosperity was not equally shared, and the disparity prompted many blacks to emigrate. First, there was a disproportionate increase in black unemployment as the federal government discontinued New Deal work relief programs. Although southern cities profited from the expansion of shipbuilding and aircraft production, black workers found few opportunities in those areas. Despite a growing labor shortage, many firms refused to hire black workers; others refused to upgrade them into higher-paying skilled positions. In other cases, defense contractors might hire skilled black workers, but vocational training programs were limited to whites. Growing frustration with local conditions, combined with promising reports from West Coast cities, encouraged many southern blacks to emigrate.

Southern defense centers were also subject to violent racial conflicts that convinced some black workers to leave the area. In May 1943, several days of rioting occurred in Mobile, Alabama, after federal authorities ordered the Alabama Dry Dock and Shipbuilding Corporation to upgrade and integrate black shipyard workers. "A lot of the colored workers got beat up, and I was afraid to go back to the yard," explained one black laborer. "White men rode around . . . [and] threw rocks at our houses." Immediately afterward, he and a group of other black workers set out for Richmond, where they hoped to practice their skills in a less hostile environment. As they would soon discover, West Coast communities experienced their share of wartime racial tensions as well.[53]

Nevertheless, the journey west promised social and economic advancement, and black migrants referred to chartered Southern Pacific trains not as "cattle cars" but as "liberty trains." For all their drawbacks, western cities offered a better alternative to life in the South for many black migrants. As Wilson Record explained in a *Crisis* article about Richmond, California offered social and political freedoms that even "poverty and unemployment cannot take away."

In California, his children go to the same schools as other children. They go for nine months during the year. The buildings are new and warm and well-lighted. He can ride on a bus without having to take a rear seat marked "colored." He can attend any movie and take any seat he likes. . . . he can walk down the street without having to move toward the curb when a white man passes. He isn't required, on perhaps pain of beating or arrest, to say "ma'am" to the woman clerks in the stores. . . . He can vote by registering and going to the polls, and no nightshirt Klansmen are going to try and stop him. . . . When he works, he knows he will be paid in cash, get all that is coming to him. His children can use the library like any other children. He can join the local chapter of the NAACP or some unions or a local anti-discrimination committee without fear of violent reprisal at the hands of law and order.

For these reasons, Record said, there was little countermigration. Approximately 85 percent of black migrants remained on the West Coast permanently.[54]

Once in the Bay Area, black migrants gravitated to the higher-paying jobs available on the waterfront. Shipbuilding was, of course, the major industry, employing approximately eighteen thousand

African-Americans in the East Bay in 1944. At Moore Dry Dock, black workers made up nearly 20 percent of the work force, while Kaiser had more than ten thousand black employees in Richmond, a town that had had only 270 black residents in 1940. Military supply centers were another major employer of black civilians in Oakland. Most of the black workers, however, were hired without civil service ratings, leaving them vulnerable to layoffs at the war's end. Black employment on the railroads and docks of the East Bay also grew. At peak employment, there were five to six thousand black longshoremen in the greater Oakland area, while the three railroads more than doubled their numbers of black employees.[55]

Overall, black employment continued to grow even after peak production in mid-1943. As whites returned to their home states, black migrants filled their jobs, thus increasing their share of total defense employment. During these years, black migrants had access to a wider range of skilled and semiskilled positions and earned higher wages than southern blacks back home or local resident blacks who remained in non–defense-related work.[56]

By transforming the racial makeup of the Bay Area, the wartime influx of black workers also transformed the racial biases of local white residents. During the war years, blacks replaced Asians as the area's largest racial minority. This shift was due not only to the growth of the black population but also to the removal and subsequent dispersion of Japanese-Americans. With the latter group confined in distant relocation centers and Chinese-Americans now allied in the anti-Japanese campaign, black migrants became the prime target of local bigotry. The antiblack racism that flourished during World War II would intensify in the postwar years, overshadowing the anti-Chinese sentiments that had historically dominated West Coast cities.

In an abrupt reversal of past practices, Chinese-Americans were mobilized for the war effort and played an active role in Bay Area shipbuilding and other defense work. For the first time, labor unions admitted Chinese workers, and Moore and other defense contractors hired Chinese women office workers. In early 1943, Kaiser employed more than two thousand Chinese workers, the majority of whom were local residents.[57] Company publicity stressed the patriotism of the Chinese, some of whom were successful entrepreneurs who closed their own businesses temporarily to aid the war effort.

A much smaller, but equally well publicized, minority was the organized group of Native Americans living in Richmond. According to

Chief Bluejacket Jack Pope, a Cherokee and leader of a major Bay Area Native American organization, more than a thousand Native Americans were living in Richmond in 1943. Most of them lived at the foot of Macdonald Avenue in converted boxcars and cottages provided by the Santa Fe Railroad, a major employer of the group. Native Americans also found work in local shipyards; at least seventy-five worked at the Kaiser yards alone. The Richmond Native American community was governed by an intertribal council that included Chippewa, Navajo, Cherokee, Apache, Creek, and Acoma members. They were an insulated, self-governing group that disciplined unruly members by returning them to the reservation. Their small numbers, strict discipline, and strong patriotism made for good relations with white workers. "The few full-blooded Indians who worked in the yards," said Katherine Archibald, "were respected, liked, and even admired by their white brethren."[58]

Although the East Bay historically contained large ethnic populations, such groups rarely appear in shipyard accounts. Older ethnic groups such as the Italians, Irish, and Eastern Europeans were relatively well assimilated by the 1940s, and some held key leadership positions in the Boilermakers Union. The East Bay's sizable Portuguese community merited only occasional comment by wartime observers. Katherine Archibald noted the presence of Portuguese workers at Moore shipyards, most of whom came from the surrounding west Oakland neighborhood. They were "held in especial contempt," she said, but they occasionally managed to move into leaderman and other supervisory positions.

The population of Mexican-Americans in the Bay Area had always been small compared with Southern California cities, but their numbers no doubt increased during the war. Since the Census Bureau did not list Hispanics in a separate category in this period (most Mexican-Americans identified themselves as "white"), we have no accurate measure of Hispanic defense migration within the United States. Data collected from 1944 police arrest records in Oakland suggest that Hispanic newcomers were less likely to come directly from Mexico than from interior southwestern states. Out of twenty arrestees with Hispanic surnames who had arrived in Oakland in the previous three years, nearly half (nine) had come from New Mexico; the remaining cases involved migrants from Texas, Arizona, and Colorado, as well as a few Mexican immigrants. The records also indicated that these migrants found work in East Bay shipyards, canneries, and railroad operations.[59]

Because most Mexican immigrants entered the United States during the war years as rural agricultural workers under the bracero program, it is likely that Hispanic newcomers to West Coast cities were mainly interstate migrants. Since the early twentieth century the Santa Fe Railroad had recruited Mexicans in the Southwest for maintenance work in East Bay cities. This practice probably accelerated during the war, and no doubt many migrants switched to more lucrative defense work once they arrived.

In the end, shipyard employers called on virtually any kind of worker they could find to meet the relentless demand for labor. Kaiser put elderly and handicapped men to work in the reclamation department sorting bolts, pipe, and other scrap materials. Beginning in 1942, the Boilermakers Union worked with shipyard managers to develop shipfitter training courses for future parolees at San Quentin Penitentiary. As one Kaiser manager put it, shipyard employers went literally "under the railway bridges and into the jails for workers."[60] By 1943, defense contractors had tapped nearly every source of labor power available, both near and far.

For the Bay Area, the defense mobilization of World War II was indeed like a "second gold rush." New shipyards and other war industries provided sudden wealth and employment for East Bay cities, attracting migrants from around the country. Unlike the boom of 1849, however, the federal government and its contractors were active in recruiting workers and directing the flow of migration. Working together, they targeted labor supply areas, selected certain kinds of workers, advanced their train fares, and provided housing and other services in East Bay communities.

As the labor shortage continued, however, employers became less selective, and the dynamic of migration changed. When employers began hiring women and youth, male migrants encouraged their friends and family members back home to join them out West. As with other immigrant groups, chain migration ensured a continuous flow of workers from southern and midwestern states to East Bay cities. This movement, particularly from southwestern states, built on earlier migrations of depression-era Okies. Unlike the thirties' migrants, however, wartime newcomers headed directly for urban defense centers. Among their ranks were thousands of black migrants—another characteristic distinguishing World War II migration from earlier westward movements.

Indeed, one of the most enduring legacies of the war was the change in the composition of the urban population. By 1944, the Bay Area population was younger, more southern, more female, and noticeably more black than in 1940. Particularly in terms of race, the population profile of the Bay Area came to resemble that of older eastern cities with their large and visible black minorities.

The population shifts in the Bay Area during these years mirrored those of other West Coast cities. The dramatic influx of war migrants into San Diego, Los Angeles, Portland, and Seattle all resulted in a younger, more female-dominated population in those areas by 1944. In all four metropolitan areas, inmigrants as a group were significantly younger than prewar residents. The number of children under age five increased by more than 60 percent from 1940 to 1944, with the greatest gains (85 percent to 95 percent) occurring around San Diego, San Francisco, and Portland—the three areas with the highest rates of defense migration. The civilian population of West Coast cities also became female-dominated during the war as local men were inducted into the military and incoming women migrants outnumbered their male counterparts. The greatest gains in female population occurred in the areas around San Diego, Seattle, and San Francisco—military centers that attracted a large number of servicemen's wives. Women's willingness to relocate during these years may help to explain why so many servicemen's families chose to settle on the West Coast permanently after the war.[61]

With some minor variations, the regional profile of Bay Area war migrants was representative of other West Coast cities. The five major metropolitan areas all drew the largest number of migrants from the Central states and Rocky Mountain region. Southern California cities showed the greatest similarity to Bay Area patterns with more than a third of all migrants coming from the West Central states. The Seattle and Portland areas also drew large numbers of migrants from the West North Central states, but noticeably fewer from the South. As in the prewar era, western migration to Pacific Northwest cities seems to have followed latitudinal lines. The population of California cities, by contrast, showed increased regional diversity as more southern migrants headed to the north of the state while more northern midwesterners now moved to Southern California. Los Angeles, in particular, drew a high percentage of out-of-state migrants from a wide geographical range, thus giving the city an especially cosmopolitan character.[62]

Other West Coast cities also experienced racial population shifts similar to those in the Bay Area. The black population of the San Diego, Los Angeles, Portland, and Seattle areas all skyrocketed during World War II. The greatest gains occurred in the shipbuilding centers of Portland and the Bay Area, where employers hired black migrants earlier and in larger numbers than did their counterparts in the aircraft industry. In retrospect, World War II marked a critical turning point in the racial patterning of West Coast cities. Traditionally, Asians had constituted the largest minority group in these areas. By 1944, because of black inmigration and Japanese relocation and dispersion, African-Americans became the largest and most visible urban minority. Los Angeles and Oakland, with their large prewar black communities, were the only exceptions to this pattern. Even in those cities, though, black wartime population gains far surpassed those of previous decades.[63]

The historian Gerald Nash has argued that the defense mobilization of World War II permanently transformed the West Coast urban economy. Other historians have been reluctant to accept this generalization, noting the prewar precedents for wartime militarization and the ephemeral nature of the defense boom in shipbuilding centers like Portland and the Bay Area.[64] What is not in dispute, however, is the long-term social and demographic impacts of the war. In the Bay Area and other West Coast cities, increased racial and regional diversity would remain a permanent feature of urban life, long outliving the economic forces that brought it about.

3

Wartime Shipyards and the Transformation of Labor

The vast majority of people seeking clearance to work in Richmond were complete strangers to this area, knew little or nothing about Unions or Union procedure, and unfortunately didn't want to learn.... Nothing but internal strife would have prevailed had this great mass of new members, uninitiated in the trade union movement, exercised control.

International Brotherhood
of Boilermakers, Iron Shipbuilders
and Helpers of America, *Richmond:
Arsenal of Democracy,* ca. 1945.

As thousands of new, largely unskilled workers streamed into East Bay communities, industrial managers faced the problem of integrating these newcomers into the workplace. Historically, California's urban migrants had found jobs in the low-paid, unskilled, and frequently unorganized ranks of industry. During World War II, however, the dramatic expansion of the defense industry required new labor power at virtually every level. To accommodate new workers, shipyard managers and other employers reorganized the work itself, breaking down traditional craft divisions and diluting skills accordingly. Nowhere was this reorganization more evident than in shipbuilding. In the East Bay, Kaiser led the nation in new industrial practices, transforming the skilled trades into assembly-line production.

Not surprisingly, old-timers and their unions resisted the new regime as an attack on their skills, job security, and organizing power. Racial, sexual, and cultural biases, however, also influenced their response. As antinewcomer bigotry clouded legitimate labor issues, shipyard unions attempted to protect control of their crafts by creating an elaborate hierarchy of auxiliary unions for migrants, blacks, and other newcomers. This unequal treatment sparked ongoing conflicts with the unions and, more important, left workers more dependent on management and the corporate welfare schemes that proliferated during the war years.

Like employers in previous periods of labor shortage and migration, wartime managers concentrated new workers in unskilled, low-paying positions. In the Bay Area, a mere 9 percent of women defense workers occupied skilled positions, compared with 46 percent of men. Black workers, concentrated on the railroads and docks and in the military supply centers, were also disproportionately represented among the unskilled. Initially, the same patterns prevailed in the shipyards, where newcomers worked as janitors, laborers, helpers, and other classifications that paid up to twenty-five cents per hour less than a regular journeyman's position.[1]

By mid-1942, however, critical labor shortages reshaped the work process and labor organization of Bay Area shipyards, allowing newcomers to enter higher-paid "skilled" employment. The ensuing transformation of both the workplace and the labor unions was most dramatic at the new emergency shipyards in Richmond. The rich documentation of Kaiser's innovations enables us to examine them in greater detail and to assess their impact on Richmond and dozens of other wartime shipyards that emulated Kaiser's ideas. Furthermore, as Nelson Lichtenstein and Ruth Milkman have shown, the de-skilling and reorganization of labor was widespread during World War II, affecting nearly all defense industries to some degree.[2] East Bay shipyards, then, provide a case study of wartime industrial trends that were then sweeping the nation.

Prior to World War II, shipbuilding had been a trade with more than 80 percent of jobs in the skilled or semiskilled categories. This pattern continued to a lesser extent in older shipyards like Moore Dry Dock, but the "overnight" shipyards established by the U.S. Maritime Commission experimented with new materials and techniques in specially designed wartime plants. The Maritime Commission proudly compared its new process to the automobile assembly line, and indeed the two systems had much in common.

Beginning in May 1942, coinciding with increased recruitment of women, black, and out-of-state workers, Kaiser instituted a new system of prefabrication adapted from previous dam-building ventures for the federal government. Under this system, whole sections of a ship's super-structure—boilers, double bottoms, forepeaks, afterpeaks, and deck-houses—were preassembled in a new prefabrication plant located between Yards Three and Four. This system allowed more work with more personnel to be conducted away from the ships with less welding, riveting, and crane lifts required during hull erection. The prefabrica-tion system was instituted at the Kaiser yards in Richmond, Portland, and Vancouver; the Bechtel yards in Marin County, California; Calship in the Los Angeles harbor area; and other war-born shipyards.

As preassembly required a large amount of space for workers, ware-houses, and cranes, the expansive new West Coast locations were ideal. Such yards differed noticeably from the tight vertical design of older East Coast shipyards. The few older western shipyards such as Moore Dry Dock expanded their facilities, incorporating preassembly design and techniques wherever feasible.[3]

For the worker, prefabrication meant increased specialization and de-skilling of basic trades. In the boilermaker trade alone, subassembly techniques fostered more than seventeen different job classifications. The occupation of shipfitter, for example, was broken down into cate-gories of layoutman, loftsman, and duplicator. Welders were confined to specific kinds of welding, and electricians were assigned specific wir-ing jobs, such as control panels or cabin lighting. With such narrow job classifications, advancement from one grade to another was quite rapid, normally under sixty days. Under the right conditions, an un-skilled newcomer could advance from trainee to journeyman status within a few months—a fraction of the time once required. As Henry Kaiser put it, "production is not labor anymore, but a process."[4]

In order to facilitate this system, Kaiser introduced a variety of new organizational techniques and practices. The proliferation of new job classifications was codified in an elaborate insignia system in which workers bore their different trade symbols on their hard hats. The list of insignias filled up several pages of the employee handbook, a printed booklet for new workers explaining basic shipyard procedures and reg-ulations. In addition, the use of security badges, timekeepers, tool checkers, pay windows, and (for the first time) income tax withholding made for a highly bureaucratized work climate.

Even the physical environment reflected the large-scale urban-industrial organization of wartime shipyards. Kaiser, for instance, designed the Richmond yards with a citylike grid system of numbered and lettered streets. As one worker explained, "It was a city without houses, but the traffic was heavy. Cranes, trucks, trains noised by." Another newcomer, a recent migrant from a small Iowa town, recalled her initial bewilderment at the immensity and seeming confusion of the yards. "It was such a huge place, something I had never been in," she said. "People from all walks of life, all coming and going and working, and the noise. The whole atmosphere was overwhelming to me." For many newcomers unfamiliar with an urban-industrial work culture, the shipyards could be a disorienting and alienating experience.[5]

The new system had other important implications for workers and their occupational mobility within the yards. The replacement of riveting with welding and the proliferation of jobs in downhand welding (considered the easiest position) facilitated quick placement of new workers. Employers channeled women, especially, into this trade, seeing them as better suited for this lighter work. At peak employment in the Richmond yards, approximately 40 percent of all welders were women. Female employees were also used extensively in "prefab," an indoor shop offering supposedly lighter, sheltered work. As Ruth Milkman has pointed out, women entered new jobs in wartime industries, but a modified version of occupational segregation remained.[6]

Similar occupational stereotypes emerged to justify the placement of other newcomer groups. Seeing them as well suited to arduous labor, shipyard employers concentrated black workers in the hull trades— hard, outdoor work on a year-round basis. By contrast, Chinese-American workers were often placed in electrical work, a lighter, detail-oriented trade considered more suitable for these immigrants. Even though such cultural stereotypes were deeply ingrained, they were not immutable. As Milkman has shown, the "idiom" of occupational segregation changed during the war to suit the needs of particular industries. As labor demands dictated, employers channeled women and minority workers into welding, burning, shipfitting, and a number of other semiskilled trades.[7]

Although the expansion of skilled and semiskilled categories offered higher status and pay for some newcomers, further occupational mobility was rarely possible. Foreman, leaderman, and other supervisory positions were dominated by old-timers and other white male workers. There were virtually no female supervisors in East Bay shipyards, and women found their occupational mobility blocked on many fronts. Even though employers were reluctant to promote women into positions overseeing men, the double burden of home and work responsibilities made such promotions even less likely. Married women especially had a higher rate of absenteeism than men or single women. Because of rationing and other wartime conditions, home responsibilities became more time-consuming than usual, and such pressures adversely affected women's job performance.[8]

Furthermore, women in nontraditional jobs found that many male coworkers resented their presence, seeing them as temporary interlopers in a male domain. Katherine Archibald commented on the constant barrage of sex jokes and innuendo directed at women, the end result of which was "to deny the possibility of the establishment of businesslike relationships between men and women on the job and to discredit them as effective workers."[9]

One of the most damning accusations against women shipyard workers was that many were prostitutes who plied their trades in remote ship compartments and warehouses. Rumors of shipyard prostitution circulated in several West Coast defense centers and gained nationwide attention following an October 1942 article on the subject in *Business Week*. The article discussed the alleged prostitution racket in Portland shipyards and the efforts of AFL unions to screen out undesirable women. The shipyard-worker-turned-prostitute also appeared in contemporary home-front novels that featured degraded southern white women as stock characters.[10]

Although a few professional prostitutes may well have worked in the yards, the sexual and racial overtones of the accusation suggest that the issue was more complex. As Amy Kesselman has pointed out, the portrayal of women as perpetually sexual beings served to reinforce men's right to harass women coworkers and undermine their legitimacy on the job. According to many women informants, sexual harassment was especially prevalent in the formerly all-male domain of shipbuilding and other defense work. Katherine Archibald, a sociologist and contemporary observer at the Moore shipyards, said as much at the time. Dismissing the prostitution claims as pernicious rumor, Archibald saw such accusations as part of a larger tendency to view women workers as sexual distractions—thus discrediting them as serious workers.

Also lurking behind the prostitution scandal was the specter of miscegenation. According to *Business Week*, Portland authorities were not only concerned with sexual misconduct in the workplace but also had "a collateral fear . . . that the prostitutes . . . may [have] consort[ed] with Negroes, who [would] then . . . try to take liberties with other

white women." Such concerns reflected white racial anxieties over miscegenation and implied that only white "prostitutes" would purposely
engage in such behavior. According to Katherine Archibald, interracial
contact between the sexes was indeed an explosive issue, particularly
among white southerners in the yards. "The Okies," she said, "were especially disturbed and found it hard to accept the casual contact between Negro men and white women.... Tales of lynching with a
background of sexual ravishment were much in demand." As a result,
she said, friendly relations between black men and white women on the
job were impossible. Archibald and other white women who dared to
fraternize with black male coworkers were labeled "nigger lovers" and
prostitutes.[11]

Fears of racial mixing had even more dire consequences for minority
workers who found themselves concentrated in the least-desirable and
lowest-paying jobs in the yards. Black workers occupied a disproportionate share of the lower-paying laborer positions, accounting for 90
percent of the members of the local Shipyard and Marine Shop Laborers Union. As skilled workers, minorities were often assigned to segregated work units, such as the all-Chinese electrical crews and the
all-black laborer and rigger gangs at Moore Dry Dock. Minority workers also encountered great difficulty breaking into supervisory ranks.
The few minority supervisors in East Bay yards generally oversaw
segregated crews, functioning as straw bosses and "pushers" of their
coworkers.[12]

Management justified such practices in terms of productivity, believ-
ing that the intermixing of races was volatile and disruptive. Where
blacks and whites did work side by side, Archibald found that racial
tensions indeed ran high. "The slightest touch," she said, "revealed the
impermanence of the surface calm and the depth of the hatred beneath." Fears of racial violence grew precipitously following the Detroit race riots in the summer of 1943. "Any incident of interracial
conflict would give rise to talk of rioting," Archibald said, and southerners had "especially dire predictions."

Ultimately, though, Archibald believed that native western workers
were equally antagonistic toward blacks and were keenly aware of the
threat to their job security. "Except for the greater emotionality of the
Southerner, and his more frequent talk of lynchings, riots, and reprisals," she explained, "the attitudes of the two groups were hard to
distinguish."[13] Southerners, then, manifested a more virulent style of
racism brought with them from the South but had not created the in-

stitutionalized racial system that dominated the shipyards and other defense plants.

In an effort to overcome social tensions and other obstacles to productivity, Kaiser implemented a number of work incentive programs based on patriotic appeals. Management conducted regular efficiency and safety contests among Richmond workers and challenged other shipyards to production races in the building of Liberty ships. In November 1942, Richmond set the all-time record with the launching of the *Robert E. Peary,* built in four days, fifteen hours, and twenty-six minutes. Although the *Peary* was a mere demonstration project designed to garner publicity and boost morale, the average construction time for Liberty ships was in fact reduced to seventeen days (see plate 6).

One of the methods for speeding production was the broadcasting of up-tempo popular music over the shipyard public address system. Although some workers enjoyed the music, others became irritated and took action to eliminate it. One fifty-year-old employee, Roy Christison, was arrested by the Federal Bureau of Investigation in 1943 for cutting the cable to the loudspeaker every other day for two months. According to a local newspaper, many employees supported Christison's protest.[14]

Kaiser also instituted a program to stem labor turnover in which the company offered membership in the "Anchormen," a kind of honor society for long-term employees. Workers received bronze pins for six months' service, silver pins after one year, and gold pins after eighteen months. Out of the estimated two hundred thousand workers who came to Richmond during the war, though, only twenty-three thousand earned the gold pins.[15] For all the hype, Kaiser's incentive programs do not seem to have been especially effective.

Despite the push for increased speed and efficiency, production bottlenecks continued to occur under the prefabrication system. A shortage of cranes or the absence or delay of one part or section could undermine the entire assembly process. Workers at both Kaiser and Moore shipyards often complained of having to "sit around" waiting for parts to arrive or of not doing a full day's work. "Many another was vaguely troubled at the ease with which he earned his wages," said Katherine Archibald, "and it was a standard joke among the men that they should walk backward to the pay window." The worst situation occurred at Pacific Bridge shipyards in Alameda, where one survey revealed that workers were idle for at least three hours per day. Indeed, production bottlenecks were common among all wartime cost-plus contractors who had easier access to labor than to parts and supplies.[16]

Production bottlenecks were further aggravated by the widespread practice of labor hoarding by major shipbuilders. Following the labor freeze measures of 1943, employers used some of their profit margins to engage excess workers to compensate for anticipated high turnover. The result was "enforced idleness" and periodic mass layoffs at Kaiser and other shipyards. In the first four months of 1943, a peak production period with full-scale labor recruitment in progress, Kaiser dismissed thousands of workers on two separate occasions because of production imbalances. Such practices prompted criticism of the pre-assembly system by the Congress of Industrial Organizations (CIO), the Oakland City Council, and other community groups.[17]

The strongest opposition to prefabrication and other labor-intensive practices came from the ranks of old-timers and their unions, who feared the effects of de-skilling on their trades. Such men, according to the Kaiser company history, tended to leave the Richmond yards for older, more traditionally organized shipyards. "One after another, their beliefs and traditions outraged, they left the ranks to give their valuable services where they would not be trampled upon by the new-fangled notions of upstarts."[18] Eventually, though, the introduction of new unskilled workers and preassembly techniques affected all Bay Area shipyards.

Reorganizing the Union

The International Brotherhood of Boilermakers, Iron Shipbuilders and Helpers of America, the union that represented the majority of West Coast shipyard workers, was the most vocal opponent of prefabrication. Although the union manifested the traditional exclusivity and conservatism of AFL craft unions, it also addressed legitimate concerns about the de-skilling of the shipbuilding trades. Throughout the war years, the Boilermakers opposed the new assembly process as an effort by management to erode the position of journeyman mechanic by breaking it down into a set of semiskilled trainee classifications. The result was "a motley collection of one-process worker Johnny-come-latelies." The Boilermakers continued to favor the "interchangeability" system in which journeyman mechanics performed a wide variety of skilled tasks in different phases of production.[19]

Once it became clear that the Maritime Commission would insist on prefabrication, however, the Boilermakers agreed to cooperate in exchange for a closed shop and other concessions secured through government-sanctioned agreements. The influx of new trainee workers also swelled union coffers and ensured the advancement of old-time workers to higher-paying supervisory positions. Acceptance of prefabrication, however, did not eliminate the problems and resentments that the system created.

As employers experimented with prefabrication, changes in production methods were reflected in labor organization. Production rearranged around subassembly areas tended to cut across older craft lines and resulted in frequent jurisdictional disputes between the Boilermakers and other AFL trades such as the Steamfitters and the Carpenters. At the same time, the proliferation of semiskilled classifications heightened craft divisions within the Boilermakers' trades, that is, shipfitting, burning, welding, rigging, caulking, and so on. The development of "crafts within crafts" created additional jurisdictional problems, including a prolonged dispute in the East Bay between Local 9 (Shipfitters) and Local 39 (Boilermakers) over the affiliation of new members. Newcomers were often caught in the middle of such disputes, and many quit in disgust over the seemingly senseless rounds of transfers, clearances, and other bureaucratic requirements.[20]

The most serious problem, though, concerned the welders, whose occupation spawned the greatest number of specialized classifications. Under prefabrication, welders and burners worked in a variety of production areas and were required to join all unions in whose jurisdictions they worked. The burden of paying multiple dues and the second-class treatment accorded an occupation that included large numbers of women and migrants stirred discontent among Burners and Welders affiliates. In response to this situation, Local 681 in Oakland and several other Burners and Welders locals in the West attempted to form the independent Welders, Burners and Helpers Union in 1942.

The Boilermakers' international was vehemently opposed to such a schism, maintaining that welding was simply one of many skills required of a good boilermaker. Retaining the still vivid memory of CIO counterorganizing drives among shipyard workers in the late thirties, the Boilermakers quickly denounced the new welders' organization as "a general nuisance to the American Labor Movement." Accordingly, the international harshly disciplined Local 681 and other dissident locals, suspending meetings, elections, and publications during the war years.[21] When newcomers also found themselves subject to undemocratic actions by the international, they would find ready allies in Local 681.

The introduction of new workers and production techniques transformed labor relations and resulted in a transitional wartime union organization based on centralized control and increased hierarchy. Under the impact of mass migration, the membership of shipyard unions mushroomed to many times their original size. The Boilermakers, who represented 65 percent to 70 percent of all West Coast shipyard workers, was the major recipient of this new membership and will thus be the focus of discussion.

During the war years, the Boilermakers Union grew by several hundred thousand nationwide, expanding from 28,609 in 1938 to 352,000 in November 1943. West Coast shipbuilding affiliates showed the greatest gains, with several local memberships exceeding 35,000—including Richmond's newly created Local 513. According to union officials, Local 513 conducted up to three initiations per day of 200–300 workers each during 1942–1943. With 36,511 members in 1943, the Richmond local was larger than the entire national membership of the Boilermakers Union five years earlier. During the war years, Local 513 became the third-largest Boilermakers' local in the country, smaller only than the Los Angeles and Portland, Oregon, branches. Other East Bay Boilermakers' affiliates, including Local 9 (Shipfitters), Local 681 (Burners and Welders), and Local 39 (Boilermakers), also grew by tens of thousands during the early 1940s.[22]

Few of these new members had had any prior experience with unions and initially tended to be somewhat distrustful of them. According to Katherine Archibald, workers had little contact with unions beyond paying their initiation fees and consequently became distrustful of union leaders, whom they suspected of bilking the membership. Unfortunately, the Boilermakers did little to dispel this attitude and in fact exacerbated suspicions in an attempt to protect the interests of its old-time membership.[23]

The economic threat posed by newcomers in the shipyards fostered resentment among old-time workers. Newcomers, they felt, had not participated in the struggle to build the union and were essentially "freeloaders" on the system. They particularly resented the easy terms under which new workers could advance to journeyman status. An article in the *Oakland Tribune* titled "From Bond Salesman to Leaderman Shipfitter in Four Easy Steps" provoked angry outcries from one skilled old-timer, who complained that "we got hard-earned conditions and wages, and now the overnight mechanics step in and collect the cream." Union leaders also claimed that newcomers were inept and accident-prone, putting old-timers at risk on the job. At its most extreme, the Boilermakers denounced newcomers as "misfits" who were lazy and irresponsible. "The 'bottom of the barrel' was being scraped," said the Boilermakers' leadership about Richmond workers, "and the human scale found thereon resented the necessity of having to go to work."[24]

To remedy this perceived deterioration of the work force, the Boilermakers attempted to influence the recruitment, job training, and education of new workers. Along with other West Coast lodges, Local 513 in Richmond hired two of its own recruiters in 1943 to "strengthen the quality of its membership."[25] There is no indication, however, that the unions were any more successful in procuring skilled workers than were Kaiser's own recruiters.

The Boilermakers also advocated the exclusive use of in-plant training and opposed all other government-sponsored training programs such as those offered by the National Youth Administration and local continuation schools. The latter offered job training to virtually all applicants, including blacks and women. By restricting training to in-plant programs, the Boilermakers ensured exclusive control of hiring by offering training only to those workers previously cleared by the union. The union's efforts to improve the quality of the work force, then, were more often used as tools for racial and sexual discrimination.

On a more constructive note, the Boilermakers did make some attempt to educate newcomers in the principles of trade unionism. Local 513 issued a pamphlet titled "What Your Union Means to You" for distribution to new members. Although containing important information on union rights and procedures, the pamphlet was condescending toward "card-packing" newcomers, who were "inclined to ride the gravy train . . . and then stab their fellow craftsmen in the back at the first opportunity." In particular, the Boilermakers derided workers who sold out their fellow unionists to "curry favor" with the boss and the even more despicable "labor-baiters" who circulated malicious rumors about union corruption, racketeering, collaboration with management, and undemocratic practices.[26] Thus in addition to conveying the principles of trade unionism, the Boilermakers also sought to warn newcomers away from union dissidents who criticized the existing power structure.

The mass infusion of new workers into shipyard locals offered potential political opportunities for those who wanted to challenge the entrenched leadership. According to the Boilermakers' international, those challenges came from a variety of sources, including the Communist party, the Ku Klux Klan (mainly in southern locals), the CIO, and organized crime. In order to "protect the interests of the Brotherhood" from those "subversive forces," the Boilermakers provided for direct international control of local affiliates that they considered suspect.[27] The Boilermakers passed this provision at their 1937 national convention in anticipation of the Merchant Marine buildup; there was no possibility of appeal for another seven years as all national conventions were postponed under the war emergency until 1944.

In the East Bay, where both the CIO and the Communist party had maintained an active network since the 1930s, the international took no chances. When Richmond Local 513 was chartered in August 1942, the international took immediate control through a governing board consisting of prominent national officers. At a time when these members most needed education and experience with unionism, the international suspended all elections, meetings, and regular publications for the duration.[28]

For women and black workers, the problem was compounded. With a widespread consensus that women's sojourn in the shipyards would be temporary, the Boilermakers' executive council ruled to admit women to membership in September 1942 in accordance with federal government and employer requests. With their brief tenure, however, women did not qualify for office-holding or other official duties and were often enrolled in the newer international-controlled locals anyway. Black workers fared even worse. Anticipating the coming shipbuilding boom, the Boilermakers provided for the establishment of auxiliary locals for blacks in 1937. The auxiliaries first appeared in the South, but during the war years they also sprang up in midwestern and West Coast cities experiencing large-scale inmigration. By 1944, forty-four auxiliary lodges had been established nationwide with 13,678 men and 2,532 women.[29]

In the East Bay, there were three active auxiliaries: A-26 (Oakland), A-36 (Richmond), and A-33 (San Francisco–based Shipfitters). The auxiliaries were controlled by their white "parent" locals and had no vote or representation at national conventions, no grievance mechanisms, no business representatives, and reduced insurance benefits. Moreover, their existence was dependent on the whims of the international, which could dissolve the auxiliaries at any time.[30]

Initially, East Bay shipyards either did not hire black workers or else referred them to Oakland's A-26, the East Bay's first black auxiliary, formed in February 1942. As black migration accelerated, discriminatory hiring practices at Kaiser and other yards came to light. In late 1942–1943, Richmond's Local 513 required black applicants to have proof of one year's residency in Contra Costa County—a requirement the union had dropped long ago for whites. The measure effectively barred all black migrants and most old-time black residents who lived in adjoining Alameda County. In addition, the War Manpower Commission received complaints from more than a hundred black job seekers (mainly women) who were turned away by Local 513 after completing welding courses under government auspices.[31]

In an attempt to curb discriminatory practices, Ray Thompson, a black shipfitter at Moore Dry Dock, founded the East Bay Shipyard Workers' Committee against Discrimination. Born in San Francisco and educated at Tuskegee Institute in Alabama, Thompson worked out of his south Berkeley home coordinating efforts to improve black housing and employment and to educate black newcomers about unions. According to Thompson, the group, founded in 1942, had more than five thousand members at its peak.

Thompson's efforts were part of a rising tide of black labor activism in West Coast shipbuilding centers. During the war years, African-American shipyard workers established antidiscrimination groups in San Francisco, Portland, and Los Angeles. The politics and tactics of these groups, however, were not identical. Thompson's group in the East Bay, for instance, grew out of the local Communist party network, but its San Francisco counterpart was closely affiliated with the National Association for the Advancement of Colored People (NAACP). These political orientations no doubt influenced their choice of tactics.[32]

The East Bay Shipyard Workers' Committee initially attempted to challenge racist union policy from within the segregated auxiliary system. This strategy was not only a tactical maneuver designed to avoid direct confrontation with the Boilermakers' international but was probably also influenced by prowar Communist party members on the committee. When the Boilermakers chartered two new East Bay auxiliaries in early 1943 (A-36 and A-33), the Shipyard Workers' Committee urged blacks to participate in auxiliary elections and to vote for progressive leaders who would spearhead the fight for equal membership. Soon after, however, the strategy backfired when the international, fearing a "subversive" takeover, suspended pending elections for A-33.[33] The experience was repeated in several auxiliaries around the country; such locals either had no officers or had them appointed by supervising white locals (as did A-36 in Richmond). Not surprisingly, black leaders became increasingly dissatisfied with the "boring from within" approach.

Across the bay, the San Francisco Committee against Segregation and Discrimination led by Joseph P. James was pursuing a more confrontational approach. As Charles Wollenberg has shown, the San Francisco group took up the cause of disgruntled black boilermakers at the Marinship yards near Sausalito. Refusing on principle to join the segregated auxiliaries, hundreds of black shipyard workers turned to the committee for legal representation when Marinship fired them for nonmembership in 1943. In February 1944, a Marin County judge ruled in favor of the fired workers, prohibiting membership in segregated auxiliaries as a condition of employment.

Encouraged by the decision, black workers in East Bay yards adopted the same strategy. When Moore Dry Dock fired 230 black workers who refused to join the local auxiliary, the East Bay Shipyard Workers' Committee filed suit against Moore and Locals 9 and 39 in Oakland and against Kaiser and Local 513 in a similar case in Richmond. While the East Bay cases were stalled or defeated, the Boilermakers appealed the Marinship case, tying it up in the state supreme court until January 1945. The state court eventually upheld the decision, ruling that a restricted union was incompatible with a closed shop agreement. Since the war was nearly over, though, the ruling had little impact; most black shipyard workers were soon laid off and their union memberships terminated.[34]

During the same period, the federal Fair Employment Practices Commission (FEPC) also conducted hearings concerning the legality of auxiliaries in Los Angeles, Portland, and San Francisco. The federal agency likewise condemned the practice, but the Boilermakers simply ignored the toothless agency, claiming it had no jurisdiction over internal union affairs. Renouncing its own role in fueling racial animosity, the Boilermakers asserted that the FEPC would "have to bear full responsibility for racial outbreaks that [would] shock the nation—if not the world." As for black activists in their locals, the Boilermakers dismissed them as "professional agitators and negro uplifters who find it more profitable to dress well and live off the contributions exacted from the negroes by appeals to their prejudice than it is for them to build ships and thus make a real contribution to the war effort."[35] The intransigence of the international, however, provoked strong rank-and-file opposition, particularly on the West Coast.

When the Boilermakers finally convened in Kansas City in 1944, the national meeting was riven with dissent. For nearly three days, West Coast delegates filibustered over the issue of international governing boards and the right to hold local elections. A couple of the locals even elected rival officers and attempted to seat them. East Bay locals alone submitted some twenty resolutions to the constitution, indicating strenuous rank-and-file activism on the local level despite repression by the international.

Welders and Burners Local 681, which at one point had lost the right to hold meetings and elections and to issue publications, was most vociferous in defending the rights of local affiliates. The suspension or delay of elections and meetings, it said, "created an anti-union sentiment among the new members." Oakland Local 39 expressed similar concerns, specifically regarding the international-controlled Richmond local. Local 681 also supported an antidiscrimination resolution prohibiting segregated auxiliaries and advocating open membership regardless of race, sex, creed, or national origin. The resolution was supported by petitions with more than six thousand signatures from East Bay shipyard workers, both black and white.[36] As with the court cases and FEPC rulings, however, the international managed to shelve most of the proposals until after the war. As massive layoffs forced most newcomers out of the shipyards, the issue of newcomer rights became moot.

In the Richmond yards in mid-1944, Kaiser began working with the Boilermakers Union to reinstitute the prewar, craft-based system of interchangeability. Using the occasion of a jurisdictional dispute between the Shipwrights and the Boilermakers unions, management and labor (represented by the Boilermakers) agreed to discontinue the prefabrication system. According to the Boilermakers, the wartime mass-production system was too costly and unwieldy to allow Kaiser to compete with older yards in postwar ship repair.[37] Although Kaiser terminated all work in Richmond by 1946, the reconversion to skilled crafts effectively excluded the more specialized newcomers from even short-term postwar employment. This episode illustrates how management and organized labor cooperated in expanding and contracting the wartime labor force, while denying newcomers any legitimate role in industrial governance.

In response to complaints by newcomers and union dissidents, the international issued a self-published book, *Arsenal of Democracy*, in 1945. Defending its actions in Richmond, the union steadfastly supported the use of governing boards and advocated international control "wherever the need for a new local arises to fill a specific need in a growing community."[38] As the book illustrates, the Boilermakers successfully preserved their craft prerogative by abrogating rank-and-file rights and dividing the work force through an elaborate organizational hierarchy. Migrants and other newcomers remained second-class workers, easily dispensable at the war's end.

Although a complete study of East Bay unions is beyond the scope of this book, it is important to note that not all unions were as inhospitable to newcomers as the Boilermakers. Shipyard unions such as the Shipwrights, Painters, and Steamfitters made attempts to encourage participation of new members through open meetings and publications. Steamfitters' Local 590 sought to promote women's membership and even elected a woman to the executive board.[39] They continued to keep their membership closed to black workers, though, as did the Teamsters Union. The black-dominated Shipyard and Marine Shop Laborers Union was one of the few AFL unions to promote equal membership for all workers.

It was the more liberal CIO unions like the Machinists, the Electrical Workers, and the Longshoremen and Warehousemen that championed the rights of newcomers in the East Bay. But the CIO's influence in the West Coast shipbuilding industry, where the largest number of new industrial workers found employment, was negligible. Most of the CIO's activities on behalf of new workers occurred outside the workplace through ad hoc committees to improve housing, transportation, health care, race relations, and other community problems associated with the war. As we will see in chapter 7, such committees were the crucible for an emerging progressive movement in East Bay urban politics. Inside the shipyards and defense plants, however, newcomers found few allies—an experience that served to heighten their feelings of distrust and alienation.

In the absence of a strong union presence, shipyard workers relied more heavily on friends and family-based networks in the workplace.

As Katherine Archibald noted, shipyard society resembled "a familial group coming to the aid of one of its own." Male workers, for instance, often related to women coworkers through familial relationships, and the large numbers of older men and younger women encouraged "fatherly" attitudes among supervisors.[40] At the same time, the gossip mill made one's personal history public knowledge:

The stranger was not strange for long. His marital condition, the number, names and ages of his children—and, preferably, pictures of each—and the principle events of his life, such as the parts of the country in which he had lived or worked and the different jobs he had held, were common property soon after his introduction into the ship or gang, and he, in turn, quickly learned all about his companions. Thereafter, momentous events—marriages, births, or deaths—were met with congratulations, advice, or sympathy, often with substantial aid if the occasion demanded.[41]

This mutual aid network impressed a middle-class Katherine Archibald, who noted that common needs—not personal affinities—motivated the system.

Joseph Fabry, author of *Swing Shift*, a collection of short stories about the Richmond shipyards, discussed similar practices among Kaiser workers. In several cases, fellow workers collected substantial sums for sick or injured coworkers and their families. Organized charity drives were unsuccessful in comparison, and unions—which might have built on such cooperative sentiments—made little effort to extend their social programs to the new membership. New workers, then, continued to rely on kinship-based habits of mutuality common in working-class communities, particularly in rural areas and small towns.

Corporate Welfare

With a deepening labor shortage and increased recruitment of black and other minority workers, however, the familial system of the shipyards began to break down. In the face of increased social diversity and conflict, employers launched an elaborate corporate welfare program designed to preserve social harmony and increase productivity. In the East Bay, the Kaiser empire became a model of corporate welfare during the war and forced other shipbuilding concerns to emulate its system in order to retain their employees in a labor-scarce market.

Corporate welfarism, though, was by no means a product of the World War II era. Emerging in the 1910s as part of the new field of personnel management, corporate welfare programs incorporated many of the social welfare practices of settlement houses, the Young Men's Christian Association, and other reform agencies. These programs, which sought to "improve" the outside community life of industrial workers through better housing, recreation, and education, proliferated during periods of economic prosperity. By improving living conditions, employers hoped to stem the high rates of turnover, absenteeism, and labor strife that plagued industry during the boom years before and during World War I.

In the 1920s, employers in the American Management Association combined elements of corporate welfare with scientific management techniques, giving rise to the open shop drive known as the "American Plan." In the East Bay, a number of companies soon adopted aspects of this antiunion program. The most well known corporate welfare plan was that of Moore Dry Dock, which in response to the growing influence of waterfront unions during World War I formed a rival company union with an elaborate array of sports teams and hobby clubs to inspire company loyalty.[42]

The World War II programs built on past experience but did so without company unions and in a spirit of wartime cooperation with local AFL affiliates. With the financial backing of the federal government, shipyard employers provided a multitude of services to employees whose needs were not being met by their unions. In fact, organized labor's neglect of and hostility toward new workers provided an opportunity for large defense contractors to intervene in employee affairs and earn widespread respect for their community service.

On the job, shipyard managers took responsibility for orienting new workers and for promoting social harmony through ongoing propaganda campaigns. For each new minority group entering the shipyards, Kaiser appointed yard counselors to help in recruitment, orientation, employee relations, grievance procedures, and, in some cases, language problems. By 1943 there were counselors for women, blacks, Chinese, Native Americans, and teenagers. Moore Dry Dock even ran a special mandatory orientation program for women workers involving both skills training and an introduction to "the mores of shipyard society."[43]

Employers also sought to alleviate racial and sexual tensions through frequent articles on the patriotism and heroism of women and minority workers and their families. *Fore 'N' Aft,* the weekly shipyard newspaper published by Kaiser, carried regular features of this type as did the Moore paper in Oakland. Employers and the federal government occasionally named ships after prominent African-Americans and used the launching celebrations as a platform for encouraging racial harmony in the workplace and the community.

Such appeals, however, were motivated largely out of practical concerns for increasing productivity and preventing the type of social strife that struck Detroit and other cities in 1943. Employers continued to chide women and minority workers for not working hard enough, not buying enough war bonds, and so forth. They also carefully monitored the activities of minority counselors. When Don H. Gipson, a black counselor at Kaiser's Yard One, challenged discriminatory layoffs and attended one of the Shipyard Workers' Committee meetings, he was summarily dismissed.[44] Likewise, when unions took exclusionary actions against black workers, employers refused to interfere, dismissing such behavior as a question of internal union policy.

In an effort to improve morale among workers with long hours and few leisure facilities, shipyard employers provided a wide array of sports and entertainment events. In addition to work-time music, Kaiser sponsored elaborate lunchtime events with the aid of former vaudeville and radio performers temporarily working in the Richmond yards. On occasion, big-time acts like Eddie Cantor, Kay Kayser, and Red Nichols would perform. Kaiser also sponsored off-site evening events such as shipyard dances at the Oakland Auditorium and the Stage Door Canteen in San Francisco. For those interested in sports, Kaiser and other defense employers sponsored athletic teams year-round for both men and women. Kaiser claimed that 32 percent of shipyard personnel participated in its sports and recreation programs.[45] White-collar and clerical workers were disproportionately represented in this group; black workers were limited in their participation because of exclusionary policies and segregated teams. Nevertheless, employer social programs provided a needed outlet for workers whose jobs and communities offered little opportunity for leisure.

Perhaps the greatest legacy of World War II corporate welfarism was the health and welfare programs instituted by Kaiser. In addition to minority counselors, Kaiser appointed a group of counselors to work in the company welfare department to help employees with financial and health-related problems. The welfare department offered financial assistance to recent migrants and other workers experiencing temporary stress due to sickness or injury. Some shipyard unions offered similar services to their members, but such efforts were usually directed more toward old-timers than to the migrants who most needed them. As the Boilermakers explained, "We were not operating a social service center for wayward mankind."[46]

Kaiser meanwhile established the Permanente Health Plan in 1942. Like so many of Kaiser's wartime practices, the idea of a prepaid health care plan for industrial workers had originated in the federal construction projects of the 1930s. Corporate managers had first initiated a health plan during the building of the Los Angeles Aqueduct in the Mojave Desert, where workers had no access to medical treatment. A Kaiser-owned insurance company was involved in the hiring of two doctors to staff an on-site clinic financed by deductions from workers' paychecks. The clinic was a resounding success and encouraged Henry Kaiser to pursue the health care business during and after World War II.

Following major flu and pneumonia epidemics in the East Bay in 1941, Kaiser inaugurated the Permanente Plan and opened the Richmond Field Hospital a few blocks from the shipyards. The hospital handled cases of illness and work-related injuries too serious to be treated in the shipyard first-aid stations; patients in critical condition were transferred to the main Kaiser Hospital in Oakland. The program was financed through paycheck deductions of fifty cents per week by the 87 percent of workers who chose to join. For Kaiser, the initial investment paid for itself many times over as better health care made for healthier workers, less absenteeism, and increased productivity.[47]

The plan's major drawback was its limited coverage. Only shipyard employees were eligible for benefits; their families, mainly women and children, had to compete for the services of the few remaining doctors in the community who had not been drafted. Nevertheless, the health plan was highly popular with workers and boosted Kaiser's image as a preferred employer. The health plan proved to be the most enduring of all Kaiser's programs. Today, the Kaiser industrial empire has all but expired, but Kaiser Permanente is among the nation's largest and most influential health maintenance organizations.[48]

Although Kaiser and other defense contractors established corporate welfare programs as a pragmatic means of increasing productivity, these programs worked to their advantage in other ways as well. In the absence of meaningful outreach by organized labor, migrants and other new workers came to rely on employers and the federal government for social initiation and services, turning their loyalty away from the unions toward their employers. As a reporter from *The Nation* explained, newcomers at the Kaiser shipyards were "quite possessive about the yards and just as paternalistic toward Kaiser as he [was] toward them, regarding him with a fond and fatherly incredulity." Some workers, it seems, believed "Pop Kaiser" had more genuine concern for their welfare than did their own unions.[49]

From its pre–World War I origins, corporate welfarism thus reemerged as an important tool in shaping the work force of World War II defense industries. Additionally, defense contractors drew on a number of other earlier industrial innovations to mobilize the West Coast war economy. These innovations, too, had far-reaching effects on work organization and workers. During the war, Kaiser and other companies adapted dam-building principles such as prefabrication, preassembly, and other mass-production techniques developed in the 1920s and 1930s and applied them to shipbuilding. The resulting job specialization and dilution of skills facilitated the entry of new unskilled workers and threatened the prewar craft system.

Opposing this reorganization of work, the Boilermakers and other AFL unions responded defensively by sealing off their organizations and relegating newcomers to subordinate auxiliaries. The undemocratic treatment of migrants, women, and especially black workers served to heighten their distrust of unions and encourage their loyalty toward management. In the East Bay, organized labor's failure to educate and organize this mass of new workers represents one of the great missed opportunities of World War II.

The sweeping changes that affected East Bay shipbuilding during the early 1940s were characteristic of national wartime trends. The sudden expansion of production, the recruitment of new unskilled workers, and the de-skilling and reorganization of work affected hundreds of thousands of workers in aircraft, auto, electrical, and other major defense industries. With the unprecedented expansion of shipbuilding and other defense industries, West Coast cities experienced these changes with particular ferocity.

The Boilermakers' treatment of newcomers in the East Bay was also typical of the larger West Coast experience. In shipbuilding centers from San Diego to Seattle, local Boilermakers' affiliates gained thousands of new members, who quickly outnumbered the prewar membership. By 1944, fear of "subversive" elements had prompted the international to take direct control of at least ten locals nationwide, including three of the largest new West Coast affiliates—Locals 513 (Richmond), 72 (Portland, Oregon), and 401 (Vancouver, Washington). Like their East Bay counterparts, disgruntled rank-and-file members of Local 72 filed at least fifteen court cases in an effort to have duly-elected officers seated.[50]

The Boilermakers' Jim Crow auxiliary system also sparked widespread protest in West Coast black communities, giving rise to groups similar to the East Bay Shipyard Workers against Discrimination. Such groups included the San Francisco Committee against Segregation and Discrimination, the Shipyard Negro Organization for Victory in Portland, and the Shipyard Workers Committee for Equal Participation in Los Angeles. Though not always in agreement with the tactics of their Communist-influenced allies in the East Bay, all of these organizations actively fought for black shipyard employment and challenged the glaring inequities of the auxiliary system.[51]

The discriminatory policies in the shipyards were equaled if not surpassed by those of the aircraft industry, the West Coast's other major defense employer. Aircraft companies like Boeing, Consolidated Vultee (later General Dynamics), and North American Aviation maintained a whites-only hiring policy for all but janitorial work. As a result, these firms relied more extensively on white women, who made up 40 percent of the wartime work force at most California aircraft plants. The aircraft industry's main union, the AFL International Association of Machinists (IAM), barred African-American workers from membership. At plants like Lockheed in Los Angeles that did hire black workers, the IAM issued temporary work permits only. Together the Machinists and the Boilermakers represented the vast majority of West Coast defense workers. Unfortunately, as Robert Zeiger has pointed out, they were also "among the most notoriously racist organizations in the labor movement."[52]

As for management, the welfare initiatives of Kaiser and other corporate newcomers forced their competitors to provide similar services. Corporate newspapers, sports teams, and entertainment were common amenities at large West Coast defense plants. Kaiser's prepaid health plan quickly spread from California to the Pacific Northwest to serve shipyard workers in the Portland-Vancouver area. Local physicians, threatened by this new competition, worked through state medical societies to organize their own health plans. The California Physicians' Service, the Oregon Physicians' Service, and others like them eventually came together to form the Blue Shield Commission after the war.

Like other corporate welfare programs, health plans encouraged workers to see employers—rather than unions—as the true guardians of
their interests.[53]

Welfare initiatives in the workplace were surpassed only by the even
more elaborate programs of housing and social services within the
community. The next chapter examines the massive wartime housing program in the East Bay and its implications for the larger urban
community.

4

The Making
of Migrant Ghettos

When Margaret Cathey arrived in Richmond from Iowa in 1942 the people she met were like her—"they were from out of state." Cathey's experience was typical of many recent migrants to the East Bay, particularly those who lived in temporary war housing. The lives of prewar residents were equally insular. Marguerite Clausen recalled, "We didn't get to know any of them [war housing residents] personally. . . . we stayed with our own little gang."[1]

The social chasm that developed between newcomers and old-timers was in large part a result of wartime federal housing policies. To facilitate defense production, housing agencies constructed a new residential zone for war migrants along the bay flatlands. The emergence of these "shipyard ghettos," as one scholar has termed them, resulted in the geographical segregation of the cities' newcomers and old-timers.[2] War housing also introduced new forms of federally sanctioned racial segregation that would influence postwar neighborhood patterns. In short, World War II transformed the urban geography of the East Bay.

The federal government was not the only architect of this transformation. Committed to a policy of decentralization, federal agencies solicited the cooperation of local governments and defense contractors in developing war housing programs. On occasion, migrant residents themselves also influenced the course of housing policies through organized tenants groups and protests. The creation of federal migrant zones was thus a negotiated arrangement reflecting an array of often conflicting objectives.

Along with public housing, the federal government sought to allay the housing shortage through private sector solutions such as home registries, home conversion programs, and building loans. Such programs increased the population density of inner-city neighborhoods, shaping class and race relations among newcomers and old-timers. In the suburbs, war-born building loan programs were the seedbed of postwar residential development, nourishing aspirations among white migrants and old-timers alike. Even though the numerous programs ultimately proved inadequate in meeting the needs of war migrants, they presaged the development of postwar community life in the East Bay.

With the entry of the United States into the war, new shipyard contracts and mass labor recruitment inundated the area with home seekers. Largely young unskilled workers and their families from the South and Midwest, the migrant group included both blacks and whites whose regional and racial backgrounds distinguished them from prewar residents. As we saw in the last chapter, mobilization and migration led to labor conflicts between newcomers and old-timers in the workplace. In the surrounding community, defense migration increased social tensions by pitting old-timers against newcomers in the search for dwindling housing. Between April 1941 and April 1942, the vacancy rate in Oakland fell from an already low 2.0 percent to 0.81 percent, plummeting to 0.06 percent by September. The rental market in nearby East Bay communities was equally tight.[3]

The impact of the housing shortage was quickly evident in the profusion of homeless migrants and their families on city streets. In the summer of 1942, Oakland Police Captain Fred Barbeau noted that "hundreds of men, women and children [were] sleeping nightly on outdoor benches in public parks, in chairs in all-night restaurants, in theatres, in halls of rooming houses, in automobiles, even in the City Hall corridors." During the summer months, many single men simply slept outdoors in a eucalyptus grove on Richmond's south side or in abandoned buildings near the shipyards. As one group of migrants told a federal investigator, working the night shift made such transiency more tolerable: "We get out [of the shipyards] at eight in the morning, have breakfast. By then it's warm enough to sleep most anywhere there's grass. Along toward evening, we get up, shave in a filling station, and bum around town—in the bars mostly; where else is there?—

until time to go to work at midnight again." In the rainy winter months, however, the transiency problem became more severe. Hotel owners requested permission from city authorities to install extra beds in their lobbies, and rooming houses in west Oakland permitted war workers to sleep in rented chairs in the hallways.[4]

The fate of homeless migrant families attracted even greater public concern. Under the headline "Nomads But Not By Choice," the *Oakland Tribune* ran a series of articles in 1942 depicting the plight of homeless shipyard workers and their families who earned good wages but could not secure housing. The *Tribune* recounted stories of Okies from the Central Valley, construction workers from the Midwest, and even a Jewish family from New York. One Richmond shipyard worker, Abraham Shugar, the *Tribune* explained, had left New York with a family of seven and set out for the Kaiser yards. Since their arrival several weeks earlier, the family had been living out of their car, eating in restaurants, and washing in service station rest rooms. Local residents, in fact, marveled at the long lines that formed at restaurants and public rest rooms serving those without kitchen or plumbing facilities.

Outside city limits, migrant families camped in tents, trailers, and other makeshift shelters. For many Okie families, in fact, transient agricultural and construction work had become a way of life. As local trailer parks quickly filled, hundreds of shipyard workers camped with their families along creeks in outer Richmond and San Pablo.[5]

Those who managed to find more permanent shelter often secured less-than-ideal accommodations. For single men, hotels and rooming houses offered "hot beds," multiple-occupancy rooms that rented beds by the shift on a round-the-clock basis. The overcrowding of such facilities worried local fire and health officials. During a fire in 1943, Richmond authorities reported that they vacated sixty-five people from one house. A few workers found more pleasant accommodations by leasing or purchasing boats that they moored at a small yacht anchorage near Richmond Yard One. The dock owner, Bill Smart, observed, "I'm not running a boat harbor anymore, just a floating hotel for shipyard workers."[6]

Among families, doubling up was common especially for those who had friends or relatives in the area. In other cases, migrant families pooled resources by sharing accommodations. During federal hearings held in 1943, Oakland officials related numerous cases of families sharing single rooms, including one instance in which twenty-eight people inhabited a partitioned storefront in a bakery. Drawing on traditional means by which working-class families economized in hard times, migrants employed such strategies for coping with the vagaries of the wartime housing market.[7]

The desperate demand for housing no doubt encouraged unlawful practices and profiteering among local landlords. During 1942–1943, federal and state authorities prosecuted East Bay landlords for health and sanitation violations in war worker housing. Inspectors found families living in converted chicken shacks, garages, and sheds with no toilets or indoor plumbing. A federal agent described one such dwelling in San Pablo:

There were at least 6 instances where clusters of shacks were so horrible that the only possible solution would be to remove their occupants immediately and burn the shacks. . . . One of these groups was housed in a chicken house, entirely without windows. . . . This room housed a shipyard welder, his wife, and 5 children. Three of the children sleep on a thin concrete floor less than 20 feet from the muddy banks of the San Pablo Creek with drainage from a privy and a garbage pile toward the house rather than toward the Creek.

In a survey conducted in late 1942, federal officials found more than five hundred such shacks in San Pablo and other unincorporated areas surrounding Richmond.[8]

Trailer camps were another source of concern to health and sanitation inspectors. The above-mentioned survey found seventy-three trailer camps housing more than sixty-two hundred people in the outer Richmond area. Inspectors judged 22 percent of these camps to be "unfit" and recommended immediate condemnation. Oakland officials found similar problems in their city, where an estimated two thousand trailers were parked within city limits in the summer of 1942. Both city and state agencies meted out fines to trailer camp owners and eviction notices to chronic offenders.[9]

These housing inspection campaigns involved several levels of government, each with its own motives. The federal government, working with local defense contractors, worried that poor housing conditions would lower efficiency, damage morale, and increase turnover among defense workers. They consequently encouraged state and local agencies to clamp down on local violators. For their part, local officials worried not only about the public health of the community but also about the social and economic impacts of "unsightly" shantytowns and trailer camps. Such developments, they argued, lowered property values and bred crime.

For the migrant residents of these areas, housing inspection campaigns were a mixed blessing. Some migrants clearly benefited from these efforts and used government apparatus to fight back against unscrupulous landlords. In 1942, for instance, forty-eight war worker-families in downtown Oakland banded together and filed suit against a notorious "slumlord" who crowded dozens of migrant families into tiny, subdivided rooms. The case garnered widespread publicity, and the city intervened, forcing the landlord to make required improvements.[10]

In other cases, though, migrants fought government intervention that threatened to render them homeless. When Oakland officials ordered Marion Larsen to shut down her trailer lot on Market and Eleventh streets, sixty tenants, all shipyard workers, refused to move out. Many of them threatened, if evicted, to ignore federal labor freeze measures and return to their homes in Oklahoma, Iowa, and Nebraska. Residents of San Pablo and north Richmond shantytowns were equally steadfast. Here federal officials found eviction proceedings to be unworkable since many of these families "partially own[ed] or . . . leased land and [were] in the process of constructing shacks which [were] satisfactory to themselves." For families like these, housing inspections seemed to be targeted more at them than at landlords and only aggravated an already critical housing shortage. Fears of vagrancy combined with genuine concerns over the plight of migrant families soon convinced federal and local officials that something had to be done.[11]

Private Sector Solutions

Fearing the prospect of public housing, federal agencies initially sought to allay the housing shortage through private sector solutions. With the creation of the U.S. Housing Administration in 1937, the federal government had retreated from direct federal action in housing construction in favor of decentralized control through local housing authorities. This policy marked a shift away from earlier communitarian schemes (such as greenbelts and cooperative farms) to greater cooperation with the private sector in urban slum clearance programs.

The establishment of the wartime National Housing Agency (NHA) in 1942 accelerated the trend toward private sector involvement. The NHA, an umbrella agency for all preexisting federal housing programs, hoped to limit public housing in favor of home registries, building conversions, and private home construction.[12] First off, the NHA encouraged local groups to conduct door-to-door canvasses, recording all vacant rooms and buildings. Empty and underoccupied hotels, college dorms, and other quarters were then converted to war worker or military lodgings.

The NHA also established local home registries in most East Bay cities to act as placement agencies for migrant war workers. These War Housing Centers, administered by local realtors and Chambers of Commerce, arranged house swaps among Bay Area defense workers in hopes of easing transportation pressures. More important, though, was the war guest program introduced in mid-1942. The program encouraged native residents to register their empty rooms and apartments and offered referrals to prospective tenants. The War Housing Centers also featured a home conversion program in which owners leased part of their homes to the federal government in exchange for low-interest loans for subdivision and remodeling.

Using a vigorous publicity campaign, the war guest program sought to convince reluctant homeowners to accept migrant war workers as tenants and boarders. Newspaper articles featured photographs of an attractive "Miss Housing," who appealed to natives (many of them women) to "Protect Your Home by Sharing It with a War Worker." Juxtaposed with gender-specific patriotic appeals were articles on migrant families who, despite their good wages, were unable to find accommodations. The War Housing Centers also enlisted the support of local churches. Ministers urged their congregants to register their spare rooms, assuring them tenants of the same denomination.[13]

During the course of the war, thousands of East Bay households responded to these appeals, particularly in blue-collar neighborhoods near the waterfront. Migrants who arrived early enough to purchase homes in these areas often sublet rooms to fellow shipyard workers. Minnesota-born Antoinette Vaara and her sister took in seven boarders in their home in south Richmond while their husbands worked at the shipyards. Their boarders were mostly friends and family from back home whom they had encouraged to move west.[14] Living arrangements like these facilitated chain migration and supplemented the earnings of newcomer families.

Boarding and subletting, though, were more common among working-class natives, who welcomed the defense mobilization as a chance to recover financially from the depression. Subletting rooms and taking in boarders thus provided a means of earning extra income while helping the war effort. With the wartime scarcity of consumer goods, old-timer families accumulated savings that would help improve their economic status in the postwar period.

As in earlier episodes of urban migration, widows and single women took in boarders as a way of earning income in their own homes. Stanley Nystrom's mother, a longtime Richmond resident whose husband died in 1941, rented out rooms to shipyard workers in their large family home. Another Richmond woman, Irene Bianchini, took in seventeen roomers, cooked for thirty-two boarders, and provided laundry service as well.

According to Nystrom, boarding and renting rooms were common practices on the working-class south side. "Everybody was renting space," he said. "In some houses they put up wires and strung drapery as a partition . . . and just gave up use of their front room."[15] Many of those who took in boarders were immigrants themselves, or the descendants of the Irish, Italians, and Eastern Europeans who populated flatland neighborhoods. These arrangements produced income for working-class families but also reversed the traditional social relationship of immigrant and native born. As landlords of white, native-born Protestants, prewar ethnic residents may have bettered their social and economic standing in East Bay communities.

The war guest program, however, was less successful in the cities' middle- and upper-class neighborhoods. Residents there, whose class sensibilities were easily offended by the ways of life of the area's new workers, were wary of opening up their homes. As one Oakland society woman put it: "Do you think people who have been brought up in refinement and luxury and own many valuable and prized possessions, care to take perfect strangers from unknown parts and of unknown character into their beautiful homes?" Despite the barbs hurled at the "unpatriotic" rich, these families cordoned off their neighborhoods, preferring to aid the war effort in other ways.

Similar sentiments existed in middle-class neighborhoods. Federal authorities in largely middle-class Alameda, for instance, noted "a general reluctance upon the part of long-time residents of Alameda to open their homes to war workers." Natives in middle-class areas accused migrants of being "trashy" and lazy, having too many children, being prone to crime, drinking too much, and so forth. Some old-time residents claimed that newcomers were too friendly. "You say hello to them twice and they're coming in your back door without knocking," said one woman.[16]

Most commonly, middle-class residents chided migrants for improper upkeep of their homes and yards. "They are transients," complained one resident about her migrant neighbors, and they "seem to have no idea of decent living standards." Landlords in middle-class areas were wary of renting to war workers, claiming that they damaged homes and property. Exclusion from such neighborhoods frustrated migrant home-seekers, who resented the natives' attitude of superiority. Said one woman war worker, "The landlords can afford to be snootier than the social blue book about the people they will condescend to take rent from."[17]

Some of the natives' accusations were directed at "Okies" and "hillbillies," terms used loosely to refer to rural and southern migrants. Among such families, down-home practices were sometimes adapted to city life to help ease wartime food shortages. Throughout the war years, natives complained about migrant neighbors keeping livestock and poultry in their yards and reported them to city health authorities. One Richmond man complained that his "Okie" neighbors kept rabbits, chickens, and six cows in their backyard. In Oakland, a midwestern woman was reported by neighbors for keeping fifty chickens in her kitchen in violation of city sanitary laws. Even shipyard workers themselves complained about the noise made by crowing roosters, which, they said, kept night-shift workers from getting adequate sleep. Noting that war workers from small towns were unfamiliar with urban restrictions, local governments periodically reiterated warnings on keeping livestock and other sanitary violations.[18]

The cultural and class differences between natives and newcomers served to hamper the war guest program in many East Bay neighborhoods. The program was most successful in ethnic and blue-collar areas in Oakland and Richmond, where the number of lodgers increased far more rapidly than in surrounding suburbs. The proximity of city neighborhoods to shipyards and other war industries and the abundance of older housing stock resulted in the subdivision of many large Victorian houses. In Oakland, where thousands of new housing units were created during the war, the number of dwellings with seven rooms or more actually declined by some fourteen hundred units, a shift that reflected the increase of subdivision and boarding.[19]

War Housing Center programs, however, were at best stop gap measures. Families with children, especially, continued to have great difficulty finding housing. In 1944, Alameda County War Housing Centers received thousands of applications but were able to place only one family in six. Housing officials in San Francisco, Portland, Detroit, and other defense centers faced similar shortages.[20]

To help remedy the situation, the Federal Housing Administration (FHA) introduced a special wartime construction program to serve the East Bay and other critical production areas. Funded by Congress in 1941, the FHA's Title 6 program guaranteed loans for private housing construction. Although federal underwriting of suburban subdivisions dates back to the New Deal, the wartime FHA program established precedents in construction techniques and business management that would influence the postwar housing boom in East Bay suburbs.

As Kenneth Jackson has pointed out, the loan program for defense housing aided the ascendance of big business construction firms that would dominate the postwar housing market. Like William Levitt back East, D. D. Bohannon, R. H. Chamberlain, Ellie Stoneman, and other major Bay Area contractors got their start in wartime projects where they experimented with new materials and mass production. Using plywood, particleboard, plasterboard, and concrete slab foundations, these contractors applied prefabrication and preassembly to home building, much as Kaiser had done in shipbuilding.[21] War migrants, then, encountered mass production not only on the job but in their homes and neighborhoods as well.

With inspiring names like "Victory Homes" and "MacArthur Villa," defense subdivisions sprang up along the East Bay urban fringe. Developers worked directly with shipyard managers in designing homes to meet the needs of defense worker families. Catering to Kaiser workers in Richmond, D. D. Bohannon and R. H. Chamberlain unveiled a seven-hundred-unit development in San Pablo in 1943. The subdivision, known as Rollingwood, featured three-bedroom houses with separate guest-room entrances to accommodate the extra family members and boarders common in war worker families. Rollingwood also provided bus service to the shipyards, a planned shopping center, and a realty office located conveniently across from the Kaiser hiring hall. For those unsure of their postwar plans, Rollingwood offered a wartime leasing arrangement with an option to buy.[22]

Albert Bernhardt and the Stoneon Brothers developed an even larger subdivision in East Oakland. Containing more than twelve hundred homes, Brookfield Village hearkened back to the garden suburbs of the early twentieth century. Located in the flatlands near the San Leandro border, the development featured winding, contoured streets lined with shade trees. Its creators advertised it as "a model village on the Pacific Coast," imitating more expensive subdivisions. Homes sold for four thousand dollars each (well below prices in most East Bay neighborhoods) and attracted large numbers of Moore and Kaiser workers. Not to be outdone, Bohannon and Chamberlain began construction a few miles south on the 1,329-unit San Lorenzo Village, the nation's largest Title 6 program at the time. Because of wartime restrictions on building materials, most of these defense subdivisions were built outside city limits to circumvent municipal building codes. Unincorporated areas like San Pablo and San Leandro were particularly popular sites.[23]

In these outlying areas, developers created "model" white migrant communities, ensuring a sanitized suburban atmosphere through written covenants among homeowners. Since its founding in 1934, the FHA had shown a strong preference for funding all-white suburban housing. That tendency continued during the war, when the FHA channeled funds into subdivisions for defense workers that restricted residence to anyone "not wholly of the Caucasian race." In addition, covenants also sought to preclude the aspects of migrant living that natives found distasteful. In Rollingwood, for example, covenants specified: "No trailer, basement, tent, shack, garage, barn or other outbuilding in the tract shall at any time be used as a residence temporarily or permanently." They also forbade the keeping of roosters or "any animal of cloven hoof."[24] Defense subdivisions became migrant enclaves, but their occupancy and appearance were carefully controlled to conform with modern suburban ideals.

For some newcomer residents, defense subdivisions promised a ready-made community atmosphere and a chance to own a piece of land, which for many had become an impossibility in their home states. One migrant woman, who complained of loneliness and alienation in Oakland, talked anxiously about her new defense home. In the suburbs, she said, "we can have a garden, family orchard, chickens and our own place, as we have never been able to do before." Their neighborhood of war workers, she believed, would be "a credit to your city." Nonessential workers, however, who were not eligible for defense subdivisions, sometimes expressed resentment at the "special privileges" accorded shipyard workers.[25]

The history of defense worker subdivisions in the East Bay highlights the importance of World War II in shaping twentieth-century suburban development. Concentrating on northeastern cities in the postwar period, urban historians have described how middle-class and white ethnic residents fled the city for new suburbs after the war. In West Coast defense centers, however, the contours of postwar suburbia clearly emerged during the war years. The new suburbanites were not urban refugees but mainly white defense migrants from small cities and rural areas in the nation's interior. Such residents were not the "organization men" of 1950s sociology but migratory blue-collar workers and their families.[26] The defense subdivisions were thus the prototypes for working-class suburbs that would proliferate throughout postwar California.

The contours of the postwar black community also took shape during World War II. For black migrants, however, the failure of private sector housing programs resulted in overcrowded and deteriorating city neighborhoods. Nearly all Title 6 construction programs were restricted to white buyers, and the war guest program offered little aid to black renters. In 1942, J. Harvey Kerns, a social worker who investigated the living conditions of blacks in Oakland, noted that there were no public housing bureaus serving blacks in that city. The plight of homeless black families grew worse in 1943, when one journalist observed "the tragic spectacle of [black] families going from door to door, begging for sleeping accommodations in sheds, garages and anyplace else they [could] have shelter."[27] Without the benefit of housing bureaus, black migrants relied more on family and neighborhood networks and on the new public housing bureaucracies.

In private housing, black migrants were limited to the same neighborhoods occupied by prewar black residents. As a result, the population density of west Oakland and north Richmond increased markedly during and after the war. In 1940, 15.2 percent of all black households in west Oakland were overcrowded; by 1950, the figure had jumped to 30.7 percent. In north Richmond the increase was even more dramatic, from 8.1 percent in 1940 to 56.1 percent in 1950 (see table 7).

In west Oakland, black homeowners took in boarders, subdivided large Victorian homes, and housed wide kin networks resulting from chain migration. Maya Angelou, who moved to the Bay Area from rural Arkansas during the war, described her family home in west Oakland in her autobiography. In an apartment that "had a bathtub in the kitchen and was near enough to the Southern Pacific Mole to shake at the arrival and departure of every train," Angelou lived with her

Table 7 Overcrowding among Black Households in West Oakland and North Richmond, 1940–1950

Census tracts	1940			1950		
	Dwelling units	No. overcrowded*	% overcrowded	Dwelling units	No. overcrowded*	% overcrowded
West Oakland						
14	237	40	16.9	1,440	416	28.9
15	357	68	19.0	1,937	628	32.4
16	599	62	10.3	1,635	474	29.0
17	224	36	16.1	1,614	442	27.4
18	98	18	18.4	772	221	28.6
21	436	73	16.7	1,626	588	36.2
Total	1,951	297	15.2	9,024	2,769	30.7
North Richmond						
CCC-3	74	6	8.1	1,111	623	56.1

SOURCES: U.S. Bureau of the Census, Sixteenth Census of the United States, 1940: Reports on Population, vol. 7, Supplementary Report—Statistics for Census Tracts: Population and Housing, "Oakland-Berkeley, Calif., and Adjacent Area," 40, 73; and U.S. Census of Population: 1950, vol. 3, Census Tracts Statistics, bulletin P-D49, "Selected Population and Housing Characteristics, San Francisco—Oakland, Calif.," 74–75.

*Overcrowded households are those with 1.01 persons or more per room.

mother, two uncles, her mother, and a brother.[28] Such households became increasingly common in west Oakland, south Berkeley, and other black neighborhoods during the war.

In the unincorporated area of north Richmond, a somewhat different housing pattern developed. Unencumbered by municipal building codes, black migrants constructed their own homes on property leased or purchased from prewar residents. In a postwar report, a local neighborhood organization explained how the area grew during the war:

Without credit and without building permits, people did the best they could. Many families moved trailers out to their lots, and gradually built additions to the trailers. Without a priority, one could buy at this time only twenty dollars worth of lumber, but many families bought that twenty dollars worth every pay-day, and went on with their building. Scrap metal and scrap lumber were pressed into service.[29]

In this manner, black migrants helped build their own community; by 1948, 60 percent of north Richmond residents owned their own homes mortgage-free. But this self-made community had its problems too. Since the city of Richmond refused to take responsibility for the area, residents suffered from frequent winter flooding, greater health hazards, and inadequate transportation, sewage facilities, and street maintenance.[30]

Most noticeably, the increase in black population density in north Richmond and west Oakland accelerated the development of eastern-style black ghettos. As large numbers of black migrants moved into these areas, white ethnic residents comprised a relatively smaller segment. In west Oakland the black percentage of the total population skyrocketed from 16.2 percent in 1940 to 61.5 percent by 1950. Compared with eastern cities, racial transition in the East Bay occurred late; in Chicago and New York, well-defined black neighborhoods had emerged by 1910, and midwestern cities like Cleveland saw their ghettos take shape in the 1920s. Such neighborhoods, which had developed in northeastern cities as a consequence of black migration before and after World War I, thus emerged in many western cities for the first time in the 1940s.[31]

Some old-time black residents in these areas blamed newcomers for the disintegration of earlier patterns of race relations. The migrants "lacked the fellowship that we had with the foreign people," said Royal Towns, a descendant of an early black pioneer family in Oakland. "All of us used to go swimming together down in the estuary. Then when this influx of blacks came, they found a separate place for themselves to go. They segregated themselves because of the way they were raised down in the South."[32]

Like white natives, black prewar residents often resented the intrusion of southern migrants into their neighborhoods. Urania Cummings, an old-time Berkeley resident, felt that the town changed for the worse during the war. Her neighborhood, she said, "used to be like a big family. Everybody seemed to get along nicely together because I think everybody owned something . . . and we had pride in what we owned." The newcomers, she said, "just didn't understand. . . . they didn't have a pride like we had in our little city."[33] Cummings's view suggests the importance of homeownership among prewar blacks and reveals a sense of class distinction between old-timers and newcomers that persists to this day.

The influx of black migrants into established black neighborhoods did, in fact, help consolidate an emerging black middle class. Black landlords, merchants, and businesspeople—primarily old-timers— prospered amid the boomtown atmosphere of the East Bay. The change was especially evident in west Oakland, where Seventh Street— long the commercial center of the black community—became a bustling boomtown district. The rapidly growing black population provided new business opportunities, and federal investigators counted at least eighty black professionals and entrepreneurs working nearby. Nathan Huggins, a historian and an old-time Bay Area resident, observed that war migrants "formed the basis of black business." With their arrival, doctors, lawyers, and other professionals emerged as the new black middle class, supplanting the redcaps and porters of the railroad era.[34]

Although many old-timers harbored ambivalent feelings toward the newcomers in their neighborhood, they offered political and economic leadership to the new black population. And despite internal tensions, prewar black neighborhoods provided a sense of community through their churches, clubs, and other social organizations. Changing demographics in these areas, then, helped shape race and class relations that would characterize the black community in the postwar period. In both black city neighborhoods and white suburban subdivisions, wartime housing arrangements prefigured many aspects of postwar community life.

Public Housing Programs

Ultimately, the failures and inadequacies of private sector housing programs prompted the federal government to turn toward public housing. The war guest program simply could not handle migrant housing demands, and shortages of labor and materials made private home building increasingly difficult. At the same time, the formation of the NHA in 1942 called a temporary truce to the jurisdictional disputes, bureaucratic infighting, and political conflicts that had hampered public housing programs in the past. By focusing strictly on temporary war housing, the director of the NHA, John Blanford, worked to bridge the gap between liberal housing reformers and conservatives representing the private construction industry. After 1942, with the intensification of the war effort, the NHA turned increasingly to public housing.[35]

Federal legislation in 1940 laid the groundwork for this program by channeling all public housing funds and resources into the defense effort. In Oakland and Richmond, as in other defense centers, existing public housing projects built before the war were converted to defense worker use in 1942.[36] That same year, the federal government approved plans for thousands of new housing units to be built with funds provided under the Lanham Act of 1940. In the East Bay, the U.S. Maritime Commission and the Federal Works Agency constructed war housing projects, but occupancy decisions and management responsibilities were left to local housing authorities under the oversight of the Federal Public Housing Authority (FPHA).

Since their establishment under the 1937 slum clearance program, local housing authorities had been dominated by realtors, builders, and other prominent business leaders. In Richmond the Chamber of Commerce actually founded the local housing authority in 1941 in an attempt to exercise control over pending federal construction. According to one political observer, the Richmond Housing Authority was a tightly controlled group "absolutely reserved to local patronage." In Oakland, organized labor had pressured the city council to take advantage of federal funding for public housing in the late thirties. When the city council created the local housing authority, however, it appointed a business-dominated board representing the banking, insurance, and real estate industries, including several past presidents of the Alameda

County Apartment House Owners Association and the California Rental Association.[37]

During the war years, the business-dominated local housing authorities remained steadfastly opposed to permanent public housing that might undercut postwar private construction. They were thus quick to cooperate with federal agencies in constructing temporary war housing projects that would be removed at the end of the war. Such a scheme, of course, presupposed that defense migrants would return to their home states, allowing the government to dispose of their dwellings.

Under normal circumstances, labor and other liberal forces might have pressed more successfully for permanent public housing. The war, however, created a peculiar set of economic and political circumstances that brought conservatives and liberals together in support of the war effort. On a practical level, mass homelessness and overcrowding called for desperate measures. Temporary housing could be prefabricated and assembled with a minimum of time and priority materials. On a political level, urban liberals, who traditionally lobbied for progressive housing reform, failed to offer any determined resistance to NHA policies for fear of hindering the war effort. Whatever idealism was left in the 1937 slum clearance program thus dissipated under the requisites of war and a mushrooming defense economy. Facing little opposition, federal and local officials embarked on what was to be the largest housing construction scheme in Bay Area history.

Guided by expediency, the FPHA and other federal agencies created, in effect, distinct zones of migrant settlement along the bay flatlands between Richmond and Alameda. Proximity to shipyards and public transportation dictated where temporary housing projects would be built, overshadowing all other social and aesthetic considerations. In addition, the FPHA gained ready access to lowland areas containing poorly drained vacant lots. In these sparsely populated areas, the federal government could lease large blocks of land with few legal obstacles.

Initially, federal agencies built temporary housing within walking distance of the shipyards and military installations. Projects like Harbor Gate, Canal, and Terrace War apartments were constructed in south Richmond; Bayview Villa and Harbor Homes sprang up near the Moore yards in west Oakland; Pacific, Encinal, and Chipman projects served Alameda shipyard and naval air station workers along the inner harbor and the island's west end. Occupancy in the temporary projects was limited to migrant war workers, who filled up new units as fast as they could be built. As the war progressed, federal facilities filled most of the open space in these areas, and housing projects soon encroached into adjoining lowland areas accessible by new wartime transportation lines.

With the majority of shipyard workers commuting between points in the East Bay, the federal government established provisional train, bus, and streetcar lines to alleviate the chronic overcrowding of local carriers. Most notable of these was the "Shipyard Railway" completed by the Maritime Commission in 1942. Constructed from old interurban track lines, the railway featured converted cars from New York City's Third Avenue elevated line. Running parallel to San Pablo Avenue, the Shipyard Railway stretched more than sixteen miles from the Moore yards in west Oakland to the Kaiser yards in Richmond and carried more than eleven thousand passengers per day.[38]

The Shipyard Railway and other new transit lines along coastal arteries opened up new areas for temporary housing development. In east Oakland, the federal government built High Street Homes and Auditorium Village to supplement the overtaxed west Oakland projects. In Richmond, the Maritime Commission expanded existing project tracts along the south side, crossing over into El Cerrito. Even Berkeley and Albany, towns that fiercely resisted war housing development, ended up with Codornices Village, a 1,900-unit complex on San Pablo Avenue. By 1945, a drive from Richmond to San Leandro along Cutting Boulevard, San Pablo Avenue, and San Leandro Boulevard revealed a waterfront corridor of federal facilities and accompanying migrant neighborhoods (see map 3).

In all, the federal government created more than 30,000 public housing units in the East Bay, holding an estimated ninety thousand war workers and family members. The impact of this development varied, depending on what percentage of a city's total population lived in public housing. In Oakland, where there were only 3,522 public housing units compared with more than 100,000 private dwellings, conflicts between migrants and old-time residents were persistent but manageable. Richmond, by contrast, housed more than half its population in temporary war housing (more than 23,000 units). Richmond's public housing program was the largest in the nation to be controlled by a single housing authority and included more units than were built in the entire state of Michigan.[39] The entire south side became a shipyard ghetto, physically dividing the city into separate

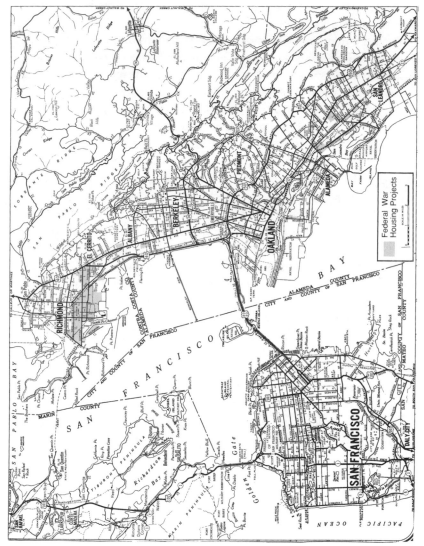

Map 3. Federal War Housing in the East Bay, 1945

communities of migrants and old-timers (see map 4). The degree of segregation in other East Bay cities fell somewhere between these two extremes.

Once established, the federal corridor allowed local governments to contain the effects of wartime social change and minimize its impact on their communities. Troublesome developments such as rooming houses and trailer camps could be safely contained and controlled in these areas. Local officials thus actively encouraged the consolidation of a federal zone within their cities.

Federally built dormitories, for instance, offered a supervised environment for young men, complete with recreation facilities. High-school-age and adult men were housed separately, in an attempt to avoid the "unhealthy" mixing that occurred in commercial rooming houses. Most important, federal dormitories physically removed this volatile population of young single males from the downtown areas, where their public behavior provoked much concern among local authorities. These young men, said the editors of the *Richmond Independent,* could now enjoy "clean amusement" at home rather than spend "the lonely hours of long evenings on street corners or in other places."[40]

The unsightly trailer camps that flanked East Bay cities were also incorporated into the federal zone through the creation of government-operated trailer parks. In fact, local officials embraced the new facilities as a means of resolving the trailer problem in their cities. Since Richmond and several other communities had previously banned trailers within city limits, Oakland, El Cerrito, and San Pablo found themselves with a proliferation of trailers in empty lots, fields, and backyards. With the opening of federal camps, both Oakland and Contra Costa County ceased issuing trailer camp licenses, dubbing such parks "a menace" to local neighborhoods and property values. Oakland officials also prosecuted individual trailer owners parked in driveways and backyards, of whom there were an estimated 600–1,500 in 1943.[41]

The federal government operated at least six trailer parks in the East Bay, including two in east Oakland, one in Alameda's west end, and three in the Richmond area. The largest of these, the El Portal Trailer Park in San Pablo, was a fully equipped community and reportedly the largest trailer facility in the nation. A few miles south, the FPHA opened Fairmount Trailer Park on the grounds of the former El Cerrito dog track.[42] As contained, supervised communities, government trailer parks provided an alternative to the makeshift migrant ac-

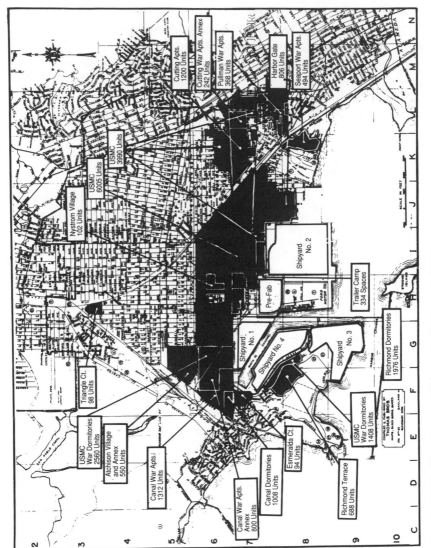

Map 4. Public Housing and Shipyards, Richmond, 1944

Cutting Apts.
1200 Units

Cutting War Apts. Annex
242 Units

Pullman War Apts.
368 Units

Harbor Gate
806 Units

Seaport War Apts.
494 Units

USMC
3990 Units

USMC
6005 Units

Nystrom Village
102 Units

Shipyard
No. 2

Pre-Fab

Shipyard
No. 1

Shipyard No. 4

Shipyard
No. 3

Trailer Camp
334 Spaces

Richmond Dormitories
1976 Units

USMC
War Dormitories
1408 Units

Triangle Ct.
98 Units

USMC
War Dormitories
2560 Units

Atchison Village
and Annex
550 Units

Canal War Apts.
1312 Units

Canal War Apts.
Annex
800 Units

Canal Dormitories
1008 Units

Esmeralda Ct.
94 Units

Richmond Terrace
688 Units

COMPILED & PUBLISHED BY
THOMAS BROS.
MAPS, BLUE PRINTS,
OAKLAND
550 9TH ST.
OAKLAND

commodations that threatened the sensibilities and property values of local middle-class residents.

The consolidation of federal migrant zones, however, was not an entirely smooth process. Some old-time residents, particularly those most directly affected by the new developments, protested federal housing policies. In west Oakland, some residents displaced by the 1937 slum clearance program expressed resentment at migrant war workers, who received priority placement in prewar housing projects. Such units were intended for the underprivileged, said one west Oaklander, but were now going to defense workers "coming in from all states [and] earning good wages." Other old-timers caught in the housing squeeze objected to the preferential treatment accorded "essential" war workers, which included access to public housing and defense subdivisions. "You know if this happened back in your hometown," said one old-timer to a recent arrival, "you wouldn't like it either."[43]

Some of the most organized opposition to public housing occurred in Alameda, Berkeley, and Albany, where white residential neighborhoods extended through the flatlands and bordered directly on federal projects. In one Albany neighborhood, residents insisted that the federal government install an eight-foot fence around the Fairmount Trailer Park. The park, they maintained, would attract transients, and war worker children would run loose in the area. "We don't feel that it is our patriotic duty to take a loss in property values," said the local homeowners' committee. Alameda residents likewise protested the creation of the FPHA's Atlantic Trailer Park, fearing the arrival of transients and the creation of an "Okie town" within city limits.[44]

The most protracted dispute occurred in 1943 with the FPHA's decision to build the Codornices housing project along San Pablo Avenue on the Albany-Berkeley line. The Berkeley city council immediately countered the proposal, objecting to the loss of prime industrial land (though no industrial uses were slated for the near future). The University of California, which owned part of the tract, also opposed the project, claiming that it needed the land for a proposed veterinary school and agricultural study station.

In Albany local citizens spearheaded an antihousing petition drive that revealed the racial and class concerns of neighboring residents. In opposing the project, the Albany city council objected to the introduction of "an undesirable element" into the community. More specifically, they feared the arrival of black migrants, who would force the integration of local schools and make Albany "like South Berkeley."

The Civil Defense Council in Berkeley echoed similar themes. "This construction is not in keeping with a university city," they said in their report. "We do not want our returning servicemen to find a transformed community."[45]

Living immediately adjacent to the federal corridor, white homeowners in Albany and Berkeley remained steadfastly opposed to its expansion. Both cities refused to create housing authorities to manage the Codornices project and continued attempts to block construction. Ironically, local resistance prompted the federal government to take direct control of the project, permitting the implementation of more radical programs at various points in its history. The Codornices case was characteristic of other war housing projects around the nation where greater federal control resulted in more progressive policies and social programs.

In the end, the federal government surmounted local opposition and succeeded in consolidating separate migrant residential zones that were geared to the needs of defense industries. This bifurcated development augmented the physical and psychological distance between war migrants and prewar residents. Among old-time residents interviewed for this study and other oral history projects, few ever ventured into the public housing areas during the war years. Migrants likewise indicated that they associated mostly with other newcomers.[46] According to Kaiser management in 1943, "Old-timers and in-migrants have not yet achieved effective working relationships."[47]

Social agencies and shipyard representatives frequently chastised both groups for their lack of civic involvement. The Kaiser newspaper urged newcomers to "accept the community duties of a good citizen," while exhorting old-timers to "accept new problems and help solve them."[48] This sense of civic disintegration, however, was not easily dispelled; economic, racial, and cultural conflicts divided newcomers and old-timers at work and in the community. With the creation of federal migrant ghettos, newcomer–old-timer divisions became embedded in the urban geography of wartime cities.

War housing programs transformed urban social relations in other ways as well, particularly in the realm of race relations. With the sanction of the federal government, local authorities introduced new racial patterns in East Bay neighborhoods, many of which would persist in the postwar era. Since the mid-1930s, the guiding principle of racial distribution in federal projects had been "local custom"—a New Deal formula that permitted local housing authorities to determine if and how segregation would be implemented. Federal housing agencies suggested that local communities follow the prevailing neighborhood patterns, thus perpetuating existing racial distribution.[49]

The massive influx of defense migrants, however, so transformed many East Bay neighborhoods that local custom became irrelevant. Local housing authorities sought to cope with this new situation through a variety of means, ranging from the "checkerboard pattern" (blacks and whites living side by side), to the "patchwork pattern" (segregation by areas or buildings), to outright segregation by housing project. In almost every case, segregation in local communities increased, as it did throughout the West Coast. Carey McWilliams, the former commissioner of housing and immigration in California, remarked at the war's end that "the federal government [had] in effect been planting the seeds of Jim Crow practices throughout the region under the guise of 'respecting local attitudes.' "[50]

In many communities, federal housing sprang up in lowland industrial areas where there was no clearly established "neighborhood pattern." Areas like south Richmond and the harbor-front tracts in Oakland and Alameda became overnight migrant ghettos, where housing authorities used segregated projects or the patchwork pattern in the absence of any prevailing racial segregation. In Oakland's Harbor Homes, adjacent to the Moore shipyards, the Oakland Housing Authority segregated black residents, though there were no adjoining neighborhoods dictating such a rigid pattern. In Alameda, where war housing was segregated by project or by building, the director of the local housing authority rejected integration policies "as a form of discrimination against whites."[51]

Richmond authorities also segregated by project, area, or building along the city's largely undeveloped south side. Here the housing authority concentrated blacks along the shoreline area south of Cutting Boulevard and west of South First Street, an arrangement that would endure into the 1950s, shaping private housing patterns as well.[52] In Richmond, as we shall see in chapter 7, wartime housing policies prefigured postwar racial patterns in city neighborhoods.

Another obstacle to the "neighborhood pattern" were the migrants themselves, many of whom came from the South and had their own "local customs." In west Oakland, where prewar public housing followed the integrated checkerboard pattern, the influx of war migrants prompted local officials to move toward segregated housing arrangements. Prior to the peak migration period, Katharine Legge, the head of tenant selection at the Oakland Housing Authority, indicated that integration was working well at west Oakland's Campbell Village, where many prewar residents lived. "Given the opportunity, Negroes and white people get along without any friction," she said, "not once have we had the slightest indication of difficulty."[53] One year later, however, Oakland housing officials claimed that the influx of southern whites had necessitated segregated projects. According to Executive Director Bernard J. Abrott, racial conflicts were common at Peralta Villa, the west Oakland project converted entirely to war worker occupancy. In response, the housing authority opened four all-black projects in west Oakland, including Bayview Villa, Cypress Village, Magnolia Manor, and Willow Manor Dorms. Corresponding all-white projects, such as Auditorium Village and High Street Homes, were built along the bay flats in east Oakland.[54]

Exactly what type of racial conflicts the Oakland Housing Authority had in mind is unclear. Certainly, racially motivated street fights and youth gang activity occurred regularly in west Oakland, particularly in the wake of the Detroit race riot and the Los Angeles zoot suit violence that spawned similar disturbances in other U.S. cities in the summer of 1943. Furthermore, rumors of lynch mobs had been reported in several West Coast defense centers.[55] With fear of racial violence running high, Oakland housing officials probably implemented segregation in hopes of reducing interracial contacts and defusing tension. The FPHA apparently accepted local segregation measures in hopes of preserving social harmony through the war emergency.

The role of local officials in determining racial distribution in public housing was revealed most vividly in the case of Codornices Village. Initially, this Berkeley-Albany project was controlled directly by the federal government and followed the patchwork pattern of segregation by building. Toward the end of the war, however, as a concession to angry Albany residents, the federal government hired a local man as head of the leasing department. According to project residents, the new administrator allowed selective transfers to white residents away from the less desirable west-side units (adjacent to the Southern Pacific railroad tracks) to conveniently located east-side units along San Pablo Avenue. By 1945 the project was solidly segregated on an east-west basis, leaving black residents the noisier, dirtier railroad frontage.[56]

In Codornices, as in Richmond, segregation measures created a kind of buffer zone between the prewar white community and new black residents. In south Richmond, housing officials concentrated black residents along the shoreline areas near the shipyards and railroads. Canal War Apartments and other projects housing blacks in this area were among the most poorly constructed, offering greater fire hazard and frequent flooding. Flanking the inland northern edge of the public housing area were all-white units that buffered the downtown area and private residences along the south side.[57] Also located inland were the prized permanent housing projects of Atchison Village, Triangle Court, and Nystrom Village—all of which admitted whites only. Segregation patterns, then, were not arbitrary but served to allocate preferred housing stock to whites while minimizing the racial impact of war migration on prewar communities.

Black residents, however, did fight back against public housing segregation. Byron Rumford, a black pharmacist and community leader in Berkeley, led an antisegregation petition drive among public housing tenants in 1944. Under the auspices of the Berkeley Interracial Committee, Rumford presented to the city council 283 signatures calling for the integration of Codornices Village. White residents of west Berkeley presented counterpetitions a few months later. Although no immediate change occurred during the war, Rumford's activities created the momentum that culminated in federally mandated integration of Codornices in 1946. And as we will see in chapter 7, the political contacts forged in these wartime housing campaigns helped in Rumford's successful bid for a state assembly seat in 1948.[58]

While segregation relegated blacks to inferior housing stock, other regulations served to restrict their access to public housing altogether. One of the most serious obstacles for black home-seekers was the informal quota system employed by local housing authorities. The FPHA encouraged racial quotas in public housing to guarantee a fair distribution of units based on need. The quotas, though, reflected the white-black ratio among defense workers, not the actual ratio among public housing applicants. As noted earlier, black migrants encountered a tightly restricted private market and relied on public housing to a greater extent than whites.

In Richmond, for instance, local housing officials maintained a ratio of four to one beginning in 1943. The 20 percent of units allocated to black families was clearly inadequate and forced many of them to double up in small apartments or procure illegal sublets. In January 1945, Richmond officials conducted a survey in one housing area that found 80 out of 360 black families living illegally but only 16 of 3,500 white families. The Richmond Housing Authority responded by evicting several black "rent chiselers," including a local leader of the National Association for the Advancement of Colored People (NAACP). The action precipitated mass meetings by the NAACP, a threatened rent strike, and eventual mediation by the FPHA.[59] The incident marked the opening round of a housing battle that would rage in Richmond for the next ten years.

Ostensibly color-blind occupancy rules in some projects also worked against black home-seekers. In Maritime Commission projects, built exclusively for shipyard workers, the federal government allowed shipyard managers to control tenant selection. These managers gave priority to "essential workers"—foremen, leadermen, and journeymen—categories into which relatively few blacks were admitted. Consequently, Harbor Homes in Oakland was 85 percent white, and Richmond's Harbor Gate and USMC Divisions 1 and 2 were 90 percent white. According to Katharine Legge, an Oakland tenant selection supervisor, she received more than forty applications per day from black families in 1943 and could not "house one of them."[60]

C. L. Dellums, a local labor leader and head of the Oakland NAACP, claimed that housing authorities were fairer in their tenant selection practices. Under shipyard managers, he said, "favored workers are getting first choice instead of the people who are most in need." He also cited a case in which black dorm dwellers in a Kaiser-controlled Richmond facility were evicted to make way for white arrivals.[61] Though technically open to blacks, Maritime Commission projects were overwhelmingly dominated by skilled white workers, who received preferential placement.

These Maritime Commission projects, along with some of the all-white permanent projects, represented the upper crust of war housing society. Selective occupancy criteria fostered class and income distinctions, and the projects' design sought to emulate a middle-class suburban setting. East Oakland's Lockwood Gardens featured landscaped duplexes with spacious front lawns and individual backyards. In Richmond, local officials touted Harbor Gate as a model war housing project with its ample outdoor play areas, its own elementary school, and a shopping center.

For the vast majority of war housing residents, however, temporary projects were bleak affairs. Located in the lowland areas, most temporary housing rested on landfill sites adjacent to railroads, industrial facilities, and the waterfront. Mosquitoes, mud, and flooding were common. An official report on Codornices Village, by no means the worst of such projects, painted an unappealing picture: "The main line of the Southern Pacific runs along the Western edge of the village. The project is directly opposite the Golden Gate and receives the cold winds from the ocean. The city dump is about a half mile from the Western edge of the Village and smoke from the burning dump is blown directly across the Village. Odors come with the smoke." Not surprisingly, such unhealthy environments witnessed polio, tuberculosis, and flu outbreaks during the war years.[62]

In the rush to build inexpensive temporary projects, federal agencies sacrificed design and safety considerations. Most buildings were wood frame two-story row houses with plasterboard siding and tar and gravel roofs. Flimsy materials and inadequate insulation led to numerous fires that killed at least ten East Bay project dwellers during the war, provoking residents' outcries that resulted in government improvements in 1944. Aerial views of the East Bay in 1945 show miles of barrackslike structures covering the flatlands. Although some projects included community centers and commercial facilities, later projects were tacked on as annexes that shared the facilities of others. The increased use of these facilities led to overcrowding and rapid deterioration of buildings and equipment. Intended as temporary shelter, these decaying structures would remain standing well into the 1950s, shaping private housing patterns in the postwar period.

War housing programs, then, proved to be more than mere temporary measures. In less than three years the federal government had created a zone of migrant settlement along the East Bay flats that transformed the urban landscape and social relations of the region. Federal housing policies created new neighborhoods and sanctioned new forms of racial segregation that would characterize postwar development. The creation of migrant ghettos within East Bay cities served to separate migrants from prewar residents, both physically and psychologically.

Local community groups also influenced wartime housing policies in more limited ways. County and municipal governments generally cooperated in creating a migrant zone, which allowed them to contain the effects of wartime social change and to preserve the character of prewar communities. Local housing authorities, dominated by business and real estate leaders, determined occupancy criteria and racial patterning. In a few instances, migrant residents themselves challenged war housing policies by protesting racial quotas, fire hazards, and other housing-related problems. War housing, then, was not a federal plot foisted on helpless localities but a product of complicated political maneuvering.

The federal government's private sector housing programs also transformed the East Bay, prefiguring residential trends of the postwar era. Home registries and conversions increased the density of working-class neighborhoods and provided economic opportunities for prewar property owners. The absence of effective programs for black migrants resulted in severe overcrowding in west Oakland and north Richmond, hastening the formation of eastern-style black ghettos. These neighborhoods would lose their multiracial character, but they fostered a new black middle class supported by an expanded wartime population.

In the suburbs, the construction of defense subdivisions under FHA financing contributed to the dominance of big business leadership and mass production techniques that would characterize postwar housing development. The requisites of war influenced the design of homes and neighborhoods and kindled the postwar aspirations of white residents. In the East Bay, defense worker subdivisions were the seedbed of postwar suburban development.

Other West Coast communities reflected the wartime housing trends of the East Bay, especially those with major shipbuilding operations. In the Bay Area, large-scale war housing areas grew up around shipyards in Hunter's Point, Marin City, and Vallejo. Elsewhere on the West Coast, federal public housing programs created migrant settlements along the Columbia River in the Portland-Vancouver region, in the Puget Sound cities of Tacoma and Bremerton, and around Los Angeles Harbor. As in the East Bay, the Maritime Commission established "Shipyard Railways" in both Vancouver and Los Angeles to facilitate transportation between new public housing areas and the yards. One of the largest war housing developments was Vanport, a planned community of more than ten thousand Kaiser workers and their families located between Portland and Vancouver. Vanport and other shipyard ghettos functioned as parallel communities with their own schools, shopping centers, and community facilities.[63]

West Coast cities dominated by aircraft production exhibited a somewhat different pattern. In the Seattle, San Diego, and Los Angeles areas, aircraft production plants were widely dispersed and often located in surrounding suburbs. Since public housing development generally followed industrial patterns, migrant settlements were widely scattered as well, thus avoiding the high urban densities that characterized the shipbuilding regions. Although Southern California cities experienced serious traffic congestion and air pollution during the war years, housing was a less critical problem than it was in the Bay Area and Portland. In Los Angeles, high prewar vacancy rates and a flurry of home construction in 1940–1941 absorbed much of the new housing demand and led to a relatively smaller amount of public housing construction compared with other West Coast cities.[64]

Despite these variations, all of these cities experienced social tensions around questions of housing and race. With the exceptions of Marin City and the municipalities of Seattle and Los Angeles—where public war housing was racially integrated—West Coast housing authorities assigned black and white tenants into different projects or areas. Some of the largest shipyard communities—Vanport, Bremerton, and Vallejo—confined black residents to separate and often less desirable quarters. In Bremerton, as in Oakland, public housing had originally been integrated. As black migration increased, however, the housing authority constructed a new all-black project called Sinclair Park several miles outside the city. In Los Angeles County, the housing authority used racial quotas to segregate tenants, a policy that sparked sustained protest by the local black community.[65]

Private sector housing policies also shaped the urban geography of these cities. The predominantly black districts of West Coast cities—Madison Street and Crosstown in Seattle, Central Avenue in Los Angeles, the Fillmore in San Francisco, and the Albina neighborhood in Portland—all became more populous and vital as a result of war migration. A racially restrictive private housing market, however, also brought overcrowding and physical deterioration. In the Fillmore, Crosstown, and Central Avenue neighborhoods, black migrants moved into housing formerly occupied by Japanese immigrant families who had been removed to internment camps. The racial transition in these areas would be permanent.[66]

Federal home loan programs also influenced urban housing patterns. According to the Census Bureau, thousands of central city homeowners in San Francisco, Los Angeles, and Portland took advantage of federal wartime loans to convert large older houses into multiple-unit dwellings for migrant families. Title 6 defense loan programs also promoted new suburban development in undeveloped areas north of Portland, south of Los Angeles, and along the San Francisco peninsula south of the Hunter's Point shipyards.[67]

In both the cities and the suburbs, the contours of postwar urban life on the West Coast took shape during the era of World War II. In the absence of any long-term social objectives, war housing programs changed the face of West Coast cities, heightening racial and social barriers that would characterize postwar urban communities. In the next chapter we turn to the experience of the urban newcomers who inhabited these migrant neighborhoods to see how individuals and families adapted to their new environment amid the chaotic climate of World War II.

5

Migrant Families
and Communities

As a worker with the Travelers Aid Society, Tarea Hall Pittman met incoming passengers at the Richmond railroad depot in 1943. Most of her clients were women and children coming to join male relatives working in the shipyards. Pittman recalled the plight of migrant families amid the turmoil and confusion of war boomtowns: "All they'd know was that their husband's name was 'Baby Lee,' but they wouldn't know where he lived. . . . Some of them found themselves in dire straits."[1]

For many newcomers, their experience in East Bay cities was indeed a "Journey through Chaos," as one writer described it.[2] More so than old-time residents, migrants faced physical and social dislocations that required considerable adaptation and adjustment. From the outset, family and kin connections were essential in helping migrants adjust to new surroundings and conditions. Transplanted into a highly diverse and transient environment, individuals relied heavily on their families for material and emotional support. Under the pressure of the unfamiliar and the more general social stress of wartime, migrant families also experienced both gender and generational conflicts, traces of which emerge periodically in the public record.

Sources on migrant family life are, unfortunately, sparse. The transient, frantic quality of boomtown life affected not only families but local service bureaucracies as well. Records of social service organizations and other investigative agencies are thus extremely limited. To gain some understanding of migrant family and community life, the historian must work from an array of diverse and often impressionistic sources, including oral histories, newspaper articles, church reports, and industry publications. When appropriate, the findings of contemporary observers in other World War II boom communities are also useful.[3]

In the war boomtowns—in contrast to many permanent working-class communities—the familial quality of defense worker households did not translate into a wider communal ethos. Long hours, high turnover, and extreme social diversity all served to hinder the growth of a common culture in war housing areas. In the short term at least, the war seems to have brought about a social rupturing, separating newcomers from the prewar community but also from one another.

Troubled by this lack of community and its adverse impact on productivity, defense employers and the federal government established a battery of social programs to help acclimate migrants to new urban-industrial conditions. In so doing, they hoped to build a sense of "community responsibility" and to instill habits of "good citizenship." Their initiatives, however, would not go unchallenged; both local officials and migrants themselves influenced the course of such programs.

Southern migrants, in particular, provided alternatives to government-sponsored activities as they imported evangelical religion, country music, the blues, and other down-home cultural traditions. With the help of migrant entrepreneurs, southern newcomers cultivated distinctive subcultures based on racial and regional ties, thus expanding and diversifying the cultural life of East Bay cities.

As noted in earlier chapters, family and kin networks were critical in facilitating defense migration. Through a process of chain migration, families, kin groups, and sometimes entire rural communities made their way to the West Coast. Among former migrants interviewed in the East Bay, a majority mentioned other family members that had gone before them to California; the remainder had family and kin that followed in their path. Family members helped each other find jobs and housing, often sharing limited space and resources.

In some cases, familial relations extended beyond blood lines to incorporate friends and neighbors back home. Antoinette Vaara remembered that her family took in not only relatives but also boys from other families back in Montana. Another migrant woman who worked as a secretary in Washington, D.C., joined up with her best friend's family to make the long drive to California in 1943. Alex Amber, a fifteen-year-old (and thus underage) newcomer to Alameda, gained quick access to the shipyards through his friend's father, who was an official in the Machinists Union. Through such extended networks, newcomers moved west and settled into their new surroundings.

Women relatives also assisted one another with child rearing and domestic work. Ophelia Hicks, who migrated from Minnesota in 1943, explained that after moving into war housing with her sister and brother-in-law, her mother came to stay with them and took care of the housekeeping. Hicks knew several other families with similar arrangements, and federal authorities reported an increasing "use of grandparents" for child care in Richmond housing areas in 1943. Younger sisters and daughters also pitched in so that mothers and older siblings could work at high-paying jobs in the shipyards.[4]

In some instances, grandmothers and other female relatives back home cared for children until their migrant parents were settled. In 1942, Margaret Cathey entrusted her two children to her mother in Iowa while she went to join her husband in the Richmond shipyards. A year or so later, when they secured adequate living space, she brought them out to California. Maya Angelou, in *I Know Why the Caged Bird Sings,* recounts a similar experience of being raised by her grandmother in rural Arkansas. Once established in Oakland, Angelou's mother sent for her children. For both black and white families, the support of kin at home facilitated the transition to urban life on the West Coast.[5]

Far from home and the familiar patterns of work and leisure, members of migrant families turned to each other to sustain themselves through the rigors of wartime life and their adjustment to a new environment. Frequently, relatives shared common housing and neighborhoods, worked at the same shipyard or defense plant, and helped each other navigate the bureaucratic maze of unions, housing offices, and other wartime agencies. Though migrants made new friends and contacts among other defense workers, high rates of turnover and geographic mobility meant that the family unit provided the main source of stability and continuity.

With so much material and emotional investment in the family relationship, migrant households also experienced a considerable degree of stress. The more general tensions of wartime society caused by war-related deaths, marital separations, and new work roles for women and youth took their toll among old-timers and newcomers alike. Migrant families thus exhibited the signs of gender and generational conflicts that were common to all Americans but were especially prevalent in the volatile environment of newcomer settlements.

One of the most obvious causes of family strain was overcrowding. In war housing, with its cramped apartments and paper-thin walls, overcrowding and lack of privacy were facts of life. Where prewar housing policies strictly regulated the size and sleeping arrangements of project families, wartime policies recognized the impracticality of such measures. Oakland housing officials authorized the use of living rooms as sleeping areas in 1942, and doubling up was widespread among project tenants. Ophelia Hicks, who shared a two-room war apartment with her mother, sister, and brother-in-law, recalled that her mother slept in a daybed in the living room while she worked the night shift. When Ophelia returned from work in the morning, she took her turn on the daybed—an arrangement that endured for several months. Nebraska migrant Helen Vaughan endured equally tight quarters when she arrived in 1943, sharing a one-bedroom Richmond war apartment with her best friend, the friend's brother, his wife, and their child.[6]

Overcrowding was especially common among black families, whose private housing options were extremely limited. Housing authorities reported a heavy doubling up among black tenants, and Charles S. Johnson found that more than 44 percent of black migrant households included non-nuclear family occupants. Conditions could be even worse in private housing, as one black migrant in north Richmond remembered: "[We] lived in this one-room trailer, one room, honest. No facilities. Twelve people lived in that trailer. Four of us went to work. . . . We'd take turns sleeping, shared beds."[7]

According to wartime sociologists, overcrowding and doubling up increased stress among defense worker families. Individuals were forced to compete for precious space and resources, and the activities of one "shift" were likely to conflict with those of another. As a result, overcrowding tended to push social life out of doors onto the streets of surrounding neighborhoods and downtown areas. In fact, the control of public space would become a major wartime issue as we will see in the next chapter. Multiple-family living arrangements also raised the possibility of dual lines of authority that provoked friction between generations or among siblings. Although such circumstances were usually temporary, they sometimes endured for months or even years.[8]

Other wartime social conditions also aggravated family tension. Longer work hours—at least forty-eight hours per week—tended to increase irritability and decrease leisure time. Even women who did not work outside the home faced heavier work loads and inconvenience due to rationing, long lines, inadequate transportation, and additional child care necessitated by shorter school sessions. Single mothers and servicemen's wives had perhaps the most difficult task as they juggled outside employment, child care, and housework. Some service wives, who moved to the Bay Area to be closer to husbands or boyfriends, sacrificed family support systems back home and suffered from loneliness and isolation in their new environment. Long-term separations, death, and other war-related trauma all added to the burdens of wartime family life.[9]

Perhaps the most difficult adjustment for many families and couples involved women's adoption of new work roles, particularly in nontraditional settings. In the East Bay, women's entry into the previously all-male shipyards provoked serious anxiety over the sanctity of marriage and the family. New female work roles not only threatened the male prerogative as breadwinner but raised fears of marital infidelity. In the advice columns of local newspapers, wives complained regularly that their husbands were having affairs with shipyard women and railed against home-wrecking "sweater gals." One woman, convinced that women shipyard workers were making advances toward her husband, claimed that such women "had a yen for a husband, and they don't care whose." Women workers responded with a barrage of counteraccusations against unpatriotic housewives. The feud served to divide women by inflaming resentments between female defense workers and other women in the community.[10]

There does, in fact, seem to be some basis for claims of increased infidelity in war boomtowns. Throughout the country, men's departure into the armed forces left a surplus of wives, girlfriends, and unattached women back home, and the war boomtowns attracted especially high proportions of them. At the same time, defense employment brought in large numbers of draft-exempt men, some of whom left their families back home. According to the special census of 1944, 13 percent of married migrant men and 18 percent of married migrant women in the Bay Area lived apart from their spouses, compared with only 5 percent of nonmigrant men and 12 percent of nonmigrant women. In fact, exceptionally high rates of temporary separation characterized migrant families in every major West Coast city.[11] With such a high percentage of lone spouses, an increase in extramarital sexual activity would not be surprising.

According to the sociologist Katherine Archibald, romantic encounters and sexual liaisons were quite common in the shipyards. Many of the encounters, she said, involved young single women "who turned to the shipyards primarily for excited roving among droves of draft-exempt men." But women were not the only ones implicated; numerous observers commented on the frequency of male philandering and marital infidelity. According to Archibald, "homes were broken and occasional irate wives or husbands raged against the temptations and sins of the shipyards . . . with sound personal reasons for their anger."[12]

In *Swing Shift,* a collection of short stories by an ex-shipyard worker, Joseph Fabry weaves a theme of romantic intrigue throughout his account of shipyard life. Based on real-life experiences from the Richmond yards, Fabry described the rise and fall of shipyard friendships, romances, and marriages. Shipyard workers themselves echoed such stories. Margaret Louise Cathey described how her marriage ended shortly after her arrival in Richmond. Before long, she began dating her leaderman at the Kaiser shipyards, and later they were married. "We worked together all the rest of our time in the shipyards . . . if they moved him to another crew, I transferred along with him." Her case was not unusual, she said, and "some marriages broke up too."[13]

This volatility in personal relationships reflected the more general instability of wartime life with its forced separations and imbalanced sex ratio. But it was also a product of wartime mobility and the disruptive influences of migration. In such a climate, new work roles for women could increase family tensions and threaten established relationships. But they could also provide women with the financial means to terminate unsatisfactory marriages or begin new ones. According to Alameda County Clerk G. E. Wade, marriage and divorce rates in 1942 had remained steady among native residents but were exceptionally high among the county's newcomers. Migrant shipyard workers, he said, accounted for much of the increase in the divorce rate; service couples tended to boost the number of marriages. The number of marriages in Alameda County, in fact, skyrocketed during the war years, from 3,862 in 1941 to 10,068 in 1945.[14]

Observers in other war boom communities found similar trends. In the Puget Sound region of Washington, marriage and divorce rates both soared. Calvin Schmid, a sociologist who studied social trends in wartime Seattle, attributed the rising divorce rate to the "increased earning power and economic independence" of women. In Los Angeles, a war housing resident also commented on the frequency of divorce among migrants there, attributing the increase to "new work roles and new contacts" for women. "What happened was that a preexisting disharmony was suddenly exploded to the surface," he said; such problems often resulted in desertion or divorce.[15]

Although the precise degree of marital strain is difficult to assess, local newspaper accounts offer a glimmer of some of the types of problems migrants faced. For one thing, a variety of living arrangements and relationships seems to have existed during the war. Newspapers regularly publicized bigamy cases involving migrant war workers who left spouses and families back home and married local war workers. Police occasionally discovered cohabiting couples, claiming to be married, living in war housing projects. In one tragic case, the *Oakland Tribune* reported that an Oklahoma man killed himself after fighting with his live-in lover in an El Cerrito housing project. Earlier, the man had moved to Southern California with his wife and family to work in the Los Angeles shipyards. Meeting another woman there, he abandoned the family, and the two ran off to find work in the Richmond yards, posing as husband and wife.[16]

The violent conclusion of the episode was, unfortunately, all too common. Throughout the war years, local newspapers carried gruesome accounts of domestic violence among war worker and service couples. Soldiers threatened their wives with bayonets, shipyard workers turned blow torches on themselves or each other, and a host of other harrowing events occurred. Women were most often the victims of such violence, with wife battering and child abuse often the common responses to family problems.[17] On occasion, however, women vented their anger as well. In one case, forty-three-year-old Maybelle Smith was arrested after decking one woman and three police officers outside the Richmond War Apartments. The fracas had started when Smith, seeing her husband follow two young women down the street, intervened. The *Richmond Record-Herald* commented humorously that Mrs. Smith, "badly outweighed, . . . managed to give a good account of herself in the first moments and carried out a running battle to the police station gouging, kicking, scratching and biting, much to the annoyance of the police officers."[18]

Although migrant family squabbles such as these may have amused Richmond readers, many serious incidents of domestic violence reflected the internal problems faced by newcomer families. Among newspaper accounts, marital infidelity was a common source of domestic tension. Perhaps the most vivid case involved a thirty-four-year-old Missouri shipyard worker who opened fire on his wife and sister-in-law in an Oakland park before turning the gun on himself. His wife, who had left him shortly after their arrival in Oakland, was living with her sister-in-law at the time. Police discovered a suicide note in the man's pocket explaining his motive: "This was my beloved wife, but she went to work in the shipyards and let some man make a fool of her. These shipyards are breaking up a lot of homes for little kids. The government should do something about it."[19] The note reflects the deadly serious nature of the infidelity issue, and the man's desperate plea for the government to "do something about it" suggests that his wife's new position had placed her beyond his control. Clearly, the glorified public image of female defense workers did not always match the private realities of wartime family life.

New work patterns also fueled generational conflict as parents and children struggled to adapt to new roles and responsibilities. Continuation schools and youth work programs, for instance, provided earlier autonomy and greater earning power for teenage migrants. In some cases, young migrants earned more than their parents, teachers, or school administrators. Conceivably, this new economic power may have disrupted traditional status hierarchies and undercut lines of family authority.[20] The proximity of young dormitory dwellers also provided a tempting vision of youthful independence, as they were seemingly unfettered by parental discipline and family obligations.

In some cases, particularly with older children, adjustment to a new environment and new friends could be quite difficult. Many parents were "at wits end" over their children, said the dean of girls at Richmond Union High School. "These kids were from small towns, farms, and they were just dropped into that unorganized mass of humanity." High rates of absenteeism, up to 25 percent at the junior-high level in Richmond, testified to the school district's lack of success at integrating newcomer children. At home, many older girls found themselves tied down with increased child care and household responsibilities while parents and brothers worked full-time defense jobs. For a variety of reasons, then, conflicts between migrant parents and children were intensified in the new environment.[21]

One of the clearest indications of generational strife was the high number of teenage runaways during the war years. Beginning in 1942, local newspapers featured regular bulletins on migrant runaways who had left their families to return to their home towns. In January 1942, for instance, two Texas girls, aged thirteen and fifteen, fled back to El Paso because of alleged unhappiness with their parents and new schoolmates in Oakland. In other cases, local authorities alerted state police to watch for runaways headed for towns in Oklahoma, Michigan, Colorado, and other points. The defection of migrant teens was also a prominent theme in two novels written about defense migrants, *Skip to My Lou* and *The Dollmaker*. In both books, older children who are unhappy in their new surroundings return home to join grandparents and other relatives left behind.[22]

For all the gender and generational conflicts, however, migrant families were remarkably durable given the stresses and strains of migration and war. Families helped each other adapt to unfamiliar places and practices and improvised to cope with new situations. Indeed, for many migrants, the family unit was the sole and central support system.

This sense of familial relations, though, does not seem to have translated into a wider sense of community within migrant settlements. Long hours, staggered shifts, high turnover, and a general sense of temporariness and anonymity all hindered the growth of a strong community ethos. Written accounts of project life and oral interviews with war housing residents do not indicate much sociability among migrants. Although some residents, especially women, cooperated for practical ends such as child care and laundry, most were simply too busy to get to know their neighbors. "Everybody was coming and going at different times," recalled Helen Vaughan, a shipyard worker who lived in the Richmond projects. "I was never around enough to really know any neighbors." Lois Harley, another former housing project resident, put it more bluntly: "You didn't have time to fraternize."[23]

The temporary nature of war housing areas also hindered the development of a sense of community. Many families planned only a brief stay in California, and others viewed war housing as a mere way station to a more permanent home on the West Coast. Tenant turnover was in fact quite high—24.4 percent in Richmond in 1943, soaring up to 104.3 percent by 1945. Amid such flux, families had little stake in cultivating a community setting within the housing areas. Furthermore, the anonymity of massive government housing projects made sociability among neighbors difficult. One story recounted in the Kaiser shipyard newspaper described how a young Texan, after his discharge from the service in 1943, came to Richmond hoping to find his father. After a fruitless eight-month search, he eventually found him living in the dorm building next to his own. Although perhaps an extreme case, the story dramatizes the sense of anonymity and lack of community that many migrants must have felt.[24]

Another obstacle to community development was the extreme social diversity of war worker settlements. Residents came from a wide variety of geographical, racial, and class backgrounds that served to divide them both on the job and at home. Katherine Archibald's characterization of the shipyards was equally true of war housing areas: "It was a society larger, more varied, and more restless . . . as to confound every local tradition of proper social relationships. . . . I found in actuality differences and gaps—social abysses so deep that the possibility of spanning them never occurred."[25] Scholars of other war boomtowns confirmed Archibald's comments, noting that class differences were particularly troublesome. The heterogeneity of tenants at many projects was in fact quite dramatic. "Many of the families have never before lived in what they consider such poor accommodations while others have never lived in such decent homes," said one student observer of Berkeley's Codornices Village. "They range in education from the completely illiterate—unable to sign their own names—to the most highly educated."[26]

Building a sense of community and citizenship among such a diverse lot became a major wartime preoccupation. Middle-class observers in the East Bay uniformly lamented the lack of community solidarity among project dwellers. When a war worker entered a housing project, said one social worker, "it is to him [sic] a place to eat and sleep, but he does not recognize or accept any responsibility to the total community."[27] To remedy this situation, defense contractors and the federal government took the offensive, attempting to "create" a community out of the diverse elements of war boom society.

Creating a Migrant Community

While shipyard employers established corporate welfare programs in the workplace, the federal government expanded this concept to the community by establishing a battery of on-site social programs within war housing areas. In an effort to improve morale and increase productivity, government and corporate leaders jointly instituted education, child care, recreation, and religious programs designed to help migrants adjust to urban-industrial life. They believed that such programs would develop "correct health habits and citizenship characteristics" among newcomers and foster a greater sense of community responsibility.[28]

This middle-class vision of community life took root most successfully among middle-class project dwellers. Participation in social activities was highest among the permanent and Maritime Commission projects, which housed families of skilled white workers and supervisors. In these projects, middle-class notions of self-help and social improvement produced a whirl of clubs, dances, orchestras, newspapers, and tenants' organizations. Lockwood Gardens in Oakland even boasted its own auxiliary police force with forty uniformed members. Improvement clubs and tenants' groups adopted a self-government approach and pressured housing agencies for better facilities and services. John Hunter, editor of the *Harbor Gate News,* praised his Richmond project as "a war-born democracy" that was much like "a little country town."[29]

Local officials were equally enthusiastic about these projects. The *Oakland Tribune* called Lockwood Gardens "an answer to government housing officials' prayers," hailing it as a place where the "theories of experts in the national capital are actually working out in practice."[30] The *Richmond Independent,* normally critical of the town's newcomers, even attempted a "society" column for Harbor Gate residents in 1943. Such gestures suggest that middle-class natives were willing to assimilate this aristocracy of shipyard society whose cultural interests resembled their own. This social tolerance would continue in the postwar era, when such projects received preferential treatment under urban redevelopment programs.

In the vast majority of war housing projects, however, reformist visions were not so easily translated into practice. Both local governments and housing residents themselves affected the outcome of federal plans. Under the Lanham Act, the federal government provided funds for community services to defense areas experiencing wartime social dislocations. With the federal government removing large tracts of land from local tax rolls, the act provided in-lieu-of-tax payments to localities where normal services were overwhelmed by the needs of an increased population. The Lanham Act, however, required that local governments take the initiative in applying for and administering specific programs.[31]

Overburdened East Bay governments responded with a series of requests to create and expand social programs throughout their cities. Indeed, they welcomed the opportunity to improve local facilities that would benefit the larger community. At the same time, though, such programs had to take into account the needs of war housing areas and their residents. Wary of setting unwanted precedents, local officials balked at the more radical aspects of these programs, forcing federal officials, defense contractors, and private agencies to intervene. Finally, war housing residents themselves influenced the course of such programs by actively organizing, participating in, or rejecting project activities. The chaotic array of agencies and interests pursuing conflicting objectives often hampered the success of on-site programs.

Perhaps the least divisive of these programs was elementary education. In the schools, inadequate resources were a critical problem, especially in the elementary grades, which had to absorb the large number of young children brought by migrant families. The high schools, depleted by the draft and teenage work programs, remained roughly at their prewar enrollment levels. Education funds were thus channeled toward the expansion of elementary education, particularly in war housing areas.

As with housing, the proportional population growth of a community was a good indicator of how much dislocation would ensue. In Oakland, where the school population grew by about 20 percent between 1940 and 1943, school authorities handled the increase with portable classroom buildings added to housing projects and prewar schools. In Richmond, by contrast, the school population grew by nearly 400 percent between the 1940–1941 and 1944–1945 school years, from 7,327 to 28,851. At the peak of the crisis, all elementary schools ran multiple sessions with an average class size of seventy-five students. In the fall of 1943, the expansion of war housing on the south side forced the nearby Stege School to operate four successive two-and-a-half-hour sessions until the completion of a ten-room addition in March 1944. Thereafter, the school ran on double sessions as did most others in the city.[32]

School authorities also secured federal funding for new school construction to alleviate the chronic overcrowding. The Richmond school department lobbied vigorously for new permanent construction in the hillside neighborhood of Mira Vista and for the new Lincoln School to serve the permanent Atchison Village housing project. The temporary residents, though, received little help from local authorities, who blamed federal housing authorities for failing to build schools inside the projects. Eventually, angry Harbor Gate residents demanded the suspension of the Richmond Housing Authority director unless he addressed the school construction issue. With the help of federal agencies and the Kaiser shipyards, the school was completed in 1944.[33]

It appears that migrants were actively interested in educational opportunities for their children. Oral history informants cited California's superior educational system as a motivation for moving to the area. The dean of girls at Richmond Union High School (a newcomer herself in the 1940s) said that the parents of migrant pupils often came to see her. "They were people who often didn't have much education themselves," she said, "but they wanted their kids to have what they didn't have so their lives would be easier."

Most school personnel, however, spoke disparagingly of migrant parents, who they felt displayed "indifference toward the welfare of their children." Newspaper articles on child abuse and neglect by war worker parents confirmed such beliefs and expressed a growing anxiety about the new roles of working mothers. As one study of the Richmond schools points out, relations between teachers and newcomer parents broke down under the pressure of war and the anxieties it provoked.[34]

Eventually, the demand for educational resources and personnel prompted the school department to begin hiring migrant women as teachers. As poor conditions and low pay had caused dozens of teachers to resign in 1943, school authorities recruited shipyard workers' wives to fill vacancies in public housing area schools. By 1945, a full one-quarter of the staff had emergency teaching credentials—many of them with previous certifications from midwestern states.[35]

With school authorities struggling to provide basic education for an expanded population, there was little time for ideological concerns over curriculum or the role of education. Major disagreements emerged, however, over the role and legitimacy of child care programs. Drawing on experiments from World War I and recent European programs, the federal government and major defense contractors advocated child care for working mothers in an effort to boost production. On the local level, though, their efforts met with less enthusiasm.

As with education, Lanham Act funding for child care programs required local initiative and direction. While communities like Berkeley and Oakland moved ahead with such programs, officials in Richmond and Albany were reluctant to create child care centers that might establish precedents for the postwar period. The Richmond superintendent of schools, Walter Helms, initially refused to take responsibility for child care for fear that it might become a permanent function of the school department. In Albany federal officials seeking to create child care programs at Codornices Village found that local school officials were "not enthusiastic" about the prospect.[36]

Faced with local reticence, federal authorities and defense contractors intervened to ensure at least minimum services. In Albany federal officials who were planning child care facilities at Codornices Village amassed statistical data on employment needs and community services. Child care centers were then "programmed" into the project, and federal authorities worked closely with school officials to expedite Lanham Act funding for staff and materials. Richmond authorities also conceded, requesting funds to operate ten nurseries in 1943.[37]

After many disputes and delays, federally funded child care facilities were established in all East Bay communities by 1944. As in the rest of the country, however, these programs were curiously underused. In January 1944, Bay Area child care centers ran at two-thirds capacity (the national average was 37 percent). East Bay officials reported openings at many centers, especially those serving black neighborhoods and housing projects. Compared with other centers, though, housing area programs were generally better attended—probably reflecting the lack of private care alternatives available to newcomer families.[38]

Several factors contributed to the low attendance, many of which stemmed from local management problems. The limited daytime-only hours of the programs prevented many families from using their services, particularly women on evening and night shifts. Inconvenient locations and transportation were a problem for some, and high fees (fifty to seventy-five cents per day) were prohibitive for larger families. In addition, reluctant local authorities sometimes failed to publicize their programs, which resulted in underattendance and early termination. Hostile Albany officials in fact closed two child care centers in August 1943, claiming poor attendance.[39]

Parental distrust of institutional care was another obstacle to the success of child care programs. Public nurseries, long associated with poverty and relief, may have seemed unappealing to many war workers. Migrant families, in particular, may not have trusted the modern "experts'" approach to child rearing. This seems to have been the case with black families, who were uniformly underenrolled throughout the East Bay. A study conducted by the Women's Bureau in 1945 found that more than 50 percent of working women in the Bay Area turned to family, friends, and neighbors for child care, but only 11 percent used nurseries.[40]

Frustrated by local programs and their problems, Kaiser established its own child care facility in Richmond's south-side housing area. One of the most heralded nursery facilities of World War II, it was designed by child welfare experts from the University of California at Berkeley and funded entirely by the Maritime Commission. Approaching child care as a productivity problem, Kaiser avoided many of the pitfalls of the Lanham Act centers by providing twenty-four-hour service, good publicity, and a convenient location. In 1943–1944, more than seven hundred children were enrolled in the program.[41]

Like other company welfare schemes, Kaiser's child care program was designed to acculturate newcomers by teaching their children how to "eat, sleep and play" and to instill "proper habits." The program included well-balanced hot meals, health care, and optional family counseling. Child care workers in other facilities echoed this approach, emphasizing a balanced diet (fruit, milk, and cod liver oil) and a wholesome family environment. As the child care director at Oakland's Lockwood Gardens explained, "When the parents first move to the area . . . it is our place to do all we can to help the parents and children adjust."[42] This acculturative mission had a long history in social reform movements among immigrants—now it was regeared toward domestic migrants under the rubric of winning the war.

The most elaborate reforms, however, were directed at recreation. With a widespread belief that recreation improved morale, both federal and local authorities sought to alleviate the overcrowding that beset existing community facilities. Furthermore, based on the experiences of World War I, government agencies anticipated a resurgence of youthful misbehavior that they hoped to counter with a battery of "wholesome" activities and amusements. Recreation programs, said one federal field representative in the East Bay, would "pay dividends to the city fathers and aid the war effort by building up a better morale in your community."[43]

In war housing areas, recreation programs involved a complicated array of activities and sponsors. Besides the usual playground and sports events, housing areas offered hobby clubs, game rooms, and dances. One Richmond project even offered a charm school that taught women shipyard workers "how to keep [their] feminine appeal despite the rigors of war-time work." Understaffed local recreation departments encouraged the participation of private service organizations to supplement government-sponsored activities. Local agencies also solicited the help of migrant group leaders to encourage self-organization among project residents. This effort included housing area youth, who organized weekend dances that proved the best attended and most successful of project events.[44]

As with other on-site programs, shipyard managers instituted their own reform-oriented recreation programs designed to facilitate production. Single male dorm dwellers, they felt, required special attention since their job performance was adversely affected by "inadequate off-hours supervision" that led to fighting, drinking, gambling, and theft. With funding from the Maritime Commission, Kaiser managed the Richmond and Canal Dormitories that housed more than two thousand men. The dorms were equipped with a bowling alley and billiards room in an effort to provide a "clean" alternative to the downtown bars and pool halls (see plate 7).[45]

For those under eighteen, Kaiser appointed a youth coordinator to arrange recreation programs and provide personal counseling. Young shipyard workers, said the Richmond coordinator, were "downright problem children and all of them need[ed] guidance." Coordinators helped young workers budget and save their earnings, which, critics claimed, were "too lavish for their own good."[46] Through recreation and counseling programs, shipyard managers hoped to keep youth out of town and out of trouble.

The enthusiasm for recreation, however, foundered on racial problems. Although federal policy stipulated that recreation be provided irrespective of race, the issue of integration and the allocation of project facilities became sources of heated controversy. The exclusion of black residents from many commercial establishments meant that they relied more heavily on project facilities. Often unaware of this inequity, many white project dwellers resented their black neighbors for "intruding" on white social activities and for making "unfair" demands for facilities and personnel. Although the federal government provided substantial funding for recreation, it offered few guidelines for handling such issues.[47]

In Richmond, the recreation program incorporated a variety of segregation practices. Many activities (such as team sports) were project based, resulting in de facto segregation. In mixed projects, where the recreation department allotted special hours for black residents based on their proportion of occupancy, the use of community space and facilities was a constant source of contention. Even more explosive was the issue of racial mixing at youth events, which some white residents feared would encourage interracial dating and marriage. Recreation leaders, many of them project residents themselves, argued bitterly over these issues with little guidance from above.[48]

Local authorities offered little assistance and did nothing to discourage racist practices among their project employees. Because of the prejudices of some white project leaders, several others resigned in 1944. For its part, the Richmond Recreation Department was pressured by the local housing authority and police department to discourage racial mixing, which they feared would lead to "trouble in the buildings" that "the police [would] have to stop." The situation became so tense in 1944 that the federal Office of Community War Services sent a representative to Richmond to try to resolve problems there. In a report that offered few solutions and reflected her own bias, the representative urged the federal government to face squarely "the Negro as the 'great problem' of the recreation program."[49]

The Richmond situation was further complicated by private service organizations that provided special programs for black service personnel and war workers. The USO (United Service Organizations), the YWCA, the YMCA, and the Boys Clubs all offered programs for civilian war workers in or adjacent to public housing areas. Federal authorities reported little cooperation between these groups and the local recreation department, who assumed that such private groups provided adequate social activities for black residents. Private facilities thus became unofficial annexes to public housing areas.

Although local officials seemed to appreciate the work done by private groups among black migrants, they restricted their activities to federal migrant settlements. When the USO attempted to build a center for black war workers in the white working-class neighborhood of Point Richmond in 1943, local residents were outraged. The *Richmond Independent* insisted it be built inside the housing area south of Cutting Boulevard amid the predominantly black projects. The editors claimed: "the shipyards, the housing authority and the other agencies involved are responsible for providing proper care and recreational facilities for these people. It is their problem."[50] A petition drive and subsequent action by the city council barred the USO from Point Richmond.

The chaotic jumble of agencies and individuals and the lack of coordination by government authorities created racial problems that hampered the effectiveness of recreation programs. The federal government's nebulous policies allowed local recreation workers to determine access to federal facilities, often on an unequal basis. As with housing policy in general, the goals of providing equal access based on need and respecting "local custom" were inherently contradictory.

Social service programs encountered many obstacles, but the federal government's efforts to build on-site commercial facilities faced even greater ones. Local housing authorities generally opposed commercial development that threatened the newfound profits of downtown businesses. Under pressure from Kaiser and other defense contractors, however, the Federal Public Housing Authority (FPHA) did build a few supermarkets in Richmond and Alameda housing projects. These markets, they hoped, would reduce absenteeism and turnover among shipyard workers. For single men and others without kitchen facilities, the FPHA and Kaiser provided on-site cafeterias in their Oakland and Richmond dormitories. Beyond these facilities, however, there were few commercial operations in the housing areas. Nearly all restaurants, bars, theaters, and other commercial amusements were located downtown.

Local churches were ambivalent toward the migrant community. On the one hand, they felt a Christian duty to provide aid and spiritual guidance to the newcomers; on the other, they feared an inundation of crude-looking "Okies" that would not "fit in" with their congregations. The solution was the United Christian Ministry, an on-site program offering religious services to war housing areas and other migrant settlements. The United Ministry was an outgrowth of the Federal Council of Churches in Christ (FCCC), a national confederation of large Protestant denominations founded in 1905 as part of the social gospel movement. Early in the war the federal government invited the FCCC into war housing areas, welcoming "a united Protestant approach as a valuable aid to community morale." Under this program, local church councils and ministerial alliances coordinated religious services in nearby housing projects, war plants, and trailer parks. FCCC ministries operated in all West Coast defense centers, but the most elaborate programs were in the shipyard communities of the East Bay and Vancouver, Washington.[51]

Designed to serve the nation's defense centers, the United Ministry sought to address the spiritual needs of migrant war workers. Practically speaking, working-class migrants could not easily assimilate into local churches. The Catholic churches of the East Bay's predominantly ethnic working class were obviously not an option for the mostly Protestant migrants. Nor were the mainstream Protestant churches, whose middle-class members were proprietary toward their church social life. The problem was particularly acute for southern white migrants, whose Southern Baptist and other evangelical denominations were sparsely represented in the prewar East Bay.

The established Protestant leadership of the FCCC worried about the mobility of war migrants and their lack of "an abiding spiritual habitat." Unlike earlier western pioneers, they said, war migrants lacked a common moral outlook; their peregrinations were planned "without genuinely promising material or moral goals, despite exhilarating temporary employment at fat wages." In their new urban setting, migrants became only "partial persons," bereft of the well-roundedness characteristic of the inhabitants of smaller communities. The temporary migrant communities, said the FCCC, "lack deep roots and do not involve the whole person in permanent basic fellowships." The United Ministry saw its role as a facilitator of moral unity, bringing the spiritual life of the prewar community to the migrant settlements. Without its efforts, the United Ministry boasted, East Bay migrants "would have been sheep without a shepherd."[52]

Beneath these discussions of the migrants' spiritual bankruptcy, however, lurked long-standing anxieties about fundamentalism and other competing forms of religious culture. The Federal Council of Churches had arisen around the turn of the century partially in response to a snowballing fundamentalist movement among southern and rural Protestants. The war and its attendant migration rearranged the social and religious landscape of the country and brought these forces face to face in northern and western cities. "The wild and desperate version of religion in sectarian movements," the FCCC said, "threaten[s] the continuity and depth of religion and its ways of long-proved vitality and consistent social responsibility."[53]

It was not so much the fervent style of the sects that the FCCC feared but their "repudiation of modern civilization." The antiunion attitudes of some sects, it said, contributed to industrial conflict and thus hindered the war effort. By contrast, the FCCC admired the sects' evangelism and saw the United Ministry as a vehicle for capturing the migrants' religious enthusiasm. "Unless the historic churches have been able to find in the war emergency a measure of new birth," the FCCC warned, "must not the postwar world belong religiously to the more ardent and unconventional sects?" The FCCC, then, saw the war and the United Ministry as an opportunity for the growth and rejuvenation of progressive Protestantism in American cities.[54]

In the East Bay, the United Ministry established active programs through local church councils in Oakland and Richmond. The ministry employed forty-eight workers in the region, including twenty-one ordained ministers, eight divinity students, and eleven lay men and women. Comprised of ten denominations, the United Ministry represented local churches, including the Methodists, Presbyterians, Lutherans, Baptists, and Congregational-Christians. These churches, along with defense industries and the migrants themselves, funded United Ministry activities.

The ministry offered Sunday school programs, religious services, and "friendly" visits to residents of war housing projects and government trailer parks. Most large housing projects retained a head minister and assistant, and if the project was racially mixed, might include a black assistant minister as well. Interdenominational services were held in community centers and were, at least in theory, interracial. Over time, though, most interracial services "fell apart into separate racial congregations after some friction and disillusionment." Pressures for separate services also arose in part from black migrant ministers working in local shipyards. These worker-preachers sought to preserve down-home religious traditions and were sometimes incorporated into the United Ministry program.[55]

Another group of United Ministry workers was drawn from the ranks of foreign missionaries awaiting reassignment abroad. Many of these workers were lay women who went door to door in housing projects, calling on families for personal consultation and friendly visits. The visiting program revealed the missionary aspects of the United Ministry, whose chief concern was the "moral hazards" facing migrant families. In towns like Richmond, where prewar social workers could not begin to keep up with the new demands of migrant families, friendly visiting also acted as a form of social casework. According to the United Ministry, friendly visiting, based on "informality and personal contacts," was highly successful.

The overall program, however, was not as effective. The United Ministry reported that in the spring of 1945 aggregate attendance at twenty-three East Bay housing projects was only 1,050 for Sunday services and 2,762 for Sunday schools. Knowing that participating East Bay housing projects accommodated some 77,000 residents, we can estimate that less than 2 percent of families attended any type of United Ministry religious activity.[56]

Certainly, a significant number of migrants simply did not attend church functions because of lack of either time or interest. Others joined local prewar churches, as increased membership rolls attest. Certain denominations, such as the Lutherans, drew hundreds of new members among migrants of Scandinavian descent from the northern midwestern and Great Plains states. Minnesota-born Antoinette Vaara and her family joined Richmond's Grace Lutheran Church during the war along with many other shipyard workers from Minnesota and the Dakotas. "It felt so much like home that we stayed with it," she recalled. Hazelle Swenson's family, North Dakota migrants of Norwegian descent, joined Trinity Lutheran Church in Richmond as well as the local branch of the Sons of Norway. In such cases, ethnic and regional ties helped newcomers gain access to mainstream community institutions. A few years after the war, a social investigator in Richmond remarked that white midwesterners seemed to have fully assimilated with old-time residents.[57]

To an even greater extent than whites, black migrants joined prewar black churches, especially those with southern evangelical roots. In north Richmond many black shipyard workers joined the Richmond Church of God, a Pentecostal church founded in 1925. A Texas migrant, Dr. Mattie McGlothen, took over the pastorate in 1945 and renamed the church McGlothen Temple.[58] As with white midwesterners, regional and cultural ties helped black migrants gain access to existing community institutions. An even greater number of migrants, however, sought to preserve their religious and cultural traditions from back home, transporting them directly to migrant settlements in the East Bay.

The Rise of Migrant Subcultures

One of the most important traditions that migrants brought with them was evangelical religion. Around the country, the Federal Council of Churches reported, storefront churches had "grown like weeds in all the less cultivated spots of the war emergency front," and the East Bay was no exception. Richmond, the FCCC noted, "became honeycombed with small sectarian organizations not in cooperation with the United Ministry." A survey conducted in 1945 found that the number of churches in the Richmond area had doubled during the war and that approximately half of these new churches were "sectarian and somewhat variant in temper and method." In west Oakland, churches sprang up in storefronts, houses, and halls "to such an extent that a study made one month later [might] reveal from three to five new religious organizations."[59]

With more than forty different Protestant churches in 1945, west Oakland Protestantism had become "almost infinitely subdivided and bereft of its older and more competent and stable religious elements," complained the FCCC. Many of the new churches were established by migrants themselves, some of whom were preachers back home who had followed their congregations to northern and western defense centers. Others were mission churches founded by local evangelical sects who sought to attract a promising new population. The Evangelical Free Church in Richmond, for example, expanded its prewar operations by opening three separate trailer missions in private camps in San Pablo.[60] Such churches did not cooperate with the United Ministry and proved to be avid competitors.

Even more distressing in the eyes of the United Ministry churches were the itinerant preachers who regularly toured the nation's defense centers. Preachers like C. L. Hunter of Texas, who dubbed himself the "Cowboy Evangelist," preached to packed halls in downtown Oakland and broadcast his message on Bay Area radio stations. Tennessee-born Bebe Patten, known as the "Girl Evangelist," conducted a nineteen-week "Crusade" in 1944, filling Oakland's largest halls with thousands of servicemen and defense workers. Patten's revival was so successful that she and her supporters soon purchased the City Club building, where she opened her Oakland Bible Institute and Evangelistic Center in 1945.[61]

Evangelism also flourished in Richmond during the war. White preachers, like their black counterparts, often followed their dwindling congregations from the South Central states to war boomtowns like Richmond. The more successful preachers established their own storefront churches on the south side and in other migrant settlements. Others, known as worker-preachers, labored in the shipyards by day and preached to small congregations in their homes in the evening. Advertisements in Richmond newspapers also indicate that itinerant Pentecostal preachers from Texas and Oklahoma conducted frequent tent and storefront revivals.[62] As entrepreneurs of southern culture, these preachers made the rounds among West Coast defense centers, where migrant communities offered eager customers flush with defense wages and hungry for home-style religion.

The greatest challenge to the United Ministry came from newcomer black preachers, who founded many of the storefront churches in Oakland and Richmond. As most surveys did not accurately count storefront churches, the exact number of them is unknown. In 1942, a social investigator, J. Harvey Kerns, counted thirty-five black churches in west Oakland alone. Such institutions, he observed, were the first sign of organized black migrant life in the city and represented "the most powerful agency for good in the community." New wartime churches served as employment and housing agencies for newcomers, and their ministers provided counseling for emotional, financial, and legal problems. Some of the new preachers became important community leaders. The Reverend Guthrie John Williams, for example, migrated to Richmond from Louisiana and founded the Mount Carmel Missionary Baptist Church in Richmond in 1944. In the postwar era, Williams became a leading force behind housing construction and other issues vital to Richmond's black community.[63]

The power and popularity of the new churches challenged the United Ministry, which surrendered religious control of the smaller housing projects to neighboring black churches. In west Oakland projects, the FCCC said, "the work of the United Ministry supplemented rather than undertook primary responsibility." Similarly, in Richmond "the Negro churches and ministers operated in considerable degree on their own," said the FCCC, "without full cooperative relations with the total movement."[64]

Migrants, then, did not tacitly accept the religious authority of the United Ministry and the local Protestant churches that dominated it. Within the areas of migrant settlement, residents created their own religious life based on evangelical traditions from the South and Midwest. In some cases, they posed a direct challenge to the Protestant reformers; in other cases, they forced the United Ministry to reformulate its programs to meet their needs. In both instances, migrants succeeded in creating a viable religious subculture based on racial and regional ties.

Migrants also imported secular traditions to the new war boomtowns. Often homesick and desperate for after-work entertainment, southern and midwestern migrants gathered together to share down-home traditions and pastimes. The annual Oklahoma state picnic, held near Vallejo (about ten miles north of Richmond), featured home-style cooking and fiddling contests and drew more than one thousand participants each year. Southern black migrants also organized state and regional clubs during the war years. In Richmond, the Mississippi Club, the Vicksburg Club, the Arkansas Club, and the Saint Landrew Parish (Louisiana) Club continue to hold annual reunions to this day.[65]

Of the many southern cultural traditions imported to West Coast boomtowns, music was among the most important. As James N. Gregory has shown, white southwesterners brought "hillbilly music" (as it was then called) to California in the 1930s. The Second World War, however, dramatically increased the popularity of country music both in California and in the nation generally. In the Bay Area, country music moved from relative obscurity in the 1930s into the musical mainstream with the influx of migrant musicians and fans to war boomtowns. As a Bay Area music writer observed in 1945, "It hasn't been so many years since Hillbilly and Western programs were a real scarcity out here. . . . Boy, OH BOY, it's a different story now! Turn the dial just any hour of the day or night and by recordings, transcriptions or live talent, you'll get a good old time program of OUR KIND of music."[66]

In praising "our kind of music," the writer addressed a growing group of fans and musicians, mainly from the South and Southwest, who worked to preserve and promote country music in California. In the East Bay, southern migrants organized bands, rented halls, and sponsored "Victory barn dances" for local shipyard workers. In Richmond, where commercial space was at a premium, country performers rented fraternal halls and reserved the East Shore and Alvarado parks several nights a week during the war years.

Heavily patronized by young shipyard workers, the barn dances replicated small-town social gatherings that migrants might have attended back home. Helen Vaughan, a Nebraska migrant and a frequent patron of barn dances at East Shore Park, remembered that "the place was always packed. . . . we often ran into other people we knew from the shipyards." The crowd included many families with children, she recalled, and young women could come alone in safety.[67]

Country music also provided an alternate avenue of opportunity for southwestern performers, many of whom were migrant defense workers. Texas-born Dave Stogner, for instance, moved to Richmond in 1943 to join his parents and other family members working in the Kaiser shipyards. Before long, Stogner met other migrant musicians and quit his job in the yards to play fiddle in a local band. A year later, he organized his own ten-piece band and played regularly throughout the area.[68]

Stogner and other country performers relied on regional loyalties to attract audiences in California boomtowns. Band names usually specified a state or regional affiliation; groups such as Elwin Cross and the Arizona Ramblers, Dave Stogner and the Arkansawyers, Bill Woods and the Texas Stars, and Leo Stevens and the Ozark Playboys used regional ties to encourage a sense of proprietary pride among their audience. Other Bay Area bands, such as Dude Martin and the Round-Up and Ray Wade and His Rhythm Riders, used western and cowboy themes to highlight their southwestern roots.[69]

Although they worked to create a sense of migrant community, country musicians were also businesspeople—cultural entrepreneurs who recognized the boomtown market for down-home music. Perhaps the most successful East Bay entertainer in this respect was Ray Wade, an Arkansas migrant who began performing in the Richmond area around 1940. Starting out with barn dances in local parks, Wade eventually established his own dance hall business in San Pablo's Maple Hall. With his twelve-piece band, the Rhythm Riders, Wade branched out from his home base of San Pablo to tour clubs throughout Northern California and started his own weekly radio show on Oakland's KWBR.[70]

In Oakland, country performers found their way into the commercial mainstream early, virtually taking over several night spots on lower Broadway. Clubs like McFadden's, Craby Joe's Big Barn, and John's Half Barrel catered to defense migrants with country-style barn dances featuring local hillbilly bands. A few blocks away on San Pablo Avenue, cheaper bars and honky-tonks offered jukeboxes full of country songs and attracted a rough and rowdy clientele. Compared with other downtown taverns, the honky-tonks were "a little tougher, a little rougher," said one informant. "There was always some fights or something going on." As James N. Gregory has pointed out, honky-tonks were a focal point for the kind of tough-guy behavior that was a source of pride for some migrant males.[71]

But not all migrants patronized such establishments or even the more family-oriented barn dances; many newcomers relied on the radio to connect them with migrant subcultures. With the mercurial growth of country music during the war years, nearly every Bay Area station added a cowboy or hillbilly show to its format. Airing in the early morning or evening hours, the programs catered to migrant defense workers. Country shows elicited an enthusiastic response from listeners, particularly among migrants, who "uprooted, . . . turn[ed] to records with a twang that reminds them of home."[72]

Like the performers, country radio announcers adopted western personas and program names to underscore their southwestern heritage. Programs such as Eddie the Hired Hand's Hillbilly Hit Parade (KLS-Oakland), Foreman Bill's Rhythm Rodeo (KYA–San Francisco), and Long Horn Joe's Cowboy Hit Parade (KROW-Oakland) filled Bay Area airwaves during the war years. Many of the announcers were, in fact, migrants themselves. Oakland's Cactus Jack, for instance, began his radio career while working at the Kaiser yards in Richmond. Starting off with twenty-five Bob Wills records donated to him by fellow workers, Cactus Jack landed a spot on station KLX in Oakland. The show's skyrocketing popularity soon enabled him to quit his shipyard job for a full-time radio career.[73]

Radio announcers like Cactus Jack provided the link between the local music scene and the big-time country music industry that was emerging in the 1940s. By playing his treasured Bob Wills records "for breakfast, dinner, and supper," Cactus Jack helped build a West Coast market for professional western swing bands from Oklahoma and Texas. Beginning in 1943, big-name bands like Bob Wills and the Texas Playboys and Bob Nolan and the Sons of the Pioneers appeared regularly in East Bay ballrooms. Moving their base of operations to California, such bands toured the dance hall circuit of West Coast defense centers. In 1944 alone, Wills's band played in Oakland four times, selling out the Oakland Civic Auditorium to capacity crowds of more than 19,000. Such turnouts topped even those of the most popular big bands of the day led by Harry James, Tommy Dorsey, and Benny Goodman.[74] The phenomenal wartime success of southwestern bands paved the way for the integration of country music into California's musical mainstream by the 1950s.

Black migrants also developed a distinct musical subculture that differed from both prewar urban black music and the dominant white culture. In contrast to white southwesterners, who had arrived in California by the thousands during the depression, the surge in southern black migration took place during the war boom some five to ten years later. The renaissance in southern black music thus occurred somewhat later in California, blossoming fully after the war. Nevertheless, the seeds of southern blues in the Bay Area first took root in the shipyard boomtowns of the East Bay.

Initially, black newcomers gravitated toward established black bars, nightclubs, and other entertainment spots in the East Bay. West Oakland, the traditional center of black social life in the Bay Area, continued to expand and prosper during the war boom, attracting migrants and service personnel from around the East Bay and San Francisco. The commercial strip on Seventh Street featured a good selection of cafes and clubs, including such jazz hot spots as the Swing Club, Harvey's Rex Club, and Slim Jenkins' Place.[75]

The latter was west Oakland's premier nightclub, founded in 1933 by Harold "Slim" Jenkins, a black Louisianan who had moved to Oakland during World War I. Attracting a racially mixed clientele, Jenkins Place contained a first-class restaurant, a large banquet room, a market, and a liquor store. Throughout the thirties and forties, the club featured some of the biggest names in black jazz and popular music and became one of the most celebrated nightclubs on the Pacific Coast. During the war years, shipyard earnings enabled some black migrants to patronize such establishments as well as the white-owned ballrooms downtown, which occasionally hosted black swing bands. Sweets Ballroom and the Oakland Auditorium, in fact, regularly sold out "colored dances" featuring the bands of Louis Jordan, Cab Calloway, Duke Ellington, and Count Basie.[76]

In addition to the music they enjoyed in these more urbane establishments, black migrants also brought with them a different kind of music, rooted in the black experience of the rural South. For these newcomers, the blues—a southern black musical form derived from slave work songs and spirituals—had a powerful appeal, helping to reinforce a sense of cultural and regional identity. The blues were certainly not new to the Bay Area in the 1940s, but the rawer country sound of the southern blues contrasted starkly with the uptown, sophisticated blues of performers who sometimes appeared in local jazz clubs.[77]

During the war, young blues musicians from Texas, Oklahoma, and other southwestern states first began to play house parties and small clubs in the East Bay. Lowell Fulson, an Oklahoma-born blues guitarist, remembers playing beach parties every weekend in Alameda while based at the nearby Naval Air Station. Jimmy McCracklin, a Missouri migrant who settled in Richmond after a stint in the navy, began playing at the local Club Savoy owned by his sister-in-law, Granny Johnson. Toward the end of the war, new juke joints and nightclubs were appearing along Seventh Street in west Oakland. In north Richmond night spots like Fred's Place, the B and L Club, Tappers Inn, and Minnie Lou's catered to a migrant clientele with down-home cooking, blues music, and dancing. For the black entrepreneurs who operated them, the blues clubs provided new economic opportunities while offering greater social and cultural autonomy from the white-owned entertainment industry.[78]

Southern gospel music also took root in the Bay Area during the war. Based on traditional choir and quartet singing in southern churches, a cappella gospel music enjoyed an upsurge in popularity as southern black migrants formed new singing groups that toured local communities. Many of the performers worked in the shipyards, and some, like the Singing Shipbuilders Quartet in Richmond, attracted the favorable attention of defense employers, who hired them to perform at ship launchings. Other gospel groups, like the Rising Stars Singers in Oakland and the Paramount Singers in San Francisco, worked independently, playing church programs and weekly radio appearances. These two groups, whose members came primarily from Texas and Louisiana, laid the groundwork for later Bay Area gospel groups like the Golden Stars, the Golden West Singers, the Swanee River Singers, the Spartonaires, the Oakland Silvertones, and many others.[79] The popularity of such groups continued into the sixties, sustained by the traditions of southern evangelical religion and folk music imported by black migrants.

As in religion, enterprising southern migrants acted as cultural transmitters of traditional blues and gospel music. Bob Geddins, a Texas migrant who settled in west Oakland during the war, was a key cultural entrepreneur in the East Bay. When Geddins first heard the Rising Stars Singers in 1944, he was favorably impressed and helped them make their first record. Sales from the record enabled Geddins to begin his own record-pressing business, and he soon discovered the power and popularity of the blues. Beginning with a Lowell Fulson record in 1946, Geddins produced dozens of local blues artists on Big Town, Trilon, Irma, Veltone, and other Oakland labels that he founded. Southern migrants were his main clientele, Geddins recalled: "Up here they was starving for blues, so the first one I put out they jumped on the bandwagon."[80]

The Bay Area blues culture blossomed fully in the postwar era as a growing cadre of blues performers learned to blend the raw intensity of the country blues with a more modern electric guitar sound. Wartime bluesmen like Fulson and McCracklin were now joined by Pee Wee Crayton, K. C. Douglas, Johnny Fuller, L. C. Robinson, Lafayette Thomas, Sugar Pie DeSanto, and many other young blues players. New clubs sprang up in the black districts of Richmond, Oakland, Vallejo, Hunters Point, and the Fillmore, creating a local "chitlin circuit" that would support the blues for decades. Nor was the Bay Area unique in this regard; Los Angeles, Detroit, Chicago, and other centers of black migration would all experience a blues boom during and after the Second World War.[81]

In the postwar era, southern music, religion, and other traditions would become an integral part of California's cultural matrix. During the war, though, such traditions were part of separate migrant subcultures that emerged in and around newcomer settlements. Building on racial and regional ties, migrant subcultures helped forge a sense of community and identity among certain migrant groups. As such, they provided an alternative to government-sponsored social programs that reflected the values of corporate leaders and middle-class urban reformers.

In the tumultuous atmosphere of war boomtowns, a newcomer's material and emotional survival often depended on his or her associations with other migrants. For most newcomers, family and kin connections were the single most important factor sustaining them in their new surroundings. Extending back to their home states, kin and friendship networks enabled migrants to move, settle, and work in West Coast cities. At the same time, however, wartime conditions such as overcrowding, long hours, and new work roles for women and youth tended to increase family stress, particularly in the highly volatile migrant settlements. Gender and generational conflicts manifested themselves in increased divorce, domestic violence, and runaway children. The family, then, was not an ideal support network but a social institution that responded to rapidly changing social conditions with varying degrees of success.

Outside the family, migrants relied on racial and regional ties that gave rise to distinctive migrant subcultures, particularly among southerners. These subcultures, however, should not be confused with the greater migrant population, which generally lacked a sense of community. Like earlier foreign immigrants, defense migrants were internally divided and tended to be mutually suspicious of one another. The temporary nature and enforced heterogeneity of public housing arrangements only enhanced their social fragmentation. Although migrant preachers, musicians, and other entrepreneurs helped cultivate regional and racial subcultures, an all-inclusive migrant community did not develop.

Hoping to create such a community through on-site social programs, corporate and federal government leaders found their initiatives challenged by both migrants and local governments. East Bay agencies generally resisted programs that they feared might set precedents for the postwar period, including child care, interracial social events, and migrant area commercial development. Migrants likewise influenced the course of social programs by demanding additional schools and community facilities in war housing areas. Some project residents also voted with their feet against certain programs such as child care and church ministries.

Ultimately, government social programs failed to create a sense of "citizenship" or "community responsibility" as migrants remained divided over racial, regional, and class differences. Nor were these programs successful in exporting the social and cultural life of the prewar community to the migrant settlements. By constructing a parallel system of community services, government programs only exacerbated the social chasm dividing old-timers and newcomers.

The migrant "cities within cities" were by no means self-sufficient, however. Migrants ventured daily into downtown areas, posing new opportunities and problems for East Bay communities. The focus of the next chapter shifts to the downtown commercial districts to examine the dynamics of public life in war boom communities.

1–2. These two panoramic views show the spectacular wartime growth of south Richmond during a six-month period. The upper photo was taken in June 1942, the lower in January 1943. The war housing projects in the lower picture are Esmeralda Court in the foreground and Canal Dormitories and War Apartments in the background. Reproduced from Joseph C. Whitnah, *A History of Richmond, California* (Richmond: Richmond Chamber of Commerce, 1944), courtesy of the Richmond Chamber of Commerce.

3. Panoramic view of shipways at Richmond Yard Two, ca. 1942. Courtesy of the Bancroft Library, Kaiser Pictorial Collection.

4. Shift change at the Richmond shipyards, ca. 1942–1944, showing the
incredible diversity of age, race, and gender among local defense workers.
Courtesy of the Dorothea Lange Collection, the City of Oakland, the
Oakland Museum, 1992.

5. Crane lift of aft section of a Liberty Ship built at the Richmond shipyards. Pioneering methods of prefabrication and assembly reduced the
average ship construction time and allowed for the introduction of
thousands of new semiskilled workers. Courtesy of the Bancroft Library,
Kaiser Pictorial Collection.

6. Launching celebration for the Liberty Ship *Robert E. Peary* at Richmond Yard Two, November 12, 1942. The *Peary*, constructed in four days, fifteen hours, and twenty-nine minutes, broke all previous construction records and provided a public relations coup for Kaiser. Courtesy of the Bancroft Library, Kaiser Pictorial Collection.

7. Young male welders' dormitory near Richmond shipyards. Kaiser
   equipped the dormitories with recreational facilities designed to keep
   young migrant men off the streets and out of trouble. Courtesy of the
   Bancroft Library, Kaiser Pictorial Collection.

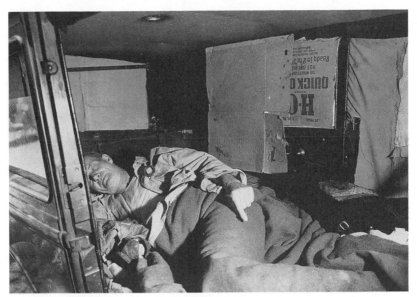

8. Night-shift shipyard worker sleeping in automobile, Richmond area, 1942. Prior to the completion of federal war housing projects, hundreds of workers slept in cars, city parks, and all-night movie theaters. Courtesy of the Bancroft Library, Kaiser Pictorial Collection.

9. Children of migrant defense workers from Oklahoma sleeping in makeshift tent beneath their trailer, Richmond area, 1942. Thousands of families camped in unsanitary, overcrowded trailer parks around the East Bay,
   prompting the federal government to build its own regulated camps in
   Richmond, El Cerrito, and east Oakland. Courtesy of the Bancroft
   Library, Kaiser Pictorial Collection.

10. Migrant woman in family trailer home, Richmond area, 1942. The cramped and chaotic conditions that many families endured added to the difficulties of housekeeping for migrant women. Courtesy of the Bancroft Library, Kaiser Pictorial Collection.

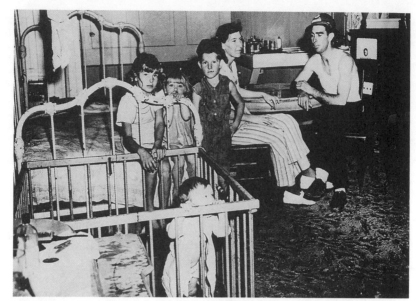

11. Migrant shipyard worker and family in their one-room apartment, Richmond area, 1942. A federal committee investigated substandard housing conditions in 1942 in preparation for launching a major public housing construction program. Courtesy of the Bancroft Library, Kaiser Pictorial Collection.

12. Richmond terminus of San Francisco commuter ferry line and the temporary "Shipyard Railway" that federal agencies assembled out of old rail lines and reconditioned trains from New York's Third Avenue elevated. Courtesy of the Bancroft Library, Kaiser Pictorial Collection.

13. Bay View Terrace, a defense worker housing subdivision under construction in Richmond, 1941. Built under the federal Title 6 housing program, suburban subdivisions like this one sprang up near defense centers around the country. Courtesy of the Dorothea Lange Collection, the City of Oakland, the Oakland Museum, 1992.

14. Woman evangelist at the Full Gospel storefront church adjacent
    to south Richmond war housing projects, ca. 1942–1944. This
    church was one of many small evangelical storefronts that pro-
    liferated in West Coast defense centers during the war, causing
    consternation among mainstream Protestant denominations.
    Courtesy of the Dorothea Lange Collection, the City of Oak-
    land, the Oakland Museum, 1992.

16. *Opposite:* The defense worker as consumer. Shipyard workers window-
    shop on Richmond's Macdonald Avenue, ca. 1942–1944. In this shot, as
    in many others, the photographer Dorothea Lange sought to capture the
    sense of prosperity and the desire to consume that gripped wartime cities.
    Courtesy of the Dorothea Lange Collection, the City of Oakland, the Oak-
    land Museum, 1992.

15. Dude Martin and the Round-Up playing a country barn dance in Richmond, ca. 1942–1944. Martin was one of many western swing performers who catered to migrant defense workers and service personnel in West Coast cities. Courtesy of the Dorothea Lange Collection, the City of Oakland, the Oakland Museum, 1992.

17. War worker couple displaying purchases outside Oakland's Tenth Street Market, ca. 1942–1944. Lange spent many hours photographing wartime consumers at this market in an attempt to document the "buying power of shipyard workers." Courtesy of the Dorothea Lange Collection, the City of Oakland, the Oakland Museum, 1992.

18. Wartime consumers exiting Oakland's Tenth Street Market, ca. 1942–1944. Here, Lange draws attention to the sensitive issue of racial mixing in urban defense centers. African-Americans and women of all races not only asserted their right to inhabit public space but also came in close physical proximity, stirring age-old fears of miscegenation. Courtesy of the Dorothea Lange Collection, the City of Oakland, the Oakland Museum, 1992.

19. Black woman patron at the Richmond Cafe, 1944. Another Lange photograph documenting the effects of wartime prosperity and social opportunity. Courtesy of the Dorothea Lange Collection, the City of Oakland, the Oakland Museum, 1992.

20. All-night movie theater in downtown Richmond, ca. 1942–1944. Movies and dance halls proliferated in East Bay boomtowns, catering to the recreational needs of defense workers twenty-four hours a day. Courtesy of the Dorothea Lange Collection, the City of Oakland, the Oakland Museum, 1992.

21. A downtown Richmond bar, ca. 1942–1944. East Bay authorities became increasingly concerned with public drunkenness and promiscuity.
As the signs in this bar indicate, tavern owners adopted a system of vol-
untary regulation aimed at controlling women's behavior in public areas—restrictions that did not apply to men. Courtesy of the Dorothea
Lange Collection, the City of Oakland, the Oakland Museum, 1992.

6

Boomtowns and the Control of Urban Space

Headlines in the March 1943 *Oakland Tribune* announced the arrival of a major crime wave on city streets. Criminal activities and juvenile delinquency had become "intolerable," said the *Tribune,* and "decent citizens [were] afraid to go out at night." The city's evening newspaper, the *Post-Enquirer,* urged city officials to take immediate action, calling for a "drastic tightening and strengthening of the forces of law and order. We cannot allow rape, murder, prostitution, robbery and gangsterism to flourish and increase in our midst."[1]

What caused this sudden hysteria? Like most crime scares, Oakland's wartime crime alert came at a critical moment in the city's history. In Oakland, as in other East Bay communities, the massive influx of new industries and workers created a tumultuous and volatile atmosphere. Almost overnight, East Bay cities turned into twenty-four-hour boomtowns with an explosion of retail business, commercial amusements, and a bustling downtown street life. The anonymous boomtown climate provided new social opportunities and freedom for its patrons, particularly for the migrants, blacks, women, and youth who enjoyed new defense earnings. Rapid urbanization, the influx of culturally and racially diverse newcomers, a breakdown in city services, and a general climate of wartime affluence and abandon resulted in a transformation of public life that shocked the sensibilities of the prewar middle class.

The complex events that transformed wartime cities affected all residents by challenging the established social customs and boundaries that governed downtown life. Rather than accept change, however, old-timers lashed out against migrants, blaming them for their cities' ills. Middle-class community leaders accused migrants of encouraging "public indecency" and leading a crime spree on city streets. In actuality, however, migrants were merely convenient targets—the most visible carriers of new social trends. Working women and youth, whose economic opportunities and autonomy also increased as a result of the war boom, were likewise deemed unruly.

Responding to residents' anxieties, East Bay leaders employed an elaborate system of municipal ordinances, business taxes, and public policing in an attempt to restore the prewar social order of their communities. At the same time, federal mandates to crack down on public disorder in critical war production areas encouraged local authorities to be more vigilant. Targeting migrants and other "unruly" groups, local authorities launched a vigorous law-and-order campaign. In time, though, old-timers would realize that the war affected not only newcomers but themselves and their families as well—forcing them to reconsider their more repressive measures.

Boomtown Social Life

As noted in chapter 1, East Bay residents remembered their cities as relatively stable, "well-ordered" communities before the war. Smaller cities like Alameda and Richmond were relatively homogeneous with few nonwhite residents, and larger cities like Oakland were spatially differentiated according to race, ethnicity, and class. In both cases, neighborhoods were relatively cohesive and self-contained with well-defined boundaries. In downtown districts, merchants and other business elites sought to preserve a sense of middle-class decorum that reflected the city's social hierarchy.

The clearly delineated social order suddenly broke down with the onset of war. With the rise of wartime shipyards, Richmond and Oakland became bustling boomtowns, catering to thousands of new war worker patrons whose round-the-clock shifts influenced the dynamics of downtown commerce. The brief sojourn of thousands of servicemen shipping to or from the Pacific through the Oakland Port of Embarkation added to the tumult. With this sudden influx of newcomers, existing public facilities and services were stretched to the breaking point.

Municipal services such as police, fire, and sanitation were the most critically affected. East Bay governments all suffered from personnel shortages because of the draft while agency workloads increased along with the population. Even with an infusion of federal aid, municipal agencies could not compete with shipyards and other high-paying defense industries in attracting personnel. Police and fire departments, faced with demands for expanded services in new neighborhoods, could barely keep pace with essential calls. Residents also complained of a deterioration of sanitation services evident in the proliferation of trash, rodents, and stray dogs on city streets. Oakland had become "a frowzy city," said the *Oakland Observer* in 1944, and newspaper editors in Richmond and Alameda echoed that complaint.[2]

Transportation services were also hard hit. Traffic congestion and lack of downtown parking were chronic wartime problems. "The streets were so jammed," said one resident, "that no car in Richmond had four good fenders." With much of the public transit system channeled into shipyards and industrial areas, streetcar and bus service was completely overburdened. Commuting between Oakland and Richmond (about twelve miles) could take up to three hours at peak periods. "Every bus was packed," remembers Alex Amber, "guys were hanging out on the bumpers."[3]

The war's impact on East Bay cities, however, was not all negative. Coming on the heels of the depression, the high wages and sudden prosperity of shipyard boomtowns were exhilarating for many migrants. Margaret Cathey, a recent arrival from Iowa, recalled that her shipyard wages were "more than [she'd] ever made in [her] life." Alex Amber, who left Los Angeles for Alameda at the age of fifteen, remembers earning fifty dollars a week: "I bought a car, nice suits . . . plus I had money in my pocket, plus I was putting money in the bank." Of course, not everyone did so well. The high cost of living in defense centers forced many families to tighten their belts, and others scrimped and saved to pay off debts or finance new defense homes. Young single workers and multiple-worker families, however, often accrued considerable savings and spent their precious off-hours shopping and taking in commercial amusements downtown. As one ex-migrant put it, "money came easy, and they spent it easy."[4]

Boosted by shipyard dollars, retail businesses flourished. During the war years, retail trade income increased by more than 50 percent in Alameda County and more than 100 percent in Contra Costa County. In 1945, many shopkeepers reported earning up to five and six times as much as they had before the war. "You know why the merchants close up at all?" said one Richmond shopkeeper. "Just because they're tired. Just exhausted."[5] The phenomenal growth of downtown business, however, was not uniform. Rationing of many consumer products, a critical labor shortage, and restrictions on building materials favored the development of large-scale businesses over smaller ones.

In the grocery business, for example, more than one thousand small stores in the East Bay closed by mid-1943 because of supply and labor shortages. Some of these stores reopened later, but others were permanently displaced by new self-service supermarkets that had successfully petitioned the federal government for building priorities in war-congested areas. The greater buying power of large-scale businesses also helped minimize the vagaries of the rationing system. Large chain stores of all types—supermarkets, department stores, and variety stores—all increased their number of outlets and volume of sales. Especially in small cities like Richmond, the war permanently diminished the prewar position of the small downtown business entrepreneur.[6] For consumers, downtown shopping became a less sociable activity, as large self-service stores provided fast-paced, impersonal service.

More marginal businesses also sprang up in abundance in war boomtowns. Business license applications for East Bay cities reveal a proliferation of secondhand jewelry and clothing stores, beauty and massage parlors, barber shops, and other businesses requiring a minimum of scarce consumer goods. The war boom also attracted a throng of street peddlers and fly-by-night businesses that sidestepped a tight real estate market by taking to the streets. Hot dog stands and lunch counters lined the streets adjacent to shipyard operations, and roving shoeshine boys, gypsy fortune-tellers, street musicians, magazine saleswomen, and others worked downtown Oakland and Richmond.

These marginal entrepreneurs found eager clients among local war workers. The State Board of Equalization commented that consumer demand, "frustrated in the quest for good, solid, lasting merchandise . . . found release in on-the-spot consumption in ersatz but high-priced articles, in knickknacks and gewgaws." Local merchants were thus challenged by both large-scale and marginal new businesses that specialized in such commodities.[7]

Illicit businesses grew as well during the war. Gambling, casual prostitution, and bootlegging were prevalent in west Oakland and other shipyard neighborhoods. One well-known bootlegger, Raincoat

Jones, became an institution in west Oakland during the war. After hours, when bars and package stores were closed, Jones sold half-pints out of his overcoat. "He was a walking liquor store," recalled one patron. Dice games were regular events near shipyard gates, on transit lines, and in local bars. "Many have been operating brazenly on the street corners, on the sidewalks, and in pool rooms and taverns," complained the *Richmond Independent*.[8]

Although the street visibility of organized prostitution generally declined during the war, federal and local authorities reported an increase in streetwalking and other casual soliciting in west Oakland, particularly among black women. Since African-American women faced a more constricted and lower-paying job market than other groups, an increase in prostitution is not surprising. Whether prostitution and other illicit operations actually rose relative to population growth, however, is impossible to determine. In any case, such activities prompted growing concern among government authorities and prewar residents.[9]

The most noticeable change in war boomtowns was the dramatic expansion of commercial amusements. Among the "knickknacks and gewgaws" purchased by war workers, meals, alcohol, and admissions to movies, shows, and dance halls accounted for a significant portion. The unhappy reality of war and long hours of defense work led many residents to seek outlets that promised quick relief from the daily war grind. Facing the prospect of death, servicemen awaiting assignment overseas also contributed to the rowdyism of East Bay boomtowns. This preoccupation with leisure and the round-the-clock wartime schedule tended to break down traditional concepts of work and leisure time. "There were no more weekends or nights," explained one Richmond old-timer. "It was just twenty-four hours a day, seven days a week."

Catering to three shifts of defense workers, many downtown restaurants and movie houses operated around the clock. In Richmond, the number of movie theaters increased from two in 1940 to twelve in 1945, four of which stayed open all night. "Movie houses sprang up all over," said one prewar resident. "They built them in former auto dealers' garages and former furniture stores or whatever was available." Even with additional theaters, movie houses were often packed, and even "fourth-rate mystery thrillers" drew a big crowd. In Oakland, palatial downtown theaters featured at least seven continuous-running movie shows as well as an assortment of burlesque and vaudeville performers.[10]

Bars, juke joints, and poolrooms also multiplied during the war years. Local proprietors expanded their prewar businesses, and out-of-town tavern owners moved their operations to shipyard towns that promised big profits. As it turned out, business was quite good, with some bars pulling in more than eight thousand dollars a month—then a fantastic sum. Many defense workers and servicemen frequented taverns as a reprieve from long hours of war work or time spent overseas. "The bars [were] always full," said one Richmond shipyard worker. "Sometimes customers [were] lined up three deep."[11]

By 1943, lower Macdonald Avenue in Richmond and lower Broadway in Oakland had become notorious saloon districts, or skid rows. Serving a working-class clientele, the bars in these areas were rough and rowdy and known for their fights and occasional bloodshed. In the bars near the Oakland waterfront, "there was fights breaking out all the time for any kind of a reason," recalled one war worker. In downtown Richmond, the Nut Club, the Denver Club, and the Red Robin were among those establishments renowned for their "tough customers." Throughout the war years, local newspapers reported on barroom brawls and shootouts, some of which involved dozens of combatants and spilled out onto nearby streets. The skid rows, though, were not the only areas affected by the tavern boom. More "respectable" piano bars and cocktail lounges appeared throughout Oakland, Richmond, and Alameda. Even Oakland's fashionable Lakeshore Avenue was dubbed "Rum Row" by local residents upset with the proliferation of cocktail lounges in their neighborhood.[12]

One of the most popular pastimes of young men and women was going to the huge dance halls that flourished during the war years. Downtown Oakland was the dance hall capital of the East Bay, with established clubs like Sweets Ballroom and the Oakland Auditorium drawing national big band acts like the Dorsey brothers, Glenn Miller, Cab Calloway, and Duke Ellington. Thousands of swing fans, both black and white, flocked to Oakland from around the Bay Area in greater numbers than ever before.

The dance hall shows were certainly not new to the city, but like the taverns and movie houses, their business increased tremendously during the war. Smaller halls like McFadden's Ballroom, Melody Lane, and New Danceland advertised extra weeknight shows to meet the increased demand for entertainment. New dance halls were also established in private clubs and hotels such as the Oakland City Club, the Hotel Alameda, and the Berkeley Women's City Club. In Richmond, a town with no commercial dance halls before the war, the old-timer Schwartz family started a dance hall on Tenth Street and Macdonald Avenue in 1943; a competing hall soon opened a few blocks away.[13] In addition, there were the many blues, western swing, and other migrant entertainment events discussed in the previous chapter.

The East Bay boomtowns also attracted more transient forms of entertainment, including traveling carnivals, boxing matches, and tent shows. An Oakland resident complained in 1944 that billboard trucks blaring "hillbilly music" were circulating around the city "just to advertise women wrestlers, barn dances and boxing matches." Circuses and carnival shows toured the Pacific Coast, stopping in major war boomtowns along the way. In the East Bay they pitched their tents adjacent to war housing areas in south Richmond and along the Oakland Estuary.[14]

Such attractions, along with the multitude of other commercial amusements, gave these cities a carny-like atmosphere. Richmond, observed one writer, was "a city that looked like carnival night every hour for three years." The crowdedness of downtown businesses and the active street culture also contributed to the liveliness. In most stores, customers waited in long lines for service; some businesses even introduced number-dispensing systems to facilitate service. Contemporary accounts noted the presence of wandering pedestrians at all hours, either window shopping or just taking in the city environment. "My husband and I often walk the downtown streets after dinner just for the pure joy of the movement all about us," explained one Oakland newcomer.[15]

The active street life also increased the anonymity of East Bay cities. "The sidewalks are blocked by gaping strangers in cowboy boots, blue jeans, and sombreros," said one journalist about Richmond. "Nobody knows anybody."[16] For many prewar residents, the sudden boom was thus a disorienting and unwelcome development. In Richmond, the small-town culture of the prewar era was permanently transformed as face-to-face social relations gave way to urban anonymity. Old-time residents suddenly found themselves in the minority. "I was amazed how many strangers there were," said Marguerite Clausen, "and how seldom you ran into people you knew." The leisurely shopping and chatting on street corners that had been so common in the prewar years quickly disappeared. One old-time businessman, J. B. Baldwin, explained: "I used to greet everyone on the street. Now I don't even look for a familiar face when I step out of my office. In fact, I don't even go out at night." This sense of alienation drove some prewar residents from the downtown area altogether in favor of outlying commercial centers or periodic shopping trips to San Francisco.[17]

For many migrants, blacks, women, and youth, however, the bustling climate of war boomtowns provided new social opportunities and freedom from the tight controls of family or small-town life. With defense wages to spend, these new workers gained entitlement to public space, where they became avid competitors for wartime goods and services. The changing uses of public space in downtown Richmond fueled resentments between old-timers and newcomers, who vied for limited resources. Throughout the war years, for instance, local residents complained to the city council about shipyard worker dances held in public parks. Such events, they felt, monopolized public facilities formerly used by fraternal lodges and community organizations. In downtown stores, some old-timers complained that they were being driven away by aggressive migrant customers. "I don't like to be tramped on by dirty cowboy boots when I go into a store," said one man. Others complained that with the influx of migrants, "casual Western living and conversation had been shoved to one side."[18] As the war transformed the civic culture of Richmond, old-timers felt that they had lost traditional public meeting places and the sense of social cohesion that had existed before the war.

In Oakland, a much larger urban center, residents reacted somewhat differently. Here, anonymity and impersonal social relations were not new. But the invasion of hundreds of hard-hatted war workers into the downtown district shocked many old-time residents. The *Oakland Observer* compared this boomtown phenomenon with California's gold rush of 1849: "when any city is suddenly overrun by a helter-skelter horde of newcomers . . . its older social barriers are inclined to be overturned and its cultural averages go backward, so that it reverts somewhat toward the mining-camp era of civilians, when everybody was uncouth and grabbed everything that he could grab." References to "mining-camp civilization" revealed the class and racial anxieties of old-time residents, who felt threatened by the newfound prosperity of war migrants. War workers—and especially blacks—were no longer content to remain in "their own portion of the city" and were now major contenders for public space and commercial activities. Native Oaklanders marveled "at the characters on the streets nowadays," and some claimed they felt like tourists in their own hometown.[19] For many old-timers, the stable and orderly prewar city was coming apart at the seams.

Blaming the Newcomers

Although newcomers were not directly responsible for the transformation of the urban social order, natives tended to blame migrants for "ruining" their cities. Many old-timers attributed trash, crime, immorality, and a host of other urban ills to outsiders who had "invaded" their communities. As one southern woman complained, "We are openly blamed for everything from trouble with garbage collection to chicken pox epidemics in the schools." Throughout the war years an "interstate debate" raged in local newspaper columns and radio programs, as natives attacked "Okies" and other newcomers and vice versa. The debate intensified in 1943, forcing an *Oakland Tribune* advice columnist "to cut out parts of the California-Okie letters" because "they would crowd out every other controversy in the column."[20]

The so-called interstate debate was not entirely new. Beginning with the vitriolic antisouthern writings of H. L. Mencken in the 1920s, novelists, journalists, and social investigators introduced the American public to a stereotyped image of the poor southern white. Usually portrayed as illiterate sharecroppers, "poor white trash" were seen as backward, lazy, and often depraved. With the onset of the dust bowl migration of the late thirties, many Californians adapted this caricature to describe migrants from the Southwest. With the influx of war migrants into coastal cities, the Okie stereotype gained new currency. Unable to distinguish the regional backgrounds of newcomers, natives applied the term indiscriminately to describe any white, working-class migrant. Similar stereotypes of "southern Negroes"—thought to be fresh off plantations—emerged to describe black migrants.[21]

Increased competition for housing, services, and public space heightened nativist feelings in overcrowded defense centers. As described in previous chapters, many old-timers resented the high wages, easy job advancement, housing, transportation, and other benefits available to war migrants. Local military personnel joined in the attack, characterizing migrant men as slackers and draft dodgers whose masculinity was suspect. "See how many servicemen would trade places with any of them who think they have it tough, or are being imposed upon because they have to work for $300 per month instead of $54, which our servicemen get," wrote one soldier.[22]

Contemporary observers frequently portrayed newcomers as "money-grabbing outsiders" who flaunted their newfound wealth in public. "Many among these migrants never dreamed that a common working stiff could make so much," one journalist commented. "This rich landfall every payday inspired a reckless exhibition of squandering—a splurge of luxuries, expensive and needless." According to the sociologist Katherine Archibald, "the richness and variety of life in the large cities soon raised the level of [migrants'] material tastes." The newcomers, she said, progressed from dime stores to department stores to fur and perfume shops. An Oakland police captain seconds this observation, noting that old-timers resented the newcomer "with his flashy clothes and pockets full of ready-cash made in the shipyards." More sympathetic observers attributed this consumerism to the migrants' supposed lack of education. "Most of these families are earning more money than they have ever earned before," said one housing project social worker, "and because they have no education on how to spend it wisely, they squander it on wasteful luxurious desires."[23]

Certain consumer items, in fact, came to symbolize the conspicuous wealth of war workers. The fur coat became a subject of heated debate in local newspaper columns. Outraged citizens attacked fur coats as "wasteful to the war effort" but seemed even more concerned over who was wearing them. "Most women, without much 'style' in the fashion magazine sense," remarked one journalist, "are garbed in fur coats, some of which are worn casually over sweaters and slacks." Others berated "the fur coat bums who hang around the booze joints." Diamond bracelets and other "credit jewelry" came under similar attack as a badge of "cheap" womanhood.[24]

Natives also regarded the wearing of cowboy attire by migrant men as a conspicuous display of shipyard wealth. One old-timer believed that Okies "spen[t] their first pay check for the biggest cowboy hat they [could] find and use[d] an affected walk in fancy cowboy boots." Katherine Archibald agreed that it was easy to identify an Okie since "his dress tended to be flamboyant, and his manner likewise."[25] Clearly, many middle-class natives resented the arrogance of working-class newcomers, who as consumers dared aspire to a higher social status.

Natives—both black and white—were likewise shocked by the conspicuous behavior of black migrants. Prewar black residents often marveled at the antics of black newcomers from the South. "You see them down in department stores with overalls on, trying on fur coats and stuff like that," said John Watkins, an Oakland native. "You'd never see any of these things before." Many white natives viewed black consumerism as a challenge to their own social status. According to a white supervisor at the California Quartermaster's Depot, "the colored girls dress[ed] much better than the white women as a rule. Jewelry and fur coats [became] basic tools to the Negroes for attaining social prestige."[26]

The photographer Dorothea Lange captured the image of the prosperous, spendthrift war worker in a series of photographs taken in the East Bay during 1942–1945. Her portrayal of shoppers at Oakland's Tenth Street Market features a parade of hard-hatted war workers emerging with packages, parcels, house plants, and other purchases (see plates 17 and 18). An even more telling shot shows a smiling, fur-clad black woman posing in front of the Richmond Cafe on Macdonald Avenue (see plate 19). The woman, standing alongside a "Free War Show" poster, exudes a sense of pride and prosperity and seems quite at home in downtown Richmond. Lange, a sympathetic observer of California migrants, nonetheless reflected in her work the stereotype of war migrants as lavish spenders who publicly asserted their newfound prosperity and social status.[27]

Migrant consumers, however, were no different from anyone else. Their patterns of consumption were shaped by the idiosyncrasies of a wartime market that offered luxuries and entertainment in lieu of durable consumer goods. Many old-timers, however, held the newcomers responsible for this new behavior and for overturning "older social barriers." Indeed, they felt, the city seemed to belong to the newcomers, who shopped and socialized with impunity. In the midst of war and on the heels of the depression, such behavior seemed somehow immoral.

Community leaders and social workers soon articulated their belief in the connection between wartime prosperity and immorality. A prominent Methodist minister in Richmond claimed: "Many of these people had before coming handled little cash. Especially where two or more in one family were employed, this sudden increase in spending money added to the moral hazards." The new prosperity of migrant families, many believed, led to drinking, gambling, fighting, and sexual misconduct among both parents and children. "This sudden prosperity for grown-ups has resulted in drinking by both fathers and mothers, indifferent to what their sons and daughters are doing," said Alameda County Probation Officer Ollie F. Snedigar. The Oakland city council concurred, noting, "there has been too much crime from the ranks of outsiders in the west end of the city."[28]

Antinewcomer sentiment reached a fever pitch during the so-called crime wave of 1943. That spring Bay Area counties conducted highly publicized grand jury investigations into the crime problem. At the specific request of the city council, Oakland newspapers publicized the proceedings, blazoning their front pages with crime wave headlines. In Richmond and Alameda, local newspapers featured week-long, front-page crime series titled "Alameda Ain't What It Used To Be" and "Richmond: What's Happening Here Every Night . . . and Day." Both the grand jury proceedings and the publicity accompanying them focused on violent crime, recounting a litany of kidnappings, stabbings, rapes, and murders.[29]

During the investigations, local authorities decried the explosion of crime and delinquency, attributing the increase to the criminal disposition of newcomers. Noting the prevalence of southern whites and blacks in criminal investigations, an Oakland police lieutenant explained that the "quality rather than the quantity" of newcomers was causing the crime increase. "The type of people that have come to Oakland have altered the character of the community considerably," he said. Local newspapers claimed that the shipyards attracted professional criminals to the area who worked defense jobs during the day and engaged in criminal activities in their off-hours. Authorities in Richmond and Alameda likewise denounced "the influx of troublemakers and law violators" into their communities.[30]

Practically, it is difficult to determine whether criminal activity actually increased. Federal Bureau of Investigation crime statistics for Oakland, Berkeley, and Alameda (Richmond statistics are not available) offer some clues, but the data raise as many questions as they answer. Between 1939 and 1944, the number of major crimes reported to police (homicide, robbery, aggravated assault, burglary, larceny, and auto theft) increased by 43 percent in Berkeley, 35 percent in Oakland, and 55 percent in Alameda (see table 8). The number of persons charged on such offenses by the Oakland police also increased markedly (see table 9). Such striking gains suggest that crime did in fact increase, justifying community fears expressed in crime wave headlines. However, these statistics tell us little about several other important factors.

The first is the issue of wartime population growth. Between 1940 and 1944, the population of Oakland and Berkeley grew by approximately 14 percent, and Alameda's increased by 21 percent—all well below the growth rates for criminal offenses. We should recognize, however, that annual crime statistics are cumulative whereas a population census captures one point in time. This distinction is particularly significant for war boomtowns that had inordinately high rates of residential turnover and mobility. Furthermore, since Oakland was a major port of embarkation, hundreds of thousands of military personnel passed through the city each year. As local arrest records indicate, conflicts between civilian and military personnel were a major source of violence and disorder.[31]

Although it is impossible to measure the impact of these other factors, they do suggest that the 1944 census significantly undercounted the day-to-day population of the East Bay. Relative to population growth and mobility, then, we can assume that the increase in criminal activity was far lower than the FBI statistics indicate. Furthermore, if we look at rates for major crimes based on the total number of people charged by the Oakland police (table 10), the wartime increases are far less significant. For example, in 1939, 0.13 percent of all persons charged were charged with murder; in 1943, the figure actually fell, to 0.09 percent. Criminal activity may well have been on the rise, but local officials cited crime statistics out of context, using them in an inflammatory and irresponsible manner.

Why did East Bay officials promote this hysteria? The most obvious explanation is that a well-orchestrated crime wave might attract federal funding for additional police personnel during a serious labor shortage. Not coincidentally, the grand jury investigations directly preceded hearings of a congressional committee visiting the nation's congested production areas.[32] In hopes of securing federal aid, Bay Area cities used grand jury investigations to publicize the need for more police and public safety services. Federal authorities encouraged and supported such enforcement efforts in an attempt to uphold discipline near military bases and reduce absenteeism and turnover in the nation's defense industries.

But beyond the practical aims of funding and personnel, the crime investigations must also be understood as part of a larger campaign to restore public order in war-affected cities. The new boomtown atmosphere and the sudden transformation of the city's public life provoked anxiety among the prewar population, especially the area's downtown ruling elite. Using inflammatory rhetoric and highly sensational publicity, East Bay leaders seized on the "crime wave" as a potent symbol of wartime urban disorder. By reasserting control of downtown areas and maintaining public order on city streets, they hoped to restore the prewar image of East Bay cities.[33]

Initially, local business leaders sought to reassert control of downtown districts through volunteer brigades, municipal ordinances, and

Table 8 *Offenses Known to Police in Three East Bay Cities, 1939–1948*

Offense	1939	1940	1941	1942
Oakland				
Homicide	12	14	13	13
Robbery	220	127	163	469
Aggravated assault	168	120	132	253
Burglary	1,473	1,430	381	1,286
Grand larceny	218	173	208	295
Petty larceny	3,935	4,088	3,779	4,062
Auto theft	727	598	645	1,134
Total	6,753	6,550	5,321	7,512
Berkeley				
Homicide	—	1	—	3
Robbery	17	6	14	22
Aggravated assault	7	8	14	31
Burglary	256	268	300	279
Grand larceny	29	26	29	53
Petty larceny	808	891	844	873
Auto theft	56	47	68	68
Total	1,173	1,247	1,269	1,329
Alameda				
Homicide	2	—	1	—
Robbery	2	1	2	4
Aggravated assault	—	1	3	—
Burglary	63	50	44	38
Grand larceny	5	5	4	8
Petty larceny	277	218	227	216
Auto theft	45	12	32	40
Total	394	287	313	306

SOURCE: U.S. Department of Justice, Federal Bureau of Investigation, *Uniform Crime Reports,* 1939–48.

business-licensing practices. Such efforts often targeted newcomers, women, and youth, whose increased visibility downtown was a source of growing public concern. Local merchants led the effort—quite literally—to "clean up" their cities. In 1943, numerous complaints about increased trash and human waste prompted the Merchants Committee of the Richmond Chamber of Commerce to organize the "Junior Merchants," a group of local schoolboys who would pick up litter in the downtown area. In Oakland, downtown merchants pressured the city

1943	1944	1945	1946	1947	1948
19	17	25	21	25	15
579	484	752	777	545	450
337	366	587	532	528	431
1,969	1,958	2,187	2,548	2,729	2,281
451	650	870	613	588	495
4,571	4,254	4,818	4,833	4,546	4,866
1,774	1,413	2,056	1,744	1,128	910
9,700	9,142	11,295	11,068	10,089	9,448
2	2	2	6	6	—
41	30	42	54	40	39
32	25	39	50	65	52
351	443	442	487	570	469
74	88	123	112	130	112
892	971	1,018	1,130	1,008	1,089
116	116	211	168	120	94
1,508	1,675	1,877	2,007	1,939	1,855
—	2	2	—	4	—
5	4	6	19	7	7
7	6	20	12	9	4
72	81	105	79	102	60
11	23	23	35	45	26
321	372	588	524	547	435
107	126	185	84	46	44
523	614	929	753	760	576

to hire a crew of high school boys as street sweepers to improve the city's "frowzy" appearance.

The merchants also assumed more responsibility for law enforcement. In Richmond, the Merchants Committee petitioned the city council for additional security and gained authorization for the merchants' patrol service to carry firearms in the summer of 1943. The *Alameda Times-Star* called for the restoration of the Civilian Defense Corps that same year. "A threat of another disaster on the home front—a wave of shocking, indecent public behavior—has risen and it

Table 9 *Persons Charged by Oakland Police, 1939–1948*

Offense	1939	1940	1941	1942
Violent crimes				
Homicide	18	21	16	23
Rape	25	11	21	30
Aggravated assault	29	14	29	40
Other assaults	505	378	386	444
Property crimes				
Robbery	66	46	43	63
Burglary	194	170	178	189
Larceny	537	576	415	557
Auto theft	99	81	117	154
Forgery and counterfeiting	83	57	35	45
Embezzlement and fraud	62	86	59	38
Stolen property	10	10	2	—
Disorderly crimes*				
Weapons	14	16	14	37
Prostitution	210	196	332	368
Sex offenses	67	68	91	72
Family and children	112	108	133	130
Narcotics	46	56	21	38
Liquor	7	3	12	14
Public drunkenness	9,354	8,664	9,367	12,321
Disorderly conduct	228	193	208	271
Vagrancy	752	1,088	1,186	877
Gambling	974	251	301	294
Other	604	605	627	922
Total	13,996	12,698	13,593	16,927

SOURCE: "Return C: Annual Return of Persons Charged," 1939–48, Planning Division, Oakland Police Department, Oakland, California.

*"Weapons" includes carrying and possession; "family and children" includes abuse, neglect, running away, etc.; "narcotics" includes both possession and sale; "liquor" includes illegal sale, possession by minors.

is fitting that the Civilian Defense Corps, organized to keep the home front safe, should be called out to meet it," said the editors. A week later, a group of merchants deputized as auxiliary police began patrolling the streets and public establishments of the city's west end to rid the area of "drunks and disorderlies." In Alameda, Oakland, and

1943	1944	1945	1946	1947	1948
16	27	20	35	46	29
53	55	51	55	52	43
49	69	96	100	93	72
648	723	913	943	858	948
95	104	140	148	189	114
290	314	282	333	334	268
828	707	584	620	594	587
244	251	341	335	228	179
36	30	51	57	63	77
17	26	14	53	25	54
7	7	6	12	4	5
54	69	66	282	278	284
447	560	584	753	339	272
77	127	58	115	80	103
85	59	63	67	136	128
50	68	48	71	56	58
46	77	46	30	20	28
11,591	13,924	13,875	13,431	14,308	12,192
327	361	345	337	385	421
407	592	611	420	472	563
657	820	719	550	380	436
1,338	1,336	774	938	1,122	1,386
17,362	20,306	19,687	19,685	20,062	18,247

Berkeley, police departments enrolled hundreds of new auxiliary members during 1942–1944.[34]

Legislation was another means of controlling public space. Using municipal ordinances and business-licensing practices, prewar elites sought to minimize the undesirable elements of boomtown life while simultaneously raising revenue to support expanded law enforcement and other municipal services. They targeted those businesses—both small and large—that challenged their commercial leadership in the city.

Table 10 *Persons Charged by Oakland Police as Percentage of Total Charges, 1939–1948*

Offense	1939	1940	1941	1942
Violent crimes				
Homicide	.13	.17	.12	.14
Rape	.18	.09	.16	.18
Aggravated assault	.21	.11	.21	.24
Other assaults	3.61	2.98	2.84	2.62
Property crimes				
Robbery	.47	.36	.32	.37
Burglary	1.39	1.34	1.31	1.12
Larceny	3.84	4.54	3.05	3.29
Auto theft	.71	.64	.86	1.13
Forgery and counterfeiting	.59	.45	.26	.27
Embezzlement and fraud	.44	.68	.43	.23
Stolen property	.07	.08	.002	—
Disorderly crimes*				
Weapons	.10	.13	.10	.22
Prostitution	1.50	1.54	2.44	2.17
Sex offenses	.48	.54	.67	.43
Family and children	.80	.85	.98	.77
Narcotics	.33	.44	.16	.23
Liquor	.05	.02	.09	.08
Drunkenness	66.83	68.23	68.92	72.79
Disorderly conduct	1.63	1.52	1.53	1.60
Vagrancy	5.37	8.57	8.73	5.18
Gambling	6.96	1.98	2.22	1.74
Other	4.32	4.77	4.61	5.45

SOURCE: "Return C: Annual Return of Persons Charged," 1939–48, Planning Division, Oakland Police Department, Oakland, California.

*"Weapons" includes carrying and possession; "family and children" includes abuse, neglect, running away, etc.; "narcotics" includes both possession and sale; "liquor" includes illegal sale, possession by minors.

Among the profusion of marginal new businesses, street peddlers were particularly vulnerable to municipal control. In Richmond, the Chamber of Commerce repeatedly petitioned the city council to take action against street peddlers, who were becoming "a nuisance" by "setting up businesses in vacant lots, doorways and lobbies in direct

1943	1944	1945	1946	1947	1948
.09	.13	.09	.18	.23	.16
.31	.27	.26	.28	.26	.24
.28	.33	.49	.51	.46	.39
3.73	3.56	4.64	4.79	4.28	5.20
.55	.51	.71	.75	.94	.62
1.67	1.55	1.43	1.69	1.66	1.47
4.77	3.48	2.97	3.15	2.96	3.22
1.41	1.24	1.73	1.70	1.14	.98
.21	.15	.26	.29	.31	.35
.10	.13	.07	.27	.12	.30
.04	.04	.03	.06	.02	.03
.31	.34	.34	1.43	1.39	1.56
2.58	2.76	2.97	3.83	1.69	1.49
.44	.63	.29	.58	.40	.56
.49	.29	.32	.34	.68	.70
.29	.34	.24	.36	.28	.32
.27	.38	.23	.15	.10	.15
66.76	68.57	70.48	68.23	71.32	66.82
1.88	1.77	1.75	1.71	1.92	2.31
2.34	2.92	3.10	2.13	2.35	3.09
3.78	4.04	3.65	2.79	1.89	2.39
7.71	6.58	3.93	4.77	5.59	7.60

competition with local merchants."[35] Besides competing with "legitimate businesses," street peddlers were predominantly newcomers who were young or female or both. The moral implications of young bootblacks plying their trade in front of barrooms and young women "soliciting" magazine subscriptions from soldiers on the street were not lost on city leaders.

In Richmond, the controversy centered on shoeshine boys, some reportedly as young as six or seven. "A serious moral question has been raised by the large number of boys now on the streets as bootblacks," said the Richmond Merchants Committee. "The boys see and hear many objectionable things in the course of an afternoon or evening along the streets in front of the bars and taverns." The boot-blacks' early exposure to adult life, city leaders maintained, introduced them to mischief and crime. Some merchants claimed that bootblacks defaced downtown shops and engaged in petty thieving, and a Contra Costa County Superior Court judge maintained that many juvenile delinquents started out as bootblacks. In July 1944, Richmond police met with some forty bootblacks to "lay down the law" concerning where and when they might conduct their trade; in October the city council effectively outlawed all street peddling by requiring a twenty-five-dollar-per-day licensing fee.[36]

Other East Bay cities passed similar antipeddling laws. In Alameda the city council enacted an ordinance prohibiting fortune-telling within city limits in late 1943. The city provided refunds to those who possessed current permits (mostly gypsy women), ending their livelihoods and forcing them out of the city.[37] Richmond, Oakland, and Alameda all enacted ordinances barring magazine soliciting, a street trade commonly practiced by young women. Oakland adopted its anti-soliciting law in 1943 following a series of newspaper articles complaining of "little girls soliciting magazines on the street." As it turned out, the "little girls" were not so little. Under the new law, Oakland authorities ordered eight women, aged eighteen to twenty-one, to leave the city in December 1943. The women had been living in downtown hotels and earning money from civilians and servicemen who were, the *Oakland Observer* said, "lonely and homesick enough to welcome attention even from a vendor."[38] Paralleling rising fears about female sexual misconduct, the concern over women's "soliciting" was a reaction to the new economic and social independence of women in war boomtowns.

The expansion of commercial amusements also attracted legislative attention. Oakland, Richmond, and several smaller East Bay towns increased their tax on traveling carnivals to prohibitive levels. Richmond's fee increased to $250 per day from $150 amid complaints from the local ministerial alliance that tent shows harmed "the moral and spiritual relations of the community." Oakland's tax jumped even more remarkably—to $500 per day from $250 per week. Applicants were also required to submit letters of recommendation from other cities, vouching for their company's moral reputation. City officials hoped to discourage carnivals from visiting Oakland, claiming that they included "gambling and immoral exhibits that contributed to the delinquency of minors." Local movie theater owners, whose business was in direct competition with the carnivals, were key participants in drafting the ordinance.[39]

Theater owners and other entrepreneurs of commercial amusements, however, also fell victim to municipal taxation. As part of a new revenue-raising plan in 1943, the Richmond city council proposed a two-cent-per-ticket amusement tax on admissions to movies, dances, and other entertainment and a five-dollar-per-month tax on all jukeboxes and pool and billiard tables. Oakland and Berkeley also passed commercial amusement taxes as well as taxes on hotels, rooming houses, advertising trucks, and transient street performers. These taxes were effective through the duration of the war and were designed, said a Richmond city council member, "to obtain revenue from those people who directly or indirectly were responsible for the need of additional police and fire protection." Rather than increase property taxes on prewar residents, the city raised revenue by taxing morally suspect commercial activities patronized by war workers.[40] Local governments thus collected thousands of dollars to expand municipal services and finance their wartime law-and-order campaigns.

Restoring Public Order

Bolstered by publicity from the 1943 grand jury crime probes, law and order became a major concern in the East Bay. Although violent crime had been the rallying cry for the investigations, the law-and-order campaigns were equally concerned with maintaining certain standards of public behavior. Intoxication, promiscuity, and other breaches of middle-class decorum seemed to preoccupy local leaders. In the minds of many officials, the increase in major crime was directly linked to the problem of "public indecency."

The link between crime and public indecency was clearly evident in the final grand jury report and in subsequent police rhetoric. Much of the twenty-seven-page report dealt with the role of alcohol consumption, promiscuity, and gambling in fueling more serious crime. According to Oakland Police Chief Brodie A. Wallman, many violent attacks and robberies were due to the intoxication of both victims and criminals. Naive newcomers who displayed their cash in bars and gambling houses, police noted, became easy marks for robbers, pickpockets, and con artists. Authorities likewise attributed cases of rape and sexual assault to the "promiscuous" behavior of women in public. By blaming the victims, East Bay authorities justified a campaign against "immoral" public behavior.[41]

Efforts to control public space and behavior targeted black and white migrants (particularly southerners) as well as women and youth—precisely those groups whose relative status and opportunities had increased as a result of the war boom. With defense wages to spend, these groups asserted their claims to public space and became more active in the social life of the streets. Often their behavior violated established community norms, prompting efforts by prewar elites to discipline them.

East Bay officials cited migrants, more than any other group, as the source of crime and disorder. A survey of Oakland arrest records from 1940 and 1944 reveals that newcomers and racial minorities did in fact represent a relatively larger proportion of those arrested during the war. The percentage of newcomers (those in residence in the Bay Area three years or less) increased from 39 percent in 1940 to 54 percent in 1944. The percentage of nonwhite arrestees also rose, from 20 percent in 1940 to 28 percent in 1944.[42]

Once again, however, statistics can be misleading. First, we should note that urban newcomers and racial minorities had always made up a disproportionately large share of those arrested in Oakland and that war migration had naturally augmented that trend. Furthermore, the migrant population was disproportionately young and male compared with the nonmigrant group. Even though women outnumbered men in the migrant population, the sex ratio was considerably higher among migrants (94 men per 100 women) than among nonmigrants (88 per 100). Among Bay Area males aged twenty to twenty-nine—an especially high-risk population for crime and disorder—migrants actually outnumbered natives, constituting 52 percent of the total. Migrants were also the most likely to suffer from inadequate schools and recreation services, weak ties with churches and other community institutions, and a smaller local support network of family and friends. Given these social and demographic factors, it is not surprising that migrants were overrepresented in East Bay police records.[43]

These extenuating factors, however, rarely surfaced in the public discourse on crime. Instead, city leaders relied on moral explanations and derogatory racial and cultural stereotypes to explain what they claimed was a dangerous crime wave. Migrant immorality—drunkenness, gambling, and other disorderly behavior—thus became the prime target of the law-and-order campaigns.

According to local newspapers, one of the most serious problems plaguing East Bay cities was drunkenness and disorderly conduct, particularly among migrant men. In 1942, these communities began petitioning the State Board of Equalization to limit the number of liquor licenses issued in their area. As a revenue-collecting agency with close ties to the liquor industry, the Equalization Board was unresponsive to these requests, choosing instead to limit the hours and conditions of service. In 1943, the Board restricted the hours of sale from 10:00 A.M. to midnight and mandated that food be served in all establishments selling liquor. The food requirement was designed to eliminate the rowdy "saloon" atmosphere, but many bars sidestepped the requirement by posting limited menus but continuing to sell liquor almost exclusively.

Local frustration and increasing pressure from federal authorities prompted East Bay cities to launch their own campaigns against drunkenness. During the grand jury probe, federal authorities warned tavern owners to "clean up or close up," charging that drunkenness was abetting absenteeism at the shipyards. The *Alameda Times-Star* agreed, denouncing "shiftless, irresponsible fellows who [did] little else but go out on 'binges' which usually land[ed] them in jail, at the expense of the city, after every pay day." Tavern owners denied their culpability, claiming, "The present crime wave has been wrongly attached to our business." They urged the authorities to go after public intoxicants who bought packaged liquor. Liquor stores and their customers, they claimed, were the real source of the crime problem.[44]

While federal authorities continued their surveillance of tavern owners, local officials focused on the consumers of alcohol. Although most newcomers were law-abiding citizens, said one local newspaper, a minority of them were "making displays of themselves," leaving downtown streets unsafe for normal citizens. "Men and women, obviously under the influence of liquor, careening down the sidewalks, lying in gutters, propped up in hallways and entrances to stores . . . have become too familiar a sight," said the *Richmond Independent*. "This city is not used to having these alcoholic playboys annoying men and women going about their business," the editors explained. "If we cannot accommodate them in our jail we will have to build a concentration camp." The *Times-Star* was equally insistent, demanding that drunks be put in jail and "ordered from the city if they continue[d] to carouse in the streets."[45]

With this mandate, East Bay police rounded up hundreds of drunks, vagrants, and other "suspicious" characters off the streets each week. Arrests for drunkenness increased in Richmond from 56 in January 1940 to 469 in January 1943, a more than eightfold increase at a time when the population had grown roughly fourfold. Rather than over-load the courts, the police department established a new streamlined processing center where defendants could gain quick release by paying a $25 fine. In 1944–1945, Richmond collected $361,500 in misde-meanor fines, primarily from traffic and drunkenness charges, com-pared with only $7,800 in 1939–1940. Misdemeanor fines helped to raise revenue, accounting for nearly 10 percent of the city's gross in-come in 1944–1945.[46]

The Alameda police court, meanwhile, increased bail for public drunkenness to $50 from $25 and instituted a $50 fine for throwing liquor or beer bottles on the streets. Arrests for drunkenness increased nearly sevenfold between 1941 and 1943. In Oakland, police cracked down on Seventh Street in west Oakland and on Broadway's skid row. The number of persons charged with public drunkenness increased by 61 percent between 1940 and 1944, with a record 13,924 persons charged in the latter year (see table 9). Police Judge Joseph A. Kennedy, who meted out ten-day sentences to drunken shipyard work-ers, remarked, "I hope they lose their jobs." According to Police Chief Wallman, fully 65 percent of Oakland's jail population in 1943 was serving time for drunkenness or vagrancy.[47]

Police cracked down on gambling as well. Authorities regularly broke up dice games in the shipyards, on transit lines, and in down-town bars and pool halls. The number of persons charged with illegal gambling in Oakland increased from a low of 251 in 1940 to 820 in 1944—or from 1.98 percent to 4.04 percent of total police charges (see tables 9 and 10). Interestingly, many of the tip-offs came from the wives and mothers of shipyard workers whose spouses or sons had lost paychecks in such games.[48] These findings suggest that war worker families may also have used the system to control unruly children and spouses.

Migrant war workers reacted adamantly against the criminal stigma. According to a journalist visiting Richmond in 1945, the law-and-order campaigns "created tenseness and hostility between shipyard workers and townspeople. Many newcomers felt (and still feel) that they were persecuted and stigmatized as hardened lawbreakers. 'If you wait for your wife on the station platform you're picked up as a vagrant.'" Even the Kaiser newspaper, *Fore 'N' Aft,* dropped its usual upbeat tone to chide local newspapers for their treatment of shipyard workers. "But let a shipyard worker get off the straight and narrow and you get three-inch headlines '*Shipyard* Worker Does This,' '*Shipyard* Worker Does That,'" complained one Kaiser employee. "They don't mind giving *all* the shipbuilders in the Bay Area a bad name because a few guys get out of line."[49]

Fueled by growing racial anxieties over black migration, the backlash against African-American migrants was even more vehement. Local officials attributed the wartime increase in crime—especially violent street crime—to the influx of black southerners. "It is very possible that the trouble comes from immigrant Negroes from the South, who are held well under control in the South but, coming North, have found themselves thrilled with a new 'freedom,'" said the *Oakland Observer.* Richmond authorities echoed this explanation, adding that the black migrant, in discovering the limits of this new freedom, "encounters many disappointments and frustrations, to which he may have an aggressive reaction." Throughout 1943, Oakland newspapers featured articles on blacks attacking servicemen and war workers in west Oakland and periodically denounced "crime waves" perpetrated by "roving Negroes."[50]

Several prominent leaders from the prewar black community joined the newspapers in denouncing the west Oakland crime problem. Shocked by the wartime transformation of their neighborhood, the Baptist Ministers' Union and a number of black businessmen appealed to the city to curb the disorder. Matthew G. Laurence, president of the black west Oakland Improvement Association, told the 1943 grand jury that local residents were "afraid to walk the streets at night because of these armed desperadoes." There were so many stabbings on Seventh Street, he said, that old-timers had renamed it "Cutting Boulevard." Laurence proposed that the city hire black police officers to staff a new west Oakland police station and called for a 7:00 P.M. closing for all taverns and a complete termination of all pool halls and other trouble spots.[51]

Laurence may have recognized the "crime wave" as an opportunity to open civil service jobs for blacks; the city's response, however, was a repressive campaign to clean up west Oakland streets and their black residents. During the grand jury probe, Oakland police conducted the first of many wartime sweeps of west Oakland, arresting hundreds of black residents on charges of vagrancy and draft evasion. Police concentrated on taverns, cafes, juke joints, and rooming houses, sealing off the entrances and searching the occupants for weapons. Men who were unable to produce draft cards were sent to jail. Police also hounded groups of black men congregating on street corners, forcing them to disperse or face arrest. With the aid of the FBI, which coordinated efforts against draft evasion, police rounded up as many as 250 men per night.[52]

Arrest records indicate that police selectively enforced the draft law against black and Hispanic men. Of thirty-eight arrests for violations of the Selective Service Act found in the 1944 sample survey, twenty-three cases, or 61 percent, involved nonwhite men. Furthermore, in 60 percent of the minority arrests, draft law violations were the sole charge compared with only 7 percent of white arrests. In nearly every case, police charged white draft violators incident to arrest on other charges such as drunkenness or assault. By contrast, police arrested nonwhite men (usually in groups of two or more) during street sweeps in west Oakland, where draft card checks served as a form of systematic harassment. Police also rounded up hundreds of "suspicious" individuals each year—typically nonwhites in white neighborhoods. Between 1940 and 1944, arrests by Oakland police for mere "suspicion" increased to 1,228 from 327, a gain of more than 275 percent.[53]

Most black arrests occurred in west Oakland, but more subtle forms of racial control emerged in the downtown district as black war workers joined the wartime rush for shopping and entertainment. Prewar East Bay cities had entertained black residents in certain downtown theaters and dance halls, but the boomtowns offered a much greater array of activities that black migrants were anxious to sample. The conservative *Oakland Observer* first sounded the alarm in May 1943 when it announced that blacks were now patronizing "downtown Oakland restaurants where formerly no local Negro ever dreamed of going." It continued, "Now we see Negroes all over the place." Despite denunciations of west Oakland as a "danger zone," the *Observer* rebuked blacks for "butting into the white civilization instead of keeping in the perfectly orderly and convenient Negro civilization of Oakland." Clearly, black residents were being chastised for crossing unmarked racial boundaries in downtown public spaces.[54]

Racial mixing in downtown establishments sometimes provoked violent conflicts that fueled racial hostilities. A black man was stabbed in a Richmond restaurant in 1943 for refusing to give up his booth to a white patron. Blacks were often warned away or attacked for entering white neighborhoods and gathering spots. Racial tensions also surfaced in a series of disturbances at the Oakland Auditorium, culminating in a street riot in May 1944. After some five thousand black swing fans were turned away from a sold-out Cab Calloway dance, the restless crowd began smashing windows and doors. The violence recommenced after the show, when a fight broke out between black fans and white sailors on a crowded streetcar. Before long, hundreds of onlookers joined in, and the melee spread down Broadway. Truck loads of city and military police were brought in to quell the disturbance, which ended with one dead and four wounded. City officials denied the disturbance was a race riot, dubbing it "a spontaneous outburst" due to inadequate transportation and security personnel.[55]

The Twelfth Street riot, though, had obvious racial implications. The *Oakland Observer* promptly denounced the outbreak, blaming it on black migrants "who insist[ed] on barging into the white man." In order to prevent future riots, they advised "orderly and respectable Negroes to tell the newcomers about the facts of life." Some black old-timers agreed that newcomers were misbehaving in public. The violence downtown, some said, was due to newcomers, "who hadn't yet learned how to behave."[56]

At the heart of these derogatory comments was an element of truth about the impact of migration. The sheer numbers of black war migrants made African-Americans more visible in East Bay cities. In downtown areas, the arrival of black southerners, unfamiliar with local mores regulating race relations, disrupted the established social order of the city. The unwritten rules and unmarked boundaries that had governed race relations since the turn of the century were now transgressed daily. As the sociologist Charles S. Johnson pointed out, southern migrants had to adjust to the racial system of the West, which, though not legally sanctioned, was confusingly similar to southern segregation.[57]

White businesspeople responded to the black influx by attempting to codify segregation measures for public establishments. After the 1944 riot, Oakland newspapers advertised separate Monday night "colored dances" at the Oakland Auditorium for all black swing band shows. Weekend performances at Sweets, meanwhile, were now reserved for white audiences. In downtown Oakland and Richmond and along San Pablo Avenue, "White Trade Only" signs appeared in many storefronts. Local bowling alleys instituted regulations prohibiting mixed teams, and Berkeley Bowl established two segregated lanes for black bowlers. Even in death, black residents were segregated. Contra

Costa's Sunset Cemetery, an integrated burial ground in the prewar era, closed its gates to black residents during World War II.

Championing the prosegregation position, the *Oakland Observer* applauded such actions and recommended they be extended to other businesses. "We don't know who or what group will have the initiative and guts to make a stand for the segregation of the colored people," said the editors, "but we might suggest that the motion picture houses could, without causing undue hardship, designate one section for our negro population." Movie theater owners did not heed the *Observer's* advice, but many other businesses did. Even local Tolerance Committees, formed by government and business leaders in the wake of the Detroit race riot, favored plans to "give the Negroes a district of their own, amusements of their own."[58]

Some old-time black residents resented the southern migrants, holding them responsible for resurgent racism. In his study of black San Francisco, Charles S. Johnson found that nearly half of old-time black residents disapproved of newcomers because they "augment[ed] racial difficulties in the city." Douglas Daniels found similar sentiments among old-timers that he interviewed in the East Bay. A few middle-class blacks even spoke out publicly against the small percentage of migrants "who were evidently of little value in their home towns and obviously had nothing worthwhile to contribute to the California commonwealth."

Some black old-timers proposed education and social settlement work for southern newcomers, much as the Urban League had done in northern cities during World War I. What was needed, they felt, was training "in civic pride and social responsibility by the better element of our own race." Berkeley old-timer Frances Albrier helped found one such group called the Little Citizens Study and Welfare Club. Using local church pulpits, black old-timers sought to educate newcomers on their dress, language, behavior, "and all those tiny things . . . they should know." Longtime black residents of San Francisco founded a similar group known as the Carpe Diem Club that taught newcomers "good behavior" including home and yard maintenance.[59]

Despite the middle-class paternalism evident in their approach, the "Big Citizens" found that they had things to learn from the newcomers. One Oakland old-timer, Eleanor Watkins, said that southern migrants had pointed out that the Bay Area was not as liberal as many had believed. Likewise, the historian Nathan Huggins explained that with the war "much of the ground for complacency disappeared." In the long run, old-timers and newcomers would unite in the struggle against racism. During the war years, old-time black leaders like C. L. Dellums and the Reverend H. T. S. Johnson began working with local black ministers, the CIO, and the Communist party to fight discrimination and segregation. Their work laid the foundation for the civil rights activities that would blossom in the postwar era.[60]

Women, Youth, and the Family

Working women and youth, the other major newcomer groups to the lucrative war economy, were also stigmatized as law-breakers in war boomtowns. While authorities were focusing on the immoral behavior of newcomers, they also began to realize that local women and teenagers, flush with new defense earnings, were also contributing to "public indecency." Although there are no age or sex breakdowns of annual crime data, Oakland police records sampled from 1940 and 1944 show that arrests of female and juvenile (under sixteen) offenders actually decreased as a percentage of total arrests. Female arrests fell from 14 percent to 11 percent, and juvenile arrests fell from 11 percent to 8 percent. Such findings suggest that we look beneath the surface of crime rhetoric to explore why the behavior of women and youth appeared as such a threat to public order.[61]

Federal and local authorities held women, in particular, accountable for a surge in sexual misconduct. Since World War I, the federal government had focused considerable attention on prostitution and venereal disease in cities located near military bases, and campaigns directed at those problems reemerged with a vengeance during World War II. In Oakland, federal authorities noted the growing activity of street-walkers and other women engaged in casual prostitution among servicemen and war workers. Under the May Act of 1941, which pressured local authorities to enforce "moral zones" around military installations, the city enacted stiffer penalties for prostitution and allocated additional funds for vice investigations. Even women merely under suspicion for prostitution were incarcerated and subjected to mandatory VD testing while their male customers went free. State and local authorities also cracked down on "B girls," or bar girls, who received a commission from management for every drink bought for them by hopeful male customers. The B girls, authorities believed, took advantage of naive servicemen and were likely to drift into prostitution.[62]

Data from the Oakland police department clearly demonstrate the growing concern with prostitution. The number of women booked on this charge increased from 196 in 1940 to 560 in 1944; in this same period, prostitution cases grew from 1.54 percent to 2.76 percent of all police charges (see tables 9 and 10). Although we will never know the actual rate of prostitution, the visibility of the practice seems to have decreased during the war as a result of stepped-up enforcement. In contrast with the prewar era, when Oakland vice officers made most prostitution arrests on the streets, the majority of wartime arrests occurred in hotel rooms and other private spaces. Such findings suggest that increased public enforcement had driven prostitution indoors.[63] Since the beginning of the war, in fact, police and private security forces had closely monitored likely contact points—bars, dance halls, and other social gathering spots. Such locales attracted not only professional prostitutes but also the more numerous young "amateurs" toward whom police increasingly directed their attention.

As in the nation generally, East Bay authorities were less concerned with organized prostitution than with casual promiscuity. According to an Oakland health officer, Dr. E. F. Carlson, certain young women were "rather enthusiastic amateurs, . . . girls who [were] largely found in bars and taverns and dance halls. Sometimes pick-ups [were] made on the street and in the theatres." These women, noted the Oakland police chief, were "primarily attracted by the uniform" of the serviceman, but they also sought companionship with male war workers "lonely like themselves."[64]

Known as "charity girls" in the working-class city of the early twentieth century, free-spirited young women who exchanged drinks and entertainment for sexual favors reemerged in World War II as "Victory girls." These women, who reportedly entered sexual relations with servicemen out of "misplaced patriotism," garnered considerable media attention during the war. Federal authorities spearheaded the campaign against such behavior, encouraging local authorities to clamp down on promiscuity and expand mandatory VD testing to all women arrested in morals cases. The Social Protection Division of the federal Office of Community War Services employed a broad definition of promiscuity, which included "lewd behavior, lascivious speech, and frequenting bars."[65]

Federal authorities feared that promiscuity would spread venereal disease among servicemen and war workers, but East Bay cities had their own reasons for cooperating with the program. Many residents, shocked by the transformation of their home towns, resented women's aggressive public behavior in the social life of war boomtowns. Local observers frequently commented on the impunity of young women who "picked up" male companions in bars, on the street, and on transit lines. One barroom spectator related: "I saw women enter these drinking emporiums . . . unescorted. I watched them pick up and be picked up. I saw some of them matching their new contacts for drinks. I saw them after an hour of drinking, go out with their arms around men who were utter strangers an hour previous. I think we know where it all ends." A naval chaplain was equally outraged by young women in Alameda and Oakland who were "chasing down soldiers" and "propositioning them."[66]

Such behavior was nothing new. Kathy Peiss has documented the activities of working-class "charity girls" in New York City as far back as the turn of the century, and Oakland no doubt had always offered similar opportunities. The war, however, vastly expanded these opportunities by freeing many young people from the watchful eyes of parents and small towns back home. In addition, a growing number of middle-class and married women now entered the wartime social world. As one Oakland man put it: "Lower class and common girls have always been cheap, . . . [but nowadays] girls are making fools out of themselves on the streets all over. . . . The so-called nice girls turn cheap, low class, and common in the night, while in the daytime they act as innocent girls."[67] As his comment suggests, the anonymous climate of boomtown nightlife allowed even middle-class women to participate in casual socializing and sexual liaisons. New wartime jobs offered them a socially acceptable—even valued—work role while providing them the income and independence to strike out on their own after hours.

During the war, the shortage of men and the separation of many couples encouraged women to seek more social outlets. The evening outings of married women, particularly in an area with an abundance of migrant men and servicemen, caused grave concern among local residents. "The majority of married soldiers and fathers get the reports of their so-called beloved wives now having the time of their lives," said an Oakland soldier. "Instead of gadding about, let them take care of the children and home, and spend a little more time encouraging their own G.I. Joe, instead of some home wrecker." Newspapers railed against dimly lit bars where servicemen's wives and their "boyfriends" could meet without fear of being identified by neighbors. As a result, women married to servicemen faced constant suspicion. "A service wife doesn't have a chance," said one woman. "She can't even say a friendly hello to a brother-in-law or cousin before she is condemned."[68]

The public behavior of women in war boomtowns was deemed responsible for other ills as well. One old-timer claimed that the upsurge of barroom brawls and violence was due to the presence of women. "The police records are full of brawls, stabbings, the result of drunken jealousy. And all these things because women frequent the saloons of today." Local officials also tended to blame women for the increase in rape and sexual assault cases that plagued most war boomtowns. They warned women to avoid "questionable public places" and "pick-up acquaintances." Some people even claimed that women accepting pick-ups were abetting the crime wave and should be punished along with male offenders.[69]

Public officials responded to women's "promiscuity" by controlling their access to bars and other public spaces. During the 1943 grand jury probe, military, federal, and state authorities met with Alameda County tavern owners to set policies on escorting and other conditions of service. A State Equalization Board member, James H. Quinn, vowed to ban promiscuous women from Alameda County bars and urged tavern owners to deny service to all unaccompanied women. The State Board also forbade women to work as bartenders despite the labor shortage. Noncomplying establishments were placed off-limits to servicemen and had their liquor licenses suspended or revoked.[70]

With only a few exceptions, bars throughout the East Bay cooperated in this system of self-regulation. Tavern owners regulated the chaperoning of women customers, posting signs reading "Attention Ladies, Unescorted Women Must Remain Without Escorts (see plate 21)." Many owners also hired private detectives, who worked with local police to "root out undesirables." In addition, both Richmond and Oakland hired additional policewomen to supervise women's activities at certain bars, dance halls, and other "contact points." By controlling public space in this manner, East Bay cities attempted to discipline women who had "gotten out of hand" during the war years.[71]

Even more unruly, in the eyes of old-timers, were the young people who became so visible on the streets of war boomtowns. The wartime crusade against juvenile delinquency was, in fact, a more emotionally charged version of the adult law-and-order campaigns. In a series of 1943 editorials, the *Richmond Independent* revealed the parallel concerns of the juvenile delinquency campaign while expressing its dismay at the wild youth that congregated in downtown streets:

Take a walk down Macdonald avenue between First and Seventh streets. . . .
You will see children in their teens drinking out of bottles while standing on
the sidewalk. . . . You will hear cuss words that you probably never have heard
in a blue moon—shouted across the sidewalk while respectable citizens are
passing by. . . . Fist fights are not an uncommon occurrence in this area. Blood
is spilled on the sidewalks regularly.

Such immoral public behavior, the *Independent* said, led to gang activity and more serious crime. Younger children, including the much-
derided bootblacks, were adopting this behavior as well. "The
strangest part," said the editors, "is they are confident they can take
care of themselves."[72]

War boomtowns did in fact foster greater autonomy among youth.
East Bay cities provided ample economic opportunities and a fluid social environment that allowed many teenagers to pass as adults. Youth
work programs freed many teenagers from all but minimal school attendance. Young people now spent less time in school and more time
earning and spending their income, making them more visible participants in the public life of the community. Younger children also enjoyed greater autonomy, as multiple school sessions released thousands
of grade school students onto the streets each day. Many headed downtown for movie houses, eateries, and street corners, where their presence camouflaged a growing number of truants, runaways, and other
rebellious youth attracted to war boomtowns.

For many East Bay residents, the public behavior of youth in such
a setting was too uncomfortably close to that of many adults. Earlier
financial independence and increased autonomy threatened to dis-
rupt traditional age hierarchies and to undermine parental authority.
"Scores have paychecks larger than any of their fathers ever had," noted
the *Oakland Tribune*. "It's going to their heads." Teachers complained
of "impudence" among students, and law enforcement officials warned
of a breakdown in parental authority. "Discipline on the home front
has fallen to the point where children are telling their parents what to
do," said a local navy official. "Parents must put a stop to this practice
of allowing their children to do just as they please." City leaders encouraged youth to participate in the war effort, but they were shocked
and dismayed by other forms of social independence that developed as
a result.[73]

Although the discovery of juvenile delinquency dates back to the
Progressive Era, it took on new meanings during the 1940s under the
impact of war. As the historian James Gilbert has pointed out, juvenile
delinquency became a code word for shifts in adolescent behavior

of which many adults disapproved. A sixteen-year-old Oakland girl recognized this fact: "We're not delinquents. That's just a word that people have come into the habit of using to describe children between the ages of twelve and eighteen."[74]

In the East Bay, the campaign against juvenile delinquency reflected anxieties, at least initially, about migration, and ultimately and more generally about the erosion of family life and women's role therein. As public attention focused on juvenile delinquency in 1942–1943, local officials assumed that migrant families were to blame. Contra Costa County Probation Officer Frederica Edgar made the outrageous claim that "an influx of moron parents into the county [was] responsible for the delinquency increase among the younger children." Such parents, she said, were impossible to train in proper child care techniques. An Alameda County Juvenile Court judge maintained that many delinquents came from regions with lower moral standards, mentioning Oklahoma specifically. Other observers echoed the "sudden prosperity" theory, which alleged that migrant parents squandered their time and money in bars, allowing their children to run wild. "The teen-age problem," noted one social worker, "grows directly out of the parents' neglect and lack of respect for the neighboring community."[75]

As in the adult morality campaigns, local authorities responded with attempts to control young people's access to public space. Following the advice of federal authorities and the example of several large western cities, Richmond officials passed a curfew law in February 1943 requiring all children under sixteen to be off the streets by ten o'clock. Later that year, the law was expanded to include sixteen and seventeen year olds, providing penalties for parents of up to five hundred dollars or six months in jail. In addition, the city enacted an antitruancy law with the same penalties for parents of children found attending movies or other admission-charging amusements between 9:00 A.M. and 5:00 P.M.[76]

Enforcement of the new laws proved to be ineffective and controversial. According to a federal field representative in September 1943, Richmond police believed that the curfew was "not effective because of the lack of cooperation from parents." Although some parents may have been just apathetic, as police maintained, many housing project residents resented police harassment of their teenage children, who were regularly picked up while returning from swing shift jobs and organized youth programs.[77] Such bad feelings only aggravated an already rocky relationship between newcomers and old-timers.

Perhaps because of the problems of public policing, Richmond authorities tried a more focused campaign aimed at families of truant children. In September 1943, the city appointed a deputy sheriff to apprehend habitual truants and arrest their parents. Ironically, the first case involved a longtime resident of the south side whose fifteen-year-old son had reportedly missed seventy-six days of school during the past year. Over the next four months, authorities arrested fifteen other parents, both old-timers and newcomers. High-profile publicity in local newspapers accompanied each arrest, offering these cases as examples to other "delinquent" parents. The campaign faded from public view in early 1944, its mission ostensibly accomplished.[78]

In Alameda County, authorities took a more moderate approach to control juvenile offenses. Police in both Alameda and Oakland relied on vagrancy, immorality, and other regulations governing public behavior to remove youth from the streets at night. Police then administered "a verbal spanking" and required parents to retrieve their children at the station. Oakland officials also secured the cooperation of local theater owners in barring admission to minors after 9:00 P.M. Underage drinking in bars, however, continued to be a major problem. The State Board of Equalization clamped down on Alameda County youth in 1944, plastering thousands of posters in streetcars and public places warning minors of a five-hundred-dollar fine or six months in jail for the purchase or consumption of alcohol.[79]

As the war progressed, local authorities also realized that the juvenile problem was not confined to migrants' children. At a meeting on juvenile delinquency in November 1943, the assistant superintendent of Oakland schools, Herbert Stolz, specifically warned against blaming migrants, explaining that their rate of delinquency was no higher than that of old-timers. Newspaper items confirmed that juvenile delinquency was striking at "better than average homes," including those of local police officials and school administrators. Alarmed by the rise of misbehavior among children of longtime residents, some observers attributed delinquency to a general wartime atmosphere of abandon and aggressiveness.[80]

Most commonly, though, local leaders feared that unruly adults—primarily newcomers—were corrupting the city's youth. Noting the wild antics of shipyard workers and sailors in Alameda, a sociologist studying the city's juvenile problem claimed: "The youth of the city cannot help noticing the apparent disregard of morals on the part of so many adults." The editors of the *Richmond Independent* concurred, denouncing "an adult element in Richmond, brought in by the war, whose company is not conducive to the welfare of the city's youth. This element frequents the streets at night and is coming into too close a contact with impressive youngsters."[81] Old-timers, then, viewed juvenile delinquency as a conduit through which migrant immorality spread from war worker settlements to other parts of the community, threatening the sanctity of old-timers' homes and families.

The belief that juvenile delinquency was spreading throughout the community was graphically illustrated in a report issued by the Oakland Council of Social Agencies in 1944. Relying on a geographical model developed by University of Chicago sociologists, the Oakland study charted juvenile delinquency arrests by census districts.[82] The maps showed the highest levels of delinquency ("red zones") in older waterfront neighborhoods in west Oakland and around the estuary. These were mainly industrial areas that coincided with the migrant settlement zones discussed in chapter 4. Comparative statistics for 1940 and 1943, however, showed a steady expansion of red zones inland and eastward along the Oakland waterfront. "Juvenile delinquency has moved to East Oakland as far as San Leandro in tracts near the estuary, while remaining a problem in the old critical areas," the report concluded. Thereafter, the troubling "eastward expanse of delinquency" became a central concern in the juvenile delinquency debate. As one community leader warned, "The problem has spread geographically as well as numerically, from a comparatively restricted area on the west Oakland waterfront to practically all sections of the city."[83]

To arrest this expansion of juvenile delinquency, Oakland officials launched a neighborhood-based campaign of reform and recreation under the banner "the Oakland Way." Eschewing public policing of juveniles and other hard-line approaches, State Superior Court Judge Frank M. Ogden led a coalition of criminal justice officials, school administrators, city recreation workers, and youth group leaders in an effort to create alternative community activities for youth. Their pilot project was Arroyo Viejo, a community center in east Oakland that encouraged youth-initiated dances, athletics, and other recreation activities under the slogan "Off the Streets." Organized on the neighborhood level, Arroyo Viejo was designed as a youth-led counterorganization to juvenile gangs.[84] Interestingly, the center was not located in a "red zone" but in an area with only average population growth and juvenile delinquency increases. However, it did lie just inland of several new housing areas and emergent red zones along the waterfront, suggesting its role as a perceived bulwark against encroaching juvenile delinquency. Arroyo Viejo soon became a model for several other neighborhood recreation programs founded in Oakland during and after the war.

The Oakland Way was a liberal alternative to the hard-line approach to juvenile delinquency. As in Richmond, San Francisco, and other West Coast cities, conservative forces in Oakland had mobilized during the war in support of youth curfews and other repressive measures. With the beginning of the defense buildup in 1939–1940, Mary Dunaway, a local club woman and military officer's wife, founded the Alameda County Coordinating Council on Juvenile Delinquency. Dunaway's group, representing fifty-nine women's clubs, church groups, and other civic organizations, demanded that the city council enact a 10:30 P.M. youth curfew, an ordinance closing all public parks to minors by 9:00 P.M., and a system of mandatory identification cards for all "girls" aged twelve to twenty-six.

Following more than a year of stormy city council meetings, the mayor appointed a special committee on juvenile crime prevention to investigate the curfew issue. The group included Dunaway, Judge Ogden, and eight other appointees. In September 1944, the committee recommended against the measure and urged the repeal of an outdated 1881 law. They questioned the constitutionality of such laws, fearing they would make "technical criminals of children following accepted standards of conduct." Furthermore, they wrote, "The passage of a law which is intended to be discretionary in its enforcement . . . would only tend to create a disrespect for all laws." Despite claims by Dunaway that the report was "a whitewash," the council acted on the committee's findings, making Oakland one of the few West Coast cities to reject the curfew in theory and practice.[85]

Underlying the more progressive reform currents, however, was a parallel movement in the later war years to prevent juvenile delinquency by correcting potential problems within the home and family. Cases of child neglect and abandonment first started appearing in local newspapers in late 1943 and were daily fare by mid-1944. At that time, Oakland officials proclaimed a crackdown on neglectful parents, who, they said, were "the real source of juvenile delinquency." Over the next few months, local newspapers featured dozens of front-page accounts of child neglect and abandonment by war worker parents and especially by working mothers.[86]

The most sensational child neglect case came out of Richmond in January 1944 when police arrested an Oklahoma couple working in the shipyards. The parents had allegedly tethered their six-year-old daughter by a rope in their kitchen to prevent her from wandering away while they worked the swing shift. The parents, who left sandwiches and milk on the table, denied any wrongdoing. Police Judge Leo Marcollo sentenced the couple to ninety days in jail, stating, "This sentence should serve as an example to people who think more of the money they earn in the shipyards than their children." In an editorial titled "Children and Money," the *Richmond Independent* applauded the sentence and recommended that such parents "have their children taken away from them."[87]

Publicized cases like these were intended as warnings to other war worker families, but they also helped natives contain their anxieties about their own children and families. As Linda Gordon has pointed out, child neglect is a recurring theme in family history, one which is subject to tremendous political manipulation. Historically, the notion of child neglect has been intertwined with fears about changes in family life resulting from the growing autonomy of women and children. In World War II boomtowns, publicity about child neglect that focused on defense migrants reassured natives that the roots of juvenile delinquency lay outside their own families. As one old-timer wrote at the height of the neglect outcry, "practically every single case of child abandonment and child neglect and cruelty was traced back to parents that hail from some other state." Juvenile delinquency was spreading throughout the city, but the source of the problem was now seen as emanating from the "inadequate homes" of migrant war workers.[88]

Working mothers also figured prominently in neglect and abandonment cases publicized in 1944. Many of the cases involved single mothers who left their children in boarding homes or with social welfare agencies while they sought work or housing. Others involved married working women who left children to shift for themselves, often with older siblings in charge. Such cases prompted increasing criticism of women's war work and demands that working mothers be required to show proof of proper child care before being hired. Not coincidentally, such sentiments grew just as mobilization efforts decelerated and patriotic rhetoric about women's war work began to fade. The use of the concept of neglect to explain juvenile delinquency, then, was influenced by the decline of support for women's work outside the home.[89]

In focusing on child neglect, public authorities shifted their enforcement efforts from the public arena to the private one of the home and family. In mid-1944, Berkeley officials initiated the "Flying Squadron" program, jointly sponsored by the city and the school department. This program featured home visitation and counseling for problem youth and their parents. With the authority to enter private homes, trained counselors were directed to "tell the parents what they should do to correct conditions, advising them as to supervision and discipline." Oakland and Richmond authorities also expanded efforts to root out neglect cases by adding more social welfare workers to their police departments.[90] Conservatives and reformers discovered they agreed on the strategy of placing responsibility for juvenile control with professional social workers inside the home.

The campaign against child neglect was the culmination of wartime social anxieties, a tidy package in which fears about migration, a changing urban environment, and greater autonomy for women and youth could be contained. Direct efforts to control public space through municipal ordinances and policing were acceptable as long as the targets were perceived as outsiders who disrupted the peace and stability of the community. But as the problem drew closer to home, touching native middle-class families and their children, the hard-line approach became less attractive. Juvenile delinquency was seen as a kind of epidemic, spreading from the "sordid" homes of migrant war workers to the children of the city's most respectable citizens.

By diagnosing child neglect as the germ of juvenile delinquency, old-timers reassured themselves once again that migrants and unruly women were to blame for their cities' ills. In so doing, they tried to ignore the more complex realities that affected everyone—changing urban demographics, overtaxed city services, the transformation of civic culture, and the increased autonomy of migrants, women, and youth that came with the war.

The Boomtown Syndrome

In defense centers around the nation, new social conditions and conflicts mirrored those of East Bay cities. On the West Coast, where newcomers made up an especially large percentage of the urban population, conflicts were particularly acute. During federal hearings on congested areas in 1943, city officials from Seattle to San Diego complained of a breakdown of social order in their communities that was expressed in more crime, vice, and delinquency. In all of these urban areas, newcomers provided a convenient scapegoat.

Shipbuilding centers around Portland and San Francisco gave war-time newcomers the most hostile reception. The Portland area, with its relatively homogeneous prewar population and its exceptionally large concentrations of migrant shipyard workers, exhibited the most viru-lent strain of nativism. Viewing itself as "a transplanted New England community," explained Carey McWilliams, Portland "resented the in-vasion of war workers in general and of Negro migrants in particular." In the nearby shipyard boomtown of Vancouver, Washington, the sociologist Calvin Schmid reported: "large segments of the popula-tion are strongly prejudiced against the in-migrants. . . . the term 'ship-yard worker' is one of opprobrium, applied to almost any stranger the speaker takes a dislike to." Newcomers themselves were acutely aware of the nativist sentiments. "The people of Portland make it clear that an Arkie or Okie is the most undesirable person on earth," said one migrant.[91]

Similar newcomer–old-timer animosities emerged in Marin City and other Bay Area shipbuilding centers with large concentrations of migrants. During a school board controversy in 1944, the migrant-oriented *Marin Citizen* charged that the area's old-time residents "didn't want shipyard workers here in the first place and . . . [were] do-ing their best to make our stay here uncomfortable."[92]

The more economically diverse and less crowded cities of Southern California were somewhat more successful in absorbing newcomers. The sprawling layout of both Los Angeles and San Diego and the dis-persed settlement patterns associated with aircraft production meant that migrants were spread more widely throughout these cities. Less likely to congregate in particular neighborhoods, newcomers remained less visible and hence less "troublesome" to old-time residents.

As the chief destination for generations of southern and midwestern migrants, Southern California also had an exceptionally high percent age of newcomers in its prewar population. As such, the residents of the region's cities were more accustomed to dealing with newcomers and less likely to treat them as scapegoats. The more favorable condi-tions, however, mainly benefited white migrants. Prewar community leaders, both black and white, routinely blamed black newcomers for increased crime, delinquency, disease, and other urban problems.

Antinewcomer sentiment was also strong in the Los Angeles Har-bor area, where thousands of newcomers congregated around Calship and other shipbuilding operations. Here, local officials voiced the usual pronouncements that newcomers were ill-adjusted and refused "to fa-miliarize themselves with the laws and habits of their new homes or communities." Strong pockets of nativist reaction also existed in the Puget Sound shipyard centers of Bremerton and Tacoma.[93]

Despite such variations, all of the West Coast cities experienced wartime crime scares and stepped up their efforts to control public space. Although crime rates varied, the five major urban areas on the West Coast all reported problems with public disorder—especially drunkenness and prostitution. The similarity of their experiences suggests that local nativist attitudes meshed well with federal mandates to suppress disorderly behavior in war production centers. The result was an exaggerated concern—at times even hysteria—over wartime crime and delinquency.

In Los Angeles, as in the East Bay, local newspapers featured periodic stories on "crime waves" perpetrated by migrants and blacks. Defense migration, claimed the Los Angeles chief of police in 1943, "seriously magnified certain of our law enforcement problems, and "the great influx of Negroes [were] largely responsible for this increase." Vice control was the biggest police problem, he said, with drunks and unescorted women constituting most of the arrests. The chief of police in Long Beach noted similar trends in his community.[94]

As the West Coast's largest naval center, San Diego authorities were most concerned with the rise in prostitution and venereal disease that they too attributed to outsiders. Many VD carriers, said a Navy medical officer, "had the disease when they arrived from Louisiana, Texas, Arkansas or wherever." According to San Diego Police Chief Clifford Peterson, many tavern owners had hired police matrons to keep undesirable women out of their establishments. Out on the streets, police used the vaguely worded state vagrancy law if they had "any reason of suspecting a girl to be a streetwalker or prostitute."[95]

Similar tactics were used in San Francisco, where federal and local authorities joined forces to crack down on "B girls" and other "immoral" women. The antiprostitution campaign was in fact part of a larger law-and-order campaign by city authorities. Claiming that police crackdowns in Oakland had driven criminal activity across the bay, San Francisco authorities announced their own anticrime campaign in March 1943. Meanwhile, in the North Bay, war workers in Marin City complained that local police were using "GESTAPO-like tactics" against blacks and teenagers.[96]

Crime scares also swept defense centers in the Pacific Northwest. The mayor of Portland, Earl Riley, decried the "Virginia City atmosphere" in his city and initiated antivice campaigns to cope with the problem. Farther north, the mayor of Seattle also noted an "increased problem in maintaining law and order." In both Seattle and Vancouver, police arrests more than doubled between 1939 and 1943. According to Calvin Schmid, the greatest increase occurred in public drunkenness and prostitution arrests.[97]

Private citizens also attempted to control public space by codifying racial segregation measures. As in the East Bay, civil rights advocates in Portland, Los Angeles, Vancouver, and Bremerton all reported an increased presence of "White Trade Only" signs in downtown stores and restaurants. According to these observers, the cosmopolitan centers of Los Angeles, San Francisco, and Seattle were more tolerant of black newcomers, but overnight boomtowns like Richmond, Vancouver, and Bremerton were very hostile. In all West Coast cities, however, the war seemed to heighten Jim Crow barriers.[98]

Young people in these communities found their access to public space more tightly controlled as well. As public concern with juvenile delinquency grew, all major West Coast cities (with the exception of Oakland) initiated youth curfews. The cities of Seattle, Los Angeles, and San Francisco prosecuted parents of delinquent children, usually after the second or third offense. In fact, the practice of arresting parents was first tried in San Francisco, where the city established a "Parental School" for the education and rehabilitation of "delinquent" parents in 1943. In lieu of jail sentences, parents could attend a series of evening lectures on such topics as child health, child employment, recreation, and parents' legal responsibilities.[99]

The growing emphasis on parental responsibility for delinquency soon manifested itself in a preoccupation with child neglect. As Linda Gordon has shown, the growing concern with neglect appeared throughout the country during World War II. In her study of wartime Seattle, Karen Anderson also observed this phenomenon. As in the East Bay, old-timers tended to see newcomers as the source of both neglect and juvenile delinquency.[100]

The persistent belief that war migrants had "ruined" West Coast cities left a bitter legacy. In the postwar era, continuing fears about urban crime and disorder would fuel white flight to the suburbs and help justify decisions about urban redevelopment. The maps, data, and proclamations of the wartime crime campaigns laid the foundation for postwar plans that would shape the modern-day landscape of the East Bay. But before turning to the postwar period, we must first examine the political realm to see how new wartime forces came to influence postwar urban policy.

7

Mobilizing Politics

On the eve of the 1947 municipal elections, an extraordinary event took place in Oakland. Starting from their respective flatland neighborhoods, hundreds of the city's working-class residents set out for the downtown district on foot, by automobile, and atop parade floats. They convened in a mass torchlight procession down Broadway, brandishing brooms and mops to dramatize the need for "municipal housecleaning." The most impressive float, constructed by the United Negro Labor Committee, showed AFL and CIO pallbearers lowering a casket labeled "The Machine" into the ground. Alongside the burial scene was a placard depicting two gloved fists—one black, one white—smashing the *Oakland Tribune* Tower (headquarters of the Knowland machine). The fists were labeled "Oakland Voters," and the banner beneath read "Take the Power Out of the Tower."[1]

The election parade vividly dramatized the urban revolt that had been gaining momentum in Oakland and other East Bay cities since the middle of World War II. Although the defense boom created a spate of urban social problems and dislocations, such events also presented an opportunity to challenge the political status quo. In the East Bay, a coalition of labor, black, and other progressive forces coalesced during the war and would become a major contender in the municipal politics of the postwar era. The most dramatic and sustained challenge occurred in Oakland, where a labor-led movement, cemented by a general strike in 1946, waged a mass electoral revolt against the powerful and conservative Knowland machine. Similar challenges in other East Bay

cities were less successful, but the renewed vitality of local politics revealed that New Deal liberalism was far from dead. The wartime city,
in fact, provided a crucible for progressives seeking to fulfill the social
ideals of the 1930s.

Standard urban histories say little or nothing about war-born political upheavals, particularly during the Second World War. Carl Abbott's work on Sunbelt cities is one of the few exceptions. In *The New
Urban America,* he chronicles the wartime boom of southern and western cities and shows how the foundations were laid for municipal
political upheavals after the war. Abbott describes these political challenges as "G.I. revolts" led by returning veterans who sought to "replace the small-time politics of city hall croneys with administrations of
growth-oriented businessmen and bureaucrats." These postwar reformers were part of a younger generation of businesspeople, professionals,
and bureaucrats who rekindled middle-class concepts of urban boost-
erism and municipal efficiency to consolidate and expand on the rapid
growth fostered by the war boom.[2]

The postwar politics of East Bay cities, however, suggests a different
pattern. In these struggles, labor, minorities, and working-class, not
middle-class, people were the driving force. Moreover, labor reformers
did not promote classic municipal reform measures such as city manager government and nonpartisan elections; business-dominated machines had already instituted such practices in the prewar era. Instead,
the labor-led insurgents of the 1940s called for an end to these practices, demanding an elected mayor, district elections, publicly owned
mass transportation, public works projects, public housing, and increased funding for education and social programs—in short, a broad-
based liberal agenda. Middle-class business reformers were thus not the
only ones to take advantage of war-born opportunities; under the right
conditions, labor and progressive forces also mounted effective political
challenges to business-dominated city governments.

The experience of East Bay cities also suggests that municipal revolts
of the late 1940s were not strictly postwar affairs but had direct roots
in wartime political arrangements. In this regard, the CIO was critical.
Nearly all of the postwar issues and personalities can be traced to the
newly formed CIO Political Action Committee (PAC) in 1944.
Though initially a creation of the CIO's national executive board, the
East Bay PACs soon took on a life of their own and became the core
of an insurgent political movement that nearly toppled Oakland's conservative Republican machine in 1947. Spurred by national political

mobilization during the war, the liberal revolt in East Bay cities fore-shadowed urban political trends that would characterize these cities in later decades.[3]

Labor's mobilization of a broad, progressive coalition in Oakland also offers a glimpse into the little-known world of 1940s politics and highlights the need for more research on the local level. Focusing mainly on national politics, labor historians have generally criticized wartime CIO political activity for fostering a rigid and ultimately det-rimental relationship between labor, the federal government, and the Democratic party.[4] When viewed at the grassroots level, however, the experience was far more fluid, democratic, and promising. By examin-ing local politics in the East Bay, we can begin to see how labor activists understood the war experience and why they chose to place their faith in the electoral system.

Urban Politics in Wartime

On the surface, the urban political scene underwent sur-prisingly little change considering the cataclysmic impact of defense migration and mobilization on East Bay cities. Existing business-dominated machines remained in power in Oakland, Alameda, Berke-ley, and Richmond with only minor personnel changes or brief interruptions of incumbents' tenures due to military service.

In Oakland, the machine dominated by the *Oakland Tribune* pub-lisher Joseph P. Knowland maintained and even strengthened its con-trol of city government after the death of rival political bosses Harry Williams and Mike Kelly in 1941. Incumbents backed by Knowland dominated the city council and mayor's seat throughout the war, a pat-tern that had been developing since the charter revisions of 1931. Like-wise, the city manager, John Hassler, remained in office from 1933 to 1954, a twenty-one-year term broken only by a three-year military stint from 1943 to 1946. During this time, the council appointed Charles Schwanenberg, a local department store president and Knowland ally, to fill in for Hassler.[5] The continuity of business leadership during the war also characterized nearby Berkeley and Alameda.

In wartime Richmond, the long-standing reign of Standard Oil–affiliated officials continued, but signs of stress were beginning to show by 1944. In a revealing set of documents contained in the Henry Kaiser collection at the Bancroft Library, an early draft of a *Fortune* article by Katherine Hamill suggests that some local officials did not weather the turmoil of war very well. Local officials, Hamill states, were overwhelmed by the severe problems and dislocations affecting their city, and some simply could not withstand the strain. According to Hamill, an overworked Mayor Mattie Chandler refused to run for reelection in 1944; City Manager James McVittie suffered a nervous breakdown the same year; and Police Judge Leo Marcollo—who had increased his time in court from one hour per day to full-time—also experienced severe stress problems.[6]

The draft is followed by a personal letter from Henry Kaiser to *Fortune* editors urging them not to publish the article, warning that it would "critically injure the war effort." Interestingly, Kaiser did not actually dispute Hamill's claims but argued only against publishing them. When the article appeared in the February 1945 issue under the title "Richmond Took a Beating," the above claims and other potentially damaging information had been deleted.[7]

Although Hamill's claims cannot be verified, the severity of Richmond's wartime plight might well have strained the best of city administrations. Richmond's business elite, however, moved quickly to heal the breach. The council elected Robert Lee, an official of the Laborers' Union—an AFL union traditionally friendly to local business interests—to succeed Chandler as mayor. Under lobbying by the Richmond Chamber of Commerce, the council hired Wayne Thompson, a plant security officer at the Kaiser shipyards, as the new city manager.

The departure of McVittie, the former city manager, was, in fact, probably a relief to local business interests, who sharply disagreed with his tactics for healing Richmond's war-born problems. Turning to desperate measures in 1944, McVittie prepared a lengthy report titled *An Avalanche Hits Richmond* that enumerated more than $6 million of postwar improvements needed by the city. Richmond, he said, believed "that the federal government ha[d] a definite responsibility to assist this war-swollen city in financing this program." Likening the city to an injured veteran, McVittie insisted that Richmond had "earned the Purple Heart" and should be treated accordingly. "No American would condone dumping a wounded veteran out of an army hospital when the guns cease firing. No more, then, should a crippled city be treated in that manner."[8]

Despite McVittie's pleas, federal aid was not forthcoming. The *Avalanche* report, the Chamber of Commerce charged, had in fact worsened the city's plight by generating adverse publicity. Under Wayne Thompson's administration, the city ceased its appeals for federal aid and turned back to private sector solutions, hoping to encourage industrial development in the postwar period. The war thus introduced some new faces into Richmond city government, but the dominance of the business community continued.[9]

Although a successful progressive challenge would not emerge until after the war, its roots lay in wartime political arrangements. Specifically, the rhetoric and ritual of wartime unity offered labor, black, and other progressive forces an opportunity to participate on citywide committees and debate public policy issues. Following the example of wartime federal agencies like the War Labor Board, local officials invited a wide range of community representatives to serve on ad hoc committees dealing with issues like defense employment, housing, mass transit, public health, child care, and rationing. Committee members included not only the conservative AFL building trades officials and black ministers traditionally appointed to represent the city's working class but left-leaning CIO members and black officials of the railroad brotherhoods as well. Organized labor embraced this opportunity to work with other community groups, and they applauded the corporatist doctrine that called for representatives of various occupational groups to come together under government sponsorship to solve social ills. The CIO even endorsed Oakland's incumbent mayor, John Slavich, in 1943 because he had been "particularly helpful in bringing labor spokesmen into committees and activity to further Oakland's war effort."[10]

Perhaps the most trenchant examples of urban corporatism were the planning committees established to promote successful reconversion after the war. As early as 1943, Mayor Slavich had appointed Oakland's Postwar Planning Committee, an ad hoc group ostensibly representing all city residents. Out of fifty members, however, thirty represented business and finance interests and only four spoke for organized labor. The committee sidestepped formal planning bodies and developed projects that would make Oakland "the leading center of the New Industrial West." The Berkeley city council organized a similar group in 1944 known as the Citizens Postwar Advisory Committee.

In an effort to provide long-deferred municipal improvements and to ease the transition to a peacetime economy, the committees developed an elaborate program of public works and civic projects. Their plans called for the repair or construction of roads, highways, sewers, schools, parks, pools, hospitals, and civic centers, many of which had languished since the depression. With fear of a postwar recession looming, such projects would create jobs for displaced veterans and defense workers—a key labor demand. For business interests, adequate facilities and services were a prerequisite to industrial growth. "Immediate and postwar civic improvements will have a far-reaching effect on Oakland's industrial development," said the Postwar Planning Committee. "Eastern concerns are more likely to locate their plants in Oakland knowing that the city of Oakland is willing to provide the facilities required by industry."[11] The business-labor unity symbolized by the postwar planning committees, however, would soon prove illusory. As we will see, the execution of postwar plans would become a source of bitter and protracted conflict.

Even during the war, labor remained at best a junior partner in this experiment in urban corporatism. As Carl Abbott has pointed out, defense contractors and federal bureaucrats, who generally favored policies acceptable to the city's business elite, dominated ad hoc committees and decision making. Labor's participation in the committees, however, brought critical experience with and exposure to urban policy issues.

During the war, labor—particularly the CIO—moved from a more narrow focus on workplace organizing to a broad-based concern with community issues such as housing, transportation, and civil rights. Communist party members, who were well represented in the International Longshoremen's and Warehousemen's Union and other West Coast CIO locals, had a long history of community organizing in the Unemployed Councils of the 1930s. In the full-employment context of East Bay boomtowns, such experience proved invaluable as the need for increased productivity to win the war provided a perfect rationale for linking community and workplace issues. For the CIO, which had had little role in organizing the masses of new shipyard workers, a community orientation offered an alternate means of addressing the needs of an expanding work force. The Alameda County CIO Council, in fact, urged every full-time union official to sit on at least one civic group or committee. They also endorsed a new course on community services offered by the Oakland-based California Labor School and urged union members to enroll. This growing concern and sophistication in dealing with community issues would not disappear at war's end.[12]

Labor not only gained experience in urban policy-making during the war but also developed an impressive organizational network. With the creation of the national CIO Political Action Committee in 1943, local PACs began forming in major industrial centers to support the reelection of Franklin Roosevelt and other prolabor candidates. The passage of the antilabor Smith-Connally Act in 1943 also served to galvanize labor forces nationwide in an effort to repeal the legislation. In California, Proposition 12, a right-to-work initiative, spurred especially enthusiastic PAC activity in the Los Angeles and San Francisco Bay areas in 1944 and helped unite the long-feuding AFL and CIO. [13] The PACs conducted mass voter registration drives in the summer and fall of 1943, enrolling a record number of voters statewide, including more than 300,000 ballot applications from migrant defense workers.

In the East Bay, sound trucks patrolled working-class neighborhoods and war housing areas all day, every day, urging residents to register. The PAC appointed registrars in both the shipyards and war housing projects, and the Democratic Club led by C. L. Dellums concentrated on reaching new black voters in west Oakland. Defense migrants were popular targets for these campaigns, since working-class and southern voters presumably backed the Democratic party. Local Republicans even suggested that a conspiracy was afoot to "colonize" California cities with southern Democrats. Migrant war workers, said the editors of the conservative *Oakland Observer,* were "being dragooned into California from the solid Democratic southern states, where their votes [were] not needed." Although no such conspiracy existed, the PACs did do extensive work in migrant neighborhoods, helping newcomers file for residency and explaining voting rights (including freedom from poll taxes and literacy tests). As a result of such efforts, Alameda County showed the greatest gains in voter registration in the Bay Area, rising from 225,000 voters before the primary election to 362,000 by late October.[14]

Labor groups made an equally impressive effort on election day. CIO and AFL members joined forces on the United Labor's Legislative Committee and organized a mass distribution of slate cards in all major shipyards. Union members and their families rallied voters by telephoning and doorbell ringing, minded children while voters went to the polls, offered information on voting rights, and served as poll watchers. When the returns were tallied, East Bay voters came in heavily for the triumphant Roosevelt and Democratic congressional candidate George Miller and helped defeat Proposition 12.[15]

To what extent PAC activity contributed to these victories is open to question, but the PAC's role as a nucleus of a progressive revolt in local politics is clear. As Joseph James, a local shipyard worker and NAACP leader, observed in 1945, a progressive coalition had formed in the Bay Area "spearheaded by CIO-PAC in the 1944 elections," and "the contacts made during the course of that political battle [had] remained intact to a surprising degree." In Alameda County, the origins of postwar progressivism were especially evident. Key local organizers of the 1944 campaign included Ruby Heide, secretary of the Alameda County CIO Council; J. C. Reynolds, chair of the Alameda County Central Labor Council; William Hollander and Earl Hall, directors of the county Democratic and Republican campaigns to reelect Roosevelt; and C. L. Dellums, an official in the Brotherhood of Sleeping Car Porters and head of the Alameda County NAACP. All of these individuals would emerge as important figures in the local revolt that first took shape in the 1945 city elections.[16]

Once again, it was the CIO that spearheaded plans for an organized labor presence in the upcoming elections. In a meeting called by the Alameda County CIO Council in December 1944, the PAC established four subcommittees to analyze the issues and candidates in spring municipal elections in Oakland, Berkeley, San Leandro, and Alameda. The PAC hoped to identify progressive, prolabor candidates who could defeat business-backed incumbents. The present leadership was "obstructionist," said the PAC, and the region's future was being "stifled by selfish interests and machine politics." Even though the war had not yet ended, the era of wartime unity was clearly over.[17]

The confrontational stance adopted by labor was the result of both changing economic conditions and disillusionment over the business community's failure to pursue postwar planning measures. By the winter of 1944–1945, labor concern was growing over the slowdown of the war economy and the specter of another depression. Shipyard employment in the East Bay had begun contracting slowly in the fall of 1943. Job layoffs increased considerably over the next year, and by early 1945 unemployment claims were five times higher than they had been the previous year. At the same time, local urban leaders had shown little enthusiasm for inaugurating the postwar public works projects designed to cushion the shock of reconversion. City officials, labor contended, had taken no concrete action on the recommendations of the postwar planning committees nor sought funding for any new projects. The issue, as one columnist put it, was whether the East Bay would "go forward or backward" in a contest pitting "prosperity versus the prewar status quo." Choosing the latter meant "a return to unemployment."[18]

The split between labor and business was not as sudden as it seemed; the rhetoric of wartime unity had merely obscured the long-standing animosity between the two groups. This is not to say that wartime rhetoric was entirely false, but rather that labor and business understood the meaning of the war experience differently. For much of the old-time business community, the war boom brought an unprecedented expansion of business, population, and economic development accompanied by a temporary, but necessary, dose of federal intervention. Business hoped to continue this growth in the postwar era, but under the control of the private sector.

The Oakland Chamber of Commerce promoted such views through conservative spokespersons such as William C. Mullendore, the president of Southern California Edison Company. In an address to the chamber in January 1946, Mullendore warned against "impossible demands by labor leaders" and "unproductive public works projects." Although excited about the economic potential of an expanded population, he lamented the dislocation of migrants and their consequent reliance on government: "In wartime, most of these people do not have to make difficult decisions for themselves. Decisions are made for them—in the Services or in the war plants—and hence when peace comes the burden of decision as to their future activities seems heavier than before and inclines them to look to the Government for direction, as well as for assistance." The free enterprise system had been temporarily suspended, he concluded, and Californians could regain true prosperity and independence only by curbing government involvement.[19]

For labor, the collectivist experiments of the war years had a different meaning. The mass mobilization of resources, personnel, and government services seemed to prove that business and government were capable of creating a humane capitalism that provided jobs, a decent standard of living, and fair treatment for all Americans. Wartime social programs such as health insurance, public housing, and child care were not just temporary expedients but models for the postwar future. Henry Kraus, a CIO organizer in California, remembered his wartime housing project as an experiment in "organized neighborliness" and "mutual self-help," populated by "little people who had once foreseen a period of unexampled security and hope coming out of the war." But as the business community's interest in social cooperation waned, labor rebelled in an attempt to preserve wartime gains. Labor's vision, then, was not a radical anticapitalist one but a more moderate vision of social democratic reform based on the war experience. Richmond's new labor coalition summed up this reformist vision in their 1945 slogan "We Can Do in Peace What We Have Done in War."[20]

Labor also had a far more positive view of the area's newcomers. Far from being disoriented and dependent, labor leaders argued, newcomers were grateful for wartime social programs and merely wanted fair treatment from local housing authorities and other agencies. City leaders had "expressed hostility toward the problems of wartime inhabitants from outside areas," said one labor supporter. "The indifference . . . is rooted in the defeatist theory that such people are here only temporarily." To help overcome the nativist and racist sentiments that plagued East Bay cities, the PAC called for the creation of civic unity committees that would bring different racial, occupational, and religious groups together to resolve community conflicts.[21]

The failure of elected officials to respond to the needs of migrants and other working people prompted the PAC to launch its own campaign and candidates in the spring of 1945. For the first time since the Progressive Era, labor-backed progressive slates challenged local business rule in municipal elections in Oakland, Richmond, Berkeley, and Alameda. The local coalitions shared common platforms calling for expanded industry and job opportunities, public works, slum clearance, public housing, civic unity committees, increased pay for civil service employees, and expanded facilities and services for education, health care, child care, recreation, and mass transit. Individual groups also addressed specific local problems. The Richmond Better Government Committee demanded an end to racial discrimination by the local housing authority and called for the creation of a publicly controlled port commission; the Allied Berkeley Citizens pressed the city to create a local housing authority to manage Codornices Village; and the United for Oakland Committee demanded district elections, an elected mayor, and other charter reforms. In all four cities, the coalitions fielded progressive candidates to oppose business-backed incumbents for city council, the school board, and other city offices.[22]

Although labor organizers set out to dismantle "machine politics," they appropriated their opponents' rhetoric of "progress" and "good government"—terms traditionally associated with business-oriented reform governments. Indeed, the labor-backed Richmond Better Government Committee sounded suspiciously like the business-dominated Non-Partisan Good Government League in Oakland. As they had in the 1930s, labor leaders also embraced the reformist mantle of nonpartisanship. Rather than denounce the charade of nonpartisan local elections, the labor coalitions praised nonpartisanship as a means of broadening their appeal beyond the labor movement and the Democratic party.

In reality, these coalitions remained overwhelmingly Democratic and labor oriented. After the war, however, they would be much more successful in forging a broad-based alliance that attracted a diverse cross-section of the urban community. First, the coalitions represented a solidly united AFL-CIO front unknown in prewar politics. Despite conservatives' efforts to split the labor vote by running machine-backed AFL candidates, labor remained united in support of its own candidates.[23]

The labor coalitions also forged links with forward-looking business interests who advocated aggressive postwar growth and opposed existing machines. The United for Oakland Committee, for example, attracted the support of former postwar planning committee members Frank Belgrano, president of the Central Bank of Oakland and regional chairman of the Committee for Economic Development; Earl Hall, a liberal Republican and chairman of the Uptown Property Owners Association (rival of Knowland's Downtown Association); and Patrick McDonough, owner of defense-oriented McDonough Steel and chairman of the Alameda County Democratic Committee.

Although both business and labor ostensibly supported industrial expansion, the labor group maintained that local machines jealously guarded their dominant position and created bottlenecks to discourage new businesses from locating in East Bay cities. Because of such attitudes, labor alleged, aircraft manufacturers like Lockheed chose to locate in Southern California instead of Oakland. One labor activist, James Kenny, described a similar proprietary attitude among local officials in Richmond, explaining that "the oil companies didn't like the competition." Other businesspeople, however, had "a sincere desire to take Oakland out of the rut it's been in," said Paul Heide, an Alameda County PAC official. "These are the people we want to work with." Carl Abbott has described these forward-looking businesspeople as the instigators of postwar "veterans revolts." In the East Bay, however, labor, not business, led the new urban coalitions.[24]

Most significantly, CIO forces worked hard to develop strong ties with the black community. Black labor leaders such as C. L. Dellums, business agent for the Brotherhood of Sleeping Car Porters, and Matt Crawford, former assistant director of the CIO Minorities Committee, provided key links between the labor movement and the larger black community. Dellums, in particular, represented a broad network of black interests in Oakland and helped deliver the support of the Railroad Brotherhoods, the local NAACP, and the Democratic Seventeenth District Citizens' League. In Berkeley, Matt Crawford and pharmacist Byron Rumford worked to mobilize the black community behind the Allied Berkeley Citizens. The newly formed Richmond NAACP likewise threw its support behind the Richmond Better Government Committee in April 1945. The labor coalitions' support for fair housing and employment practices, civic unity committees, and other civil rights measures made such interracial alliances possible.[25]

Finally, the labor coalitions also drew support from middle-class white liberals, particularly those in progressive religious circles. Religious support was most evident in Berkeley, where faculty members from the Pacific School of Religion occupied key positions in the Allied Berkeley Citizens. One faculty member, Dr. A. C. McGiffert, was a co-founder and chair of the ABC. Reflecting the social gospel tendencies of liberal Protestantism, members of the Pacific School of Religion, the interracial war housing ministries, and the local Councils of Churches all united with labor coalitions in support of fair labor practices and civil rights. As Joseph James, leader of the San Francisco NAACP, explained, "there [was] a large group of prominent white persons who [were] outspokenly liberal on the question of racial equality." These people joined with "an overwhelming preponderance of working people, combined with the strength of the CIO" to form a truly broad-based progressive coalition in Bay Area cities.[26]

The liberal coalitions, however, were far less successful in actually turning out the vote on election day. In the spring municipal elections of 1945, voters swept nearly all incumbent candidates back into office. To help elect machine candidates, the *Oakland Tribune* and the *Berkeley Gazette* had waged a fierce red-baiting campaign against the labor challengers. Both papers highlighted the fact that the local Communist party supported the progressive slate, and the *Oakland Tribune* claimed that such support provided "indisputable proof that a Communist group [was] entering the April 17 Oakland city elections." Although there was no evidence linking labor candidates to the Communist party, such charges no doubt hurt their campaigns.[27]

More important, though, was the dismally low turnout that plagued all the municipal elections. In Oakland, a turnout of only 26 percent of the city's registered voters allowed incumbents to roll over their United for Oakland Committee (UOC) challengers; equally light turnouts in other East Bay cities brought similar results. Only in Berkeley and Richmond, where the progressives backed renegade liberal incumbents, did the labor coalitions score any victories. Assessing their losses, liberals realized they needed to redouble their efforts to reach new and disaffected voters. "Our job until the next city elections is clear," said PAC chairman John Bittman. "We must continue and increase an educational program in order to acquaint voters with the importance of voting in city elections."[28]

In all likelihood, labor's message was as much a problem as the poor turnout. By appropriating the progrowth, reform rhetoric of their opponents, liberal candidates were at times indistinguishable from machine incumbents. Future labor candidates would discover that a more frankly left-wing platform had more grassroots appeal than a watered-down reform agenda.

The 1945 challenge, however, was more than just a painful learning experience. In Oakland, pressure by the UOC served to push local machines into action on key community issues. Just prior to the elections, the city raised the wages of police and fire personnel, and Mayor John Slavich established a civic unity committee despite prior statements that no such body was necessary. In May 1945, the city council finally presented a bond measure to provide modest funding for roads, sewers, libraries, swimming pools, parks, and a new Hall of Justice. The measure passed decisively with Knowland and UOC support. In a separate election in September, the city council offered a second bond measure to fund new school facilities. Heartened by these small victories, the UOC vowed to continue the fight by extending its outreach and education efforts until the next election.[29]

Postwar Politics

The economic conditions and political events of the immediate postwar period would provide the organizing spark that progressive forces needed. At the end of the war, the contraction of the defense sector spurred unemployment, creating a short-term economic crisis for East Bay workers. A continuing influx of interstate migrants and returning veterans only aggravated the problem. As in other U.S. cities, the postwar crisis would come to a head in 1946, when Alameda County labor forces declared a general strike that virtually shut down

Oakland and adjoining East Bay cities. Although unsuccessful, the strike would galvanize local labor organizations and serve as a springboard into the hotly contested municipal elections of 1947.

To understand the political events of 1946–1947, we first need to examine the historical context in which these events occurred. Unemployment was the most pressing issue for East Bay workers, and statistics from the Richmond shipyards indicate the dimensions of the problem. By August 1945, employment at the Kaiser yards had fallen from a peak of more than 90,000 workers to less than 35,000. Although the company retained a small proportion of these employees for postwar ship repair, such contracts were short-lived. By November 1946, the U.S. Employment Service (USES) in Richmond reported that shipbuilding activities had "virtually ceased." The sudden jump in unemployment reduced turnover and allowed employers to become extremely selective in hiring. During 1946, USES reported increasing numbers of job seekers at factory gates in Richmond and noted that employers were hiring male veterans only. The bulk of the unemployed workers were unskilled, said USES: "Job opportunities do not now exist for the majority of this labor pool." Approximately 20 percent of that labor pool was nonwhite.[30]

Women manufacturing workers faced the most severe dislocations. Although surveys conducted by the Women's Bureau indicated that 70 percent of working women in the Bay Area wanted to keep their jobs after the war (20 percent of whom were the sole supporters of families), most were unable to do so. During 1944–1945, the number of women working in California shipyards declined by 63 percent, compared with only 25 percent for men. By June 1946, only 300 out of a wartime peak of 41,000 women remained employed in shipyards statewide. Although less dramatic, layoffs in other defense industries also affected women disproportionately.

In the East Bay, USES reported a large percentage of female unemployment claimants, noting that women were the largest "hard-to-place" group. Women lost ground not only in industrial jobs but in traditional female fields as well. In clerical work, for instance, employers often requested male applicants, many of whom had learned clerical skills in the service. According to USES, even women "willing to do house work [had] difficulty finding jobs where they [didn't] have to 'live in.' " Black women experienced the highest unemployment rates—more than 40 percent in the Bay Area. Eventually, an expanded trade and services sector would absorb many of these female workers, but in the immediate postwar period, competition for all jobs remained keen.[31]

With the closing of defense industries, the debilitating effects of postwar unemployment and economic dislocation were most glaring in small boomtowns like Richmond. By 1946, the city had the highest proportion of unemployment claimants anywhere in the Bay Area. A visiting journalist observed that the bars in downtown Richmond were open at 10:00 A.M. "These emporia of good cheer," he explained, "are the unofficial clearing houses for the late war plant workers." Defense migrants and other displaced workers, however, did not disappear; most stayed on in hopes of finding work and housing in a reconverted peacetime economy. Describing this human residue, one writer dubbed Richmond "Hangover Town," likening the postwar recession to a civic illness resulting from the economic excesses of the war boom. Berating them as welfare freeloaders, some old-timers urged migrants to "go back wherever they came from and get in their own breadlines."[32]

Immediately after the war, natives had seen encouraging signs that the mass exodus might indeed occur. "Day by day," wrote a local journalist, "carloads of families toting their mattresses, pots and pans, tables and chairs streamed out of the vast housing projects back to the corn belt, the wheat belt, the cotton belt, from which they had come to build ships." The sudden exodus seemed to confirm the views of East Bay officials, who had drafted postwar planning measures based on significant levels of outmigration. The Oakland Housing Authority had predicted outmigration rates of 40 percent to 60 percent in 1945, and the city manager of Richmond had based his 1944 report on a probable outmigration rate of 50 percent.[33]

The initial exodus proved illusory, however. Most migrants remained in their new homes, and many more continued to come. Even before the war ended, Chamber of Commerce surveys conducted in East Bay shipyards revealed that 75 percent to 80 percent of migrant workers intended to stay in the area after the war, with even higher percentages among black workers.[34] After an initial burst of outmigration, the flow of emigrants dwindled. In addition, some of the departing families returned to the East Bay within the next year. The Debneys, for example, a black family from the Texas Panhandle, headed home shortly after the war. Finding no work and few opportunities, they soon returned to Richmond, where Henry Debney's brother, a returning veteran, and his wife joined them in war housing. Many oral history informants described similar sojourns to their home states to visit family and friends after the war. Some went for short-term visits only, but others intended to stay but became disillusioned with the lack of opportunities in their home towns. As the Oakland Housing Authority reported in 1945, substantial numbers of migrants "having become accustomed to local climate, people and conditions, came back in a short time, bringing friends and relatives with them."[35]

Federal migration studies confirm these observations, revealing a continuing pattern of inmigration. A 1947 USES survey of employment applicants in the Bay Area found that 14 percent had moved to the region during the past three months. Of those coming from outside the state, the largest number came from Texas, Louisiana, and Oklahoma—the same states from which wartime migrants had come. Nearly 50 percent of the newcomers were veterans and 23 percent were nonwhite. Among the black migrants, reported Wilson Record in the *Crisis*, some had relocated from shipyards in Portland and Seattle, where layoffs of black workers had been even more severe.[36] Much to the disappointment of many old-timers, migrants did not disappear from the East Bay after the war.

Veterans constituted the single largest group of new arrivals. Some were prewar residents returning home; others relocated to California after being stationed there during the war. For veterans throughout the state, educational opportunities motivated their move to the East Bay. As the home of the University of California at Berkeley, where thousands of veterans enrolled under the G.I. bill, Alameda County hosted 84,760 veteran residents in 1947. With the exception of Los Angeles County, Alameda attracted the largest number of veterans in the state. The veteran influx spilled into adjoining Contra Costa County, where the initial exodus of Richmond war workers had left some four thousand public housing units vacant. The state assigned available apartments to returning veterans and their families, including many University of California students.[37]

High rates of inmigration, combined with relatively slow outmigration, produced a marked increase in East Bay population. Despite declining defense employment, the cities of Oakland, Berkeley, Alameda, and Richmond all registered population gains of anywhere from 6 percent to 46 percent from 1944 to 1950 (see table 4). The greatest increases occurred among the black population; Oakland's black community grew by more than 118 percent during this period and

Richmond's by approximately 135 percent (see table 6). Such statistics dashed any remaining hopes that East Bay cities would "return to normal" after the war.

In the immediate postwar period, then, unemployment remained a problem for many East Bay residents, particularly recent migrants and black workers. In a postwar survey of welfare recipients conducted in Contra Costa County, Tarea Hall Pittman found migrants heavily represented in the monthly case load. Better than half the clients had moved to the area since 1940, and 20 percent were still nonresidents. In line with migration patterns, the greatest proportion of these people came from the southwestern states of Oklahoma, Texas, and Louisiana. For nonresidents, securing relief could take months or even years. Since California had a three-year residence requirement, state agencies required these clients to apply through their home states, a protracted process involving voluminous correspondence and documentation. Applicants from states where residency was lost after one or two years' absence found themselves without recourse to public assistance.[38]

An abrupt withdrawal of social services in war housing areas in December 1945 further aggravated the plight of poor and working-class families. State and local governments maintained minimal recreation and child care services but refused to invest in the upkeep of playgrounds and other facilities. In 1947, the state instituted a means test for all child care clients, approximately three-quarters of whom were single mothers. Thereafter, Richmond and other localities closed down many of their centers. Health care facilities were also overwhelmed; with the cessation of shipbuilding, thousands of former Kaiser employees lost access to local clinics. Likewise in Contra Costa County, the California Physicians Service also curtailed its medical programs soon after the war. Anxious to tear down war housing, local officials offered its residents few incentives to stay, reducing social services to a bare minimum.[39]

Even those who kept their jobs after the war saw their standard of living deteriorate. Despite record corporate profits, the take-home pay of many workers declined because of the reduction of hours and the loss of overtime and bonus pay. With the termination of wartime price controls in the summer of 1946, consumer prices skyrocketed nationwide while real wages fell. Furthermore, the existence of a growing pool of unemployed benefited local employers, who adopted an increasingly hostile stance toward labor organizing. The same trends prevailed throughout the country, where employers, aided by a conservative Republican Congress, attempted to roll back New Deal labor gains through open shop legislation and other antilabor measures later embodied in the Taft-Hartley Labor Act of 1947. In reaction to these trends, labor discontent erupted in a nationwide strike wave in 1945–1946.

Oakland was one of six cities nationwide that experienced a general strike in this tumultuous period. The conflict began in October 1946, when some four hundred members—mainly women—of the AFL Department and Specialty Store Employees Union walked off their jobs at Kahn's and Hastings downtown department stores. Demanding employer recognition of the union as a legitimate bargaining agent, striking workers picketed the stores throughout November with the support of the Teamsters and other AFL trades. On December 1, Kahn's brought in nonunion drivers to deliver twelve truckloads of merchandise to its store under the protection of 250 Oakland police officers.

The police complicity triggered a sharp outcry against city officials, and on December 2 the Alameda County Labor Council declared a "labor holiday." The next day, 142 unions with more than 100,000 workers took to the streets, successfully shutting down streetcar and bus lines, factories, shipyards, stores, restaurants, hotels, and three local newspapers. The Oakland protest garnered widespread support, reflecting workers' dissatisfaction over postwar economic dislocations and threats to union organizing rights.

After two and a half days, as the strike threatened to spread to adjoining Contra Costa County, leaders of the Teamsters' and Machinists' internationals ordered their members back to work. With the loss of these critical unions, local labor leaders reluctantly accepted an agreement with the city manager to end the general strike in exchange for the city's pledge to observe workers' civil rights in the future. The general strike thus ended inconclusively, but the store workers' strike continued as a separate dispute. Within weeks, however, the city again deployed police to protect scab workers at the downtown stores.[40]

Feeling angry and betrayed, labor forces rebounded into the electoral arena in 1947. Outraged by the brazen proemployer sentiments of the mayor and city council, the labor coalition of 1945 reorganized as the Oakland Voters League (OVL) and revitalized its efforts to build a unified progressive movement. In the May elections, the OVL ran a slate of five candidates for city council with a platform reminiscent of the 1945 campaign by the United for Oakland Committee. As the UOC had two years earlier, the OVL dubbed the Knowland machine "obstructionist" and demanded that postwar public works projects begin immediately. "Two years ago, $15,754,000 was voted for parks and playgrounds, swimming pools and recreational facilities, health services, street improvements, and other needed civic projects," the OVL asserted. "Where are they?"[41]

The 1947 platform also added some new planks, giving the OVL a more radical edge. Specifically, the OVL called for city council neutrality in all labor disputes; repeal of antipicketing and antihandbill ordinances often used against labor; investigation of police brutality against black residents; the restoration of rent control; repeal of the sales tax; and more equitable tax assessment procedures to eliminate unfair advantages for downtown property owners. The OVL also gave top priority to building public housing, establishing a city fair employment commission, and constructing new school facilities. Disputing Chamber of Commerce data on industrial growth, the OVL noted that the majority of new industries had located in suburban areas outside the city. In contrast with 1945, though, Oakland progressives talked less about attracting new business. Their main thrust was employment, community services, and social justice.[42]

Like the labor coalition of 1945, the OVL represented a broad spectrum of community interests—from Communists and left-wing CIO members to local veterans and church members. Labor remained the centerpiece of the coalition, and in the wake of the failed 1946 strike and the pending Taft-Hartley legislation, union forces closed ranks as never before. The AFL, CIO, and Railroad Brotherhoods all endorsed the OVL, and in early April they held a mass support rally of more than ten thousand union members at the Oakland Auditorium. Labor support from west Oakland's black community was also strong; black unionists formed the United Negro Labor Committee, which was a particularly active and visible campaigner for the OVL.[43]

Because of labor's outspoken concern for returning G.I.s, the OVL won support from veterans groups as well. Back in 1945, the United for Oakland Committee had called for housing and job placement services for returning veterans. The following year, labor joined with the Oakland Veterans Council, the NAACP, the Council of Churches, and other community organizations to pressure the city into taking advantage of new federal funding for temporary veterans' housing. After several months of lobbying, the council finally agreed to accept 500 temporary units to be placed adjacent to existing west-side projects.[44] By supporting housing and other pressing community concerns, labor built a broad-based urban coalition in support of the OVL.

The coalition's main obstacle was its lack of access to mainstream media. Both Knowland's *Tribune* and the Hearst-owned *Post-Enquirer* were machine supporters and functioned, the OVL claimed, "as bulletin boards for the incumbents." The *Tribune* renewed its red-baiting tactics against "Communists" and "CIO political bosses" and featured headlines such as "Oakland Primary Hailed as Communist Victory." One of the Bay Area's leading radio stations, the *Tribune*-owned KLX, refused to sell air time to the OVL, prompting the latter to file complaints with the Federal Communications Commission. In the meantime, OVL workers established their own publication, the *Oakland Voters Herald*, a four-page news sheet offering information and views on campaign issues and developments.[45]

To combat the low turnout that had hampered the United for Oakland Committee in the 1945 elections, the OVL established a broad-based community network based on a grassroots precinct-level system. OVL precinct workers canvassed Oakland neighborhoods in the weeks prior to the election, distributing thousands of copies of the *Voters Herald*. In west Oakland, the United Negro Labor Committee sponsored a street dance and other activities to help turn out the vote. The campaign culminated in the dramatic torchlight procession described at the beginning of this chapter.[46]

On election day the OVL's organizing efforts paid off. With a record turnout of 97,520 voters—65 percent of the city's registered voters—OVL candidates Vernon Lantz, Raymond Pease, Joseph Smith, and Scott Weakley defeated the Knowland-backed incumbents. The other OVL candidate, Ben Goldfarb, a former Richmond shipyard worker, lost by less than a thousand votes. Although no precinct voting records have survived, local newspapers agreed that the OVL's strongest support came from the working-class districts of east and west Oakland. The latter, inhabited predominantly by blacks and migrants, contributed the strongest support with residents voting three to one in favor of the OVL. The landslide vote prompted the *Labor Herald* to chide that the "Old Guard's Waterloo was in west Oakland."[47]

The triumph of the four OVL candidates was an unprecedented event that demonstrated the power of an interracial labor coalition. But Goldfarb's loss was a damaging blow. The new city council still stood five to four in favor of the Knowland machine. The latter, however, did not always act as a coherent unit. When selecting a mayor a few months later, feuding Knowland forces could not agree on a single candidate. As a result, OVL council members elected their own favorite, Joseph Smith.[48] The mayoral contest was an indication that OVL council members might be able to win a majority by trading favors with one of their opponents. As we will see in the next chapter, this strategy would be key in the fight over public housing.

Labor mounted a similar but somewhat less effective challenge to Richmond's probusiness leadership in the 1947 municipal elections. As in Oakland, a climate of postwar labor strife in Richmond helped galvanize labor forces. The nationwide strike wave of 1945–1946 included many oil- and autoworkers at Standard Oil and Ford in Richmond and increased the visibility of local labor leaders, like James Kenny, vice president of CIO Oil Workers Local 326. In the 1947 city council elections, labor supported Kenny along with Louis Richardson, a member of the AFL Laundry Workers Union, president of the Richmond NAACP, and the city's first black candidate for municipal office. Both candidates upheld much of the 1945 platform of the Richmond Better Government Committee, including public housing, improved city services, abolition of the sales tax, equitable tax assessment, fair employment practices, and public control of the waterfront. In the May runoff, Richmond voters elected Kenny but turned down his black ally—a fate shared by all black candidates who sought municipal office in the late 1940s. Kenny ran successfully for reelection in 1949 and was joined by Gay Vargas, a tavern owner and an official in the AFL Musicians Union. Together, they became known as "the labor bloc," a force that the established business leadership now had to contend with.[49]

Although no precinct voting data from Richmond remains for the early postwar years, other evidence suggests that demographic changes in the electorate were central to the success of the labor revolt. War migration seems to have disrupted the prewar political system, challenging the power of local business elites. Voter participation rates generally dropped during the war (with the exception of the 1944 presidential election), but they increased in the postwar years, particularly in local elections. In a study of postwar voting patterns in Richmond, a Berkeley political scientist concluded that the war made local residents more keenly aware of community conditions and more willing to take action.[50]

Many migrants and war housing residents were outspoken in their criticism of local machine politicians. Several former migrants interviewed for this study still expressed outrage at the attitudes of old-time

East Bay leaders. One woman from Arkansas recalled that such politicians hoped "all of us would just disappear as if we was zombies. . . . they couldn't seem to realize what change was." Black migrants, especially, resented the callousness of city leaders, who regarded them as temporary residents. "The Negro does not think of the temporary housing units as temporary," said W. Miller Barbour, an Urban League investigator. "He knows that very little housing is available to him and the reasons that it will not be provided."[51]

Labor worked hard to bring these newcomers into the liberal fold. James Kenny, a city council member in the late forties, recalled that he had found little support among longtime Richmond residents and that most of his votes "were from the southside." Kenny explained how the members of the United Auto Workers and their families acted as precinct workers in war housing areas. "We had them work out here in the lower part of town. . . . They would talk to people, go to each home." On election day, sound trucks toured the south-side housing projects, and union members served as building captains to turn out the vote. In the 1949 city council election, the *Richmond Independent* reported that Kenny "was particularly strong in the south side" and implied that he would have lost without those votes. Other labor candidates also had good showings in these areas, suggesting that migrant votes may indeed have contributed to the success of liberal challengers.[52]

The fight against urban machine rule was less successful in the more middle-class communities of Alameda and Berkeley. Wartime political enthusiasm appears to have waned in Alameda after 1945, judging from the absence of any organized progressive slates in subsequent municipal elections. In Berkeley, however, progressives channeled their efforts toward backing Byron Rumford, a black pharmacist, for state representative in 1948. With the support of labor, the black Ministerial Alliance, and the Berkeley Interracial Committee, Rumford won a state assembly seat in the Seventeenth District covering west Oakland and parts of Berkeley. Like other African-Americans who entered electoral politics after the war, Rumford owed his margin of victory to the political support of southern newcomers. Along with Augustus Hawkins, a black representative from south central Los Angeles, Rumford would lead the fight for fair employment and housing legislation over the next fifteen years.[53]

Black candidates for municipal office did not fare as well. Although sharing the same platforms and support networks as white progressives, pioneer black candidates like Louis Richardson were limited by the racial biases of an at-large white electorate. For this reason, the Oakland Voters League's support of district elections and other charter reforms was particularly appealing to black voters. But despite their losses, the postwar campaigns of black candidates helped build an organizational infrastructure for later black victories in the 1970s. Their appearance thus marked a new departure in the urban politics of the East Bay.

In many ways the 1940s provided a dress rehearsal for many of the progressive movements that would emerge in East Bay cities beginning in the 1960s. Civil rights legislation, district elections, rent control, and progressive education and social programs were eventually implemented in one or more East Bay cities. In retrospect, World War II was the springboard for an effective urban political mobilization.

The political arrangements of wartime cities offered labor leaders a new voice in municipal affairs and encouraged them to expand their political horizons from the workplace to the city at large. The formation of political action committees by the CIO gave this impulse an organizational coherence, and defense migrants provided an expanded working-class constituency. After the war, recessionary pressures served to galvanize labor and other progressive forces, helping them defeat business-backed incumbents in both Oakland and Richmond. By the late 1940s, progressives were poised to begin a new era of municipal rule in East Bay cities.

Labor's role in forging a progressive political coalition was not limited to the East Bay; labor forces in San Francisco and Los Angeles also established local Voters Leagues after the war. The San Francisco league resembled the OVL and included activists from many of the same CIO unions. The Los Angeles Voters League, founded in 1948, was a direct descendant of the United AFL Committee for Political Action organized in 1943 as an AFL counterpart to the CIO Political Action Committee. Like the OVL, the San Francisco and Los Angeles Voters Leagues worked to bring labor together with other local progressive groups to pursue a broad-based, multiple-issue program. Explicitly rejecting the role of political lobbying groups, the Voters Leagues organized from the precinct level up, stressing grassroots political participation and leadership development among rank-and-file union members and community activists.[54]

Although further research is needed on labor politics in California cities, the early experience of the Oakland Voters League reveals an innovative and exciting experiment in grassroots democracy and urban coalition-building. In its emphasis on multi-issue politics, grassroots leadership development, and community mobilization, the OVL resembled the People's Organization founded by the CIO organizer Saul Alinsky in Chicago during this same period. Like Alinsky's group, the OVL grew out of a left-wing organizing tradition that labor leaders reformulated and revitalized during and after World War II. Even as labor's role in national politics became increasingly rigid and tied to the fate of the Democratic party during this era, we should not let this obscure these genuinely progressive organizing efforts of labor on the local level.

The experience of the OVL in the 1940s thus suggests a kind of organizational bridge between the class-based movements of the 1930s and the cultural or community-based social movements that have emerged since the 1960s (i.e., civil rights, women's liberation, community organizing, and so forth). Although the conservatism of the 1950s posed a historical chasm between these two types of movements, the new social activism did not emerge suddenly in the sixties; the urban movements of the 1940s provided important precedents.[55]

Unfortunately, the efforts of the 1940s would be short-lived. If distant events had spurred changes in East Bay politics during the war, subsequent national and international events would also influence these cities after 1947. As we shall see in the next chapter, the housing issue would become the focal point of urban conflict and a barometer of the nation's shifting economy, demographics, and ideology.

8

Boomtown Blues

Today most Bay Area residents see Richmond only when driving along Interstate 580 to or from the San Rafael Bridge. Few know of the city's illustrious history, and most wonder why so much vacant space exists along this south-side freeway. The answer goes back to the early 1950s, when Richmond razed hundreds of acres of war housing to open up land for private development. In so doing, the city evicted thousands of minority and low-income tenants, sowing the seeds of racial discontent that would plague Richmond and other East Bay cities for decades.

The controversy over war housing proved to be a critical turning point in East Bay politics after the war. War housing areas occupied strategic land and housed people who were culturally and racially distinct from prewar residents. Waged in the politically charged atmosphere of the late forties and early fifties, the war housing conflict would be the final struggle over the future of the migrant community in the East Bay.

Although prohousing progressives mounted a successful challenge to business leadership shortly after the war, the liberal momentum expired by the early fifties. Returning prosperity, changing urban demographics, a pervasive climate of anti-Communism, and a rising tide of white racial fear all undermined the liberal initiatives of the labor coalition. Conservatives, led by banking and real estate interests, thus used the housing controversy to reestablish their hegemony in East Bay cities.

A Shifting Job Market

In the immediate postwar period, progressives had won electoral victories in the midst of an economic recession and a business backlash that contrasted markedly with the wartime growth and social cooperation that labor had hoped to preserve. The gap between expectations and reality was the key to labor's successful revolt in Oakland in 1947. Returning prosperity, however, tended to undercut labor's message and made many working people—especially whites—less receptive to progressive appeals.

Following the initial postwar recession, the Bay Area economy began to recover in the late 1940s. As the Cold War intensified, expanding U.S. military commitments around the world fueled the local defense economy. Although shipbuilding was not part of this expansion, increased military activity provided new jobs at East Bay installations like the Oakland Army Base, the Naval Supply Center, and the Alameda Naval Air Station. Other East Bay residents commuted to nearby military facilities in Benecia, Vallejo, Hunter's Point, and Port Chicago. Between 1940 and 1947, government became the fastest-growing employment sector, increasing 186 percent.

The growth of government employment was part of a larger Bay Area trend away from manufacturing and toward trade and services. After the war, pent-up consumer demand resulted in explosive growth in wholesale and retail trade, and a wartime population boom required expanded services of all types. By 1947, manufacturing jobs represented a smaller share of total Bay Area employment than in 1940; trade and services showed the largest gains. In addition to government and wholesale and retail trade, the fastest-growing fields included construction, transportation, and communications.[1]

As in the nation generally, the growth of the service sector in the Bay Area expanded opportunities for women workers, particularly married women. Following an initial period of postwar layoffs, the burgeoning trade and service sectors absorbed thousands of displaced women workers. Between 1940 and 1947, the number of working women grew by 84 percent in the San Francisco–Oakland area, compared with 49 percent for men. Much of the work, however, was concentrated in lower-paying, traditionally female fields.[2]

Black women, and black workers generally, did not share in the postwar expansion of trade and services because of discriminatory hiring practices. Black workers displaced from shipbuilding and other defense industries often turned to federal government operations, which were more susceptible to pressures for fair employment. Black men continued to find employment on railroads and docks in the East Bay, and a few managed to break into the building trades and automobile plants. Black women worked in local canneries, government installations, and domestic work but displayed a firm resistance to the latter—often preferring unemployment to live-in service. Despite economic growth, unemployment remained a serious problem for black workers. During the 1949 recession, unemployment in the predominantly black area of north Richmond reached 32 percent—more than four times the rate of all Richmond workers. Clearly, the fruits of postwar prosperity were not equally shared.[3]

Changing urban demographics after the war also resulted in economic inequities. To a greater extent than ever before, suburban areas grew at the expense of the older central cities, leaving urban residents with relatively fewer economic opportunities. While white residents found employment in the burgeoning service sector and new homes in federally financed suburbs, blacks competed for a dwindling number of manufacturing jobs and central city housing units. This dilemma was part of a larger economic transformation that transcended the immediate problems of the East Bay. Throughout the northern United States, central city areas lost industry and manufacturing jobs to suburban areas and to newer cities in the South and West.

Collectively, the Bay Area benefited from this economic shift, but the gains were by no means uniform. Rural and suburban counties in the South Bay experienced phenomenal growth in the postwar years, but the older industrial cities of the Bay Area decelerated accordingly. The Bay Area was a microcosm of the nation at large— with San Francisco, Oakland, and Richmond exemplifying older, declining cities and the South Bay representing the emergent "Sunbelt" economy.

This shift of economic activity was not accidental; national and local business leaders made deliberate decisions to de-emphasize central city development. East Bay business leaders had begun promoting the "metropolitan Oakland area" back in the 1930s, but the suburban exodus accelerated dramatically after the war under the leadership of the Bay Area Council. Founded by local business interests in 1944, the Bay

Area Council was a regional planning organization dedicated to promoting economic development in the entire nine-county Bay Area. The council hoped to rechannel labor and industrial resources away from the sagging war economy toward new projects in industry, public works, home building, commerce, and transportation. By luring "footloose factories" into the region's urban periphery, however, the council's plan served the interests of suburban areas at the expense of the cities. In the suburbs, business leaders explained, industry could escape the housing shortage, traffic jams, crowded streetcars, swollen land prices, and high taxes and living costs that characterized war-bloated cities. And, they might have added, industry could also escape the cities' growing minority populations and an increasingly powerful labor movement. Suburban employers, the council claimed, "testify that their employees are more loyal, more cooperative, more productive workers than those in big cities."[4]

The fastest-growing suburban area in the postwar era was Santa Clara County in the South Bay. Largely fruit orchards before the war, Santa Clara first attracted Westinghouse and a few other defense contractors during World War II. Launching an elaborate public relations campaign at the end of the war, the county successfully encouraged the postwar expansion of Westinghouse, Lockheed, and other aircraft and electrical industries. Santa Clara County was thus able to profit from new patterns of federal defense spending in the 1950s, a development that laid the groundwork for the later emergence of "Silicon Valley." By the 1980s, San Jose would be the largest city and Santa Clara the most populous county in the Bay Area.

Other adjoining South and East Bay counties also boomed. Southern Alameda County, dominated by truck farms in the prewar period, attracted an array of automobile plants, food-packaging facilities, and other industries after the war. Central Contra Costa County and the suburbs north of Richmond also showed rapid residential and industrial expansion.

Much of this growth, however, came directly at the expense of Oakland and Richmond. Both cities lost major industries to the suburbs, including a General Motors plant that relocated from Oakland to Fremont and Ford Motors—Richmond's largest prewar employer—which moved to Milpitas in 1955. By the late fifties, Oakland's industry accounted for only 28 percent of all industrial investment in Alameda County. Not surprisingly, unemployment rates in central city areas grew in response to the suburban exodus of industry.[5]

The Housing Crisis

Jobs were not the only thing in short supply in East Bay cities; poor and working-class families also faced a critical housing shortage. The housing problem in war boomtowns did not abate after after the war but actually worsened. As thousands of veterans returned to the area and private property owners evicted tenants to make room for returning family members, the waiting list for public housing reached record length in 1945–1946. By the late forties, housing officials reported that more than 12 percent of East Bay families were doubled up with friends or relatives. The most severe shortage occurred in Oakland, where housing authorities estimated the need for at least twenty-three thousand new units to accommodate families currently residing in temporary war housing or sharing quarters with others.

Lower-income families encountered the tightest market conditions. With federally guaranteed loans provided under the Servicemen's Readjustment Act (G.I. bill) of 1944, many middle-income residents found housing among the burgeoning subdivisions of surrounding suburbs. In the central cities, however, low-income families competed for a limited stock of low-cost houses and apartments. Based on housing surveys in the late forties and early fifties, the Housing Authority concluded that there were "practically no housing units . . . offered at rentals within the reach of lower-income families." Furthermore, black families of all income levels were barred from most suburban developments through restrictive covenants, a practice resulting in additional pressure on the central city housing market.[6]

In this desperately tight housing market, federal authorities sought to aid returning veterans by granting them priority placement in temporary war housing projects. This policy substantially changed the occupancy pattern in East Bay public housing. In Richmond, temporary projects had accepted only migrant war workers and their families during the war; by 1950, two-thirds of all tenants were the families of veterans or of those still in active service. A similar shift occurred in Codornices Village in Berkeley and in the temporary projects in Oakland and Alameda. According to a Berkeley graduate student who investigated Codornices in 1953, large war worker families who could afford new quarters moved out of the project when they outgrew the small, cramped apartments. Veterans' families, often younger and with fewer children, quickly replaced them.[7]

As noted earlier, many of the veterans were migrants themselves who came to the East Bay to join up with friends and relatives. These younger migrants tended to earn less than their predecessors of the war years, and their incomes compared unfavorably with other residents of the community. In the early fifties, Richmond had a per-capita income of $1,111, but housing project dwellers earned an average of only $849. In Oakland, the average income of public housing tenants also declined because of the reestablishment of income ceilings in permanent housing projects in 1947. With the eviction of hundreds of over-income tenants, low-income residents once again dominated public housing.[8]

The housing shortage itself contributed to the impoverishment of public housing tenants. Although the Bay Area offered a variety of new job opportunities, many were physically inaccessible to East Bay residents. An extremely tight housing market severely limited the geographic mobility of labor, literally freezing some families into unemployment. This was especially true in Richmond, where public war housing had become a refuge for homeless veterans' families.[9]

The postwar period also saw a growing percentage of minority occupants in public housing. One of the newest groups to move in after the war was the Japanese. The Richmond Housing Authority assigned several hundred Japanese-American families to segregated areas in the Cutting War Apartments and Cutting Annex in El Cerrito. Generally spurned by other residents, the Japanese occupants were the families of nisei veterans, servicemen, and returning evacuees. Some of the exiled families had been prewar residents of the East Bay who had lost their homes and livelihoods as a result of relocation. Forced to start over, Japanese-Americans joined other migrants in the war housing projects that served as a portal to East Bay cities.[10]

Southern black migrants constituted the fastest-growing minority in public housing areas. Between March 1945 and May 1946, black occupancy in temporary housing in the East Bay increased 22 percent. New migrants streamed in by the thousands in the postwar era, and wartime migrants remained trapped in public housing because of racial discrimination in the private market. From 1949 to 1951, for instance, Bay Area cities issued more than 75,000 building permits for private dwellings of which only 600 were open to black buyers. Black residents of public housing thus tended to remain in the projects after the war. According to an Oakland Housing Authority survey in 1946, turnover among black residents during a sixty-day period was only 1.5 percent compared with 15.7 percent for whites. With negligible turnover rates, an increasing number of black families competed for a limited quantity of public housing units.[11]

The severe housing shortage among black families prompted some cities to liberalize their racial policies. In response to wartime protests the Public Housing Authority (PHA—the agency dropped the adjective "Federal" in 1947) strengthened its stand on racial equality in the postwar period, encouraging local authorities to abandon segregation and liberalize racial quotas. Berkeley and Oakland both revised their quotas upward so that by the late forties blacks made up the majority of public housing tenants. In the Bay Area overall, more than half of the total black population lived in temporary war housing in 1946.[12]

The shifts in occupancy and racial composition did not bode well for the future of public housing in East Bay cities. With their residents suffering the effects of unemployment and racism, war housing areas had higher rates of crime, disease, and infant mortality than other neighborhoods. Such problems, combined with the rising rate of black occupancy, no doubt strengthened the determination of conservative leaders to rid their cities of unwanted temporary housing. Although city officials avoided blatant racial epithets, more strident denunciations of "slums," "blight," and "squalor" in the late forties had definite racist overtones.

At the same time, internal racial tensions among housing project residents themselves probably hindered effective political organizing. The wholesale turnover of tenants in the postwar years resulted in a lack of continuity and organization as more established members of the community moved away. Migrant settlements had never been tightly knit communities, but the postwar turnover reduced whatever cohesion existed. In later political disputes, the lack of effective organization would leave these residents ill equipped to fight redevelopment programs and their own dispossession.[13]

Finally, the loss of major industries and white workers to the suburbs was a blow for urban labor coalitions that fought on behalf of public housing residents. Increasingly, public housing and other urban programs would be viewed as minority issues, alien to the interests of white working-class voters who aspired to homeownership in the suburbs. Race would thus become the main dividing line in postwar urban politics, eclipsing the wartime division between newcomers and old-timers and the class-based political battles of the mid-1940s.

War Housing:
Reconstruction versus Removal

Changing economic, demographic, and racial patterns presented urban policymakers with difficult problems in the postwar years. In an effort to revitalize the urban core, professional planners called for slum clearance projects in several East Bay cities. Although such programs had originated under the New Deal, the major thrust did not come until after the war. Under the California Community Redevelopment Act of 1945, East Bay cities established local agencies to develop master plans in preparation for future federal funding. Urban redevelopment was to have a long and complex history, and a full discussion of the subject is beyond the scope of this study. During the late forties and early fifties, however, the removal of war housing was the number one redevelopment issue in East Bay cities and led to a showdown between conservative and liberal forces in local politics.

Planning administrations in Oakland and Richmond promptly turned to the wartime data on crime, juvenile delinquency, and other social conditions to justify their policies. In Richmond, the Planning Commission correlated data on housing stock with social characteristics such as welfare cases, police calls, and incidences of juvenile delinquency. The highest concentrations were tagged with black triangles and labeled "blighted." In Oakland, where the wartime juvenile delinquency campaigns had been most sophisticated, planners took data directly from the Council of Social Agencies. Rather than blaming the problem on newcomers as public officials had done during the war, planners adopted an environmental explanation. "The rapid turnover of residents experienced in most of the problem areas," said the planners, "suggests that this environment is like an infectious disease which affects new and old residents alike." Although they could not identify the exact causes of delinquency, they believed it was a problem "which, *like blight itself,* result[ed] from a wide variety of factors" (emphasis mine).[14] In equating crime and delinquency with "blight," planners applied perceptions of wartime social disorder to generate postwar redevelopment plans.

Not surprisingly, migrant settlements emerged as the primary targets of "slum clearance." In Oakland, the City Planning Administration published its report in 1949, recommending redevelopment of the predominantly black west Oakland area; the East-of-the-Lake district (a white working-class neighborhood that included the Auditorium

Village war housing project); and tracts along the Oakland Estuary containing other temporary projects. The following year, Richmond planning officials issued a report that targeted the black neighborhood of north Richmond and extensive areas of public housing in south Richmond.

Vocal protests by local property owners caused the city to shelve redevelopment schemes in private neighborhoods, but city officials remained committed to prompt demolition of temporary war housing. Federal law required that such housing be removed after the war, and many old-time residents were anxious to see it go. Local officials had been calling for its removal since 1945, but the federal government postponed demolition for several years because of the housing shortage. By the late forties, city leaders had grown impatient, claiming such projects were blighting their communities. In 1949, the City Planning Administration dubbed war housing projects "Oakland's sorest blight problem," adding that they were "beyond the salvage point. Squalid and unkempt, they [were] unsuitable for housing or any other use." Richmond planners agreed, noting that the south-side public housing area was becoming "a vast ugly slum, a reproach to the City and a constant source of trouble, conflict and expense."[15]

As in the war years, conservative city leaders continued to view temporary housing residents as temporary citizens. According to W. Miller Barbour, a National Urban League representative, "the core community of Richmond ha[d] always thought of this housing as temporary and its inhabitants as being equally temporary." Among old-time residents, said the West Contra Costa Community Welfare Council, "there was the opinion, prevalent in many areas, that they [migrants] were here only as temporary residents."[16] As a result, conservative officials felt little responsibility toward these citizens and actively sought to move their "blighted" neighborhoods off of city lands.

Removal of the housing, conservatives maintained, was the key to the city's future. "If Richmond can remove the stigma of its temporary war housing and attendant economic and social conditions, it would appear to have bright prospects for attracting many of the industries which are locating or relocating in the Bay Area."[17] Housing lands, then, assumed a strategic significance in the postwar reconstruction effort—"temporary" residents would have to leave, taking their undesirable social and economic traits with them.

Although acknowledging the need for redevelopment and slum clearance, progressive officials placed greater emphasis on tenant relocation and the construction of new public housing. Liberals and conservatives thus approached the redevelopment issue from different perspectives. Liberals saw it as an opportunity to rehouse needy veterans and war migrants; conservatives embraced it as a means of removing undesirables and returning housing project lands to private development.

The federal housing acts of 1949–1950 offered something to please both camps. Under the 1949 act, the federal government provided the long-awaited funding and apparatus for public housing and urban redevelopment, including an allocation of 135,000 public housing units nationwide to rehouse displaced residents. The following year, a second act transferred title of all war housing projects from federal to local authorities. The latter could either continue operation of the projects or clear the land for redevelopment. The federal government would demolish any projects not claimed by their host cities, and remaining tenants would have to vacate by July 1, 1952. The act also required federal and local authorities to assist in relocating displaced tenants.

In overcrowded West Coast cities, new public housing was essential to replace aging war housing units. Under the 1949 program, Richmond applied for 4,230 new units, and Oakland requested 3,000. Although they contained significantly fewer units than existing war housing, the new projects promised to provide shelter for at least the neediest of the displaced families.

The public housing program, however, hit several snags over the next few years. First, the outbreak of the Korean War and the consequent need to conserve building supplies resulted in a reduction of federally allocated units for Oakland, Richmond, and most other cities. The war also caused Congress to postpone the transfer of war housing for another two years, until July 1, 1954. Most critically, the National Association of Real Estate Boards (NAREB), the main opponent of public housing since the 1930s, renewed its attacks against "socialized housing." Although they lost the initial battle against the Housing Act of 1949, NAREB soon regrouped and shifted its focus to the state and local levels.[18]

NAREB selected California as a test case for its anti–public housing campaign. As the state Chamber of Commerce pointed out, California contained more federally owned public housing than any state in the union. As landlord of 270,000 people (including 60,000 black families), the U.S. government was "the largest single operator of residential real estate in California." With California communities applying for some 36,000 new public housing units under the 1949 program, business and real estate interests expressed fear that an additional 90,000 people would leave the private housing market.

Seeking to prevent this occurrence, NAREB quickly organized its forces in California, a state in which real estate developers had long had a central role in local politics. NAREB formed the Committee for Home Protection (CHP), led by Fred D. Parr, the East Bay developer who had masterminded the construction of the Port of Richmond in the 1920s and later helped bring in Kaiser during the war. Backed by massive funding from the real estate industry and the state Chamber of Commerce, the CHP claimed to be "made up of Californians from all walks of life." According to housing reformers of the California Housing Association, though, the CHP was a real estate industry front group, a "ruthless and unprincipled opposition which [would] resort to any stratagem to accomplish its ends."[19]

Along with Los Angeles County, Oakland became the main battleground for the housing issue. In 1948, the Oakland Real Estate Board and the Apartment House Owners Association joined forces under the local CHP branch and launched an anti–public housing referendum. Attacking public housing as "socialistic," the CHP appealed to voters' patriotism, fiscal conservatism, and belief in free enterprise. In the midst of an economic upswing and growing anti-Communism, such rhetoric had strong appeal, particularly among the white middle class. The initiative won, defeating public housing in principle but without force of law.

In the meantime, labor representatives on the city council had been working hard to secure support for the housing cause. Now that the liberal Oakland Voters League occupied four of nine council seats, it needed only one defector to win the housing vote. By trading their support for the mayoral candidacy of one of the Knowland-backed council members, the OVL members stood a good chance of winning the housing vote.[20]

In the summer of 1949, anti–public housing forces waged a fierce, emotional, and often misleading campaign directed at black homeowners in west Oakland. Real estate groups working through the local CHP branch rented sound trucks to tour the neighborhood blaring, "your homes are about to be torn down; you will have no place to live; public housing will not admit you; go down to the city council meeting and fight this menace." Building on legitimate black fears of "slum clearance," the CHP mobilized hundreds of west Oakland residents to turn out for the heated meeting of August 20.

During this meeting the city council, after much debate, approved the Housing Authority's request for three thousand new units. Bowing to the wishes of west Oakland homeowners and merchants, the council passed an ordinance restricting all construction to vacant or federally owned land occupied by temporary housing.[21]

The CHP was outraged by this compromise. Filing affidavits for the recall of three of the five prohousing council members (the other two had not yet served six months and were thus ineligible for recall), the CHP launched an elaborate and vicious red-baiting campaign associating the labor coalition with "socialized housing" and "CIO Communism." Although red-baiting tactics had been largely unsuccessful in past elections, a rising tide of anti-Communism made the public more suspicious and susceptible to such appeals. In a special election held in February 1950, two members were reelected but a third, Scott Weakley, was ousted. Losing his job as a radio announcer because of alleged employer blacklisting, Weakley committed suicide shortly thereafter. In a low-turnout election the following year, two other liberal council members, Joseph Smith and Raymond Pease, also lost to CHP-backed candidates running on an anti–public housing, anti-Communist platform. The remaining OVL representative died in office.[22]

By 1951, then, the liberal challenge in Oakland had run its course— defeated over the housing issue that had come to symbolize the future of the city. Conservative anti–public housing forces regained firm control of the city government and rescinded federal housing contracts. That year, Mayor Clifford Rishell filled two vacancies on the Housing Authority with appointees who promptly scrapped the one east Oakland project that had reached the planning stage. According to Edmund Horwinski, executive director of the Oakland Housing Authority, "there was such strong opposition from the Apartment House Owners Association and the Real Estate Board that [the Housing Authority] didn't get anywhere at all." In fact, between 1945 and 1965, the city constructed a total of only five hundred public housing units. During those same years, the city leveled one temporary housing project after another, displacing thousands of migrants, veterans, and low-income residents.[23]

What had happened between 1947 and 1951 to so shift the course of Oakland politics? Most critically, the pervasive climate of Cold War anti-Communism worked to the advantage of conservatives, who used red-baiting to discredit liberals. But the internal divisions that wracked the labor coalition were even more damaging. Under the impact of

Taft-Hartley loyalty oaths and the bitterness of the 1948 presidential election, the CIO was torn by raids, ousters, and infighting. With the most progressive labor forces in disarray, leadership fell to the AFL contingent led by J. C. Reynolds, chairman of the Central Labor Council.

Reynolds's leadership was damaging to the coalition in several ways. Most obviously, Reynolds's 1951 indictment on federal bribery and conspiracy charges critically harmed the credibility of the labor coalition. The *Tribune*'s age-old cries of "labor bossism" now seemed disturbingly close to reality. Unlike his predecessors, Reynolds scorned any attempt to enlist the support of the local black community. From their perspective, black leaders had little cause to back labor candidates. Those elected in 1947 had not delivered on their campaign promises to pass a fair employment practices act and to deal with police brutality against minority citizens. Admittedly, the conservative council majority had derailed labor's efforts to do so, but progressives had also defected on other issues such as the city sales tax increase. In the conservative climate of postwar Oakland, labor representation was not the progressive panacea that many had hoped it would be. As the CIO *Labor Herald* explained, the coalition's defeat "was a tragic lesson in the cost of disunity and political opportunism."[24]

The success of anti–public housing forces in Oakland and in a similar dispute in Los Angeles encouraged the Committee for Home Protection to try out its electoral tactics on the state level.[25] Later that year, the CHP sponsored Proposition 10, which called for an amendment to the state constitution to prohibit the establishment of any low-rent housing project without the express approval of a majority of voters in the locality. Those opposing the measure included the AFL, the CIO, the Railroad Brotherhoods, the American Legion, the Veterans of Foreign Wars, and an array of religious and community groups. After a bitter campaign in which the CHP vastly outspent its opponents, Proposition 10 passed by some thirty-seven thousand votes. Thereafter, construction of public housing in California required a protracted and costly electoral campaign, an effort that few localities were willing or able to make.[26]

The housing debacle disheartened liberal leaders in East Bay cities. The Oakland recall election was a trenchant example of conservative power, said the California Housing Association, "used to intimidate city councilmen in every other California community." According to State Assemblyman Byron Rumford in 1956, "any politician who espoused . . . public housing as such was threatened with political finality."[27] With the opposition effectively silenced, conservative leaders in other Bay Area cities moved ahead with redevelopment plans, removing temporary housing projects and their residents with impunity.

Housing Removal in Richmond

With the nation's largest war housing program, Richmond was a prime site for redevelopment—at least from the perspective of the city's conservatives. The demolition program that ensued displaced tens of thousands of residents and caused grave hardships that highlighted the racial issues underlying redevelopment.

In 1950, 50.5 percent of the city's population still lived in war housing, including 78 percent of all black residents (more than twenty-eight hundred families). Up through 1951 the Richmond Housing Authority had maintained a four-to-one ratio between white and black residents and had practiced the "patchwork pattern," segregating black residents by building and by area. Because of such policies, housing officials routinely turned away black applicants despite an increasing number of vacancies in Richmond projects after 1949. This practice continued until 1952, when, under pressure from the federal Public Housing Authority, Richmond passed a resolution banning segregation in public housing. However, the permanent projects of Atchison Village, Nystrom Village, and Triangle Court remained heavily white with only token integration after 1952.[28]

Since the end of the war, various factions in Richmond had debated the merits of postwar redevelopment. As in Oakland, most city officials urged the prompt removal of temporary war housing, which they saw as a deterrent to industrial growth. The lack of permanent housing, it was rumored, had been behind Ford's 1953 decision to move its assembly plant to the South Bay. According to City Assessor Forest J. Simoni, Richmond had been unable to participate in the postwar industrial expansion of the Bay Area and needed south-side housing lands for this purpose.

On the other side, a group of downtown merchants opposed redevelopment, fearing the loss of business due to displacement of thousands of housing residents. The NAACP, the CIO, and other progressive groups also questioned redevelopment policies, pressing for public housing construction to meet the needs of the displaced. According to one political observer, financial and industrial leaders in the Chamber of Commerce eventually persuaded the merchants' committee to accept redevelopment, convincing them that public housing tenants were transient, made poor credit risks, and bought few durable goods. With the defection of the merchants, progressives lost critical support in their fight to modify city redevelopment plans.[29]

Although planners promised to use south-side lands for both new industry *and* housing, the city in fact built little housing. During the early fifties, Richmond abandoned its original request for 4,230 public housing units, settling for one 300-unit complex (Easter Hill) and encouraging private contractors to make up the difference. Ultimately, of course, private enterprise would be unable to meet the needs of many low-income tenants, and thousands of them would have to leave the city. George Tobing, director of the Redevelopment Agency, said as much in 1953:

The only way we can have both industry and the present population is to build skyscrapers for houses. . . . Obviously, many people now living in Richmond are going to have to move. We want them to stay in this area, of course, but we don't care if they go to Pinole [an outlying suburb]. . . . That doesn't mean that anybody is going to be kicked out of Richmond. It means that over the years, there will be population attrition and orderly rebuilding.

According to a *San Francisco Chronicle* reporter, Richard Reinhardt, this was also the unstated policy of the city council, the Housing Authority, and other Richmond planning bodies.[30]

Although no one was "kicked out" of Richmond, inadequate relocation arrangements forced many residents to leave the city. This situation first came to light in 1952 with the evacuation and demolition of Canal and Terrace War Apartments. The selection of Canal and Terrace as the first demolition sites was in itself an indication of racial bias. With a total of 911 units, these projects housed more than seven hundred black families and represented the heart of black settlement on the south side.

Local officials added insult to injury by conducting eviction proceedings abruptly and insensitively. Initially, the Richmond Housing Authority made no effort to alert project tenants of their future relocation; Canal and Terrace residents first learned of it from an article in the *Richmond Independent*. A few days later, the Housing Authority sent out a rather flippant letter to the affected tenants. "We regret the necessity of asking you to move," the letter said. "We know that many of you like the low rent, the spaces for your children to play and many other things in Canal. But as many of you who were in the Army and Navy know, 'orders is orders.' " Hundreds of veterans' families were the recipients of this callous official notice.[31]

The city offered little information on the actual mechanics of relocation or what actions it would take to rehouse displaced tenants. As a result, a storm of protest erupted among black residents, who feared they would be pushed out of the city. Led by Father John Garcia, the Reverend W. Lee La Beaux, and other housing project religious leaders, black tenants staged a series of protests at city hall demanding priority in other public housing projects. With rumors of racial violence afoot, the Redevelopment Agency created a placement center downtown to assist residents in finding private housing. For those who could not find accommodations, the agency would place them in public housing vacancies as required by state and federal law.[32]

Although 35 percent of white families found housing in the private market, only 16 percent of black families did—the rest were funneled back into war housing. According to a black real estate agent, Neitha Williams, in 1953, "there was nothing, absolutely nothing in private rentals or sales available to the minority groups. They had to take what the housing authority offered." In this case, the Housing Authority moved most of the displaced tenants into vacancies on State and Fall streets, a dilapidated area high on the list for future demolition. A few years later, these tenants would have to move again, as south-side redevelopment claimed their homes.[33]

In effect, the city forced black housing residents into a holding pattern, moving them from one temporary project to another. "The unhappy housing tenants," noted one newspaper reporter, "concluded that the leaders of Richmond [were] more anxious to divest their city of vestiges of the past than to include 'housing people' in the city's future." The Reverend W. Lee La Beaux, a black pastor at the Canal project's Providence Baptist Church, remarked: "[Ultimately,] our people will be driven away. . . . Sometimes I am sure that's what the people running this town really want."[34]

The following year, in 1953, a second redevelopment conflict erupted when the city moved to tear down Harbor Gate, a predominantly white project. The Richmond Housing Authority had originally slated this better-quality project as "reservoir housing" for displaced families, making it a low priority for demolition. All that changed, however, when the Safeway supermarket chain expressed interest in the site for its new regional warehouse. The Chamber of Commerce immediately formed a "Get Safeway" recruiting committee and after thirteen months of closed negotiations delivered city support for the deal. With demolition scheduled for the following year, eviction of Harbor Gate residents began in March 1953.

As with the Canal and Terrace projects, city agencies displayed little sense of responsibility in their handling of relocation proceedings. Once again, project residents were not consulted on redevelopment plans and learned of their impending displacement from the newspapers. Outraged tenants, including some veterans attending the University of California, organized to fight the plan. Led by Hugh Hansen, a graduate student in economics at Berkeley, the tenants took their case to the city council, the federal Public Housing Authority and the U.S. Congress. They asked local officials to delay the demolition of Harbor Gate and demanded representation on "extra-governmental committees that [were] deciding the fate of the city."[35]

Although the tenants' group did not succeed in saving Harbor Gate, they did win important concessions from the city—a fact that underscores the racial dimensions of the redevelopment issue. As noted in chapter 4, Harbor Gate had been one of the model wartime projects, housing the "aristocracy" of shipyard labor—predominantly skilled white workers. In the postwar years, the Richmond Housing Authority maintained the wartime racial quota of at least 90 percent white occupancy. Consequently, tenants' protests that they would be forced out of the community struck a responsive chord with local merchants and industrial leaders who sought to retain these more "desirable" residents.

While plans for the Safeway facility moved forward, city leaders secured replacement housing for Harbor Gate tenants in Atchison Village, the city's largest permanent housing project. Arguing against Atchison's conversion back to low-rent housing, the city set forth its position in a letter to the federal housing administration on September 10, 1953:

The above projects [Atchison Village and Atchison Annex] meet a pressing and immediate need in Richmond's redevelopment programs. They provide housing for skilled and key workers in our City whose incomes, while greater than the limits of eligibility for permanent public low rent accommodations, are too low to permit them to purchase or rent privately owned housing on the local market. . . . Richmond desires to retain these skilled and key workers and their families. A too rapid transfer of these projects to low-rent use . . . will result in the loss of these families to the City, its trading area and perhaps its industries.

By keeping Atchison Village as "temporary housing" with no income ceilings, the city retained many of its skilled white workers from Harbor Gate and hundreds of moderate-income white residents then residing at the Atchison project. Despite promises to reconvert the buildings to low-rent occupancy later on, Richmond sold the project to a private tenants' cooperative in 1957, eliminating the city's largest permanent public housing facility.[36]

The city's failure to reconvert Atchison to low-income use also resulted in a delay of federal funding for the new Easter Hill project. Easter Hill, whose tenants would be primarily low-income black families, was eventually completed, but the city council's intransigence on the Atchison issue precluded any further federal funding. City officials, most of whom opposed public housing anyway, gladly accepted the trade-off. Like neighboring Oakland, Richmond continued to raze its war housing over the next decade but built virtually no public housing to replace it.[37]

Even on its own terms, Richmond's redevelopment policy failed. Although aimed at attracting industry and middle-income whites at the expense of poor, black, and unskilled residents, redevelopment programs did not prevent whites from abandoning the city. According to Helene Conant, a relocation specialist employed by the city from 1957 to 1959, only 46.3 percent of white war housing residents remained in Richmond compared with 56.0 percent of black tenants. Many white residents made use of attractive financing terms under the G.I. bill to purchase homes in surrounding suburban areas such as San Pablo, Pinole, and El Sobrante. One Contra Costa County builder reported in 1950 that he sold more than half of new homes under $9,000 to former war housing tenants from Richmond.[38] Continuing the trend of wartime defense subdivisions, west Contra Costa County attracted an increasing number of white war migrants who brought evangelical churches, country music, and other southern cultural traditions and institutions along with them.

Black public housing tenants did not have this suburban option. The case of the Garys, a black Richmond family, illustrates the degree of white resistance faced by black families that attempted to break the color line in East Bay suburbs. Wilbur Gary, a navy veteran and ex–shipyard worker, had previously lived with his wife and seven children in a four-room apartment in Richmond's Harbor Gate war housing project. Having outgrown the unit, the Garys purchased a home in

1952 in Rollingwood, a defense worker subdivision built in San Pablo during the war (see chapter 4). Because of its war origins, Rollingwood was heavily dominated by defense workers and white war migrants, some of whom were stridently racist. When the Garys moved in, a crowd of more than 150 neighbors greeted them with jeers, rocks, a white cross planted on their lawn, and a brick through their front window. After several hours under siege, the county sheriff arrived and dispersed the crowd, but the attacks on the Garys continued intermittently for several weeks.

The local homeowners' group, the Rollingwood Improvement Association, offered to buy out the Garys at a $1,200 profit—a considerable sum at the time. But the Garys refused to sell at any price, determined to keep their home. At that point, several white neighbors, including four board members of the Rollingwood Association, acquiesced and sent a letter of welcome to the Garys. At the group's next meeting, angry residents voted to recall the four board members by a three-to-one margin. Throughout the controversy, sympathetic white neighbors and local church ministers were denounced as "nigger lovers" and "Communists."[39]

The Garys most effective support came from the local NAACP, which provided round-the-clock volunteers to help protect the house, paid for floodlights on the property, and alerted Governor Earl Warren to the problem. Thereafter, state and local authorities increased efforts to protect the home, and the attacks subsided. The overall effect of this widely publicized incident, however, was to discourage black families from even attempting to move to the suburbs. Similar violent incidents occurred in other California communities affected by defense migration, including South San Francisco and several Los Angeles area neighborhoods.[40]

Some black residents did manage to leave Richmond in these years, settling in north Richmond and other black neighborhoods outside city limits. The county housing authority constructed public housing projects in San Pablo and north Richmond, and a few private contractors experimented with new interracial developments. The latter, however, were too expensive for most war housing tenants, and white reprisals scared off many who might have afforded them.[41] In Richmond, the city continued to demolish war housing but built no new public housing to take its place.

Some of the displaced families ended up on the city's south side, which would become predominantly black by the late fifties. According to oral testimony by south-side homeowners, local real estate agents made a concerted effort to "sell" the neighborhood to black buyers, triggering panic sales by white homeowners. Predictably, the transition began along the southern and western edges, closest to the waterfront and former black public housing areas. From there the new black community expanded north and east, until by the 1960s there was a solid belt of black settlement along the south side.[42] Wartime housing programs, it would appear, affected the private housing market, fostering a new black community in south Richmond. This transformation was not unique; Hunters Point, Marin City, Vallejo, and other shipyard boomtowns in the Bay Area developed similar racial patterns in the postwar period.

The Codornices Conflict

In Berkeley and Albany, the tenuous federal sponsorship of the Codornices Village project made it easier for local officials to rid their communities of war housing and its nonwhite tenants. Ironically, progressive desegregation measures in this project worked to the detriment of black residents by making Codornices predominantly nonwhite and thus a target for removal.

From the project's inception in 1943, the two cities had opposed its construction and had refused to sponsor it in any way. As a result, the Federal Public Housing Authority (FPHA) had taken direct administrative control of the project. Unlike local housing authorities dominated by real estate and business interests, the FPHA proved more responsive to calls for racial equality, particularly in the postwar period. Since 1944, the Berkeley Interracial Committee, led by Byron Rumford, a future state assemblyman, had conducted petition drives calling for the desegregation of Codornices. Their efforts bore fruit in August 1946, when the FPHA appointed a new housing manager for the project and implemented an antidiscrimination policy. Thereafter, all units were open to all applicants regardless of race, and the FPHA conducted mandatory staff training sessions in race relations. Within a year, Codornices integrated 82 percent of its buildings, with black residents now making up 60 percent of its tenants.

The attrition of white tenants, however, posed a problem for Codornices' managers. While black families continued to seek apartments in the complex, an increasing number of white tenants moved out as private housing became available. With a growing number of vacancies in formerly white units, the FPHA decided to drop its sixty-forty racial quota in 1950. In contrast to the situation in Richmond, where thousands of white units remained vacant, Codornices opened its doors to the backlog of black applicants. The new policy, however, undercut integration efforts as the percentage of black applicants shot upward and several buildings became all-black once again. By 1954, 88 percent of Codornices' tenants were minorities, nearly all of them black. Such "open-door" policies increased the visibility of minority tenants, confirming the suspicions of nearby white residents, who feared their neighborhoods would be "overrun" by southern blacks.[43]

The changing racial composition of Codornices Village thus strengthened the resolve of local officials to disassociate themselves from the project. Both the Berkeley and Albany city councils continued to oppose public housing and rejected opportunities to take over management of Codornices. In March 1950, the Berkeley city council voted against conducting a housing survey that would have enabled the city to acquire federal funding to replace the project. Officials at the University of California, which owned approximately 40 percent of the Codornices land, refused to extend the lease, claiming that the university would not "get involved in the housing business." With no eligible local agency willing to adopt Codornices, in March 1954 the federal government announced the closing of the project.[44]

With a termination date set for June 30, 1956, the Public Housing Authority began eviction proceedings on a rolling basis in March 1954. Beginning with couples and small families, federal housing authorities gave six months' notice to approximately one-quarter of Codornices residents; thereafter, the PHA served notices on another five hundred families every six months. The initial notification elicited a sharp reply from angry Codornices residents, who formed a "Save Our Homes Committee" to protest the evictions. Drawing support from the Berkeley NAACP and local members of the Socialist and Communist parties, the committee launched a petition drive calling on the Berkeley city council to save the project. If the city tried to remove tenants without adequate replacement housing, said Arthur Green, a Codornices resident and vice president of the Berkeley NAACP, it would "have to do it at the point of bayonets."[45]

In the end, though, no unified resistance developed. Tenants' organizations throughout the East Bay, in fact, were wracked by internal disputes. The federal Gwinn Amendment of 1952 required all public housing residents to take a loyalty oath, denying allegiance with "Communists, Fascists, and other subversives." Such tactics aggravated tensions between Communists and other tenant groups and helped dissolve the alliance between the local Communist party and the NAACP that had endured through the war. Communist party members then accused the NAACP and other liberals of soft-peddling the housing issue in Berkeley. The NAACP defended its actions around Codornices and accused the Communists of political opportunism on the housing issue. Although all the charges are difficult to assess, they clearly reflect the impact of McCarthyism in heightening tensions between progressives.[46] Under these conditions, broad-based political action around public housing was difficult, if not impossible. With the opposition in disarray, city officials moved forward with relocation plans.

Acting on the recommendations of a special relocation committee, the cities of Berkeley and Albany established placement and counseling centers for evicted families. As in Richmond, few black residents could find affordable private housing through these channels. According to the *San Francisco Chronicle*, Berkeley City Manager John D. Phillips "broadly hinted that residents of the village would do better to hunt for housing in other areas." But with thousands of families recently displaced from war housing in Richmond, housing for blacks was in short supply throughout the East Bay. According to the NAACP, most moved into already overcrowded black neighborhoods, doubling up with friends or relatives.[47]

In June 1955, Berkeley and Albany officials hired a professional relocation specialist to help find accommodations for the remaining 250 families still on site. These families were the "hardship cases": most were large families, many of them with unemployed adults, female-headed, or on public assistance. In these cases, the relocation specialist arranged transfers to public housing facilities in Oakland, thus removing such "problem" families from Berkeley and Albany.[48]

By 1956, all nineteen hundred families had left Codornices, and the federal government returned the land to its original owners. Not all the housing was razed, however. Once the tenants were gone, state and local authorities willingly accepted such federal facilities. The University of California—that had earlier declined to "get involved in the housing business"—eventually took over several hundred units of the project for use as married student housing. Albany officials also negotiated with the federal government for title to the Codornices school and administration buildings. Clearly, the race and class of the tenants—not the deterioration of project buildings—was the main issue.

By the mid-fifties, Berkeley, Oakland, and Richmond had disposed of most of their temporary war housing. The removal of public housing struck minority tenants the hardest; indeed, by 1956, these three cities together had displaced close to three thousand black families—or approximately twelve thousand people. With no new public housing and a costly and racially restricted private market, housing demolition forced these families into already overcrowded black neighborhoods. For both older and newer residents, the quality of life in these flatland neighborhoods steadily deteriorated. East Bay cities thus became rigidly segregated in the postwar period with blacks expanding into and across older central city neighborhoods and whites migrating to new outlying suburbs with the help of federally guaranteed housing loans.

In retrospect, World War II was a critical turning point in the social history of East Bay cities, particularly in terms of race relations. The federal government, which had done so much to encourage migration and urban development during the war, precipitously withdrew from defense centers in the postwar era, leaving the burden of reconversion to local communities. Much as they tried, conservative leaders could not rid their communities of migrants and war-born social problems by simply eliminating war housing. Black newcomers were there to stay, and the callous execution of redevelopment plans only aggravated class and racial tensions.

During the late fifties and early sixties, black inmigration to the East Bay continued and the black population grew accordingly. At the same time, local governments refused to build public housing even as the final remnants of war housing came down for freeway construction, mass transit, and other redevelopment projects. As a result, black settlement spilled over its old boundaries, expanding out along the bay flatlands to north and east Oakland, west Berkeley, and south Richmond.

The postwar black residential pattern mirrored migrant settlement during World War II and was in fact linked to the fate of public war housing. Where the wartime city segregated newcomers and old-timers, the postwar city divided minority and white residents. As white migrants gravitated toward the suburbs and black occupancy in public housing increased, racial divisions eclipsed the newcomer—old-timer conflict of the war years. Antimigrant and anti—public housing rhetoric took on distinctly racial connotations.

Forced together in postwar cities and lumped together in the minds of whites, black newcomers and old-timers forged a new alliance based on race. "Communists, Uncle Toms, preachers, and everybody had to pull together," explained Margaret Starks, a former NAACP leader. "Where you were born wasn't the issue, but where you could go was the problem." For blacks especially, racial mobilization overshadowed the cultural and class conflicts of the World War II era.[49]

Over the next decade, racial tensions increased and finally exploded in the mid-1960s, when both Oakland and Richmond experienced several days of rioting and racial unrest. As in Watts, Newark, and dozens of other cities, black rioters responded not only to immediate civil rights issues but to a long history of racial oppression. In the East Bay, the roots of this violence stretched back more than twenty years—to the racial troubles accompanying war migration and to the ruthless displacement of black war housing residents under postwar redevelopment programs.

The tragic saga of housing removal and migrant and minority displacement was common among West Coast cities. The postwar experiences of Los Angeles and Portland, in fact, were remarkably similar to those of the East Bay. In both those areas, the unraveling of war boom society produced heated battles over public housing construction that pitted middle-income white homeowners against minority tenants. Although liberals had found widespread support for public housing construction just after the war, by the early 1950s a conservative counteroffensive had thwarted their plans.

In postwar Los Angeles, where a vast influx of veterans joined hundreds of thousands of wartime migrants, a broad-based coalition of labor and other progressive forces helped rally unanimous city council support for the construction of ten thousand public housing units in 1949. By 1951, however, the real estate industry, the Chamber of Commerce, and the *Los Angeles Times* organized an anti–public housing lobby known as the Citizens Against Socialist Housing (CASH). Like the Committee for Home Protection in Oakland, CASH orchestrated an expensive and ultimately successful campaign against a 1952 public housing referendum, attacking the program as "creeping socialism." CASH also waged a pernicious red-baiting campaign against housing supporters on the city council and local housing authority. In 1953, CASH allegations led to an investigation of the City Housing Authority by the California Senate Committee on Un-American Activities and the firing of three of its members who had taken the Fifth Amendment. Occurring only weeks before the city's mayoral election, the McCarthy-like hearings contributed to the defeat of Fletcher Bowron, the incumbent and prohousing mayor. The new mayor, Norris Poulson, an anti–public housing crusader, negotiated a compromise with the City Housing Authority, effectively scrapping more than half of the planned units. As in the East Bay, the city removed acres of temporary war housing but built few units to replace them.[50]

Portland Mayor Dorothy Lee had faced a similar defeat a year earlier amid a storm of sentiment against public housing. Back in 1948, Lee had successfully defeated machine incumbent Earl Riley by offering a reform agenda promising to clean up police corruption, institute a city manager system, and expand municipal services—including public housing. The need for replacement housing in the area was particularly critical after a flood destroyed the 10,000-unit Vanport war housing project in May 1948. But as in Oakland and Los Angeles, Portland voters rejected a 1950 referendum allocating funds for 2,000 units of public housing under the 1949 federal program. White middle-class residents who "associated public housing with undisciplined war workers and blacks" were the strongest opponents. Lee's support for this unpopular issue ensured her defeat to conservative Fred Peterson two years later.[51] The city thus continued to dismantle its temporary war housing, relegating Portland's migrant black residents to deteriorating and overcrowded north Portland neighborhoods.

In several West Coast cities, then, public housing became, quite literally, a referendum on the future of the migrant community. The conflict, however, was no longer between newcomers and old-timers but between whites and blacks. In Oakland and other California cities, labor and progressive forces had struggled to build an interracial coalition that addressed the needs of urban newcomers and working people generally. But by the early 1950s, returning prosperity, changing urban demographics, and an increasingly conservative political climate had made such alliances untenable. Under conservative rule, the callous treatment of black migrants in the postwar era fueled growing racial resentments that would explode in the urban riots of the 1960s. In the East Bay, as in other West Coast defense centers, racial conflict would be the most enduring and troublesome legacy of World War II.

Conclusion

West Coast cities experienced dramatic upheavals during the Second World War, producing domestic social conflicts that proved as significant as those overseas. Military mobilization, the creation of new defense industries, and massive inmigration transformed the urban landscape of Oakland, Richmond, and other western defense centers. The influx of war migrants radically increased the racial and cultural diversity of such cities, shaping urban social and political relations both during and after the war. For these communities, the impact of World War II was immense and undeniable.

Historians of the home front have long disputed the significance of World War II as an agent of social change in the United States. Some argue that the war was a watershed in American history; others find that it merely accelerated existing social and economic trends. Clearly, there is some validity to both claims.

Although this study emphasizes the war's role in transforming urban life, wartime developments in the East Bay were not wholly unprecedented. Beginning in the 1920s, Kaiser and other defense contractors gained valuable experience with federal government contracting, prefabrication, and corporate welfare schemes that would be used extensively in the war effort. In the 1930s, "Okie" migrants blazed an early trail to California and provided direct personal links in a chain of migration that would culminate in the war years. Patterns of migration, family networks, and survival strategies—particularly among white southwesterners—were clearly established in this earlier period.

In California cities, federal-local cooperation, public housing programs, suburban development, and other urbanization trends all date back to the prewar era. New patterns of labor relations also arose in response to New Deal initiatives of the 1930s as did some of the progressive political alliances spawned by the CIO. The war experience, then, resulted in both continuity and change, accelerating many existing trends while at the same time introducing new urban populations and policies.

The preoccupation with the war-as-watershed has blinded historians to more important questions regarding the impact of World War II. Rather than tallying the forces of change and continuity, historians of the home front would do better to identify exactly *where* and *how* specific changes occurred and how the war reshaped existing social and economic trends. Furthermore, we should consider the pace at which these events transpired, understanding that rapid, unplanned social change produces different results than the same phenomenon spread over several decades.

First, we must acknowledge that the war affected various regions of the country quite differently, boosting the fortunes of some at the expense of others. On the positive side, urban areas in the South and West—and especially West Coast cities—grew tremendously in terms of both population and economic development. Unlike eastern cities and many rural areas, western defense centers were visibly and permanently transformed by the war as new industries, residents, housing, and services sprang up along the urban periphery. In these communities, change—not continuity—was the dominant theme.

Interstate migration, though by no means a new development in California, took an important new direction during the war years. Unlike the depression-era Okies, defense migrants shunned agricultural work and headed directly for coastal defense centers. The arrival and subsequent settlement of these migrants changed the population composition of West Coast cities, making them markedly younger, more southern, and more black than ever before.

No doubt the most significant shift in western migration patterns during the war was the new influx of southern black residents. Black migration radically expanded the African-American population of West Coast cities, permanently transforming residential patterns, race relations, and political culture. As a result, the small black communities of the prewar East Bay increasingly resembled eastern-style ghettos, posing both social problems and political opportunities for their black residents.

The suddenness and rapidity of the war boom had serious implications for the physical and social development of West Coast communities. Cataclysmic defense migration precluded any kind of gradual accommodation of newcomers, forcing the federal government to intervene in the organization of work, housing, and community services. In many cases, federal efforts to accommodate newcomers resulted in the creation of parallel organizations and structures that augmented the social distance between migrants and prewar residents.

In East Bay shipyards, for example, defense contractors worked with government agencies to simplify, reorganize, and de-skill the work process to facilitate the entry of new workers. To protect their skilled crafts, prewar workers responded by creating a system of second-class union auxiliaries for women, blacks, and other newcomers. At the end of the war, employers and unions easily disposed of these marginalized workers, creating serious economic dislocations for East Bay cities. Outside the workplace, federal war agencies constructed elaborate migrant settlements with parallel systems of urban services that segregated newcomers and old-timers in the community. Although intended as temporary arrangements, many of these housing projects would remain standing well into the 1950s, shaping neighborhood patterns in the postwar era.

Perhaps the most serious consequence of rapid inmigration was the growing animosity between newcomers and old-timers in war boomtowns. In the resource-scarce climate of war, old-time residents tended to resent newcomers for their well-paid defense jobs, new housing, and conspicuous behavior as downtown consumers. More important, with the transformation of East Bay communities into raucous boomtowns, city leaders blamed disorderly newcomers (and newly employed blacks, women, and youth) for "ruining" their cities. In the guise of combating a massive "crime wave," city officials sought to limit access to urban space through a law-and-order campaign that only aggravated existing social and racial tensions.

Not all East Bay residents reacted so inhospitably to the newcomers. Outside the AFL-dominated shipyards, progressive labor forces mobilized around community issues, defending the interests of an expanded working class that included old-timer and newcomer alike. Building on the experience gained through wartime committee work and the organizational infrastructure of the 1944 political action committees, CIO members launched a major political offensive against local machines. Such oppositional movements flourished at the end of the war as an economic recession and housing shortage fueled working-class discontent. But as prosperity returned, suburbanization accelerated, and the Cold War intensified, progressives found themselves ousted or silenced over the public housing issue, which had come to symbolize the future of East Bay cities.

Although overt political conflict dissipated by the early fifties, the unresolved problems of the war era left a bitter racial legacy for East Bay cities. As white migrants moved out to the suburbs and black urban migration continued, federal migrant settlements became the minority enclaves of postwar cities. In these areas, wartime social programs shaped postwar urban community life, setting the boundaries for what the Kerner Commission would call "two societies, one black, one white," some twenty years later.[1] Over the next decades, black residents would remain the preeminent "newcomers" in town, regarded as temporary, disorderly, and undesirable by city leaders.

Newcomer–old-timer conflicts and the wartime crime campaigns they engendered influenced urban policy in the postwar period. The persistent belief that war migrants had "ruined" East Bay cities by bringing a scourge of crime and delinquency fueled white flight to the suburbs and helped justify decisions about urban redevelopment that targeted and eventually eradicated many war housing areas then dominated by black residents. Callous efforts to displace these families from their homes, jobs, and communities after the war planted the seeds of racial discontent that would explode so violently in these same communities in the 1960s.

Defense migration also left a more positive political and cultural legacy, however. By increasing the diversity of East Bay cities, the war ended the social and political complacency of the prewar era. Boosted by new population and votes, labor and minority candidates challenged elite rule in the late 1940s, setting the agenda for many of the liberal programs of the 1960s—district elections, mass transit improvement, fair employment legislation, rent control, and new education and social service facilities. By the 1970s, machine rule was coming to an end, pushed out by a new generation of progressives seeking to fulfill the lost hopes of the wartime coalitions.

New churches, musical styles, and other traditions imported by war migrants also left their cultural mark on Bay Area communities. Among whites, most of whom dispersed and were assimilated into postwar suburbs, these influences are not easily discerned. Within East Bay cities, only a few war-born churches and other migrant institutions have survived. The Christian Cathedral in east Oakland is a case in point. Founded in 1944 by Bebe Patten, a visiting revivalist of the World War II era, this evangelical church has grown into a major religious center with a cathedral, elementary and secondary schools, a Bible college, and weekly television and radio programs. Patten has remained true to her fundamentalist roots, but she has also adjusted to the needs of a diverse urban congregation by integrating the schools and actively supporting minority rights. Such war-born institutions have not been static entities but have reacted and adjusted to new conditions in California communities.[2]

On venturing into San Pablo, Brisbane, or any of the Bay Area's old shipyard suburbs, the impact of defense migration is readily apparent. The sprinkling of Southern Baptist and Full Gospel churches, the country music honky-tonks, and the down-home restaurants testify to the enduring cultural impact of white war migration. Over the years, such institutions have broadened their appeal, attracting not only southwesterners but a wide range of white working-class Californians. In fact, one of the Bay Area's most successful country music band leaders was "Shorty Joe" Quartuccio, a second-generation Italian-American who made his career in postwar San Jose as white defense migrants were moving into South Bay suburbs. Far outside his own ethnic background, Quartuccio's love of country music illustrates how migrant traditions have become part of the larger culture of postwar California.[3]

The legacy of southern black migration in the Bay Area has been even more pervasive. Several black churches founded during the war boom have become influential religious institutions. Founded by southern migrants during World War II, churches like Mount Carmel Missionary Baptist Church in Richmond and Mount Zion Spiritual Temple in Oakland grew from small storefront operations into major churches in the postwar era. The newcomer churches also influenced the area's more staid prewar churches, which gradually adopted some of the emotional style and enthusiasm of their competitors. Liberal Protestant churches like Easter Hill Methodist in Richmond also grew out of the war experience. Founded in 1942 as a war housing ministry by the mainly white Saint Luke's Methodist Church, Canal Community Church faced extinction when the city demolished surrounding black housing projects in the early fifties. With financial assistance from the United Methodist church, the Canal church was renamed Easter Hill and moved to a new location on the south side, where it now serves hundreds of African-American members.[4]

Perhaps the most well-known cultural legacy of the war is the vibrant and expressive blues tradition that figures so prominently in contemporary Bay Area music. From the seedbed of wartime juke joints, Bay Area blues has evolved from the raw, Texas- and Oklahoma-style country blues into a more modern electric blues sound. As several musicologists have noted, however, the "Oakland blues"—more so than other regional blues—has preserved a distinctive down-home style. The small size of the prewar black community in the Bay Area and the wartime inundation of southern newcomers may explain how the down-home styles came to be dominant. The large numbers of black migrants from Louisiana also imported a hybrid form of the blues known as Zydeco. Combining blues and Cajun swamp music, Zydeco bands began playing concerts in Oakland and Richmond church basements in the 1950s. Growing from these roots, Cajun-Zydeco music now enjoys wide popularity throughout the Bay Area.[5]

Like country music, the blues have attracted newcomers and old-timers alike, and the common experience of postwar black urban life has shaped its style and content. In recent years, increasing numbers of young whites have also become interested in the blues. The larger, interracial audience provides a substantial clientele for the spate of blues clubs—many serving home-style southern specialties—that thrive in Oakland, Berkeley, and other Bay Area cities. The Bay Area has thus emerged as one of the major regional blues centers in the country.

The blues, country music, evangelical religion, southern-style food, and other traditions brought by war migrants produced unique Bay Area styles and institutions that have enriched local cultural life. For all their problems, East Bay cities today are remarkably diverse, tolerant, and culturally rich communities. Like other West Coast cities, they are still enjoying the benefits and paying the costs of a war that profoundly and permanently transformed urban life.

Notes

Introduction

1. Joseph C. Whitnah, *A History of Richmond, California* (Richmond: Richmond Chamber of Commerce, 1944).

2. Roger W. Lotchin, ed., "Introduction," in *The Martial Metropolis: U.S. Cities in War and Peace* (New York: Praeger, 1984), xi–xii.

3. U.S. Bureau of the Census, *Current Population Reports, Population Characteristics*, ser. P-20, no. 14, *Internal Migration in the United States: April 1940 to April 1947* (Washington, D.C., Bureau of the Census), 1.

4. Ibid., 1–2.

5. On rural-urban migration in early America see, for example, Thomas Dublin, *Women at Work: The Transformation of Work and Community in Lowell, Massachusetts, 1826–1860* (New York: Columbia University Press, 1979); Mary P. Ryan, *Cradle of the Middle Class: The Family in Oneida County, New York, 1790–1865* (New York: Cambridge University Press, 1981); Paul S. Boyer, *Urban Masses and Moral Order in America, 1820–1920* (Cambridge: Harvard University Press, 1978). For examples of work on the impact of nineteenth- and twentieth-century migration, see Herbert G. Gutman, "Work, Culture, and Society in Industrializing America, 1815–1919," *American Historical Review* 78 (June 1973): 531–88; John E. Bodnar, *Immigration and Industrialization: Ethnicity in an American Mill Town, 1870–1940* (Pittsburgh: University of Pittsburgh Press, 1977); Daniel J. Walkowitz, *Worker City, Company Town: Iron and Cotton-Worker Protest in Troy and Cohoes, New York, 1855–1884* (Urbana: University of Illinois Press, 1981); Virginia Yans-McLaughlin, *Family and Community: Italian Immigrants in Buffalo, 1880–1930* (Urbana: University of Illinois Press, 1982); Olivier Zunz, *The Changing Face of Inequality: Urbanization, Industrial Development, and Immigrants in Detroit, 1880–1920* (Chicago: University of Chicago Press, 1982).

6. Jacquelyn Dowd Hall et al., *Like a Family: The Making of a Southern Cotton Mill World* (Chapel Hill: University of North Carolina Press, 1987); James N. Gregory, *American Exodus: The Dust Bowl Migration and Okie Culture in California* (New York: Oxford University Press, 1989).

7. For national studies, see John Morton Blum, *V Was for Victory: Politics and American Culture during World War II* (New York: Harcourt Brace Jovanovich, 1976); Gerald D. Nash, *The Great Depression and World War II: Organizing America, 1933–1945* (New York: St. Martin's Press, 1979); and Richard Polenberg, *War and Society: The United States, 1941–1945* (Philadelphia: J. B. Lippincott, 1972). For state and regional treatments, see Alan Clive, *State of War: Michigan in World War II* (Ann Arbor: University of Michigan Press, 1979); C. Calvin Smith, *War and Wartime Changes: The Transformation of Arkansas, 1940–1945* (Fayetteville: University of Arkansas Press, 1986); and Gerald D. Nash, *The American West Transformed: The Impact of the Second World War* (Bloomington: Indiana University Press, 1985).

8. Marc Scott Miller, *The Irony of Victory: World War II and Lowell, Massachusetts* (Urbana: University of Illinois Press, 1988), 205–9.

9. Louis Wirth, "The Urban Community," in *American Society in Wartime,* ed. William Fielding Ogburn (Chicago: University of Chicago Press, 1943), 72. In keeping with Wirth's conceptual framework, other sociologists produced community studies of war boomtowns in the immediate postwar period that have influenced my thinking about the East Bay. See Lowell J. Carr and James E. Stermer, *Willow Run: A Study of Industrialization and Social Inadequacy* (New York: Harper, 1952); and Robert J. Havighurst and H. Gerthon Morgan, *The Social History of a War Boom Community* (New York: Longmans, Green and Co., 1951).

10. Bureau of the Census, *Internal Migration in the United States,* 1.

11. Catherine Bauer, "Cities in Flux," *American Scholar* 13 (Winter 1943–1944): 74.

12. Bureau of the Census, *Internal Migration in the United States,* 5; Nash, *The American West Transformed,* 56; U.S. Bureau of the Census, *Population,* ser. CA-2, *Wartime Changes in Population and Family Characteristics,* no. 3, "San Francisco Bay Congested Production Area, April 1944" (Washington, D.C.: Bureau of the Census, 1944), 1; and idem, *Population,* ser. CA-1, *Final Population Figures for the Area and Its Constituent Parts,* no. 11, "Total Population of Ten Congested Production Areas: 1944" (Washington, D.C.: Bureau of the Census, 1944), 2–3. Population figures for West Coast cities include both military and civilian population growth; the rate of civilian population growth alone in the Bay Area between 1940 and 1944 was 25.9 percent.

13. Beth Bagwell, *Oakland: The Story of a City* (Novato, Calif.: Presidio Press, 1982), 234; Commonwealth Club of California, *The Population of California* (San Francisco: Parker Printing Co., 1946), 197; Bureau of the Census, *Wartime Changes in Population,* "San Francisco," 1.

14. Bureau of the Census, "Total Population of Ten Congested Production Areas," 2–3; Lotchin, *The Martial Metropolis,* 225.

15. Industrial Survey Associates, *The San Francisco Bay Area: Its People, Prospects, and Problems* (San Francisco: n.p., 1948), 9; "Detour through Purgatory," *Fortune* (February 1945): 182.

1. Prelude to War

1. Robert Wenkert, *An Historical Digest of Negro-White Relations in Richmond, California* (Berkeley: Survey Research Center, University of California, 1967), 5.

2. Beth Bagwell, *Oakland: The Story of a City* (Novato, Calif.: Presidio Press, 1982), 38, 56, 156.

3. Edgar J. Hinkel and William E. McCann, eds., *Oakland, California, 1852–1938: Some Phases of the Social, Political, and Economic History,* 2 vols. (Oakland: U.S. Work Projects Administration and the Oakland Public Library, 1939), 1:367.

4. William Sokol, "Richmond during World War II: Kaiser Comes to Town," (University of California, Berkeley, 1971, typescript; copy in Richmond Collection, Richmond Public Library), 4–6.

5. John T. Cumbler, *A Social History of Economic Decline: Business, Politics, and Work in Trenton* (New Brunswick, N.J.: Rutgers University Press, 1989), 7. For the colonialism argument, see Gerald D. Nash, *The American West Transformed: The Impact of the Second World War* (Bloomington: Indiana University Press, 1985), 3–14; Walter Prescott Webb, *Divided We Stand: The Crisis of a Frontier Democracy* (New York: Farrar, 1937); and Gene M. Gressley, "Colonialism and the American West," *Pacific Northwest Quarterly* 54 (January 1963): 1–8.

6. Hinkel and McCann, *Oakland: 1852–1938,* 1:354–56; Bagwell, *Oakland: The Story of a City,* 87.

7. Carey McWilliams, "Profiles: Los Angeles," in "The New Race Relations Frontier," ed. L. D. Reddick, *Journal of Educational Sociology* 19 (November 1945): 188; Bagwell, *Oakland: The Story of a City,* 82; Lawrence P. Crouchett, Lonnie G. Bunch III, and Martha Kendall Winnacker, eds., *Visions toward Tomorrow: The History of the East Bay Afro-American Community, 1852–1977* (Oakland: Northern California Center for Afro-American History and Life, 1989), 9–10, 37.

8. Hinkel and McCann, *Oakland: 1852–1938,* 1:356. Many of the Portuguese residents of west Oakland were descendants of the Azorean whaling crews that worked the Pacific Coast in the early nineteenth century. During the mid-twentieth century most of these families moved out to east Oakland or to nearby San Leandro, where many took up dairy farming. Oakland, however, remained the cultural center of the Luso-American community in California. See Tim Stirling Hallinan, "The Portuguese of California," Ph.D. diss., University of California, Berkeley, 1968.

9. Because of changing definitions of ethnicity and race (white versus nonwhite), census statistics on Mexican and Mexican-American populations in California are erratic and have no doubt undercounted the seasonal migratory labor force. Nevertheless, the Mexican population of Bay Area cities prior to World War II was relatively small—especially compared with Southern California cities.

10. Edward C. Hayes, *Power Structure and Urban Policy: Who Rules in Oakland* (New York: McGraw-Hill, 1972), 10–12.

11. Ibid., 12–14.

12. Bagwell, *Oakland: The Story of a City*, 179.

13. Ibid., 189–90, 192.

14. Hinkel and McCann, *Oakland, California: 1852–1938*, 2:864.

15. Bagwell, *Oakland: The Story of a City*, 196.

16. Sokol, "Richmond during World War II," 9.

17. William H. Mullins, *The Depression and the Urban West Coast, 1929–1933* (Bloomington: Indiana University Press, 1991), 5, 92; Bagwell, *Oakland: The Story of a City*, 217.

18. As James N. Gregory point out, the West South Central states of Texas, Oklahoma, Missouri, and Arkansas are not traditionally considered part of the South or the West. Culturally, they combine elements of both regions, constituting a type of border zone that Gregory designates as the "Southwest." In this book, I have borrowed Gregory's terminology (and applied it to northern Louisiana as well) except where otherwise noted. See James N. Gregory, *American Exodus: The Dust Bowl Migration and Okie Culture in California* (New York: Oxford University Press, 1989).

19. Gregory, *American Exodus*, 6–13. For an in-depth discussion of California's reaction to the Okie migration, see Walter J. Stein, *California and the Dust Bowl Migration* (Westport, Conn.: Greenwood Press, 1973).

20. Gregory, *American Exodus*, 40.

21. Bruce Nelson, *Workers on the Waterfront: Seamen, Longshoremen, and Unionism in the 1930s* (Urbana: University of Illinois Press, 1988), 127–29, 137, 219–21; Bagwell, *Oakland: The Story of a City*, 218; *East Bay Labor Journal*, May 18 and 23, June 8, July 27, 1934.

22. Nelson, *Workers on the Waterfront*, 259–60; Crouchett et al., *Visions toward Tomorrow*, 37–39; Frances Mary Albrier, "Determined Advocate for Racial Equality" (interview by Malca Chall, 1979, Regional Oral History Office, Bancroft Library, University of California, Berkeley), 120; Gretchen Lemke, "Blacks in Berkeley, 1859–1987" (Northern California Center for Afro-American History and Life, Oakland, 1987, typescript), 16, 27.

23. *Labor Herald*, June 8, August 24, September 22, October 13, November 17, December 1, 22, and 29, 1937. For general information on CIO organizing activities in the Bay Area, see the CIO *Labor Herald*, which began publication in 1937.

24. *East Bay Labor Journal*, August 24, 1934; *Labor Herald*, June 8 and 15, July 27, October 6, 1937; idem, July 7, August 11, 1938.

25. Labor's Non-Partisan League of Alameda County, "Bring the New Deal to California" (Oakland, n.d.); Labor's Non-Partisan League of California, *Minutes and Report*, December 1937, June 1938, January 1939 (copies of above documents are in Institute for Governmental Studies Library, University of California, Berkeley); *Labor Herald*, July 7, August 4, September 8, 1938.

26. Wenkert, *Historical Digest*, 9; Sokol, "Richmond during World War II," 7; Roy Hamachi, "Postwar Housing in Richmond, California" (M.A. thesis, University of California, Berkeley, n.d. [copy in Richmond file, carton 6, Catherine Bauer Wurster Papers, Bancroft Library, University of California, Berkeley]), 52; International Brotherhood of Boilermakers, Iron Shipbuilders

and Helpers of America, *Richmond: Arsenal of Democracy* (Berkeley: Tam, Gibbs Co., n.d.), 22.

27. U.S. Bureau of the Census, *Sixteenth Census of the United States, 1940: Reports on Population,* vol. 2, *Characteristics of the Population,* pt. 1, "California," 601, 637. Breakdowns on second-generation immigrants ceased after the 1930 census, but based on previous census figures we can assume that the number of residents with foreign-born parents equaled or exceeded the number of foreign-born.

28. Harry and Marguerite Williams, "Reflections of a Longtime Black Family in Richmond" (interview by Judith K. Dunning, 1985, Regional Oral History Office, Bancroft Library, University of California, Berkeley, 1990), 41; Lee Hildebrand, "North Richmond Blues," *East Bay Express,* February 9, 1979; Shirley Ann Moore, "The Black Community in Richmond, California, 1910–1963" (Ph.D. diss., University of California, Berkeley, 1989), 72–73.

29. *Oakland Observer,* March 11, 1944.

30. "Richmond Took a Beating," *Fortune* (February 1945): 262; Stanley Nystrom, "A Family's Roots in Richmond: Recollections of a Lifetime Resident," 34, and Marguerite Clausen, "Memories of a Lifelong Richmond Resident, 1912 to 1987," 26 (interviews by Judith K. Dunning, 1985, Regional Oral History Office, Bancroft Library, University of California, Berkeley, 1990); Wenkert, *Historical Digest,* 1.

31. Hubert Owen Brown, "The Impact of War Worker Migration on the Public School System of Richmond, California: 1940–1945" (Ed.D. diss., Stanford University, 1973), 32.

32. Hayes, *Power Structure and Urban Policy,* 47–48.

2. The Second Gold Rush

1. Milton Silverman, "The Second Gold Rush Hits the West," series of articles in the *San Francisco Chronicle,* April 25–May 20, 1943.

2. Roger W. Lotchin, *Fortress California* (New York: Oxford University Press, 1992), 42–63; *Oakland Tribune Yearbook, 1941* (Oakland: Oakland Tribune Company, 1941), 13; Sheila Tropp Lichtman, "Women at Work, 1941–1945: Wartime Employment in the San Francisco Bay Area" (Ph.D. diss., University of California, Davis, 1981), 73; Stanley Nystrom, "A Family's Roots in Richmond: Recollections of a Lifetime Resident" (interview by Judith K. Dunning, 1985, Regional Oral History Office, Bancroft Library, University of California, Berkeley, 1990), 73–74.

3. Gerald D. Nash, *The American West Transformed: The Impact of the Second World War* (Bloomington: Indiana University Press, 1985), 66; Lichtman, "Women at Work," 74.

4. William Sokol, "Richmond during World War II: Kaiser Comes to Town" (University of California, Berkeley, 1971, typescript; copy in Richmond Collection, Richmond Public Library), 13–14.

5. Permanente Metals Corporation, *A Booklet of Illustrated Facts about the Shipyards at Richmond, California* (Richmond, June 30, 1944; copy in Richmond Collection, Richmond Public Library), 30–31.

6. *Oakland Tribune Yearbook, 1944,* 25; House Subcommittee of Committee on Naval Affairs, *Hearings on Congested Areas,* pt. 3, "San Francisco Bay Area, April 12–17, 1943," 78th Cong., 1st sess., 858 (hereafter cited as *Hearings on Congested Areas,* "San Francisco").

7. "Trend of Employment, Earning, and Hours," *Monthly Labor Review* 60 (January 1944): 140.

8. U.S. Bureau of the Census, *Population,* ser. CA-2, *Wartime Changes in Population and Family Characteristics,* no. 3, "San Francisco Bay Congested Production Area, April 1944" [Washington, D.C.: Bureau of the Census], 1 (hereafter cited as *Wartime Changes in Population,* "San Francisco"); U.S. Federal Works Agency, Work Projects Administration, "Recent Migration into Oakland, California, and Environs," February 3, 1942, 2–3 (copy in Oakland History Collection, Oakland Public Library); *Richmond Independent,* February 2, 1941.

9. Marguerite Clausen, "Memoirs of a Lifelong Richmond Resident, 1912 to 1987" (interview by Judith K. Dunning, 1985, Regional Oral History Office, Bancroft Library, University of California, Berkeley, 1990), 34–35; Nystrom, "A Family's Roots in Richmond," 12–13; Louis Campbell quoted in Shirley Ann Moore, "The Black Community in Richmond, California, 1910–1963" (Ph.D. diss., University of California, Berkeley, 1989), 86.

10. Senate Committee on Military Affairs, *Labor Shortages in the Pacific Coast and Rocky Mountain States,* 78th Cong., 1st sess., September 9–10, 1943, 58 (hereafter referred to as *Labor Shortages Hearings*). Northern California had a brief resurgence of gold mining in the late 1930s when the United States abandoned the gold standard. As a result, many unemployed urban dwellers left the Bay Area and other California cities during the depression for mining areas in the Sierra foothills.

11. Industrial Relations Department, "Report: Contract Recruits," memo from William Beck to C. H. Day and J. C. Egan, March 31, 1943, carton 23, Henry Kaiser Papers, Bancroft Library, University of California, Berkeley.

12. *Oakland Tribune,* October 22 and 23, 1942.

13. Hubert Owen Brown, "The Impact of War Worker Migration on the Public School System of Richmond, California; 1940–1945" (Ed.D. diss., Stanford University, 1973), 117; International Brotherhood of Boilermakers, Iron Shipbuilders and Helpers of America, *Richmond: Arsenal of Democracy* (Berkeley: Tam, Gibbs Co., n.d.), 45.

14. Alyce Mano Kramer, "The Story of the Richmond Shipyards" (typescript, copy in carton 330, Henry Kaiser Papers, Bancroft Library, University of California, Berkeley), 57–58.

15. Kaiser recruiting pamphlet quoted in Deborah Ann Hirschfield, "Rosie Also Welded: Women and Technology in Shipbuilding during World War II" (Ph.D. diss., University of California, Irvine, 1987), 124; Kramer, "The Story of the Richmond Shipyards," 58.

16. Boilermakers, *Arsenal of Democracy,* 44; "Workers West," *Business Week* (October 3, 1942): 74–75; Brown, "The Impact of War Worker Migration," 116.

17. Industrial Relations Report, Jean Johnson to James C. Egan, February 7, 1943, 1, Kaiser Papers. In a novel about an Arkansas family's odyssey to Richmond in 1942, William Martin Camp, a writer for the *San Francisco Chronicle,* implied that company recruiters worked with local sheriffs to ensure the departure of local contract laborers. If true, recruits would have had to leave the area but might have headed elsewhere in the country (William Martin Camp, *Skip to My Lou* [Garden City, N.Y.: Doubleday, 1945]), 113.

18. Industrial Relations Report, Jean Johnson to James C. Egan, February 7, 1943, and D. J. Robertson to J. J. Boney, January 1, 1943, Kaiser Papers.

19. Industrial Relations Report, Jean Johnson to James C. Egan, February 7, 1943, and Jean Johnson to William Beck, February 13, 1943, Kaiser Papers.

20. *Daily People's World,* December 21, 1942.

21. Industrial Relations Report, Jean Johnson to J. C. Egan, March 9, 1943, Kaiser Papers.

22. Camp, *Skip to My Lou,* 193–94.

23. Commonwealth Club of California, *The Population of California* (San Francisco: Parker Printing Co., 1946), 129; *Wartime Changes in Population,* "San Francisco," 2.

24. Commonwealth Club, *The Population of California,* 123; interview with Agnes Ginn Moore by author, June 29, 1990. Note that the regional migration statistics cited here and in the next few paragraphs refer to *interstate* migration only. The figures in table 5 refer to *total* migration (intra- and interstate) and are thus somewhat lower.

25. Commonwealth Club, *The Population of California,* 123; Marion Clawson, "What It Means to Be a Californian," *California Historical Society Quarterly* 24 (June 1945): 139–61.

26. *Wartime Changes in Population,* "San Francisco," 2.

27. Percentages calculated from figures provided by the U.S. Bureau of the Census, *Population,* ser. CA-3, *Characteristics of the Population, Labor Force, Families, and Housing,* no. 3, "San Francisco Bay Congested Production Area, April 1944" [Washington, D.C.: Bureau of the Census], 14 (hereafter cited as *Characteristics of the Population,* "San Francisco").

28. Katherine Archibald, *Wartime Shipyard: A Study in Social Disunity* (Berkeley: University of California Press, 1947; New York: Arno Press, 1977), 192.

29. Charles S. Johnson, *The Negro War Worker in San Francisco* (San Francisco: YWCA, 1944), 80; Lichtman, "Women at Work," 85; Work Projects Administration, "Recent Migration into Oakland," 4.

30. *Oakland Tribune,* January 19, March 2, 1943.

31. *Labor Shortages Hearings,* 15, 59.

32. Office of Defense Health and Welfare Services and National Resources Planning Board, "Composite Report on Richmond Area, Contra Costa County, California," June 2, 1942, 8, Community Reports file, Region 12,

U.S. Office of Community War Services, Record Group 215, National Archives, Washington, D.C. (hereafter cited as OCWS, RG 215, NA).

33. Amy Kesselman, *Fleeting Opportunities: Women Shipyard Workers in Portland and Vancouver during World War II and Reconversion* (Albany: State University of New York Press, 1990), 17; Archibald, *Wartime Shipyard,* 2.

34. Lichtman, "Women at Work," 77; percentages calculated from figures included in *Characteristics of the Population,* "San Francisco," 4, 18.

35. Clawson, "What It Means to Be a Californian," 148. The exceptions to the male-dominated migration occurred in the 1910s, because of the influence of the draft on migration caused by World War I, and in the 1890s, when Chinese exclusion resulted in the countermigration of thousands of Chinese males.

36. Lichtman, "Women at Work," 77, 298; Karen Anderson, *Wartime Women: Sex Roles, Family Relationships, and the Status of Women during World War II* (Westport, Conn.: Greenwood Press, 1981), 36; Charles Wollenberg, *Marinship at War: Shipbuilding and Social Change in Wartime Sausalito* (Berkeley: Western Heritage Press, 1990), 60.

37. *Oakland Tribune,* October 7, 1943.

38. Lichtman, "Women at Work," 148, 156; Permanente Metals Corp., *A Book of Illustrated Facts,* 36; Archibald, *Wartime Shipyard,* 16.

39. Lichtman, "Women at Work," 128.

40. Davis McEntire, "Postwar Status of Negro Workers in the San Francisco Area," *Monthly Labor Review* 70 (June 1950): 614.

41. *Oakland Tribune,* October 22, 1988; *Hearings on Congested Areas,* "San Francisco," 774.

42. Brown, "The Impact of War Worker Migration," 252.

43. Anne Roller Issler, "Shipyards and the Boys," *Survey Graphic* 33 (March 1944): 175; Sokol, "Kaiser Comes to Town," 31; *Fore 'N' Aft,* April 2, 1943.

44. Issler, "Shipyards and the Boys," 175.

45. California Youth Authority, "A Study of Youth Services in Contra Costa County" (typescript, 1945, copy in Richmond Collection, Richmond Public Library), 107–8; Brown, "The Impact of War Worker Migration," 255–56; Issler, "Shipyards and the Boys," 174.

46. Brown, "The Impact of War Worker Migration," 256, 296.

47. Oakland, California, Housing Authority of the City of Oakland, *Annual Report, 1942–1943* (Oakland, 1944), 15.

48. Archibald, *Wartime Shipyard,* 45; *Wartime Changes in Population,* "San Francisco," 3; Commonwealth Club, *The Population of California,* 129–30; Clawson, "What It Means to Be a Californian," 152.

49. L. D. Reddick, "The New Race Relations Frontier," in "Race Relations on the Pacific Coast," *Journal of Educational Sociology* 18 (November 1945): 129–45.

50. Federal Regional Advisory Council, Region 12, "Minutes of the Eleventh Meeting, Friday, August 20, 1943," 4, Community Reports file, Region 12, OCWS, RG 215, NA; Commonwealth Club, *The Population of California,* 128.

51. Moore, "The Black Community in Richmond," 80–82; Archibald, *Wartime Shipyard,* 60; Federal Regional Advisory Council, "Minutes," 4; *Fore 'N' Aft,* October 19, 1945.

52. Wilson Record, "Willie Stokes at the Golden Gate," *Crisis* 56 (June 1949): 176; Johnson, *The Negro War Worker,* 8, 80. Although Johnson's study was conducted in the Fillmore neighborhood of San Francisco, there is little reason to believe that this migrant population differed from that of the East Bay.

53. Merl E. Reed, "The FEPC, the Black Worker, and the Southern Shipyards," *South Atlantic Quarterly* 74 (Autumn 1975): 447–56; Mobile laborer quoted in Moore, "The Black Community in Richmond," 82–83.

54. Carey McWilliams, *PM,* April 26, 1945; Record, "Willie Stokes at the Golden Gate," 187.

55. Lois Markus, "The Problem of the Negroes in Oakland," in *Problems of American Communities,* Department of Economics and Sociology, Mills College, 3 vols. (collection of unpublished papers, 1945, copy in Mills College Library, Oakland), 1:150; J. Harvey Kerns, "A Study of the Social and Economic Conditions Affecting the Local Negro Population" (Council of Social Agencies, Oakland, 1942, copy in vertical files, Oakland History Room, Oakland Public Library), 2.

56. Johnson, *The Negro War Worker,* 17.

57. *Oakland Tribune,* February 1, 1943.

58. Archibald, *Wartime Shipyard,* 105; *Richmond Record-Herald,* October 21, 1943; *Richmond Independent,* March 18, 1943; *Fore 'N' Aft,* March 12, 1943.

59. Archibald, *Wartime Shipyard,* 101; Oakland, California, Oakland Police Department, Records Division, Oakland police arrest records (microfilm), April 1944.

60. *Fore 'N' Aft,* December 10, 1942; Lichtman, "Women at Work," 89.

61. U.S. Bureau of the Census, *Population,* ser. CA-2, *Wartime Changes in Population and Family Characteristics,* reports on congested production areas, no. 2, "San Diego, March 1944"; no. 3, "San Francisco, April 1944"; no. 5, "Los Angeles, April 1944"; no. 6, "Portland-Vancouver, May 1944"; no. 8, "Puget Sound, June 1944" [Washington, D.C.: Bureau of the Census].

62. U.S. Bureau of the Census, *Population,* ser. CA-3, *Characteristics of the Population, Labor Force, Families, and Housing,* reports on congested production areas, no. 2, "San Diego, March 1944"; no. 3, "San Francisco, April 1944"; no. 5, "Los Angeles, April 1944"; no. 6, "Portland-Vancouver, May 1944"; no. 8, "Puget Sound, June 1944" [Washington, D.C.: Bureau of the Census].

63. *Wartime Changes in Population,* "San Diego," "San Francisco," "Los Angeles," "Portland-Vancouver," and "Puget Sound."

64. Gerald D. Nash, *World War II and the West: Reshaping the Economy* (Lincoln: University of Nebraska Press, 1990). Dissenting opinions include Roger W. Lotchin, "The Metropolitan-Military Complex in Comparative Perspective: San Francisco, Los Angeles, and San Diego, 1919–1941," in *The Making of Urban America,* ed. Raymond A. Mohl (Wilmington, Del.: SR Books, 1988), 202–13; see also reviews of Nash's book by Daniel Cornford,

California History 70 (Spring 1991): 117–19, and by James N. Gregory, *Reviews in American History* 19 (June 1991): 249–54.

3. Wartime Shipyards and the Transformation of Labor

1. Sheila Tropp Lichtman,"Women at Work, 1941–1945: Wartime Employment in the San Francisco Bay Area" (Ph.D. diss., University of California, Davis, 1981), 119, 124–26; J. Harvey Kerns, "A Study of the Social and Economic Conditions Affecting the Local Negro Population" (Council of Social Agencies, 1942, Oakland, copy in vertical files, Oakland History Room, Oakland Public Library), 2.

2. See Nelson Lichtenstein, *Labor's War at Home: The CIO in World War II* (New York: Cambridge University Press, 1982); and Ruth Milkman, *Gender at Work: The Dynamics of Job Segregation by Sex during World War II* (Urbana: University of Illinois Press, 1987).

3. Lichtman, "Women at Work," 118; Alyce Mano Kramer, "The Story of the Richmond Shipyards" (typescript, copy in carton 330, Henry Kaiser Papers, Bancroft Library, University of California, Berkeley), 22, 26–28; Frederick C. Lane, *Ships for Victory: A History of Shipbuilding under the U.S. Maritime Commission in World War II* (Baltimore: Johns Hopkins Press, 1951), 213.

4. International Brotherhood of Boilermakers, Iron Shipbuilders and Helpers of America, *Richmond: Arsenal of Democracy* (Berkeley: Tam, Gibbs Co., [1945]), 66; Office of Defense Health and Welfare Services, "Composite Report on Richmond Area," June 2, 1942, 1, Community Reports file, Region 12, U.S. Office of Community War Services, Record Group 215, National Archives, Washington, D.C.; Lichtman, "Women at Work," 119.

5. William Sokol, "Richmond during World War II: Kaiser Comes to Town" (typescript, University of California, Berkeley, 1971, copy in Richmond Collection, Richmond Public Library), 36; Joseph Fabry, *Swing Shift: Building the Liberty Ships* (San Francisco: Strawberry Hill Press, 1982), 16; Margaret Louise Cathey, "A Wartime Journey: From Ottumwa, Iowa, to the Richmond Shipyards, 1942" (interview by Judith K. Dunning, 1985, Regional Oral History Office, Bancroft Library, University of California, Berkeley, 1990), 7.

6. Lane, *Ships for Victory,* 239, 258; Lichtman, "Women at Work," 119; Milkman, *Gender at Work,* 9.

7. Katherine Archibald, *Wartime Shipyard: A Study in Social Disunity* (Berkeley: University of California Press, 1947; New York: Arno Press, 1977), 104; Wilson Record, "Willie Stokes at the Golden Gate," *Crisis* 56 (June 1949): 176; *Oakland Tribune,* February 1, 1943; Milkman, *Gender at Work,* 60–64.

8. Lichtman, "Women at Work," 171.

9. Archibald, *Wartime Shipyard,* 19.

10. The *Business Week* article is discussed in Amy Kesselman, *Fleeting Opportunities* (Albany: State University of New York Press, 1990), 61. Two con-

temporary writers helped advance the prostitute stereotype in the characters of Mamie and Madge—degraded southern white women who turn to prostitution after their arrival in California defense centers; see William Martin Camp, *Skip to My Lou* (Garden City, N.Y.: Doubleday, 1945); and Chester Himes, *If He Hollers Let Him Go* (London: Falcon Press, 1946; New York: Thunder's Mouth Press, 1986).

11. Archibald, *Wartime Shipyard*, 19, 63, 70, 72; Deborah Ann Hirschfield, "Rosie Also Welded: Women and Technology in Shipbuilding during World War II" (Ph.D. diss., University of California, Irvine, 1987), 181; *Business Week* article quoted in Kesselman, *Fleeting Opportunities*, 54–55, 61.

12. Archibald, *Wartime Shipyard*, 84, 104; *Oakland Tribune*, February 1, 1943; Fred Stripp, "The Relationship of the San Francisco Bay Area Negro-American Worker with Labor Unions Affiliated with the American Federation of Labor and the Congress of Industrial Organizations" (Th.D. thesis, Pacific School of Religion, 1948), 168.

13. Archibald, *Wartime Shipyard*, 61, 70–75, 94.

14. *Richmond Record-Herald*, September 18, 1943.

15. Kramer, "The Story of the Richmond Shipyards," 64.

16. Archibald, *Wartime Shipyard*, 195; *Daily People's World*, June 5, 1943.

17. *Daily People's World*, January 5, April 10, 1943.

18. Kramer, "The Story of the Richmond Shipyards," 28

19. Boilermakers, *Arsenal of Democracy*, 68.

20. Lane, *Ships for Victory*, 241–43.

21. Lane, *Ships for Victory*, 243; International Brotherhood of Boilermakers, Iron Shipbuilders and Helpers of America, *Report and Proceedings of the Seventeenth Consolidated Convention* (Kansas City, Mo.: n.p., 1944), 64 (hereafter referred to as *Proceedings*); *Daily People's World*, September 26, 1942.

22. Boilermakers, *Proceedings*, 72, 114–22, and *Arsenal of Democracy*, 43.

23. Archibald, *Wartime Shipyard*, 131, 134.

24. *Oakland Tribune*, August 27, 1942; Boilermakers, *Arsenal of Democracy*, 45, 59.

25. Boilermakers, *Arsenal of Democracy*, 63.

26. Ibid.,90–94.

27. Boilermakers, *Proceedings*, 64.

28. Boilermakers, *Arsenal of Democracy*, 83; idcm, *Proceedings*, 123, 170.

29. Boilermakers, *Proceedings*, 56.

30. Charles Wollenberg, "James vs. Marinship," *California History* 60 (Fall 1981): 267. East Bay auxiliaries were the subject of frequent allegations of corruption and fiscal mismanagement. However, as Shirley Moore points out, Richmond's A-36 also acted as an advocate for the local black community by pressuring the city to improve recreation facilities in black neighborhoods and to hire black recreation department employees (Shirley Ann Moore, "The Black Community in Richmond, California, 1910–1963" [Ph.D. diss., University of California, Berkeley, 1989]), 95.

31. *Daily People's World*, February 4, May 7, 1943.

32. Ibid., May 13, 1943; William H. Harris, "Federal Intervention in Union Discrimination: The FEPC and West Coast Shipyards during World

War II," *Labor History* 22 (Summer 1981): 331; Ray Thompson, interview by Jesse J. Warr III, October 11, November 6, 1978, transcript, Oral History Project, Afro-Americans in San Francisco prior to World War II, Friends of the San Francisco Public Library and San Francisco African-American Historical and Cultural Society, 52, 60; Charles Wollenberg, *Marinship at War* (Berkeley: Western Heritage Press, 1990), 75.

33. *Daily People's World,* May 5, 8, 13, 1943.

34. Wollenberg, "James vs. Marinship," 267, 272; *Daily People's World,* April 3, May 10, 1944.

35. Boilermakers, *Proceedings,* 58, 61.

36. Wollenberg, "James vs. Marinship," 272; Boilermakers, *Proceedings,* 317.

37. Boilermakers, *Arsenal of Democracy,* 68–75. Ironically, as American companies discarded prefabrication and other mass-production practices, Japanese shipbuilders successfully adopted them in the postwar era. Such construction techniques helped make Japan one of the world's leaders in the shipbuilding industry; see Hirschfield, "Rosie Also Welded," 224.

38. Boilermakers, *Arsenal of Democracy,* 84.

39. Archibald, *Wartime Shipyard,* 38.

40. Ibid., 17, 217.

41. Ibid., 215.

42. David Montgomery, *The Fall of the House of Labor* (New York: Cambridge University Press, 1987), 236–42; Beth Bagwell, *Oakland: The Story of a City* (Novato, Calif.: Presidio Press, 1982), 218.

43. Archibald, *Wartime Shipyard,* 37.

44. *Daily People's World,* April 15, 1943.

45. Kramer, "The Story of the Richmond Shipyards," 62.

46. Boilermakers, *Arsenal of Democracy,* 57; Kramer, "The Story of the Richmond Shipyards," 63.

47. Kaiser Industries, *The Kaiser Story* (Oakland: Kaiser Industries, 1963), 56.

48. One of the ironies of the health-oriented Kaiser shipyards is the large number of former workers who later developed asbestosis as a result of their wartime work. Class action suits against employers and asbestos manufacturers are still pending in court as of this writing.

49. Archibald, *Wartime Shipyard,* 133; *Nation* article quoted in Mark S. Foster, *Henry Kaiser: Builder in the Modern American West* (Austin: University of Texas Press, 1989), 81.

50. Boilermakers, *Proceedings,* 123, 145, 170, and *Arsenal of Democracy,* 83.

51. Harris, "Federal Intervention in Union Discrimination," 331.

52. Gerald D. Nash, *World War II and the West: Reshaping the Economy* (Lincoln: University of Nebraska Press, 1990), 77; Robert H. Zieger, *American Workers, American Unions, 1920–1985* (Baltimore: Johns Hopkins University Press, 1986), 83.

53. Rickey Lynn Hendricks, "A Necessary Revolution: The Origins of the Kaiser Permanente Medical Care Program" (Ph.D. diss., University of Denver, 1987), 147, 185.

4. The Making of Migrant Ghettos

1. Margaret Louise Cathey, "A Wartime Journey: From Ottumwa, Iowa, to the Richmond Shipyards, 1942," 25, and Marguerite Clausen, "Memories of a Lifelong Richmond Resident, 1912 to 1987," 42 (interviews by Judith K. Dunning, 1985, Regional Oral History Office, Bancroft Library, University of California, Berkeley, 1990).

2. Hubert Owen Brown, "The Impact of War Worker Migration on the Public School System of Richmond, California: 1940–1945" (Ed.D. diss., Stanford University, 1973), 137.

3. *Oakland Tribune*, September 27, 1942; Oakland, California, Housing Authority of the City of Oakland, *Annual Report, 1941–1942*, 2.

4. An extraordinary source on wartime homelessness is a 1942 collection of photographs and annotations taken in conjunction with a federal housing investigation in Richmond; see Kaiser Pictorial Collection (1983.19), Bancroft Library, University of California, Berkeley. *Oakland Tribune*, July 21, August 16, 1942; *Daily People's World*, January 26, 1943.

5. Susan D. Cole, *Richmond: Windows to the Past* (Richmond: Wildcat Canyon Books, 1980), 86; *Oakland Tribune*, August 5 and 6, November 8, 1942.

6. Kaiser Pictorial Collection (1983.19); House Subcommittee of Committee on Naval Affairs, *Hearings on Congested Areas*, pt. 3, "San Francisco Bay Area, April 12–17, 1943," 78th Cong., 1st sess., 791, 847 (hereafter cited as *Hearings on Congested Areas*, "San Francisco").

7. *Hearings on Congested Areas*, "San Francisco," 1011.

8. Paul E. Carrico, "Visual Inspection of Trailer Camps and Shack Developments in the Unincorporated Area Surrounding Richmond, California," January 1, 1943, Federal Security Agency, Office of Defense Health and Welfare Services, War Area Reports and Correspondence, Region 12, U.S. Office of Community War Services, Record Group 215, National Archives, Washington, D.C. (hereafter referred to as OCWS, RG 215, NA).

9. *Oakland Tribune*, August 5, 1942.

10. Ibid.

11. Ibid., February 11, 1943; Carrico, "Visual Inspection of Trailer Camps and Shack Developments," 3.

12. Among the most significant of the New Deal housing programs were those of the U.S. Housing Authority (USHA) and the Federal Housing Administration (FHA). The USHA, originally the emergency housing division of the Public Works Administration, was established under the U.S. Housing Act of 1937 to fund slum clearance and the construction of public housing projects. The FHA, created under the 1934 Housing Act, encouraged suburban home construction by insuring long-term mortgage loans by private lenders. Later Congress established the NHA as an umbrella agency for all preexisting federal housing programs including those of the FHA, the USHA, and the Farm Security Administration. See John F. Bauman, *Public Housing, Race, and Renewal* (Philadelphia: Temple University Press, 1987), 70; Kenneth

Jackson, *Crabgrass Frontier* (New York: Oxford University Press, 1985), 204; and John Mollenkopf, *The Contested City* (Princeton, N.J.: Princeton University Press, 1983), 67–70.

13. *Oakland Tribune,* July 21, September 13 and 27, 1942; idem, April 16, 1943.

14. Interview with Antoinette Vaara by author, November 21, 1988.

15. Stanley Nystrom, "A Family's Roots in Richmond: Recollections of a Lifetime Resident" (interview by Judith K. Dunning, 1985, Regional Oral History Office, Bancroft Library, University of California, Berkeley, 1990), 59; California Archeological Consultants, Inc., *Investigation of Cultural Resources within the Richmond Harbor Redevelopment Project 11-A,* (Richmond: n.p., March 1981), 5.45.

16. *Oakland Tribune,* November 12, 1943; idem, June 9, 1944; Federal Security Agency, "Composite Report on Alameda Area, California," June 7, 1943, 15, Community Reports file, Region 12, OCWS, RG 215, NA.

17. *Oakland Tribune,* December 13, 1942; idem, October 6, 1943.

18. *Oakland Tribune,* May 18, August 4, October 18 and 30, 1943.

19. U.S. Bureau of the Census, *Population,* ser. CA-3, *Characteristics of the Population, Labor Force, Families, and Housing,* no. 3, "San Francisco Bay Congested Production Area, April 1944" [Washington, D.C.: Bureau of the Census], 8, 20.

20. *Oakland Tribune,* January 7, 1944.

21. Jackson, *Crabgrass Frontier,* 233.

22. *Oakland Tribune,* July 4, 1943.

23. Ibid., February 19, October 18, 1942; idem, April 14, 1944; *Oakland Post-Enquirer,* February 20, 1942.

24. Jackson, *Crabgrass Frontier,* 233; Bauman, *Public Housing, Race, and Renewal,* 70, 95; *Declaration of Establishment of Protective Restrictions, and Covenants, Affecting the Real Property Known as Rollingwood,* sec. 8, 11, 12, (July 1, 1943; property of George Eldredge, who graciously shared his personal files with me).

25. *Oakland Tribune,* January 9, March 25, 1943.

26. The best and most influential example of this view of middle-class suburbia is William H. Whyte's *The Organization Man* (New York: Simon and Schuster, 1956).

27. J. Harvey Kerns, "A Study of the Social and Economic Conditions Affecting the Local Negro Population," Council of Social Agencies, Oakland, 1942 (copy in vertical files, Oakland History Room, Oakland Public Library), 3; *Daily People's World,* January 26, 1943.

28. Maya Angelou, *I Know Why the Caged Bird Sings* (New York: Random House, 1969; Bantam Books, 1973), 173.

29. Quoted in Roy Hamachi, "Postwar Housing in Richmond, California" (M.A. thesis, University of California, Berkeley, n.d., copy in Richmond file, carton 6, Catherine Bauer Wurster Papers, Bancroft Library, University of California, Berkeley), 27.

30. Douglas Maher, "The Pattern of a Generation" (typescript, University of California, Berkeley, 1966; copy in Richmond Collection, Richmond Public Library), 5, 30.

31. Percentages based on calculations from Oakland census tracts 14, 15, 16, 17, 18, and 21. U.S. Bureau of the Census, *Sixteenth Census of the United States, 1940, Reports on Population,* vol. 7, *Supplementary Reports—Statistics for Census Tracts: Population, and Housing,* "Oakland-Berkeley, Calif., and Adjacent Area," 4; and *U.S. Census of Population, 1950,* vol. 3, *Census Tracts Statistics,* Bulletin P-D49, "Selected Population and Housing Characteristics, San Francisco–Oakland, California," 15. As the historian Kenneth Kusmer points out, the process of ghetto formation was by no means uniform in American cities. Cleveland's black ghetto took shape later and more slowly than did the ghettos of Chicago and New York. The experience of East Bay cities during World War II substantiates Kusmer's argument by showing an even later and slower development of black neighborhoods on the West Coast. Kenneth L. Kusmer, *A Ghetto Takes Shape* (Urbana: University of Illinois Press, 1976).

32. Quoted in Lee Hildebrand, "West Side Story," *East Bay Express* (September 28, 1979).

33. Quoted in Douglas Henry Daniels, *Pioneer Urbanites* (Philadelphia: Temple University Press, 1980), 173.

34. Memo from Charlotte Moton to Harry H. Stoops, Federal Security Agency, n.d., General Classified files, Region 12, OCWS, RG 215, NA; Nathan I. Huggins, "Preface" in Daniels, *Pioneer Urbanites,* xiv–xv.

35. For a detailed discussion of federal housing policy and administration, see chapter 3 of Philip J. Funigiello, *The Challenge to Urban Liberalism* (Knoxville: University of Tennessee Press, 1978), 80–119.

36. Out of some 300 public housing projects nationwide, at least 175 were converted to war worker occupancy. In the East Bay, the prewar public housing projects of Campbell Village, Peralta Villa, and Lockwood Gardens in Oakland and Nystrom Village, Triangle Court, and Atchison Village in Richmond were converted to war worker use by 1942. The conversion of these projects, however, added only a few hundred units to a desperately tight housing market.

37. Jackson, *Crabgrass Frontier,* 226; Robert Wenkert, *An Historical Digest of Negro-White Relations in Richmond, California* (Berkeley: Survey Research Center, University of California, 1967), 21; Hamachi, "Postwar Housing in Richmond," 52; biography files for Thomas M. Robinson, Henry W. Haler, C. M. Walter, Bernard J. Abrott, John P. Brennan, and other Oakland Housing Authority commissioners, Oakland History Room, Oakland Public Library.

38. Frederick C. Lane, *Ships for Victory* (Baltimore: John Hopkins Press, 1951), 430; Alyce Mano Kramer, "The Story of the Richmond Shipyards" (typescript, copy in carton 330, Henry Kaiser Papers, Bancroft Library, University of California, Berkeley), 63.

39. Housing Authority of the City of Oakland, *Annual Report, 1943–1944,* 1; Alan Clive, *State of War: Michigan in World War II* (Ann Arbor: University of Michigan Press, 1979), 105.

40. *Richmond Independent,* October 29, 1943; *Hearings on Congested Areas,* "San Francisco," 847.

41. *Oakland Tribune,* February 15, October 15, 1943; idem, February 29, 1944; Housing Authority of the City of Oakland, *Annual Report, 1943–1945,* 28.

42. *Oakland Tribune,* August 23, 1943; *Richmond Record-Herald,* August 18, 1943.

43. *Oakland Tribune,* December 23, 1941; idem, March 25, 1943.

44. Ibid., July 29, 1942; idem, February 16, 1943.

45. Helen Smith Alancraig, "Codornices Village: A Study of Non-Segregated Public Housing" (M.A. thesis, University of California, Berkeley, 1953), 35–49.

46. See Brown, "The Impact of War Worker Migration," 138; and interviews with Richmond residents by Judith K. Dunning, Regional Oral History Office, Bancroft Library, University of California, Berkeley, 1990.

47. Memo from Elsa Reisner, Housing and Transportation Department, Kaiser Shipyards, Richmond, October 25, 1943, box 122, Central files, Committee for Congested Production Areas, Record Group 212, National Archives, Washington, D.C.

48. "Boom Town," *Fore 'N' Aft,* June 4, 1943.

49. Alancraig, "Codornices Village," 21, 58. The "local custom" approach was incorporated into the 1937 U.S. Housing Act in an effort to appease southern Democrats in Congress, who otherwise might have defeated the bill.

50. James M. Burns, *Roosevelt: Soldier of Freedom* (New York: Harcourt Brace Jovanovich, 1970), 466; Carey McWilliams, *PM,* April 26, 1945.

51. Alancraig, "Codornices Village," 73.

52. Hamachi, "Postwar Housing in Richmond," 31.

53. *Daily People's World,* September 23, 1942.

54. *Hearings on Congested Areas,* "San Francisco," 803, 1013. The local housing authority introduced the patchwork pattern of segregation at Peralta Villa under pressure from local real estate interests in 1941. The practice of segregating entire projects in west Oakland, however, appears to have been a consequence of the war.

55. Rumors of lynch mobs were reported in Portland, Los Angeles, and Oakland. See Henry Kraus, *In the City Was a Garden: A Housing Project Chronicle* (New York: Renaissance Press, 1951), 87–98; Katharine Archibald, *Wartime Shipyard* (Berkeley: University of California Press, 1947; New York: Arno Press, 1977), 70; Mark S. Foster, *Henry Kaiser: Builder in the Modern American West* (Austin: University of Texas Press, 1989), 76.

56. Alancraig, "Codornices Village," 101–3.

57. Hamachi, "Postwar Housing in Richmond," 31, 108.

58. Alancraig, "Codornices Village," 52.

59. Newspaper clippings in Richmond files, NAACP West Coast Region Papers, Bancroft Library, University of California, Berkeley.

60. Housing Authority of the City of Oakland, *Annual Report, 1942–1943,* 19; Hamachi, "Postwar Housing in Richmond," 110; *Hearings on Congested Areas,* "San Francisco," 799.

61. *Daily People's World,* January 26, 1943.

62. Codornices description quoted in Alancraig, "Codornices Village," 99; *Richmond Independent,* March 18, 1943; *Daily People's World,* July 24, 1943; Kerns, "A Study of the Social and Economic Conditions," 8; *Hearings on Congested Areas,* "San Francisco," 880.

63. Lane, *Ships for Victory,* 430; Foster, *Henry Kaiser,* 76; Carl Abbott, *Portland: Politics, Planning, and Growth in a Twentieth-Century City* (Lincoln: University of Nebraska Press, 1983), 134; Charles Wollenberg, *Marinship at War* (Berkeley: Western Heritage Press, 1990), 86; House Subcommittee of Committee on Naval Affairs, *Hearings on Congested Areas,* pt. 8, "Los Angeles–Long Beach Area, November 10–13, 1943," 78th Cong., 2d sess., 1891, 1971.

64. Calvin Schmid, *Social Trends in Seattle* (Seattle: University of Washington Press, 1944; New York: Greenwood Press, 1969), 323; Gerald D. Nash, *The American West Transformed* (Bloomington: Indiana University Press, 1985), 60, 63; House Subcommittee of Committee on Naval Affairs, *Hearings on Congested Areas,* pt. 2, "San Diego Area, April 6–10, 1943," 78th Cong., 1st sess., 393, 524, 546, 549, and pt. 8, "Los Angeles," 1760, 1971, 1973.

65. Wollenberg, *Marinship at War,* 91; Abbott, *Portland,* 143; Lawrence B. de Graaf, "Negro Migration to Los Angeles, 1930–1950" (Ph.D. diss., University of California, Los Angeles, 1962), 200; House Subcommittee of Committee on Naval Affairs, *Hearings on Congested Areas,* pt. 6, "Puget Sound, October 25–27, 1943," 78th Cong., 2d sess., 1374, 1524, and pt. 8, "Los Angeles," 1859; Charles Bratt, "Profiles: Los Angeles," 186, and Robert W. O'Brien, "Profiles: Seattle," 150, both in series "The New Race Relations Frontier," *Journal of Educational Sociology* 19 (November 1945).

66. De Graaf, "Negro Migration to Los Angeles," 199; *Hearings on Congested Areas,* "Los Angeles," 1761; O'Brien, "Profiles: Seattle," 148.

67. Abbott, *Portland,* 135; U.S. Bureau of the Census, *Population,* ser. CA-2, *Wartime Changes in Population and Family Characteristics,* reports on congested production areas, no. 3, "San Francisco," 7; no. 5, "Los Angeles," 7; no. 6, "Portland-Vancouver," 6.

5. Migrant Families and Communities

1. Tarea Hall Pittman, "NAACP Official and Civil Rights Worker" (interview by Joyce Henderson, 1974, Regional Oral History Office, Bancroft Library, University of California, Berkeley), 34.

2. Agnes Meyer, *Journey through Chaos* (New York: Harcourt, Brace and Co., 1944).

3. The most notable of these studies are Henry Kraus, *In the City Was a Garden: A Housing Project Chronicle* (New York: Renaissance Press, 1951); Robert J. Havighurst and H. Gerthon Morgan, *The Social History of a War Boom Community* (New York: Longmans, Green and Co., 1951); and Lowell J. Carr and James E. Stermer, *Willow Run: A Study of Industrialization and Social Inadequacy* (New York: Harper, 1952).

4. Interview with Antoinette Vaara by author, November 21, 1988; interview with Ophelia M. Hicks by author, March 30, 1989; interview with Alex Amber by author, November 22, 1988; Memoranda from conference with Elsa Reisner, Housing and Transportation Department, Kaiser Shipyards, Richmond, October 23, 1943, box 122, Central files, San Francisco Area, U.S.

Committee for Congested Production Areas, Record Group 212, National Archives; *Fore 'N' Aft,* September 1, 1944.

5. Margaret Louise Cathey, "A Wartime Journey: From Ottumwa, Iowa, to the Richmond Shipyards, 1942" (interview by Judith K. Dunning, 1985, Regional Oral History Office, Bancroft Library, University of California, Berkeley, 1990), 19; Maya Angelou, *I Know Why the Caged Bird Sings* (New York: Random House, 1969; Bantam Books, 1973). Female kin networks have been especially important to black migration in the United States. For a detailed view, see Carol Stack, *All Our Kin: Strategies for Survival in a Black Community* (New York: Harper and Row, 1974).

6. Oakland, California, Housing Authority of the City of Oakland, *Annual Report, 1941–1942,* 11, 24; Helen Smith Alancraig, "Codornices Village: A Study of Non-Segregated Public Housing" (M.A. thesis, University of California, Berkeley, 1953), Appendix 5, Table 1; interview with Ophelia M. Hicks, March 30, 1989; interview with Helen M. Vaughan by author, June 12, 1990.

7. North Richmond migrant quoted in Sheila Tropp Lichtman, "Women at Work, 1941–1945: Wartime Employment in the San Francisco Bay Area" (Ph.D. diss., University of California, Davis, 1981), 289; Charles S. Johnson, *The Negro War Worker in San Francisco* (San Francisco: YWCA, 1944), 23. Although Johnson collected his data in San Francisco, we can assume that overcrowding was comparable if not worse in East Bay black communities given the more critical housing shortage that existed there.

8. Johnson, *The Negro War Worker,* 25; Francis Merrill, *Social Problems on the Home Front: A Study of Wartime Influences* (New York: Harper, 1948), 33.

9. Karen Anderson, *Wartime Women: Sex Roles, Family Relationships, and the Status of Women during World War II* (Westport, Conn.: Greenwood Press, 1981), 85–86; Lichtman, "Women at Work," 83.

10. See "Problems, by Geraldine" column in *Oakland Tribune,* December 27, 1942, and succeeding issues.

11. U.S. Bureau of the Census, *Population,* ser. CA-2, *Wartime Changes in Population and Family Characteristics,* reports on congested production areas, no. 3, "San Francisco, April 1944, 8; no. 2, "San Diego, March 1944," 3; no. 5, "Los Angeles, April 1944," 8; no. 6, "Portland-Vancouver, May 1944," 7; no. 8, "Puget Sound, June 1944," 7 (Washington, D.C.: Bureau of the Census, 1944).

12. Katherine Archibald, *Wartime Shipyard: A Study in Social Disunity* (Berkeley: University of California Press, 1947; New York: Arno Press, 1977), 31–32.

13. Joseph Fabry, *Swing Shift: Building the Liberty Ships* (San Francisco: Strawberry Hill Press, 1982); Cathey, "A Wartime Journey," 20.

14. *Oakland Tribune,* January 1, 1943; U.S. Bureau of the Census, *Population,* ser. PM-1, no. 4, *Marriage Licenses Issued in Cities of 100,000 or More, 1939 to 1944* ([Washington, D.C.: Bureau of the Census], 1945), 6; and *Population,* ser. PM-3, no. 3, *Marriage Licenses Issued in Cities of 100,000 or More, Annual Summary: 1945* ([Washington, D.C.: Bureau of the Census], 1946), 6. Unfortunately, divorce statistics for East Bay counties are not available for this period.

15. Anderson, *Wartime Women,* 76; Calvin Schmid, *Social Trends in Seattle* (Seattle: University of Washington Press, 1944; New York: Greenwood Press, 1969), 321; Kraus, *In the City Was a Garden,* 124; Carr and Stermer, *Willow Run,* 274.

16. *Oakland Tribune,* January 4, 1944; for examples of bigamy cases, see *Oakland Tribune,* November 29, 1943, and May 5, 1944; and *Richmond Record-Herald,* July 20, 1943.

17. See, for example, *Oakland Tribune,* March 25, December 10, 1942; idem, August 7, 17, 30, November 16, December 5, 23, 24, 1943; and *Richmond Record-Herald,* June 18 and 30, July 4 and 12, August 4 and 31, and October 1 and 12, 1943.

18. *Richmond Record-Herald,* June 10, 1943.

19. *Oakland Tribune,* September 9, 1943.

20. Hubert Owen Brown, "The Impact of War Worker Migration on the Public School System of Richmond, California; 1940–1945" (Ed.D. diss., Stanford University, 1973), 250–52.

21. Ibid., 231, 233; *Fore 'N' Aft,* September 1, 1944.

22. *Oakland Tribune,* January 16, 1942; see also *Tribune* items on November 21, December 8, 1943, and October 20, 1944; William Martin Camp, *Skip to My Lou* (Garden City, N.Y.: Doubleday, 1945); Harriette Arnow, *The Doll-maker* (New York: Macmillan, 1954; New York: Avon, 1972).

23. Interview with Helen M. Vaughan, June 12, 1990; interview with Lois Harley by author, February 22, 1989.

24. Robert Wenkert, *An Historical Digest of Negro-White Relations in Richmond, California* (Berkeley: Survey Research Center, University of California, 1967), 22; *Fore 'N' Aft,* December 3, 1943.

25. Archibald, *Wartime Shipyard,* 4–6.

26. Beth Noel, "Codornices Village: A Project of the Federal Public Housing Authority, Berkeley-Albany, California," in *Problems of American Communities,* Department of Economics and Sociology, Mills College, 3 vols. (collection of unpublished papers, 1945, copy in Mills College Library, Oakland), 2:186. Outside the East Bay, studies of other war boomtowns also highlighted this class conflict; see Kraus, *In the City Was a Garden,* 78; and Havighurst and Morgan, *The Social History of a War Boom Community,* 78, 91, 95.

27. Quoted in Barbara Chudley, "Social Problem: The Lockwood Gardens Housing Project," in *Problems of American Communities,* Mills College, 2:230.

28. House Subcommittee of Committee on Naval Affairs, *Hearings on Congested Areas,* pt. 3, "San Francisco Bay Area, April 12–17, 1943," 78th Cong., 1st sess., 884.

29. *Fore 'N' Aft,* March 5, 1943; *Oakland Tribune,* February 3, 1944; *Richmond Independent,* March 13, 1943.

30. *Oakland Tribune,* February 3, 1944.

31. Alan Clive, *State of War: Michigan in World War II* (Ann Arbor: University of Michigan Press, 1979), 99.

32. *Hearings on Congested Areas,* "San Francisco," 789; Brown, "The Impact of War Worker Migration," 195–98, 213.

33. Brown, "The Impact of War Worker Migration," 204, 221, 226; *Richmond Independent*, March 13, 1943.

34. Brown, "The Impact of War Worker Migration," 228–30.

35. Ibid, 281.

36. Lichtman, "Women at Work," 299; Memo from conference with Elsa Reisner, October 23, 1943 (see note 4 above).

37. Memo from conference with Elsa Reisner, October 23, 1943.

38. Lichtman, "Women at Work," 310; Housing Authority of the City of Oakland, *Annual Report, 1943–1945,* 23; *Fore 'N' Aft,* September 3, 1943; California Youth Authority, "A Study of Youth Services in Contra Costa County" (typescript, 1945; copy in Richmond Collection, Richmond Public Library), 112.

39. Lichtman, "Women at Work," 310; *Daily People's World,* July 31, 1943; *Oakland Tribune,* August 6, 1943.

40. Lichtman, "Women at Work," 317.

41. Ibid., 319–21; Brown, "The Impact of War Worker Migration," 270.

42. Chudley, "Social Problem," 229.

43. Letter from George R. Vestal to Eleanor Ten Broeck, April 20, 1943, box 73, Director's files, San Francisco Area, U.S. Office of Community War Services, Record Group 215, National Archives, Washington, D.C. (hereafter referred to as OCWS, RG 215, NA).

44. *Fore 'N' Aft,* May 5, 1944; Questionnaire on Youth Centers, Director's files, "Recreation," San Francisco Area, OCWS, RG 215, NA.

45. Anne Roller Issler, "Shipyards and the Boys," *Survey Graphic* 33 (March 1944): 175; *Richmond Independent,* October 29, 1943.

46. Issler, "Shipyards and the Boys," 177.

47. Alancraig, "Codornices Village," 120.

48. Report from Charlotte Moton to Sherwood Gates, March 24, 1944, 5, Director's files, "Recreation," OCWS, RG 215, NA.

49. Ibid.

50. *Richmond Independent,* May 27, 1943.

51. H. Paul Douglass, *The City Church and the War Emergency* (New York: Friendship Press, 1945), 17. For a comparative look at FCCC ministries, see David W. Barry, "Survey of the Protestant Churches of Metropolitan Seattle, Washington" (Council of Churches and Christian Education, Seattle, 1945); H. Paul Douglass et al., "The Portland Church Survey" (Portland Council of Churches, Portland, Ore., 1945); Ross W. Sanderson, "The Churches of Los Angeles, California" (Committee for Cooperative Field Research, New York, 1945); and Ross W. Sanderson, "San Diego Churches and Their Prospects" (Committee for Cooperative Field Research, New York, 1945), all in H. Paul Douglass, *Social Problems and the Church* (microfiche collection).

52. Douglass, *The City Church,* 2–3; H. Paul Douglass, A. Ronald Merrix, and John Halko, Committee for Cooperative Field Research, *The San Francisco Bay Area Church Study* (San Francisco: Federal Council of Churches in Christ, 1946), 103.

53. Douglass, *The City Church,* 4.

54. Ibid., 19, 23.

55. *San Francisco Bay Area Church Study,* 104–5. Statistics on the number of United Christian Ministry personnel include Solano County—an area not included in my study of the East Bay. Actual figures for the East Bay, as I have defined it, would thus be slightly lower.

56. Ibid., 102, 104. Again, these calculations are based on figures that include Solano County.

57. Interview with Antoinette Vaara by author; interview with Hazelle Swenson and Gladys Enstad by author, June 29, 1990; W. Miller Barbour, "An Exploratory Study of Socio-Economic Problems Affecting the Negro-White Relationship in Richmond, California" (United Community Defense Services and the National Urban League, Pasadena, 1952; copy in Richmond Collection, Richmond Public Library), 9.

58. Shirley Ann Moore, *The Black Community in Richmond, California, 1910–1987* (typescript, Northern California Center for Afro-American History and Life, Oakland, 1987), 62.

59. *San Francisco Bay Area Church Study,* 96, 105–6; J. Harvey Kerns, "A Study of the Social and Economic Conditions Affecting the Local Negro Population" (Council of Social Agencies, Oakland, 1942; copy in vertical files, Oakland History Room, Oakland Public Library), 20.

60. Douglass, *The City Church,* 19; Richmond Chamber of Commerce, *Handbook of Richmond, 1944–1945.*

61. See advertisements in the *Oakland Tribune,* February 12, March 17, 1944; Gary Moncher, ed., *Bebe Patten: Her Ministry, Then and Now* (San Francisco: Peter Wells Press, 1976), 4–12.

62. *Richmond Independent,* May 13, June 3, July 15, and August 13, 1944; idem, April 13, 1945.

63. Kerns, "Study of the Social and Economic Conditions," 20; Moore, "The Black Community in Richmond," 55.

64. *San Francisco Bay Area Church Study,* 105.

65. *Richmond Independent,* June 24, 1944; Moore, "The Black Community in Richmond," 84. Newcomers to California first formed state clubs in the migrant-dominated Los Angeles area back in the 1920s. The most famous of these was the Iowa Club, which held annual picnics in Long Beach attended by hundreds of ex-Iowans. See Carey McWilliams, *Southern California: An Island on the Land* (New York: Ducll, Sloan and Pierce, 1946; Santa Barbara, Calif.: Peregrine Smith, 1973), 165–71.

66. James N. Gregory, *American Exodus: The Dust Bowl Migration and Okie Culture in California* (New York: Oxford University Press, 1989), 226; Janie B. Hamilton, "West of the Mississippi," *Tophand* 3 (March 1945): 24.

67. See, for example, advertisements in the *Richmond Independent,* January 27, May 11, and June 28, 1944; *Richmond Record-Herald,* June 25, 1944; and Hamilton, "West of the Mississippi," 24; interview with Helen M. Vaughan, June 12, 1990.

68. Viola Stogner, liner notes from LP *Dave Stogner: The King of West Coast Country Swing,* Cattle Records, Mono LP 63; telephone interview with Viola Stogner by author, August 30, 1989; *Richmond Independent,* May 11, 1944.

69. Gregory, *American Exodus,* 231.

70. *Tophand* 3 (June 1946) and 6 (October 1946); see also Wade's obituary in the *Oakland Tribune*, November 9, 1976.

71. Interview with Alex Amber by author, November 22, 1988; Gregory, *American Exodus*, 143–46. For examples of Oakland barn dances, see advertisements in the *Oakland Tribune*, September 26, October 2 and 23, 1942.

72. *Daily People's World*, July 21, 1943.

73. Hamilton, "West of the Mississippi," 24; *Tophand* 3 (June 1946) and 5 (September 1946).

74. *Tophand* 5 (September 1946); Charles R. Townsend, *The Life and Music of Bob Wills* (Chicago: University of Illinois Press, 1986), 241; see also advertisements in the *Oakland Tribune*, January 18, February 22, May 5 and 22, September 4, 1944.

75. Johnson, *The Negro War Worker*, 88; see also advertisements in local Armed Forces Edition for black service personnel, *We Also Serve*, 1945 (copy in vertical files, San Francisco Labor Archives).

76. Lee Hildebrand, "Oakland Blues: The Thrill Goes On," *Museum of California*, September–October 1982, 5; see also advertisements in the *Oakland Tribune* for colored dances at Sweets Ballroom and Oakland Auditorium during the war.

77. Hildebrand, "Oakland Blues," 5; see also Hildebrand's liner notes for LP *Oakland Blues*, Arhoolie 2008, 1970.

78. Interview with Lowell Fulson by Bruce Iglauer, Jim O'Neal, and Bea Van Geffen, *Living Blues* 5 (Summer 1971): 25; interview with Bob Kelton by Tom Mazzolini, *Living Blues* 62 (Winter 1984): 106; Lee Hildebrand, "North Richmond Blues," *East Bay Express* (February 9, 1979); Moore, "The Black Community in Richmond," 132–36.

79. Catherine Schutz, "That Old-Time Gospel Lives Again," *Contra Costa Independent*, June 2, 1982; see liner notes by Ray Funk for LP *San Francisco Bay Gospel*, Interstate Music Limited HT 314, 1987.

80. Interview with Bob Geddins by Tom Mazzolini, *Living Blues* 34 (September–October 1977): 19–20.

81. For a fuller discussion of regional blues traditions during the 1940s, see Arnold Shaw, *Honkers and Shouters: The Golden Years of Rhythm and Blues* (New York: Collier Books, 1978).

6. Boomtowns and the Control of Urban Space

1. *Oakland Tribune*, March 12, 1943; *Oakland Post-Enquirer*, March 16, 1943.

2. Richmond, California, City Manager (James A. McVittie), *An Avalanche Hits Richmond*, 1944; *Oakland Observer*, September 16, 1944.

3. Leon Loofbourow, *In Search of God's Gold* (San Francisco: Methodist Church, Historical Society of the California-Nevada Annual Conference, 1950), 297; International Brotherhood of Boilermakers, Iron Shipbuilders and

Helpers of America, *Richmond: Arsenal of Democracy* (Berkeley: Tam, Gibbs Co., [1945]), 33; interview with Alex Amber by author, November 22, 1988.

4. Margaret Louise Cathey, "A Wartime Journey: From Ottumwa, Iowa, to the Richmond Shipyards, 1942" (interview by Judith K. Dunning, 1985, Regional Oral History Office, Bancroft Library, University of California, Berkeley, 1990), 15; interview with Alex Amber by author; interview with Antoinette Vaara by author, November 21, 1988.

5. California State Board of Equalization, *Wartime Changes in Retail Outlets and Sales Volume* (Sacramento, January 1945), 24; "Richmond Took a Beating," *Fortune* (February 1945): 264.

6. *Oakland Tribune,* May 30, 1943; Hubert Owen Brown, "The Impact of War Worker Migration on the Public School System of Richmond, California; 1940–1945" (Ed.D. diss., Stanford University, 1973), 144.

7. State Board of Equalization, *Wartime Changes in Retail Outlets,* 18; for an indication of the types of business licenses issued, see city council minutes for Oakland, Richmond, and Alameda.

8. Interview with Alex Amber by author; Lee Hildebrand, "Oakland Blues: The Thrill Goes On," *Museum of California* (September–October 1982): 5; *Richmond Independent,* April 3, 1943; *Oakland Tribune,* January 6 and July 3, 1943.

9. Cindy Eckert, "Setting Limits: The Enforcement of Prostitution Laws, Oakland, California, 1934–1954" (senior honors thesis, Stanford University, 1989), 38–39; Report by F. G. Straka, October 30, 1945, Director's files, Social Protection Division, U.S. Office of Community War Services, Federal Security Agency, Region 12, Record Group 215, National Archives, Washington, D.C. (hereafter cited as OCWS, RG 215, NA).

10. *Oakland Tribune,* July 5, 1944; Stanley Nystrom, "A Family's Roots in Richmond: Recollections of a Lifetime Resident" (interview by Judith K. Dunning, 1985, Regional Oral History Office, Bancroft Library, University of California, Berkeley, 1990), 44, 65; Robert Wenkert, *An Historical Digest of Negro-White Relations in Richmond, California* (Berkeley: Survey Research Center, University of California, Berkeley, 1967), 23; "Boom Town," *Fore 'N' Aft,* June 4, 1943, 4.

11. "Richmond Took a Beating," *Fortune,* 267; "Boom Town," *Fore 'N' Aft,* 4; see also city council minutes for Oakland, Richmond, and Alameda for business licenses issued during the war years.

12. Interview with Alex Amber by author; "Richmond Took a Beating," *Fortune,* 267; *Oakland Observer,* December 23, 1944.

13. Richmond City Council, *Minutes,* December 20, 1943; see also advertisements for dance halls and cabarets in the *Oakland Tribune* and *Oakland Post-Enquirer.*

14. *Oakland Tribune,* March 26, 1944; see also carnival advertisements in *Oakland Tribune* and *Richmond Independent.*

15. Marshall Maslin, ed., *Western Shipbuilders in World War II* (Oakland: Shipbuilding Review Publishing Association, 1945), 56; Loofbourow, *In Search of God's Gold,* 297; "Boom Town," *Fore 'N' Aft,* 4; *Oakland Tribune,* December 29, 1942; "Richmond Took a Beating," *Fortune,* 262.

16. "Richmond Took a Beating," *Fortune*, 264.

17. Marguerite Clausen, "Memories of a Lifelong Richmond Resident, 1912 to 1987" (interview by Judith K. Dunning, 1985, Regional Oral History Office, Bancroft Library, University of California, Berkeley, 1990), 38; "Boom Town," *Fore 'N' Aft*, 2.

18. Richmond City Council, *Minutes*, February 28, 1944; "Richmond Took a Beating, *Fortune*, 264; Boilermakers, *Arsenal of Democracy*, 23.

19. *Oakland Observer*, March 11, 1944; *Oakland Tribune*, June 9, 1944; Douglas Henry Daniels, *Pioneer Urbanites: A Social and Cultural History of Black San Francisco* (Philadelphia: Temple University Press, 1980), 172.

20. "Problems, by Geraldine," *Oakland Tribune*, February 18, 1943, and July 13, 1944. See also "Tell It to Hazel" column in the *Oakland Post-Enquirer*; *Daily People's World*, August 5, 1943, for article on radio station KROW's comment on the debate; and Katherine Archibald, *Wartime Shipyard: A Study in Social Disunity* (Berkeley: University of California Press, 1947; New York: Arno Press, 1977), 53, for description of California-Okie graffiti war in shipyard rest rooms.

21. James N. Gregory, *American Exodus: The Dust Bowl Migration and Okie Culture in California* (New York: Oxford University Press, 1989), 106–8; Daniels, *Pioneer Urbanites*, 173.

22. *Oakland Tribune*, June 23, 1944; see also April 13–15 and September 20, 1942.

23. *San Francisco Chronicle*, March 20, 1944; *Oakland Tribune*, December 13, 1942; Archibald, *Wartime Shipyard*, 7; Irma Jean Smith, "The Wartime Population Increase in Oakland, California," 194, and Barbara Chudley, "Social Problem: Lockwood Gardens Housing Project," 228, both in *Problems of American Communities*, Department of Economics and Sociology, Mills College, 3 vols. (collection of unpublished papers, 1945, copy in Mills College Library, Oakland).

24. William Hogan, "Hangover Town," *Salute Magazine* (June 1946): 33; *Oakland Tribune*, June 13 and 29, 1944.

25. *Oakland Tribune*, April 26, 1943; Archibald, *Wartime Shipyard*, 44–45.

26. Daniels, *Pioneer Urbanites*, 172; Smith, "The Wartime Population Increase in Oakland," 195.

27. Dorothea Lange Collection, vols. 35–36, Oakland Museum, Oakland.

28. Loofbourow, *In Search of God's Gold*, 297; *Oakland Tribune*, October 23, 1942, and February 13, 1943.

29. Oakland City Council, *Minutes*, March 16, 1943; *Oakland Tribune* and *Oakland Post-Enquirer*, March 12–April 16, 1943; *Richmond Independent*, April 1–3, 1943; *Alameda Times-Star*, March 18–26, 1943.

30. *Oakland Tribune*, March 18 and 26, 1943; *Richmond Independent*, April 2–3, 1943; Brown, "The Impact of War Worker Migration," 164; Smith, "The Wartime Population Increase in Oakland," 204.

31. Senate Committee on Military Affairs, *Labor Shortages in the Pacific Coast and Rocky Mountain States*, 78th Cong., 1st sess., Sept. 9–10, 1943, 14–

15; *House Subcommittee of Committee on Naval Affairs, Hearings on Congested Areas,* "San Francisco Bay Area, April 12–17, 1943," 78th Cong., 1st sess., 788 (hereafter cited as *Hearings on Congested Areas*); Oakland arrest files (microfilm), April 1944, Records Division, Oakland Police Department.

32. The congressional committee investigating congested areas held hearings in San Francisco, Oakland, Richmond, Alameda, and Vallejo in April 1943; see *Hearings on Congested Areas* cited above.

33. Brown, "The Impact of War Worker Migration," 158.

34. *Richmond Independent,* June 3, 1944; *Oakland Tribune,* March 27, June 18, 1943; *Alameda Times-Star,* March 22 and 29, 1943; Richmond City Council, *Minutes,* August 23, 1943; U.S. Department of Justice, Federal Bureau of Investigation, *Uniform Crime Reports,* 1942–1944. At their wartime peak, Oakland had 2,360 auxiliary police, Alameda had 435, and Berkeley 281. The FBI does not indicate whether military police are included in these figures.

35. Richmond City Council, *Minutes,* June 26, 1944.

36. Richmond City Council, *Minutes,* October 9, 1944; *Richmond Independent,* June 27, July 3 and 19, 1944.

37. *Alameda Times-Star,* December 16, 1943. A band of some five hundred gypsies living in the Stockton, California, area was one of many groups recruited for wartime harvesting work in the Central Valley. Following the crops from Lodi to Dixon, some gypsies left the fields for coastal defense centers, often supporting themselves by street peddling. *Oakland Tribune,* July 3, 1944.

38. *Oakland Observer,* November 27, 1943; *Oakland Tribune,* December 2, 1943.

39. Richmond City Council, *Minutes,* January 15, 1943, and September 25, 1944; *Oakland Tribune,* July 20, October 6 and 20, 1943.

40. *Richmond Independent,* March 18, 1943; *Oakland Tribune,* October 27, 1942; Richmond City Council, *Minutes,* January 29, 1943. The greatest source of new revenue came through the business taxes leveled at newcomer defense contractors and other large businesses. Under the guidance of State Attorney General Robert W. Kenney, war-affected California cities and counties taxed federal defense contractors for their "possessory interest" in equipment (not property, which was leased by the federal government and thus tax-exempt). By May 1944, East Bay cities and counties had collected $132,213 from nearby shipyard operations. Brown, "The Impact of War Worker Migration," 151; *Oakland Tribune,* October 27, 1942, and May 2, 1944.

41. *Oakland Tribune,* January 30, March 18, April 16, 1943.

42. To assess changing law enforcement patterns during the war, I surveyed a sample of consecutive police arrest reports from the first week of April 1940 (123 cases) and April 1944 (291 cases). The arrest records offered information on the age, race, residence, birthplace, occupation, marital status, and previous offenses of the arrestee, as well as the date, time, place, and nature of the offense. Data were collected on all records for which adequate information was available. In some cases, particularly arrests made on out-of-town warrants, information was incomplete and was thus not included in the sample. See Oakland arrest files (microfilm), April 1940, April 1944.

43. U.S. Bureau of the Census, *Population*, ser. CA-3, *Characteristics of the Population, Labor Force, Families, and Housing in Ten Congested Production Areas*, no. 3, "San Francisco Bay Area" [Washington, D.C., 1944], 15.

44. *Oakland Tribune*, March 20 and 30, 1943; *Alameda Times-Star*, March 26, 1943.

45. *Alameda Times-Star*, March 18, 1943; *Richmond Independent*, March 13, 1942, and March 20, 1944.

46. *Hearings on Congested Areas*, "San Francisco," 871; Brown, "The Impact of War Worker Migration," 162, 166.

47. *Alameda Times-Star*, March 19 and 29, 1943; *Oakland Tribune*, June 5, 1942; *Oakland Post-Enquirer*, March 20, 1943.

48. *Oakland Tribune*, August 22, 1942, and June 18, 1944.

49. "Richmond Took a Beating," *Fortune*, 267; *Fore 'N' Aft*, December 24, 1943.

50. *Oakland Tribune*, November 7, 1942, and September 13, 1943; *Oakland Observer*, May 15, 1943; California Department of Justice, *A Guide to Race Relations for Police Officers* (Sacramento, 1946), 26.

51. *Oakland Tribune*, March 25, 1943, and November 30, 1944; *Oakland Post-Enquirer*, March 25, 1943.

52. *Oakland Tribune*, March 15 and 20, April 9, 1943; August 5, 1944; *Oakland Post-Enquirer*, March 20, April 9, 1943.

53. Oakland arrest files (microfilm), April 1940, April 1944; and "Return C: Annual Return of Persons Charged," 1940, 1944, Planning Division, Oakland Police Department.

54. *Oakland Observer*, May 15, 1943, and March 11, 1944; *Oakland Tribune*, January 18, 1943.

55. *Oakland Post-Enquirer*, August 10, 1943, and March 7, 1944; *Richmond Independent*, October 30, 1943, and February 10, 1944; *Oakland Tribune*, March 8, 1944.

56. *Oakland Observer*, March 11, 1944; Nathan Huggins, "Preface," in Daniels, *Pioneer Urbanites*, xiv.

57. Huggins, "Preface," xiv; Charles S. Johnson, *The Negro War Worker in San Francisco* (San Francisco: YWCA, 1944), 77. One notable example of confusing racial customs was at Sweets Ballroom in Oakland, where black swing bands had traditionally played two successive nights, the first one for whites, the second for blacks. There were no written rules or advertisements to this effect, but everyone complied. Black migrants, who often had little contact with old-timers, simply had to learn by experience.

58. *Oakland Observer*, May 15, August 7, 1943; *Oakland Tribune*, October 12, 1944; *Daily People's World*, April 9, 1943; "Richmond Took a Beating," *Fortune*, 264; Shirley Ann Moore, "The Black Community in Richmond, California, 1910–1963" (Ph.D. diss., University of California, Berkeley, 1989), 43.

59. Johnson, *The Negro War Worker*, 18; Daniels, *Pioneer Urbanites*, 173; William V. F. Scott, "Eliminate the Stokes Willies," *Crisis* 57 (January 1950): 10; *Oakland Tribune*, August 13, 1943; Frances Mary Albrier, "Determined Advocate for Racial Equality" (interview by Malca Chall, 1979, Regional Oral

History Office, Bancroft Library, University of California, Berkeley), 150–56; Joseph James, "Profiles: San Francisco," in "Race Relations on the Pacific Coast," ed. L. D. Reddick, *Journal of Educational Sociology* 19 (November 1945): 173.

60. Daniels, *Pioneer Urbanites*, xiv, 174; *Daily People's World*, March 29, April 9, 1943.

61. Oakland arrest files (microfilm), April 1940, April 1944.

62. *Hearings on Congested Areas*, "San Francisco," 768; *Oakland Tribune*, March 25, July 6, 1943; Oakland City Council, *Minutes*, May 27, 1943.

63. Cindy Eckert, "Setting Limits," 22.

64. *Hearings on Congested Areas*, "San Francisco," 778, 787; *Oakland Tribune*, August 8, 1943.

65. Karen Anderson, *Wartime Women: Sex Roles, Family Relationships, and the Status of Women during World War II* (Westport, Conn.: Greenwood Press, 1981), 104.

66. *Oakland Tribune*, November 12 and 19, 1944; *Alameda Times-Star*, November 3, 1943; Jane Hamilton, "Survey of Juvenile Delinquency for Oakland, California," 340, and Joy Hickok, "Juvenile Delinquency in Oakland, California," 357, both in *Problems of American Communities*, Department of Economics and Sociology, Mills College, 3 vols. (collection of unpublished papers, 1945, copy in Mills College Library, Oakland).

67. *Oakland Tribune*, October 15, 1944.

68. *Oakland Tribune*, September 28, November 16, 1944.

69. *Oakland Tribune*, January 30, May 16, 1943; *Oakland Post-Enquirer*, March 20, 1943; *Newsweek* (November 15, 1943): 49.

70. *Hearings on Congested Areas*, "San Francisco," 788; *Oakland Tribune*, March 20, 1943, and February 4, 1944; *Oakland Post-Enquirer*, March 25, 1943.

71. *Oakland Tribune*, March 30, November 16, 1943; *Richmond Independent*, March 6, 1944; memo from F. G. Straka to Thomas Devine, April 5, 1945, Classified files, Social Protection Division, OCWS, RG 215, NA; Willard Waller, as quoted in William Chafe, *The Unfinished Journey: America since World War II* (New York: Oxford University Press, 1986), 8–9.

72. *Richmond Independent*, April 1 and 2, 1943.

73. Brown, "The Impact of War Worker Migration," 238–40, 250–51; *Oakland Post-Enquirer*, February 17, March 16, 1943; Irvin C. Futter, "Juvenile Delinquency in a California Defense Area" (M.A. thesis, Stanford University, 1943), 47; *Alameda Times-Star*, November 3, 1943; *Oakland Tribune*, November 4, 1943.

74. James Gilbert, *Cycle of Outrage: America's Reaction to the Juvenile Delinquent in the 1950s* (New York: Oxford University Press, 1986), 25, 29, 40; *Oakland Tribune*, August 1, 1944.

75. Brown, "The Impact of War Worker Migration," 248; *Richmond Independent*, March 18, 1943; *Oakland Tribune*, February 13, 1943, and February 21, 1944; Chudley, "Social Problem: Lockwood Gardens Housing Project," 226. The tendency of local officials to blame migrants for the city's ills reached ludicrous proportions during an epidemic of dog biting in Alameda County in

September 1944. An increased canine population and a lack of municipal dog-catchers had resulted in a proliferation of stray dogs on city streets and an accompanying rabies scare. In a statement that bore remarkable parallels to the juvenile delinquency arguments, Oakland Poundmaster Richard Trotter claimed: "Most of the biting dogs in quarantine are from out of town, brought here by war workers from Texas, Oklahoma, Kansas and other points. . . . We do not believe these animals to be inflicted with rabies. They are, in my opinion, just nervous in their efforts to acclimate themselves in the Oakland environment." Trotter warned owners to keep proper identification on their dogs "as they [were] now being picked up off streets on the slightest suspicion" (*Oakland Tribune*, September 21, 1944).

76. Richmond City Council, *Minutes,* February 8, 1943, and November 6, 1944; Brown, "The Impact of War Worker Migration," 244.

77. Memo from George R. Vestal to Mark McCloskey, September 29, 1943, box 73, Director's files, Recreation Division, OCWS, RG 215, NA; *Oakland Tribune,* October 17, 1944; Brown, "The Impact of War Worker Migration," 247; Richmond City Council, *Minutes,* November 20, 1944.

78. *Richmond Independent,* October 23, November 22, 1943; Brown, "The Impact of War Worker Migration," 233–34.

79. *Oakland Tribune,* February 12, March 31, April 20, July 5, 1944.

80. *Oakland Tribune,* November 11, 1943.

81. *Oakland Tribune,* March 27, May 12, 1944; Futter, "Juvenile Delinquency in a California Defense Area," 22–23; *Richmond Independent,* January 20, 1943.

82. The geographical model of juvenile delinquency was first developed by the sociologists Robert Park and Ernest Burgess in Chicago in the 1920s. Explaining juvenile delinquency in terms of differential city growth, they found delinquency rates highest among immigrant groups that inherited the old urban core. Such areas soon became slums that bred family disorganization and delinquency. In the absence of positive community organization, they argued, young people would model themselves after local criminals and form delinquent gangs. Robert M. Mennel, *Thorns and Thistles* (Hanover, N.H.: University Press of New England, 1973), 188.

83. *Oakland Tribune,* March 30, April 20, 1944; Council of Social Agencies/Community Chest, Research Department, "Our Community: A Factual Presentation of Social Conditions" (Oakland, August 22, 1945; copy in Oakland History Room, Oakland Public Library), 2.

84. California Assembly, Interim Committee on Juvenile Delinquency, *Reports on Juvenile Delinquency* (Sacramento, 1944), 39–40; *Oakland Tribune,* April 13, August 8, November 17, 1943.

85. Oakland, California, Mayor's Committee on Juvenile Crime Prevention, *Report* (Oakland, September 1944; copy in Institute for Governmental Studies Library, University of California, Berkeley); *Oakland Tribune,* June 10, December 4, 1943; April 20, October 4 and 20, 1944. Judge Ogden became a leader of the California State-wide Committee on Youth in Wartime and subsequent postwar organizations. His struggles with conservatives in wartime Oakland foreshadowed later conflicts between conservative law-and-order proponents and more liberal reformers in both California and the nation. Dun-

away's group, by contrast, frequently expressed support of J. Edgar Hoover and the repressive stance on wartime delinquency championed by the FBI. Ogden's reformers reflected the more cautious position of the federal Children's Bureau led by Katherine Lenroot. Gilbert, *Cycle of Outrage,* 25.

86. *Oakland Tribune,* April 20, June 4, 1944; for some examples of child neglect and abandonment cases see *Oakland Tribune,* January 3, June 5, August 4, 1944.

87. *Richmond Independent,* January 27 and 31, 1944. A surprisingly similar case of child tethering by a Louisiana migrant was reported in a Portland area war housing project. The similarity of the two cases suggests that tethering may have been a common practice in some areas of the rural South. Amy Kesselman, *Fleeting Opportunities: Women Shipyard Workers in Portland and Vancouver during World War II and Reconversion* (Albany: State University of New York Press, 1990), 71.

88. Linda Gordon, *Heroes of Their Own Lives: The Politics and History of Family Violence* (New York: Viking Press, 1988), 118; *Oakland Tribune,* June 9, 1944; *Richmond Independent,* January 28, 1944.

89. *Oakland Tribune,* November 23, 1943, and March 17, June 4, August 4, 1944. Linda Gordon argues that in the Progressive Era the concept of neglect became a preoccupation of social welfare workers just as the impact of feminism was declining. A similar short-term cycle seems to have occurred during the war years as patriotic rhetoric about working women rose and fell between 1942 and 1945. Gordon, *Heroes of Their Own Lives,* 80.

90. *Oakland Tribune,* December 9, 1943, and April 25, 1944.

91. Carey McWilliams, "Jim Crow Goes West," *Negro Digest* 3 (August 1945): 71; Calvin Schmid, *Social Trends in Seattle* (Seattle: University of Washington Press, 1944; New York: Greenwood Press, 1969), 309; Carl Abbott, *Portland: Planning, Politics, and Growth in a Twentieth-Century City* (Lincoln: University of Nebraska Press, 1983), 128;

92. Charles Wollenberg, *Marinship at War: Shipbuilding and Social Change in Wartime Sausalito* (Berkeley: Western Heritage Press, 1990), 94.

93. Gregory, *American Exodus,* 174–76; Gerald D. Nash, *The American West Transformed: The Impact of the Second World War* (Bloomington: Indiana University Press, 1985), 62, 65, 80; House Subcommittee of Committee on Naval Affairs, *Hearings on Congested Areas,* pt. 8, "Los Angeles–Long Beach Area, November 10–13, 1943," 78th Cong., 2d sess., 1763, 1770, 1916; McWilliams, "Jim Crow Goes West," 72; Lawrence B. de Graaf, "Negro Migration to Los Angeles, 1930–1950" (Ph.D. diss., University of California, Los Angeles, 1962), 202.

94. *Hearings on Congested Areas,* "Los Angeles," 1770.

95. House Subcommittee of Committee on Naval Affairs, *Hearings on Congested Areas,* pt. 2, "San Diego Area, April 6–10, 1943," 78th Cong., 1st sess., 404, 408, 414, 433.

96. Wollenberg, *Marinship at War,* 92; *Oakland Tribune,* March 23, 1943.

97. Schmid, *Social Trends in Seattle,* 311, 331; Abbott, *Portland,* 129; House Subcommittee of Committee on Naval Affairs, *Hearings on Congested Areas,* pt. 6, "Puget Sound Area, October 25–27, 1943," 78th Cong., 2d sess., 1320, 1330.

98. *Hearings on Congested Areas,* "Puget Sound," 1524; Nash, *The American West Transformed,* 95; McWilliams, "Jim Crow Goes West," 72; Schmid, *Social Trends in Seattle,* 320. For a comparative view of West Coast race relations, see Reddick, ed., "Race Relations on the Pacific Coast," a special issue of the *Journal of Educational Sociology.*

99. *Hearings on Congested Areas,* "Los Angeles," 1772, 1918, and "Puget Sound," 1323; Gilbert, *Cycle of Outrage,* 36.

100. Gordon, *Heroes of Their Own Lives,* 116–67; Anderson, *Wartime Women,* 91, 98.

7. Mobilizing Politics

1. Edward C. Hayes, *Power Structure and Urban Policy: Who Rules in Oakland* (New York: McGraw-Hill, 1972), 21; *Labor Herald,* May 20, 1947; *Daily People's World,* May 7 and 9, 1947.

2. Carl Abbott, *The New Urban America: Growth and Politics in Sunbelt Cities* (Chapel Hill: University of North Carolina Press, 1981), 120–42.

3. For another example of the role of national wartime developments in shaping urban politics, see Robin Einhorn, "The Civil War and Municipal Government in Chicago," in *Toward a Social History of the American Civil War,* ed. Maris A. Vinovskis (New York: Cambridge University Press, 1990).

4. Proponents of this view include Nelson Lichtenstein, *Labor's War at Home: The CIO in World War II* (New York: Cambridge University Press, 1982), 171–77, and James C. Foster, *The Union Politic: The CIO Political Action Committee* (Columbia: University of Missouri Press, 1975).

5. Hayes, *Power Structure and Urban Policy,* 34–36.

6. The Hamill manuscript and Kaiser letter are located in the "Time, Life, and Fortune" file, carton 27, Henry Kaiser Papers, Bancroft Library, University of California, Berkeley.

7. Ibid.

8. Richmond, California, City Manager (James A. McVittie), *An Avalanche Hits Richmond* (Richmond, 1944), 6, 24.

9. "Richmond Took a Beating," *Fortune* (February 1945): 269; "Richmond: A City of High Hopes and Big Headaches," *Fortnight* (December 19, 1947): 18–19.

10. *Labor Herald,* April 16, 1943. For specific examples of labor's involvement in citywide committees, see back issues of the *Labor Herald* for 1943–1945.

11. Oakland Postwar Planning Committee, *Oakland's Formula for the Future* (Oakland, 1945); Hayes, *Power Structure and Urban Policy,* 145–46; Berkeley Citizens Postwar Advisory Committee, "Report of the Sub-Committee on Project Studies and City Planning" (Berkeley, September 14, 1944).

12. Carl Abbott, "Planning for the Home Front in Portland and Seattle, 1940–1945," in *The Martial Metropolis: U.S. Cities in War and Peace,* ed. Roger W. Lotchin (New York: Praeger Publishers, 1984), 181–82; *Labor Herald,* De-

cember 12, 1944. For the shifting priorities of labor, see back issues of the CIO's *Labor Herald* for the war and prewar years.

13. Nelson Lichtenstein suggests that the founding of the CIO-PAC was also a reaction to the internal threat from left-wing CIO members (primarily in New York and Michigan) who supported a radical third-party alternative. I have found no evidence of a similar split in California CIO ranks. Lichtenstein, *Labor's War at Home*, 172–73; Robert H. Zeiger, *American Workers, American Unions, 1920–1985* (Baltimore: Johns Hopkins University Press, 1986), 115; Foster, *The Union Politic*, 14.

14. *Labor Herald*, June 20, October 6, November 3, 1944; *Daily People's World*, October 23 and 24, 1944; *Oakland Observer*, June 17, 1944.

15. *Daily People's World*, November 4 and 5, 1944. For an insider's view of PAC organizing in a war housing project, see Henry Kraus, *In the City Was a Garden: A Housing Project Chronicle* (New York: Renaissance Press, 1951).

16. Joseph James, "Profiles: San Francisco," in "Race Relations on the Pacific Coast," ed. L. D. Reddick, *Journal of Educational Sociology* 19 (November 1945): 175; *Daily People's World*, November 10, 1944. James C. Foster argues that the CIO-PAC was not the effective vote-getting machine that contemporaries believed. See Foster, *The Union Politic*, 1–2.

17. *Labor Herald*, December 22, 1944, and March 2, 1945.

18. U.S. Department of Labor, War Manpower Commission, "Summary of Monthly Narrative Reports, June 14, 1945," Labor Market Survey Reports, box 27, Bureau of Employment Security, Record Group 183, National Archives, Washington, D.C.; *Labor Herald*, February 16, April 20, 1945; *Daily People's World*, March 17, April 6, 1945.

19. Mullendore's address was subsequently published and widely distributed in East Bay business circles. William C. Mullendore, "What Price Prosperity" (Oakland Chamber of Commerce, Oakland, 1946; copy in the Institute for Governmental Studies Library, University of California, Berkeley).

20. Kraus, *In the City Was a Garden*, 254; *Daily People's World*, April 20, 1945. Ironically, some of the most avid proponents of this social democratic vision were Communist party members such as Henry Kraus and the writers at the *Daily People's World*.

21. *Labor Herald*, February 16, 1945; *Daily People's World*, April 6, 13, 20, 1945.

22. *Labor Herald*, February 16, March 9 and 30, 1945; *Daily People's World*, April 6, 9, 13, 18, 20, 1945.

23. In an attempt to split the labor vote, the Knowland forces pressured incumbent councilman James DePaoli to resign one month before the Oakland elections of 1945. They appointed James D'Arcy, an official of the AFL Culinary Workers Union and a Knowland supporter, to replace him and then announced D'Arcy's candidacy as an incumbent. The United for Oakland Committee denounced D'Arcy, noting that his union had followed exclusionary and undemocratic policies during the war. Labor forces thus remained united behind their candidate, Herman Bittman, shop steward of the CIO steelworkers. *Labor Herald*, March 16, 1945; *Daily People's World*, March 15, 1945.

24. *Labor Herald,* February 16, March 16, 1945; *Daily People's World,* March 15, April 6 and 13, 1945; Oakland Tribune Publishing Co., *Oakland Tribune Yearbook: 1944,* 45; interview with James P. Kenny by author, June 11, 1991; Abbott, *The New Urban America,* 121. Kaiser industries also accused Richmond officials of sandbagging their plans for a gypsum processing plant and other postwar ventures. *San Francisco Chronicle,* February 10, 1946.

25. *Labor Herald,* April 20, 1945; *Daily People's World,* March 16, April 13 and 25, 1945.

26. *Labor Herald,* March 30, 1945; James, "Profiles: San Francisco," 175.

27. *Labor Herald,* April 13, May 4, 1945; *Daily People's World,* April 19, 1945; *Oakland Tribune,* March 25, April 15, 1945.

28. *Labor Herald,* March 16, May 4, 1945; *Daily People's World,* April 19, May 3, 1945; *Oakland Tribune,* April 18, 1945.

29. Hayes, *Power Structure and Urban Policy,* 145; *Daily People's World,* April 19, 1945. The school measure was subsequently defeated; Hayes speculates that the separation of the bond measures indicated lukewarm business support for school funding.

30. War Manpower Commission, "Summary of Monthly Narrative Reports, June 14, 1945"; U.S. Dept. of Labor, U.S. Employment Service, "Monthly Area Statement, Richmond, California," October–November 1946, January 1947, Labor Market Survey Reports, box 20, Bureau of Employment Security, RG 183, NA; "Richmond: A City of High Hopes and Big Headaches," 18–19.

31. Sheila Tropp Lichtman, "Women at Work, 1941–1945: Wartime Employment in the San Francisco Bay Area" (Ph.D. diss., University of California, Davis, 1981), 348, 352; War Manpower Commission, "Summary of Monthly Narrative Reports, June 14, 1945"; U.S. Employment Service, "Monthly Area Statement, Richmond, California," November 1946; Karen Anderson, *Wartime Women: Sex Roles, Family Relationships, and the Status of Women during World War II* (Westport, Conn.: Greenwood Press, 1981), 170; Davis McEntire, "Postwar Status of Negro Workers in the San Francisco Area," *Monthly Labor Review* 70 (June 1950): 616.

32. William Hogan, "Hangover Town," *Salute Magazine* (June 1946): 33; Charles Raudebaugh, "Richmond, a Town with a Purple Heart, Looks to the Future," *San Francisco Chronicle,* March 18, 1946; Richmond Redevelopment Agency, *A Report on Housing and Redevelopment,* January 1950, 31; Milton Silverman, "The Second Gold Rush Hits the West," series of articles from the *San Francisco Chronicle,* April 25–May 20, 1943.

33. Richard Reinhardt, "Richmond: The Boom That Didn't Bust," *San Francisco Chronicle,* August 16, 1953; Housing Authority of the City of Oakland, *Annual Report, 1943–1945,* 33; Richmond City Manager (McVittie), *An Avalanche Hits Richmond.*

34. California State Reconstruction and Reemployment Commission, pamphlet no. 3, *The Bay Region Takes Stock* (Sacramento, August 1944), 8; California State Chamber of Commerce, Research Department, "Survey of the Housing Problem in California" (February 1946; copy in Bancroft Library, University of California, Berkeley), 4; "Detour through Purgatory," *Fortune* (February 1945): 183.

35. Hogan, "Hangover Town," 33; Housing Authority of the City of Oakland, *Annual Report, 1943–1945,* 33.

36. California Department of Employment, "Immigration Study: San Francisco Bay Area Labor Market Area, April, 1947," Labor Market Survey Reports, box 28, Bureau of Employment Security, RG 183, NA; Wilson Record, "Willie Stokes at the Golden Gate," *Crisis* 56 (June 1949): 188.

37. Industrial Survey Associates, *The San Francisco Bay Area: Its People, Prospects, and Problems* (San Francisco: n.p., 1948), 8; California Chamber of Commerce, "Survey of the Housing Problem," 6; Raudebaugh, "Richmond, a Town with a Purple Heart," 14.

38. Tarea Hall Pittman, "The Operation of State and County Residence Requirements under the California Indigent Aid Law in Contra Costa County" (M.A. thesis, University of California, Berkeley, 1946), 21–45.

39. *San Francisco Chronicle,* June 8, 9, 17, 24, 1953; Lichtman, "Women at Work," 329; Nancy Reeves, "California: Child Care Centers," *Frontier* (May 1955): 11–12.

40. William Chafe, *The Unfinished Journey: America since World War II* (New York: Oxford University Press, 1986), 93; Zeiger, *American Workers, American Unions,* 100–108; *Oakland Tribune,* December 2 and 5, 1946; *San Francisco Chronicle,* December 4, 1946; Hayes, *Power Structure and Urban Policy,* 19–20.

41. *Oakland Voters Herald,* May 9, 1947 (copy in election files, Oakland History Room, Oakland Public Library); *Labor Herald,* April 22, 1947.

42. Hayes, *Power Structure and Urban Policy,* 21–22; *Labor Herald,* May 6, 1947; Oakland Voters League circular, March 24, 1947 (copy in election files, Oakland History Room, Oakland Public Library).

43. The only labor unions not participating in the OVL campaign were the fourteen locals of the Teamsters Union led by conservative Knowland-supporter Charles Real. Real had been instrumental in getting the international to call off striking Oakland teamsters in 1946, thus breaking the general strike. *Oakland Voters Herald,* May 9, 1947.

44. Helen Smith Alancraig, "Codornices Village: A Study of Non-Segregated Public Housing" (M.A. thesis, University of California, Berkeley, 1953), 15; Hayes, *Power Structure and Urban Policy,* 81–82; Housing Authority of Oakland, *Annual Report, 1946–1947,* 2.

45. *Daily People's World,* May 2 and 12, 1947; *Oakland Voters Herald,* May 9, 1947. The *Oakland Tribune, Post-Enquirer,* and other mainstream newspapers were strangely mute about the electoral challenge. Except for the editorial red-baiting just prior to the elections (see, for example, April 1947 issues of the *Oakland Tribune*), the Knowland-owned *Tribune* and the Hearst-owned *Post-Enquirer* provided no sustained coverage. In ignoring their opponents, I suspect, the Knowland machine hoped to render them invisible and thus ineffective. By contrast, the labor and left press devoted extensive coverage to these events. Used carefully, these sources provide vital information on Oakland municipal politics unavailable elsewhere in the written record.

46. *Labor Herald,* May 9, 1947; *Daily People's World,* May 6 and 9, 1947.

47. *Oakland Tribune,* May 14, 1947; *Labor Herald,* May 20, 1947; *Daily People's World,* May 14, 1947; Hayes, *Power Structure and Urban Policy,* 21.

Hayes and other observers have suggested that anti-Semitism was significant in Goldfarb's defeat in this predominantly Protestant city.

48. *Labor Herald,* July 8, 1947.

49. *Labor Herald,* April 9 and 22, May 6, 1947; *Richmond Independent,* May 9 and 11, 1949; Roy Hamachi, "Postwar Housing in Richmond, California" (M.A. thesis, University of California, Berkeley, n.d.; copy in Richmond file, carton 6, Catherine Bauer Wurster Papers, Bancroft Library, University of California, Berkeley), 53.

50. *Oakland Observer,* June 17, 1944; James Orosco, "A Survey of Voting Behavior in the City of Richmond, California, 1936–1956" (typescript, University of California, Berkeley, 1963; copy in Richmond Collection, Richmond Public Library), 16, 29.

51. Interview with Lois Harley by author, February 22, 1989; W. Miller Barbour, "An Exploratory Study of Socio-Economic Problems Affecting the Negro-White Relationship in Richmond, California" (United Community Defense Services and the National Urban League, Pasadena, 1952; copy in Richmond Collection, Richmond Public Library), 24.

52. Interview with James P. Kenny, by author, June 11, 1991; *Labor Herald,* April 29, 1947; Hamachi, "Postwar Housing," 53, 59; *Richmond Independent,* May 11, 1949.

53. Robert Wenkert, *An Historical Digest of Negro-White Relations in Richmond, California* (Berkeley: Survey Research Center, University of California, 1967), 67; Gretchen Lemke, "Blacks in Berkeley, 1859–1987" (typescript, Northern California Center for Afro-American History and Life, Oakland, 1987), 36; William Byron Rumford, "Legislator for Fair Employment, Fair Housing, and Public Health" (interview by Joyce A. Henderson, Amelia Fry, and Edward France, 1973, Regional Oral History Office, Bancroft Library, University of California, Berkeley), 32.

54. Richard Baisden, "Labor in Los Angeles Politics" (Ph.D. diss., University of Chicago, 1958), 309–14; James, "Profile: San Francisco," 175; William Issel, "Liberalism and Urban Policy in San Francisco from the 1930s to the 1960s," *Western Historical Quarterly* 22 (November 1991): 431–50.

55. For an insightful analysis of "old" and "new" social movements, see Bob Fisher and Joe King, "Popular Mobilization in the 1990s: Prospects for the New Social Movements," *New Politics* 25 (Winter 1991): 71–84; and Robert Korstad and Nelson Lichtenstein, "Opportunities Lost and Found: Labor, Radicals, and the Early Civil Rights Movement," *Journal of American History* 75 (December 1988): 786–811.

8. Boomtown Blues

1. Industrial Survey Associates, *The San Francisco Bay Area: Its People, Prospects, and Problems* (San Francisco: n.p., 1948), 11–13.

2. Ibid., 12.

3. Ibid., 14; Davis McEntire, "Postwar Status of Negro Workers in the San Francisco Area," *Monthly Labor Review* 70 (June 1950): 614–16; W. Miller Barbour, "An Exploratory Study of Socio-Economic Problems Affecting the Negro-White Relationship in Richmond, California" (United Community Defense Services and the National Urban League, Pasadena, 1952), 13–15; Shirley Ann Moore, "The Black Community in Richmond, California, 1910–1987" (typescript, Northern California Center for Afro-American History and Life, Oakland, 1987), 66.

4. Edward C. Hayes, *Power Structure and Urban Policy: Who Rules in Oakland* (New York: McGraw-Hill, 1972), 141–42; California State Reconstruction and Reemployment Commission (hereafter referred to as SRRC), pamphlet no. 3, *The Bay Region Takes Stock* (Sacramento, August 1944), 14, 20; SRRC, pamphlet no. 11, *New Factories for California Communities* (Sacramento, 1946), 3–7. The State Reconstruction and Reemployment Commission, it should be noted, was the parent organization of the big business–dominated Bay Area Council.

5. Charles Wollenberg, *Golden Gate Metropolis* (Berkeley: Institute of Governmental Studies, University of California, 1985), 259–62; Hayes, *Power Structure and Urban Policy,* 49.

6. Housing Authority of the City of Oakland, *Annual Report, 1948–1949,* 7, and "Analysis of the Oakland Housing Shortage as of January 1946," 1 (copy of latter in the Institute of Governmental Studies Library, University of California, Berkeley); California Senate, Interim Committee on Community Redevelopment and Housing, *Community Redevelopment and Housing,* 1949, 16–18; *Oakland Tribune,* November 8, 1945; *San Francisco Chronicle,* August 19, 1952.

7. Richmond Redevelopment Agency, *A Report on Housing and Redevelopment* (Richmond: n.p., January 1950), 49; Helen Smith Alancraig, "Codornices Village: A Study of Non-Segregated Public Housing" (M.A. thesis, University of California, Berkeley, 1953), 113.

8. Barbour, "The Negro-White Relationship in Richmond," 10; Housing Authority of the City of Oakland, *Annual Report, 1946–1947,* 2.

9. Tarea Hall Pittman, "The Operation of State and County Residence Requirements under the California Indigent Aid Law in Contra Costa County" (M.A. thesis, University of California, Berkeley, 1946), 7; California State Chamber of Commerce, Research Department, "Survey of the Housing Problem in California" (February 1946; copy in Bancroft Library, University of California, Berkeley), 6.

10. Roy Hamachi, "Postwar Housing in Richmond, California" (M.A. thesis, University of California, Berkeley, n.d.; copy in Richmond file, carton 6, Catherine Bauer Wurster Papers, Bancroft Library, University of California, Berkeley), 5–6.

11. Alancraig, "Codornices Village," 138; untitled housing survey, Oakland, 1946, copy in carton 23, C. L. Dellums Papers, Bancroft Library, University of California, Berkeley. Black occupancy rates in temporary housing in Richmond, Oakland, Berkeley, and Alameda were calculated from PHA figures provided by Alancraig, see Appendixes 4 and 5.

12. Alancraig, "Codornices Village," 66, 104, 114, Appendix 4; Housing Authority of the City of Oakland, *Annual Report, 1946–1947,* 2, and *Annual Report, 1948–1949,* 5. Under an administrative reorganization in July 1947, the National Housing Agency became the Housing and Home Finance Agency, an umbrella organization for all federal housing programs. At that time, the Federal Public Housing Authority, which oversaw management of public housing around the country, became the Public Housing Authority.

13. Postwar observers frequently commented on the lack of leadership and organization among public housing residents. See Raymond Paul DeRomanett, "Public Action and Community Planning: A Case Study of Richmond, California" (M.A. thesis, University of California, Berkeley, 1956), 87, 94; Alancraig, "Codornices Village," 123; Barbour, "The Negro-White Relationship in Richmond," 48.

14. Oakland City Planning Administration, *Redevelopment in Oakland* (Oakland, 1949), 27; Richmond Redevelopment Agency, *A Report on Housing and Redevelopment,* 34.

15. Robert Wenkert, *An Historical Digest of Negro-White Relations in Richmond, California* (Berkeley: Survey Research Center, University of California, 1967), 36; Hayes, *Power Structure and Urban Policy,* 110–11; Oakland City Planning Administration, *Redevelopment in Oakland,* 43; Richmond Redevelopment Agency, *Report on Housing and Redevelopment,* 18.

16. Barbour, "An Exploratory Study," 24; West Contra Costa Welfare Council report quoted in Hamachi, "Postwar Housing in Richmond," 4.

17. Richmond Redevelopment Agency, *Application for Preliminary Advance* (Richmond, September 12, 1950), 59.

18. Alancraig, "Codornices Village," 17–18; John F. Bauman, *Public Housing, Race, and Renewal* (Philadelphia: Temple University Press, 1987), 136; *California Housing Association Newsletter,* November 18, December 27, 1949 (copy in "Housing in California" pamphlets, Bancroft Library, University of California, Berkeley).

19. California Chamber of Commerce, "Survey of the Housing Problem," 4, 15; *San Francisco Chronicle,* October 29, 1950; *California Housing Association Newsletter,* December 27, 1949. The first California housing battle occurred in 1948, when forerunners of the CHP mobilized to fight a statewide proposition creating a state housing agency, a bureaucratic requisite for obtaining federal funds. Outspending its opponents $128,675 to $4,107, the group succeeded in defeating the measure, Proposition 14, by a narrow margin. Thereafter, the CHP turned its attention to the local level, hoping to derail public housing measures through a campaign of "grassroots democracy."

20. Under the council-manager form of government, city council members elected a mayor from among their own ranks. Several of the older conservative council members were bidding for the position, which meant that liberals would cast the deciding vote. See Edward C. Hayes, "Power Structure and the Urban Crisis" (Ph.D. diss., University of California, Berkeley, 1968), 56; *San Francisco Chronicle,* November 17, 1949.

21. *California Housing Association Newsletter,* November 18, 1949; Hayes, "Power Structure and the Urban Crisis," 153; Alancraig, "Codornices Village," 82.

22. *San Francisco Chronicle,* November 17, 1949, and January 4, 1950; Hayes, "Power Structure and the Urban Crisis," 59–60.

23. Alancraig, "Codornices Village," 85; Hayes, *Power Structure and Urban Policy,* 83; see also Housing Authority of the City of Oakland, annual reports for 1948–1949 through 1959–1960.

24. Robert Zeiger, *American Workers, American Unions, 1920–1985* (Baltimore: Johns Hopkins University Press, 1986), 131; *Labor Herald,* May 22, 1951; *Daily People's World,* May 18, 1951; *Oakland Tribune,* May 11, 1951.

25. In Los Angeles County, a similar dispute raged over the fate of fifteen hundred public housing units on the county's west side. As in Oakland, anti–public housing forces on the county board of supervisors used voter referendums to shut down public housing programs and battled with the housing authority to abandon projects contracted under the 1949 program. *San Francisco Chronicle,* June 13, August 1, and September 6, 1952.

26. California Senate, *Community Redevelopment and Housing,* 32; *San Francisco Chronicle,* October 29, November 11, 1950. Proposition 10 was not a balanced measure; a "no" vote barred local governments from using federal or state funds to build public housing, but a "yes" vote did not require them to do so.

27. *California Housing Association Newsletter,* December 27, 1949; W. Byron Rumford, letter to the editor, *Frontier* (February 1956): 26.

28. Wenkert, *Historical Digest,* 21; Richmond Redevelopment Agency, *A Report on Housing and Redevelopment,* 49; Hamachi, "Postwar Housing," 30–32, 112; "Annual Report of the Richmond Branch, 1952," carton 26, Field Office Reports, NAACP West Coast Region Papers, Bancroft Library, University of California, Berkeley.

29. Hamachi, "Postwar Housing," 66; Selden Menafee, "America at War: California Gold Rush," *Washington Post,* January 6, 1944; Richard Reinhardt, "The Boom That Didn't Bust," *San Francisco Chronicle,* August 20, 1953; DeRomanett, "Public Action and Community Planning," 92–93.

30. Reinhardt, "The Boom That Didn't Bust," August 17, 1953.

31. Ibid., August 18, 1953; Hamachi, "Postwar Housing," 118.

32. Hamachi, "Postwar Housing," 63; Reinhardt, "The Boom That Didn't Bust," August 17–18, 1953; *San Francisco Chronicle,* August 12, 1952.

33. Wenkert, *Historical Digest,* 40; Reinhardt, "The Boom That Didn't Bust," August 18, 1953.

34. Reinhardt, "The Boom That Didn't Bust," August 17 and 18, 1953.

35. Reinhardt, "The Boom That Didn't Bust," August 19, 1953; Hamachi, "Postwar Housing," 124; Richmond Redevelopment Agency, *A Report on Housing and Redevelopment,* 40.

36. Hamachi, "Postwar Housing," 73–86; Reinhardt, "The Boom That Didn't Bust," August 21, 1953.

37. *San Francisco Chronicle,* July 18, 1953; Hamachi, "Postwar Housing," 86. In 1956, Richmond officials put the public housing issue to rest once and for all by hiring Paul Wendt, a Berkeley professor of business administration, to conduct a local housing survey. Based on Wendt's findings, which were hotly disputed by local housing advocates, Richmond planning agencies concluded that the city needed no additional public housing.

38. *Bay Area Real Estate Report,* January 1950, 30; Hamachi, "Postwar Housing," 129, 166.

39. *San Francisco Chronicle,* March 6, April 20, 1952; letter from Franklin Williams to Walter White, March 19, 1952, and memo from Douglas Stout to Franklin Williams, March 21, 1952, Wilbur Gary files, carton 40, NAACP Papers. The latter records indicate that there was considerable tension between the NAACP and the Communist-dominated Civil Rights Congress over the handling of the Gary case. At Gary's request the NAACP took over as the official representative for the case.

40. Letter from Williams to White, March 19, 1952, NAACP Papers; Barbour, "The Negro-White Relationship in Richmond," 26; Wollenberg, *Golden Gate Metropolis,* 265. For information on other instances of harassment of nonwhite homeowners in California cities, see Mike Davis *City of Quartz* (London: Verso Press, 1990), 163–64, 399–400; and Robert Lee, "Christian Ethics and Race Relations" (M.A. thesis, Pacific School of Religion, 1952).

41. Barbour, "The Negro-White Relationship in Richmond," 20; Hamachi, "Postwar Housing," 130–31. One of the "interracial" private developments was Parchester Village in Point Pinole, financed by Fred Parr, waterfront developer and head of the Committee for Home Protection. Working with a local black minister, the Reverend Guthrie John Williams, Parr constructed Parchester as a "community for all Americans." Before long, though, many white buyers withdrew their bids, leaving the development predominantly black owned. Hailed by many as a model community, Parchester (like other "interracial" subdivisions) attracted a large number of middle-income black families from outside the Richmond area. See Moore, "The Black Community in Richmond," 62–64.

42. Interview with George Eldredge by author, February 8, 1988; Harry and Marguerite Williams, "Reflections of a Longtime Black Family in Richmond" (interview by Judith K. Dunning, 1985, Regional Oral History Office, Bancroft Library, University of California, Berkeley, 1990), 125; Hamachi, "Postwar Housing," 147–64.

43. Alancraig, "Codornices Village," 104–11, 138–41; "Proposed Citizens Committee to Deal with the Emergency at Codornices Village," Codornices Village files, carton 37, NAACP Papers. According to an NAACP survey, blacks made up 84 percent of all Codornices residents.

44. Alancraig, "Codornices Village," 134–36; *San Francisco Chronicle,* March 13, 1954; Herman Schein, "Debacle in Berkeley: How the Codornices Housing Project Was Sabotaged," *Frontier* (October 1955): 10.

45. "Report on the Relocation Problem of Families Residing at Codornices Village," Berkeley files, carton 14, NAACP Papers; *San Francisco Chronicle,* March 13 and 24, 1954.

46. *San Francisco Chronicle,* September 14, 1952; Schein, "Debacle in Berkeley," 11, and responses to the article in letters to the editor, *Frontier* (February 1956): 25–26. During the early fifties, when McCarthyism was at its peak, NAACP branches around the country purged Communist party members from their ranks. In the Richmond branch, a conservative faction red-baited and forced the resignation of President Cleophus Brown and other

radicals; similar red-baiting and infighting occurred in Berkeley and Oakland. See Moore, "The Black Community in Richmond," 66.

47. *San Francisco Chronicle,* March 13, 1954.

48. "Report on the Relocation Problem"; letter from Herman Schein to Lester Bailey, July 6, 1955, Codornices Village files, carton 37, NAACP Papers; letters to the editor, *Frontier* (February 1956): 25–26.

49. Quoted in Shirley Ann Moore, "The Black Community in Richmond, California, 1910–1963" (Ph.D. diss., University of California, Berkeley, 1989), 187.

50. For a detailed account of the Los Angeles housing controversy, see Richard Baisden, "Labor in Los Angeles Politics" (Ph.D. diss., University of Chicago, 1958), 359–78; and Thomas S. Hines, "Housing, Baseball, and Creeping Socialism," *Journal of Urban History* 8 (February 1982): 137–40.

51. Carl Abbott, *Portland: Planning, Politics, and Growth in a Twentieth-Century City* (Lincoln: University of Nebraska Press, 1983), 156–58.

Conclusion

1. The National Advisory Commission on Civil Disorders, otherwise known as the Kerner Commission, was appointed by President Lyndon Johnson in 1967 to study the causes and possible solutions to the race riots of the 1960s. Its report, published in 1968, became the best-known liberal policy statement on urban racial violence.

2. Gary Moncher, ed., *Bebe Patten: Her Ministry, Then and Now* (San Francisco: Peter Wells Press, 1976), 18–25.

3. Cammy Blackstone, "Cowtown California: The Bay Area's Country Music Heritage," *SF Weekly* (November 1, 1989); *San Jose Mercury News,* January 10, 1979; May 29, 1985; April 30, 1986.

4. Shirley Ann Moore, "The Black Community in Richmond, California, 1910–1963" (Ph.D. diss., University of California, 1989), 146, 150–51; W. Edgar Gregory, "Protestantism in a Northern California Industrial Satellite County: A Study of Contra Costa County" (Northern California–Western Nevada Council of Churches, San Francisco, 1947), 9, in H. Paul Douglass, ed., *Social Problems and the Churches,* microfiche collection; interview with George Eldredge by author, February 8, 1988.

5. Arnold Shaw, *Honkers and Shouters: The Golden Years of Rhythm and Blues* (New York: Collier Books, 1978), 256–60; Lee Hildebrand, "Oakland Blues: The Thrill Goes On," *Museum of California* (September–October 1982): 5–7.

Bibliography

Unpublished Materials

Alameda, California. City Council. *Minutes,* 1940–1955.

Alancraig, Helen Smith. "Codornices Village: A Study of Non-Segregated Public Housing." M.A. thesis, University of California, Berkeley, 1953.

Baisden, Richard. "Labor in Los Angeles Politics." Ph.D. dissertation, University of Chicago, 1958.

Barbour, W. Miller. "An Exploratory Study of Socio-Economic Problems Affecting the Negro-White Relationship in Richmond, California." United Community Defense Services and the National Urban League, Pasadena, 1952. Copy in Richmond Collection, Richmond Public Library.

Barry, David W. "Survey of the Protestant Churches of Metropolitan Seattle, Washington." Council of Churches and Christian Education, Seattle, 1945. In *Social Problems and the Churches* (microform collection), ed. H. Paul Douglass. New York: National Council of Churches, 1971.

Berkeley, California. Berkeley Citizens Postwar Advisory Committee. "Report of the Sub-Committee on Project Studies and City Planning." September 14, 1944.

Brown, Hubert Owen. "The Impact of War Worker Migration on the Public School System of Richmond, California: 1940–1945." Ed.D. dissertation, Stanford University, 1973.

California Archeological Consultants, Inc., Peter M. Banks, and Robert I. Orlins. *Investigation of Cultural Resources within the Richmond Harbor Redevelopment Project 11-A.* Richmond, March 1981.

California State Chamber of Commerce. Research Department. "Survey of the Housing Problem in California." February 1946. Copy in Bancroft Library, University of California, Berkeley.

California. Youth Authority. "A Study of Youth Services in Contra Costa County." Typescript. Sacramento, 1945. Copy in Richmond Collection, Richmond Public Library.

Council of Social Agencies/Community Chest. Research Department. "Our Community: A Factual Presentation of Social Conditions." Oakland, August 22, 1945. Copy in Oakland History Room, Oakland Public Library.

———. "Studies in Population and Juvenile Delinquency, 1944–1945." Oakland, August 1945.

Declaration of Establishment of Protective Restrictions, and Covenants, Affecting the Real Property Known as Rollingwood. July 1, 1943. Property of George Eldredge.

de Graaf, Lawrence B. "Negro Migration to Los Angeles, 1930–1950." Ph.D. dissertation, University of California, Los Angeles, 1962.

DeRomanett, Raymond Paul. "Public Action and Community Planning: A Case Study of Richmond, California." M.A. thesis, University of California, Berkeley, 1956.

Douglass, H. Paul, et al. "The Portland Church Survey." Portland Council of Churches, Portland, Ore., 1945. In *Social Problems and the Churches* (microform collection), ed. H. Paul Douglass. New York: National Council of Churches, 1971.

Douma, Frank H. "The Oakland General Strike." M.A. thesis, University of California, Berkeley, 1951.

Eckert, Cindy. "Setting Limits: The Enforcement of Prostitution Laws, Oakland, California, 1934–1954." Senior honors thesis, Stanford University, 1989.

France, Edward E. "Some Aspects of the Migration of the Negro to the San Francisco Bay Area since 1940." Ph.D. dissertation, University of California, Berkeley, 1962.

Futter, Irvin C. "Juvenile Delinquency in a California Defense Area." M.A. thesis, Stanford University, 1943.

Gregory, W. Edgar. "Protestantism in a Northern California Industrial Satellite County: A Study of Contra Costa County." Northern California–Western Nevada Council of Churches, San Francisco, 1947. In *Social Problems and the Churches* (microform collection), ed. H. Paul Douglass. New York: National Council of Churches, 1971.

Hamachi, Roy. "Postwar Housing in Richmond, California." M.A. thesis, University of California, Berkeley, n.d. Copy in Richmond file, carton 6, Catherine Bauer Wurster Papers, Bancroft Library, University of California, Berkeley.

Hayes, Edward C. "Power Structure and the Urban Crisis." Ph.D. dissertation, University of California, Berkeley, 1968.

Hendricks, Rickey Lynn. "A Necessary Revolution: The Origins of the Kaiser Permanente Medical Care Program." Ph.D. dissertation, University of Denver, 1987.

Hirschfield, Deborah Ann. "Rosie Also Welded: Women and Technology in Shipbuilding during World War II." Ph.D. dissertation, University of California, Irvine, 1987.

Kerns, J. Harvey. "A Study of the Social and Economic Conditions Affecting the Local Negro Population." Council of Social Agencies, Oakland, 1942. Copy in Oakland History Room, Oakland Public Library.

Labor's Non-Partisan League of Alameda County. "Bring the New Deal to California." Oakland, n.d. Copy in Institute for Governmental Studies Library, University of California, Berkeley.

Labor's Non-Partisan League of California. *Minutes and Report.* December 1937, June 1938, January 1939. Copy in Institute for Governmental Studies Library, University of California, Berkeley.

Labor Unions Unemployed Council of Alameda County. "Starve or Fight." Oakland, n.d.

League of Women Voters, Richmond Chapter. "Local Government Responsibility in the Solution of Interracial Problems." 1963.

Lee, Robert. "Christian Ethics and Race Relations." M.A. thesis, Pacific School of Religion, 1952. Copy in Graduate Theological Union Library, University of California, Berkeley.

Lemke, Gretchen. "Blacks in Berkeley, 1859–1987." Northern California Center for Afro-American History and Life, Oakland, 1987. Typescript.

Lichtman, Sheila Tropp. "Women at Work, 1941–1945: Wartime Employment in the San Francisco Bay Area." Ph.D. dissertation, University of California, Davis, 1981.

Luke, Sherrill D. "The Problem of Annexing North Richmond to the City of Richmond." M.A. thesis, University of California, Berkeley, 1954.

Maher, Douglas. "The Pattern of a Generation." University of California, Berkeley, 1966. Typescript. Copy in Richmond Collection, Richmond Public Library.

Mills College. Department of Economics and Sociology. *Problems of American Communities.* 3 vols. Mills College Library, Oakland, 1945.

Moore, Shirley Ann. "The Black Community in Richmond, California, 1910–1987." Northern California Center for Afro-American History and Life, Oakland, 1987. Typescript.

———. "The Black Community in Richmond, California, 1910–1963." Ph.D. dissertation, University of California, Berkeley, 1989.

Mullendore, William C. "What Price Prosperity." Oakland Chamber of Commerce, Oakland, 1946. Copy in the Institute for Governmental Studies Library, University of California, Berkeley.

Oakland, California. City Council. *Minutes.* 1940–1955.

———. City Planning Administration. *The Civic Center and Lake Merritt Improvement.* Oakland, 1947.

———. *Redevelopment in Oakland.* Oakland, 1949.

———. Housing Authority of the City of Oakland. "Analysis of the Oakland Housing Shortage as of January 1946." Oakland. Copy in Institute of Governmental Studies Library, University of California, Berkeley.

———. *Annual Report.* Oakland, 1939 to 1957–58.

———. Mayor's Committee on Juvenile Delinquency Prevention. *Report.* Oakland, September 1944. Copy in Institute of Governmental Studies Library, University of California, Berkeley.

————. Oakland Postwar Planning Committee. *Oakland's Formula for the Future*. Oakland, 1945.

————. Police Department. Records Division. Arrest reports (microfilm). Oakland, April 1940, April 1944.

————. Police Department. Planning Division. "Return C: Annual Return of Persons Charged." Oakland, 1939–1948.

Oakland Voters Herald. May 9, 1947. Copy in election files, Oakland History Room, Oakland Public Library.

Oakland Voters League. March 24, 1947. Circular. Copy in election files, Oakland History Room, Oakland Public Library.

Orosco, James. "A Survey of Voting Behavior in the City of Richmond, California, 1936–1956." University of California, Berkeley, 1963. Typescript. Copy in Richmond Collection, Richmond Public Library.

Pittman, Tarea Hall. "The Operation of State and County Residence Requirements under the California Indigent Aid Law in Contra Costa County." M.A. thesis, University of California, Berkeley, 1946.

Richmond, California. City Council. *Minutes*. 1940–1955.

————. City Manager (James A. McVittie). *An Avalanche Hits Richmond*. Richmond, 1944.

————. Housing Authority of Richmond. *Annual Report*. 1942–1945.

————. Redevelopment Agency. *Application for Preliminary Advance*. Richmond, September 12, 1950.

————. *A Report on Housing and Redevelopment*. Richmond, January 1950.

Sanderson, Ross W. "The Churches of Los Angeles, California." Committee for Cooperative Field Research, New York, 1945. In *Social Problems and the Churches* (microform collection), ed. H. Paul Douglass. New York: National Council of Churches, 1971.

————. "San Diego Churches and Their Prospects." Committee for Cooperative Field Research, New York, 1945. In *Social Problems and the Churches* (microform collection), ed. H. Paul Douglass. New York: National Council of Churches, 1971.

Sokol, William. "Richmond during World War II: Kaiser Comes to Town." University of California, Berkeley, 1971. Typescript. Copy in Richmond Collection, Richmond Public Library.

Stripp, Fred. "The Relationship of the San Francisco Bay Area Negro-American Worker with Labor Unions Affiliated with the American Federation of Labor and the Congress of Industrial Organizations." Th.D. thesis, Pacific School of Religion, 1948. Copy in Graduate Theological Union Library, University of California, Berkeley.

U.S. Federal Works Agency. Work Projects Administration. "Recent Migration into Oakland, California, and Environs." February 3, 1942. Copy in Oakland History Collection, Oakland Public Library.

Woodington, Donald. "Federal Public Housing in Relation to Certain Needs and the Financial Ability of the Richmond School District." Ed.D. dissertation, University of California, Berkeley, 1954.

Oral Histories

Albrier, Frances Mary. "Determined Advocate for Racial Equality." Interview by Malca Chall, 1979. Regional Oral History Office, Bancroft Library, University of California, Berkeley.

Cathey, Margaret Louise. "A Wartime Journey: From Ottumwa, Iowa, to the Richmond Shipyards, 1942." Interview by Judith K. Dunning, 1985. Regional Oral History Office, Bancroft Library, University of California, Berkeley, 1990.

Clausen, Marguerite. "Memories of a Lifelong Richmond Resident, 1912 to 1987." Interview by Judith K. Dunning, 1985. Regional Oral History Office, Bancroft Library, University of California, Berkeley, 1990.

Dellums, C. L. "International President of the Brotherhood of Sleeping Car Porters." Interview by Joyce Henderson, 1973. Regional Oral History Office, Bancroft Library, University of California, Berkeley.

Eaton, Eddie. "In Search of the California Dream: From Houston, Texas, to Richmond, California, 1943." Interview by Judith K. Dunning, 1986. Regional Oral History Office, Bancroft Library, University of California, Berkeley, 1990.

Nystrom, Stanley. "A Family's Roots in Richmond: Recollections of a Lifetime Resident." Interview by Judith K. Dunning, 1985. Regional Oral History Office, Bancroft Library, University of California, Berkeley, 1990.

Pittman, Tarea Hall. "NAACP Official and Civil Rights Worker." Interview by Joyce Henderson, 1974. Regional Oral History Office, Bancroft Library, University of California, Berkeley.

Rumford, William Byron. "Legislator for Fair Employment, Fair Housing, and Public Health." Interview by Joyce Henderson, Amelia Fry, and Edward France, 1973. Regional Oral History Office, Bancroft Library, University of California, Berkeley.

Thompson, Ray. Interview by Jesse J. Warr III, 1978. Oral History Project, Afro-Americans in San Francisco prior to World War II, Friends of the San Francisco Public Library and San Francisco African-American Historical and Cultural Society. Transcript.

Williams, Harry and Marguerite. "Reflections of a Longtime Black Family in Richmond." Interview by Judith K. Dunning, 1985. Regional Oral History Office, Bancroft Library, University of California, Berkeley, 1990.

Interviews Conducted by Author

Amber, Alex. November 22, 1988.
Eldredge, George. February 8, 1988.
Enstad, Gladys. June 29, 1990.
Green, Archie. February 7, 1989.
Harley, Lois P. February 22, 1989.
Hicks, Ophelia M. March 30, 1989.
Hubert, Leigh. May 9, 1989.

Kenny, James P. June 11, 1991.
Moore, Agnes Ginn. June 29, 1990.
Patten, Bebe. June 10, 1991.
Quartucchio, "Shorty Joe." June 12, 1990.
Searcy, Ethel. March 30, 1989.
Swenson, Hazelle. June 29, 1990.
Vaara, Antoinette. November 21, 1988.
Vaughan, Helen M. June 12, 1990.

Archival and Manuscript Collections

Dellums, C. L. Papers. Bancroft Library, University of California, Berkeley.
Kaiser, Henry. Papers. Bancroft Library, University of California, Berkeley.
Kaiser Pictorial Collection. Bancroft Library, University of California, Berkeley.
Lange, Dorothea. Collection. Oakland Museum, Oakland.
National Association for the Advancement of Colored People, West Coast Region. Papers. Bancroft Library, University of California, Berkeley.
U.S. Committee for Congested Production Areas. Record Group 212. National Archives, Washington, D.C.
U.S. Department of Labor. Bureau of Employment Security. Labor Market Survey Reports. Record Group 183. National Archives, Washington, D.C.
U.S. Office of Community War Services. Record Group 215. National Archives, Washington, D.C.
U.S. Office of Public Housing Administration. Record Group 196. National Archives, Washington, D.C.
Wurster, Catherine Bauer. Papers. Bancroft Library, University of California, Berkeley.

Published Materials

Abbott, Carl. *The New Urban America: Growth and Politics in Sunbelt Cities.* Chapel Hill: University of North Carolina Press, 1981.
———. *Portland: Planning, Politics, and Growth in a Twentieth-Century City.* Lincoln: University of Nebraska Press, 1983.
Anderson, Karen. *Wartime Women: Sex Roles, Family Relationships, and the Status of Women during World War II.* Westport, Conn.: Greenwood Press, 1981.
Angelou, Maya. *I Know Why the Caged Bird Sings.* New York: Random House, 1969; Bantam Books, 1973.
Archibald, Katherine. *Wartime Shipyard: A Study in Social Disunity.* Berkeley: University of California Press, 1947; New York: Arno Press, 1977.

Arnow, Harriette. *The Dollmaker.* New York: Macmillan, 1954; New York: Avon Books, 1972.

Bagwell, Beth. *Oakland: The Story of a City.* Novato, Calif.: Presidio Press, 1982.

Bauer, Catherine [Wurster]. "Cities in Flux." *American Scholar* 13 (Winter 1943–1944): 70–84.

Bauman, John F. *Public Housing, Race, and Renewal.* Philadelphia: Temple University Press, 1987.

Berger, Bennett. *Working-Class Suburb.* Berkeley: University of California Press, 1968.

Blackstone, Cammy. "Cowtown California: The Bay Area's Country Music Heritage." *SF Weekly* (November 1, 1989): 1, 13.

Blum, John Morton. *V Was for Victory: Politics and American Culture during World War II.* New York: Harcourt Brace Jovanovich, 1976.

Bruce, J. Campbell. "Bay Area Migrants." *San Francisco Chronicle,* March 19–22, 1944.

Burns, James M. *Roosevelt: Soldier of Freedom.* New York: Harcourt Brace Jovanovich, 1970.

California. Department of Justice. *A Guide to Race Relations for Police Officers.* Sacramento, 1946.

———. State Board of Equalization. *Wartime Changes in Retail Outlets and Sales Volume in California.* Sacramento, January 1945.

———. State Reconstruction and Reemployment Commission. *The Bay Region Takes Stock.* Pamphlet no. 3. Sacramento, August 1944.

———. *California's Housing Crisis.* Sacramento, January 1946.

———. *New Factories for California Communities.* Pamphlet no. 11. Sacramento, 1946.

———. *Postwar Housing in California.* Sacramento, 1945.

———. *Richmond, California: A City Wins the Purple Heart.* Pamphlet no. 2. Sacramento, August 1944.

———. Special Crime Study Commission. *Social and Economic Causes of Crime and Delinquency.* Sacramento, 1949.

———. State Legislature. Assembly. Interim Committee on Juvenile Delinquency. *Final Report.* H.R. no. 268. Sacramento, February 16, 1945.

———. *Reports on Juvenile Delinquency.* Sacramento, 1944.

———. *Report on Crime Prevention and Correction.* H.R. no. 132. Sacramento, 1946.

———. Joint Senate Assembly. Committee on the Housing Problem. *Report on the Housing Problem.* 57th sess. Sacramento, 1947.

———. Senate. Interim Committee on Community Redevelopment and Housing. *Community Redevelopment and Housing.* Sacramento, 1949.

California Housing Association Newsletter. November–December issues, San Francisco, 1949. Copies in "Housing in California" pamphlets, Bancroft Library, University of California, Berkeley.

Camp, William Martin. *Skip to My Lou.* Garden City, N.Y.: Doubleday, 1945.

Carr, Lowell J., and James E. Stermer. *Willow Run: A Study of Industrialization and Social Inadequacy.* New York: Harper, 1952.

Chafe, William. *The Unfinished Journey: America since World War II.* New York: Oxford University Press, 1986.

Clawson, Marion. "What It Means to Be a Californian." *California Historical Society Quarterly* 24 (June 1945): 139–61.

Clive, Alan. *State of War: Michigan in World War II.* Ann Arbor: University of Michigan Press, 1979.

Cohen, Lizabeth. *Making a New Deal: Industrial Workers in Chicago, 1919–1939.* New York: Cambridge University Press, 1990.

Cole, Susan D. *Richmond: Windows to the Past.* Richmond: Wildcat Canyon Books, 1980.

Commonwealth Club of California. *The Population of California.* San Francisco: Parker Printing Co., 1946.

Cookingham, L. P. "The Effect of War upon Our Cities." *Planning: 1943.* Chicago: American Society of Planning Officials, 1943, 15–26.

Crouchett, Lawrence P., Lonnie G. Bunch III, and Martha Kendall Winnacker, eds. *Visions toward Tomorrow: The History of the East Bay Afro-American Community, 1852–1977.* Oakland: Northern California Center for Afro-American History and Life, 1989.

Cumbler, John T. *A Social History of Economic Decline: Business, Politics, and Work in Trenton.* New Brunswick, N.J.: Rutgers University Press, 1989.

Daniels, Douglas Henry. *Pioneer Urbanites: A Social and Cultural History of Black San Francisco.* Philadelphia: Temple University Press, 1980.

Davis, Mike. *City of Quartz.* London: Verso Press, 1990.

"Detour through Purgatory." *Fortune* (February 1945).

Douglass, H. Paul. *The City Church and the War Emergency.* New York: Friendship Press, 1945.

Douglass, H. Paul, A. Ronald Merrix, and John Halko. Associates of the technical staff of the Committee for Cooperative Field Research. *The San Francisco Bay Area Church Study.* San Francisco: Federal Council of Churches in Christ, 1946.

Fabry, Joseph. *Swing Shift: Building the Liberty Ships.* San Francisco: Strawberry Hill Press, 1982.

Fisher, Bob, and Joe King. "Popular Mobilization in the 1990s: Prospects for the New Social Movements." *New Politics* 25 (Winter 1991): 71–84.

Foster, James Caldwell. *The Union Politic: The CIO Political Action Committee.* Columbia: University of Missouri Press, 1975.

Foster, Mark S. *Henry Kaiser: Builder in the Modern American West.* Austin: University of Texas Press, 1989.

Funigiello, Philip J. *The Challenge to Urban Liberalism: Federal-City Relations during World War II.* Knoxville: University of Tennessee Press, 1978.

Gaer, Joseph. *The First Round: The Story of the CIO Political Action Committee.* New York: Duell, Sloan and Pearce, 1944.

Gilbert, James. *Cycle of Outrage: America's Reaction to the Juvenile Delinquent in the 1950s.* New York: Oxford University Press, 1986.

Gordon, Linda. *Heroes of Their Own Lives: The Politics and History of Family Violence.* New York: Viking Press, 1988.

Gothberg, John A. "The Local Influence of J. R. Knowland's Oakland 'Tribune.'" *Journalism Quarterly* 45 (Autumn 1968): 487–95.

Gregory, James N. *American Exodus: The Dust Bowl Migration and Okie Culture in California.* New York: Oxford University Press, 1989.

Gruenberg, Sidonie. *The Family in a World at War.* New York: Harper and Bros., 1942.

Hall, Jacquelyn Dowd, et al. *Like a Family: The Making of a Southern Cotton Mill World.* Chapel Hill: University of North Carolina Press, 1987.

Hamilton, Janie B. "West of the Mississippi." *Tophand* 3 (March 1945): 24.

Harris, Sheldon. *Blues Who's Who.* New Rochelle, N.Y.: Arlington House, 1979.

Harris, William H. "Federal Intervention in Union Discrimination: The FEPC and West Coast Shipyards during World War II." *Labor History* 22 (Summer 1981): 325–47.

Hartman, Susan M. *The Homefront and Beyond.* Boston: Twayne Publishers, 1982.

Havighurst, Robert J., and H. Gerthon Morgan. *The Social History of a War Boom Community.* New York: Longmans, Green, 1951.

Hayes, Edward C. *Power Structure and Urban Policy: Who Rules in Oakland.* New York: McGraw-Hill, 1972.

Hildebrand, Lee. "North Richmond Blues." *East Bay Express* (February 9, 1979): 1, 4–5.

———. "Oakland Blues: The Thrill Goes On." *Museum of California* (September–October 1982): 5–7.

———. "West Side Story." *East Bay Express* (September 28, 1979).

Himes, Chester. *If He Hollers Let Him Go.* London: Falcon Press, 1946; New York: Thunder's Mouth Press, 1986.

Hines, Thomas S. "Housing, Baseball, and Creeping Socialism." *Journal of Urban History* 8 (February 1982): 123–43.

Hinkel, Edgar J., and William E. McCann, eds. *Oakland, California, 1852–1938: Some Phases of the Social, Political, and Economic History.* 2 vols. Oakland: U.S. Work Projects Administration and the Oakland Public Library, 1939.

Hogan, William. "Hangover Town." *Salute Magazine* (June 1946): 32–43.

Industrial Survey Associates. *The San Francisco Bay Area: Its People, Prospects, and Problems.* San Francisco: n.p., 1948.

International Brotherhood of Boilermakers, Iron Shipbuilders and Helpers of America. *Report and Proceedings of the Seventeenth Consolidated Convention.* Kansas City, Mo.: n.p., 1944.

———. *Richmond: Arsenal of Democracy.* Berkeley: Tam, Gibbs Co., [1945].

Issel, William. "Liberalism and Urban Policy in San Francisco from the 1930s to the 1960s." *Western Historical Quarterly* 22 (November 1991): 431–50.

Issler, Anne Roller. "Shipyards and the Boys." *Survey Graphic* 33 (March 1944): 174–77, 187–88.

Jackson, Kenneth T. *Crabgrass Frontier: The Suburbanization of the United States*. New York: Oxford University Press, 1985.

Johnson, Charles S. *The Negro War Worker in San Francisco*. San Francisco: YWCA, 1944.

Kaiser Industries. *The Kaiser Story*. Oakland: Kaiser Industries, 1963.

Kesselman, Amy. *Fleeting Opportunities: Women Shipyard Workers in Portland and Vancouver during World War II and Reconversion*. Albany: State University of New York Press, 1990.

Korstad, Robert, and Nelson Lichtenstein. "Opportunities Lost and Found: Labor, Radicals, and the Early Civil Rights Movement." *Journal of American History* 75 (December 1988): 786–811.

Kraus, Henry. *In the City Was a Garden: A Housing Project Chronicle*. New York: Renaissance Press, 1951.

Kusmer, Kenneth. *A Ghetto Takes Shape*. Urbana: University of Illinois Press, 1976.

Lane, Frederick C. *Ships for Victory: A History of Shipbuilding under the U.S. Maritime Commission in World War II*. Baltimore: Johns Hopkins Press, 1951.

Lichtenstein, Nelson. *Labor's War at Home: The CIO in World War II*. New York: Cambridge University Press, 1982.

Loofbourow, Leon L. *In Search of God's Gold*. San Francisco: Methodist Church Historical Society of the California-Nevada Annual Conference, 1950.

Lotchin, Roger W. *Fortress California*. New York: Oxford University Press, 1992.

———. "The Metropolitan-Military Complex in Comparative Perspective: San Francisco, Los Angeles, and San Diego, 1919–1941." In *The Making of Urban America*, ed. Raymond A. Mohl, 202–13. Wilmington, Del.: SR Books, 1988.

———, ed. *The Martial Metropolis: U.S. Cities in War and Peace*. New York: Praeger Publishers, 1984.

Malone, Bill C. *Country Music U.S.A.* American Folklore Society, 1968. Rev. ed. Austin: University of Texas Press, 1985.

Maslin, Marshall, ed. *Western Shipbuilders in World War II*. Oakland: Shipbuilding Review Publishing Association, 1945.

McEntire, Davis. "Postwar Status of Negro Workers in the San Francisco Bay Area." *Monthly Labor Review* 70 (June 1950): 612–17.

McWilliams, Carey. "Jim Crow Goes West." *Negro Digest* 3 (August 1945): 71–74.

———. *PM*, April 22–26, 1945.

Menafee, Selden. "America at War: California Gold Rush." *Washington Post*, January 6, 1944, 8.

Mennel, Robert M. *Thorns and Thistles*. Hanover, N.H.: University Press of New England, 1973.

Merrill, Francis. *Social Problems on the Home Front: A Study of Wartime Influences*. New York: Harper, 1948.

Meyer, Agnes. *Journey through Chaos* New York: Harcourt, Brace and Co., 1944.

Milkman, Ruth. *Gender at Work: The Dynamics of Job Segregation by Sex during World War II.* Urbana: University of Illinois Press, 1987.

Miller, Marc Scott. *The Irony of Victory: World War II and Lowell, Massachusetts.* Urbana: University of Illinois Press, 1988.

Mollenkopf, John. *The Contested City.* Princeton, N.J.: Princeton University Press, 1983.

Moncher, Gary, ed. *Bebe Patten: Her Ministry, Then and Now.* San Francisco: Peter Wells Press, 1976. Copy available from Christian Cathedral, Oakland.

Montgomery, David. *The Fall of the House of Labor.* New York: Cambridge University Press, 1987.

Mullins, William H. *The Depression and the Urban West Coast, 1929–1933.* Bloomington: Indiana University Press, 1991.

Nash, Gerald D. *The American West Transformed: The Impact of the Second World War.* Bloomington: Indiana University Press, 1985.

———. *The Great Depression and World War II: Organizing America, 1933–1945.* New York: St. Martin's Press, 1979.

———. *World War II and the West: Reshaping the Economy.* Lincoln: University of Nebraska Press, 1990.

Nelson, Bruce. *Workers on the Waterfront: Seamen, Longshoremen, and Unionism in the 1930s.* Urbana: University of Illinois Press, 1988.

Oakland Tribune Yearbook. 1938–1945. Oakland: Oakland Tribune Co.

Ogburn, William Fielding, ed. *American Society in Wartime.* Chicago: University of Chicago Press, 1943.

Permanente Metals Corporation. *A Booklet of Illustrated Facts about the Shipyards at Richmond, California.* Richmond: Permanente Metals Corp., June 30, 1944. Copy in Richmond Collection, Richmond Public Library.

Polenberg, Richard. *War and Society: The United States, 1941–1945.* Philadelphia: J. B. Lippincott, 1972.

Raudebaugh, Charles. "Richmond, a Town with a Purple Heart, Looks to the Future." *San Francisco Chronicle,* March 18, 1946, 14.

Record, Wilson. "Willie Stokes at the Golden Gate." *Crisis* 56 (June 1949): 175–79, 187–88.

Reddick, L. D., ed. "Race Relations on the Pacific Coast." *Journal of Educational Sociology* 19 (November 1945).

Reed, Merl E. "The FEPC, the Black Worker, and the Southern Shipyards." *South Atlantic Quarterly* 74 (Autumn 1975): 446–67.

Reinhardt, R. "The Boom That Didn't Bust." *San Francisco Chronicle,* August 16–21, 1953.

"Richmond: A City of High Hopes and Big Headaches." *Fortnight* (December 19, 1947): 18–19.

Richmond Chamber of Commerce. *Handbook of Richmond.* 1943–1945 and 1948–1953. Richmond: n.p., n.d.

———. *Richmond News.* 1942–1943.

"Richmond Took a Beating." *Fortune* (February 1945): 262–70.

Schein, Herman. "Debacle in Berkeley: How the Codornices Housing Project Was Sabotaged." *Frontier* (October 1955): 9–10, 14.

Schlegel, Marvin W. *Conscripted City: Norfolk in World War II.* Norfolk, Va.: Norfolk War History Commission, 1951.

Schmid, Calvin. *Social Trends in Seattle.* Seattle: University of Washington Press, 1944; New York: Greenwood Press, 1969.

Scott, William V. F. "Eliminate the Stokes Willies." *Crisis* 57 (January 1950): 9–11.

Shaw, Arnold. *Honkers and Shouters: The Golden Years of Rhythm and Blues.* New York: Collier Books, 1978.

Silverman, Milton. "The Second Gold Rush Hits the West." *San Francisco Chronicle,* April 25–May 20, 1943.

Smith, C. Calvin. *War and Wartime Changes: The Transformation of Arkansas, 1940–1945.* Fayetteville: University of Arkansas Press, 1986.

Stack, Carol. *All Our Kin: Strategies for Survival in a Black Community.* New York: Harper and Row, 1974.

Stein, Walter J. *California and the Dust Bowl Migration.* Westport, Conn.: Greenwood Press, 1973.

Thompson, Wayne E. "A Unique Civic Center for Richmond, California." *American City* (January 1953): 94–96.

Townsend, Charles R. *The Life and Music of Bob Wills.* Chicago: University of Illinois Press, 1986.

"Trend of Employment, Earning, and Hours." *Monthly Labor Review* 60 (January 1944): 140.

Tuttle, William M., Jr. *Race Riot: Chicago in the Red Summer of 1919.* New York: Atheneum, 1980.

U.S. Bureau of the Census. *Twelfth Census of the United States, 1900: Population.* Vol. 1, pt. 1., "California." Washington, D.C.: Government Printing Office.

———. *Thirteenth Census of the United States, 1910: Population.* Vol. 2, *Reports by States.* "California," 137–87. Washington, D.C.: Government Printing Office.

———. *Fourteenth Census of the United States, 1920: Population.* Vol. 3, *Composition and Characteristics of the Population by States.* "California," 106–33. Washington, D.C.: Government Printing Office.

———. *Fifteenth Census of the United States, 1930: Population.* Vol. 3, pt. 1, *Reports by States.* "California," 231–87. Washington, D.C.: Government Printing Office.

———. *Sixteenth Census of the United States, 1940: Reports on Population.* Vol. 2, *Characteristics of the Population.* Pt. 1, "California," 513–689. Washington, D.C.: Government Printing Office.; vol. 7, *Supplementary Report—Statistics for Census Tracts: Population and Housing.* "Oakland-Berkeley, California, and Adjacent Area"; *Reports on Housing.* Vol. 2, *General Characteristics of Housing—By States.* Pt. 2, "California," 211–323.

———. *U.S. Census of Population, 1950.* Vol. 2, *Characteristics of the Population.* Pt. 5, "California," and vol. 3, *Census Tracts Statistics,* Bulletin P-D49, "Selected Population and Housing Characteristics, San Francisco–Oakland, California." Washington, D.C.: Government Printing Office.

———. *Population*. Series CA-1. *Final Population Figures for the Area and Its Constituent Parts*. [Washington, D.C.: Bureau of the Census, 1944.] No. 4, "San Francisco Bay Congested Production Area: April, 1944"; no. 11, "Total Population of Ten Congested Production Areas: 1944."

———. *Population*. Series CA-2. *Wartime Changes in Population and Family Characteristics*. No. 2, "San Diego Congested Production Area, March 1944." [Washington, D.C.: Bureau of the Census]; no. 3, "San Francisco Bay Congested Production Area, April 1944"; no. 5, "Los Angeles Congested Production Area, April 1944"; no. 6, "Portland-Vancouver Congested Production Area, May 1944"; no. 8, "Puget Sound Congested Production Area, June 1944."

———. *Population*. Series CA-3. *Characteristics of the Population, Labor Force, Families, and Housing*. [Washington, D.C.: Bureau of the Census.] No. 2, "San Diego Congested Production Area, March 1944"; no. 3, "San Francisco Bay Congested Production Area, April 1944"; no. 5, "Los Angeles Congested Production Area, April 1944"; no. 6, "Portland-Vancouver Congested Production Area, May 1944"; no. 8, "Puget Sound Congested Production Area, June 1944."

———. *Population*. Series PM-1. No. 4, *Marriage Licenses Issued in Cities of 100,000 or More, 1939 to 1944* [Washington, D.C.: Bureau of the Census], 1945.

———. *Population*. Series PM-3. No. 3, *Marriage Licenses Issued in Cities of 100,000 or More, Annual Summary: 1945* [Washington, D.C.: Bureau of the Census], 1946.

———. *Population—Special Reports*. Series P-S, no. 5. *Civilian Migration in the United States, December 1941 to March 1945*. [Washington, D.C.: Bureau of the Census.]

———. *Current Population Reports, Population Characteristics*. Series P-20, no. 14, *Internal Migration in the United States: April 1940 to April 1947*. [Washington, D.C.: Bureau of the Census,] April 15, 1948.

U.S. Congress. House. Select Committee to Investigate National Defense Migration. *Hearings, Pursuant to HR 16*. 77th Cong., 1941.

———. Subcommittee of Committee on Naval Affairs. *Hearings on Congested Areas*. 78th Cong., 1st and 2d sess., 1943.

———. Senate. Committee on Military Affairs. *Labor Shortages in the Pacific Coast and Rocky Mountain States, Pursuant to SR 88 and 113*. 78th Cong., 1st sess., September 9–10, 1943.

U.S. Department of Justice. Federal Bureau of Investigation. *Uniform Crime Reports*. Washington, D.C.: Government Printing Office, 1939–1948.

U.S. Department of Labor. Women's Bureau. Bulletin 209, *Women Workers in Ten War Production Areas*. Washington, D.C.: Government Printing Office, 1946.

U.S. Work Projects Administration. *Berkeley: The First Seventy-five Years*. Berkeley: Gillick Press, 1941.

Wenkert, Robert. *An Historical Digest of Negro-White Relations in Richmond, California*. Berkeley: Survey Research Center, University of California, 1967.

Whitnah, Joseph C. *A History of Richmond, California*. Richmond: Richmond Chamber of Commerce, 1944.

Whyte, William H. *The Organization Man*. New York: Simon and Schuster, 1956.

Wirth, Louis. "The Urban Community." In *American Society in Wartime*, ed. William Fielding Ogburn, 63–81. Chicago: University of Chicago Press, 1943.

Wollenberg, Charles. *Golden Gate Metropolis: Perspectives on Bay Area History*. Berkeley: Institute of Governmental Studies, University of California, 1985.

———. "James vs. Marinship: Trouble on the New Black Frontier." *California History* 60 (Fall 1981): 262–79.

———. *Marinship at War: Shipbuilding and Social Change in Wartime Sausalito*. Berkeley: Western Heritage Press, 1990.

"Workers West." *Business Week* (October 3, 1942): 74–75.

Zeiger, Robert H. *American Workers, American Unions, 1920–1985*. Baltimore: Johns Hopkins University Press, 1986.

Newspapers

Alameda Times-Star
Berkeley Gazette
Daily People's World
East Bay Labor Journal
Fore 'N' Aft (Kaiser shipyard newspaper)
Labor Herald (newspaper of the Northern California CIO)
Oakland Observer
Oakland Post-Enquirer
Oakland Tribune
Richmond Independent
Richmond Record-Herald
San Francisco Chronicle
San Jose Mercury

Sound Recordings

Bay Area Blues Blasters. Ace Records CHD 224, 1987.

Oakland Blues. Arhoolie 2008, 1970.

San Francisco Bay Gospel. Interstate Music Limited HT 314, 1987.

Stogner, Dave. *Dave Stogner: The King of West Coast Country Swing*. Cattle Records Mono LP 63, 1984.

Western Swing Blues, Boogie, and Honky Tonk. Old Timey 121, 1981.

Index

Compositor: BookMasters, Inc.
Text: 10/13 Galliard
Display: Galliard
Printer: BookCrafters, Inc.
Binder: BookCrafters, Inc.